PostgreSQL

Introduction
and
Concepts

PostgreSQL
Introduction
and
Concepts

Bruce Momjian

ADDISON–WESLEY

Boston • San Francisco • New York • Toronto • Montreal • London • Munich
Paris • Madrid • Cape Town • Sidney•Tokyo •Singapore • Mexico City

The publisher offers discounts on this book when ordered in quantity for special sales. For more information, please contact:

Pearson Education Corporate Sales Division
One Lake Street
Upper Saddle River, NJ 07458
(800) 382-3419
corpsales@pearsontechgroup.com
Visit AW on the Web: www.awl.com/cseng/

Library of Congress Cataloging-in-Publication Data

Momjian, Bruce.
PostgreSQL : introduction and concepts / Momjian,
Bruce.
p. cm.
ISBN 0-201-70331-9
1. Database management. 2. PostgreSQL. I. Title.
QA76.9.D3 M647 2000
005.75'85–dc21   00-045367
                                                              CIP

This book was prepared with LyX and LATEX and reproduced by Addison–Wesley from files supplied by the author.

Text printed on recycled and acid-free paper

1 2 3 4 5 6 7 8 9-MA-0403020100

First Printing, November 2000

To my wonderful wife, Christine,
and my fine boys, Matthew, Luke, and Peter

Contents

List of Figures

List of Tables

Foreword

Most research projects never leave the academic environment. Occasionally, exceptional ones survive the transition from the university to the real world and go on to become a phenomenon. POSTGRESQL is one of those projects. Its popularity and success are a testament to the dedication and hard work of the POSTGRESQL global development team. Although developing an advanced database system is no small feat, maintaining and enhancing an inherited code base are even more challenging. The POSTGRESQL team has managed to not only improve the quality and usability of the system, but also expand its use among the Internet user community. This book marks a major milestone in the history of the project.

Postgres95, later renamed POSTGRESQL, started as a small project to overhaul Postgres. Postgres was a novel and feature-rich database system created by the students and staff at the University of California at Berkeley. Our goal with Postgres95 was to keep the powerful and useful features of this system while trimming down the bloat caused by much experimentation and research. We had a lot of fun reworking the internals. At the time, we had no idea where we were going with the project. The Postgres95 exercise was not research, but simply a bit of engineering housecleaning. By the spring of 1995 however, it had occurred to us that the Internet user community really needed an open source, SQL-based multiuser database. Happily, our first release was met with great enthusiasm, and we are very pleased to see the project continuing.

Obtaining information about a complex system like POSTGRESQL is a great barrier to its adoption. This book fills a critical gap in the documentation of the project and provides an excellent overview of the system. It covers a wide range of topics, from the basics to the more advanced and unique features of POSTGRESQL.

In writing this book, Bruce Momjian has drawn on his experience in helping beginners with POSTGRESQL. The text is easy to understand and full of practical tips. Momjian captures database concepts using simple and easy-to-understand language. He also presents numerous real-life examples throughout the book. In addition, he does an outstanding job of covering many advanced POSTGRESQL topics. Enjoy reading the book and have fun exploring POSTGRESQL! It is our hope this book will not only teach you about using POSTGRESQL, but also inspire you to delve into its innards and contribute to the ongoing POSTGRESQL development effort.

Chen and Andrew Yu, co-authors of Postgres95

Preface

This book is about POSTGRESQL, the most advanced open source database. From its origins in academia, POSTGRESQL has moved to the Internet with explosive growth. It is hard to believe the advances during the past four years under the guidance of a team of worldwide Internet developers. This book is a testament to their vision, and to the success that POSTGRESQL has become.

The book is designed to lead the reader from their first database query through the complex queries needed to solve real-world problems. No knowledge of database theory or practice is required. However, basic knowledge of operating system capabilities is expected, such as the ability to type at an operating system prompt.

Beginning with a short history of POSTGRESQL, the book moves from simple queries to the most important database commands. Common problems are covered early, which should prevent users from getting stuck with queries that fail. The author has seen many bug reports in the past few years and consequently has attempted to warn readers about the common pitfalls.

With a firm foundation established, additional commands are introduced. The later chapters outline complex topics like transactions and performance.

At each step, the purpose of each command is clearly illustrated. The goal is to have readers understand more than query syntax. They should know *why* each command is valuable, so they can use the proper commands in their real-world database applications.

A database novice should read the entire book, while skimming over the later chapters. The complex nature of database systems should not prevent readers from getting started. Test databases offer a safe way to try queries. As readers gain experience, later chapters will begin to make more sense. Experienced database users can skip the early chapters on basic SQL functionality. The cross-referencing of sections allows you to quickly move from general to more specific information.

Much information has been moved out of the main body of the book into appendices. Appendix A lists sources of additional information about POSTGRESQL. Appendix B provides information about installing POSTGRESQL. Appendix C lists the features of POSTGRESQL not found in other database systems. Appendix D contains a copy of the POSTGRESQL manual pages which should be consulted anytime you have trouble with query syntax. Also, do not overlook the excellent documentation that is part of POSTGRESQL. This documentation covers many complex topics, including much POSTGRESQL-specific functionality that cannot be covered in a book of this length. Sections of the documentation are referenced in this book where appropriate.

   This book uses *italics* for identifiers, SMALLCAPS for SQL keywords, and a `monospaced` font for SQL queries. The Web site for this book is located at `http://www.postgresql.org/docs/awbook.html`.

Acknowledgments

POSTGRESQL and this book would not be possible without the talented and hard-working members of the POSTGRESQL Global Development Team. They took source code that could have become just another abandoned project and transformed it into the open source alternative to commercial database systems. POSTGRESQL is a shining example of Internet software development.

Steering

- Fournier, Marc G., in Wolfville, Nova Scotia, Canada, coordinates the entire effort, provides the server, and administers the primary Web site, mailing lists, ftp site, and source code repository.

- Lane, Tom, in Pittsburgh, Pennsylvania, United States, is often seen working on the planner/optimizer, but has left his fingerprints in many places. He specializes in bug fixes and performance improvements.

- Lockhart, Thomas G., in Pasadena, California, United States, works on documentation, data types (particularly date/time and geometric objects), and SQL standards compatibility.

- Mikheev, Vadim B., in San Francisco, California, United States, does large projects, like vacuum, subselects, triggers, and multi-version concurrency control (MVCC).

- Momjian, Bruce, in Philadelphia, Pennsylvania, United States, maintains FAQ and TODO lists, code cleanup, patch application, training materials, and some coding.

- Wieck, Jan, near Hamburg, Germany, overhauled the query rewrite rule system, wrote our procedural languages PL/PGSQL and PL/TCL, and added the NUMERIC type.

Major Developers

- Cain, D'Arcy, J. M., in Toronto, Ontario, Canada, worked on the TCL interface, PyGreSQL, and the INET type.

- Dal Zotto, Massimo, near Trento, Italy, created locking code and other improvements.

- Eisentraut, Peter, in Uppsala, Sweden, has added many features, including an overhaul of psql.

- Elphick, Oliver, in Newport, Isle of Wight, United Kingdom, maintains the POSTGRESQL package for Debian Linux.

- Horak, Daniel, near Pilzen, Czech Republic, did the WinNT port of POSTGRESQL (using the Cygwin environment).

- Inoue, Hiroshi, in Fukui, Japan, improved btree index access.

- Ishii, Tatsuo, in Zushi, Kanagawa, Japan, handles multibyte foreign language support and porting issues.

- Martin, Dr. Andrew C. R., in London, United Kingdom, created the ECPG interface and helped in the Linux and Irix FAQs including some patches to the POSTGRESQL code.

- Mergl, Edmund, in Stuttgart, Germany, created and maintains pgsql_perl5. He also created DBD-Pg, which is available via CPAN.

- Meskes, Michael, in Dusseldorf, Germany, handles multibyte foreign language support and maintains ECPG.

- Mount, Peter, in Maidstone, Kent, United Kingdom, created the Java JDBC interface.

- Nikolaidis, Byron, in Baltimore, Maryland, United States, rewrote and maintains the ODBC interface for Windows.

- Owen, Lamar, in Pisgah Forest, North Carolina, United States, maintains the RPM package.

- Teodorescu, Constantin, in Braila, Romania, created the PGACCESS interface.

- Thyni, Göran, in Kiruna, Sweden, has worked on the Unix socket code.

Non-code Contributors

- Bartunov, Oleg, in Moscow, Russia, introduced the locale support.

- Vielhaber, Vince, near Detroit, Michigan, United States, maintains our Web site.

All developers are listed in alphabetical order.

Chapter 1

History of POSTGRESQL

1.1 Introduction

POSTGRESQL is the most advanced open source database server. In this chapter, you will learn about databases, open source software, and the history of POSTGRESQL.

Three basic office productivity applications exist: word processors, spreadsheets, and databases. *Word processors* produce text documents critical to any business. *Spreadsheets* are used for financial calculations and analysis. *Databases* are used primarily for data storage and retrieval. You can use a word processor or spreadsheet to store small amounts of data. However, with large volumes of data or data that must be retrieved and updated frequently, databases are the best choice. Databases allow orderly data storage, rapid data retrieval, and complex data analysis.

1.2 University of California at Berkeley

POSTGRESQL's ancestor was Ingres, developed at the University of California at Berkeley (1977–1985). The Ingres code was later enhanced by Relational Technologies/Ingres Corporation,[1] which produced one of the first commercially successful relational database servers. Also at Berkeley, Michael Stonebraker led a team to develop an object-relational database server called Postgres (1986–1994). Illustra[2] took the Postgres code and developed it into a commercial product. Two Berkeley graduate students, Jolly Chen and Andrew Yu, subsequently added SQL capabilities to Postgres. The resulting project was called Postgres95 (1994–1995). The two later left Berkeley, but Chen continued maintaining Postgres95, which had an active mailing list.

---

[1] Ingres Corporation was later purchased by Computer Associates.

[2] Illustra was later purchased by Informix and integrated into Informix's Universal Server.

1.3   Development Leaves Berkeley

In the summer of 1996, it became clear there was great demand for an open source SQL database server, and a team formed to continue development. Marc G. Fournier of Toronto, Canada, offered to host the mailing list and provide a server to host the source tree. One thousand mailing list subscribers were moved to the new list. A server was configured, giving a few people login accounts to apply patches to the source code using cvs.[3]

Jolly Chen has stated, "This project needs a few people with lots of time, not many people with a little time." Given the 250,000 lines of C[4] code, we understood what he meant. In the early days, four people were heavily involved: Marc Fournier in Canada; Thomas Lockhart in Pasadena, California; Vadim Mikheev in Krasnoyarsk, Russia; and me in Philadelphia, Pennsylvania. We all had full-time jobs, so we participated in the effort in our spare time. It certainly was a challenge.

Our first goal was to scour the old mailing list, evaluating patches that had been posted to fix various problems. The system was quite fragile then, and not easily understood. During the first six months of development, we feared that a single patch might break the system and we would be unable to correct the problem. Many bug reports left us scratching our heads, trying to figure out not only what was wrong, but how the system even performed many functions.

We had inherited a huge installed base. A typical bug report came in the following form: "When I do this, it crashes the database." We had a long list of such reports. It soon became clear that some organization was needed. Most bug reports required significant research to fix, and many reports were duplicates, so our TODO list included every buggy SQL query. This approach helped us identify our bugs, and made users aware of them as well, thereby cutting down on duplicate bug reports.

Although we had many eager developers, the learning curve in understanding how the database worked was significant. Many developers became involved in the edges of the source code, like language interfaces or database tools, where things were easier to understand. Other developers focused on specific problem queries, trying to locate the source of the bug. It was amazing to see that many bugs were fixed with just one line of C code. Because Postgres had evolved in an academic environment, it had not been exposed to the full spectrum of real-world queries. During that period, there was talk of adding features, but the instability of the system made bug fixing our major focus.

1.4   POSTGRESQL Global Development Team

In late 1996, we changed the name of the database server from Postgres95 to POSTGRESQL. It is a mouthful, but honors both the Berkeley name and its SQL capabilities. We started distributing the source code using remote cvs, which allowed people to keep up-to-date copies of the development tree without downloading an entire set of files every day.

---

[3]cvs sychronizes access by developers to shared program files.
[4]C is a popular computer language first developed in the 1970s.

Releases occurred every three to five months. Each period consisted of two to three months of development, one month of beta testing, a major release, and a few weeks to issue sub-releases to correct serious bugs. We were never tempted to follow a more aggressive schedule with more releases. A database server is not like a word processor or game, where you can easily restart it if a problem arises. Instead databases are multiuser, and lock user data inside the database, so they must be as reliable as possible.

Development of source code of this scale and complexity is not for the novice. We initially had trouble interesting developers in a project with such a steep learning curve. However, over time, our civilized atmosphere and improved reliability and performance helped attract the experienced talent we needed.

Getting our developers the knowledge they needed to assist with POSTGRESQL was clearly a priority. We had a TODO list that outlined what needed to be done, but with 250,000 lines of code, taking on any item was a major project. We realized developer education would pay major benefits in helping people get started. We wrote a detailed flowchart of the database modules.[5] We also wrote a developers' FAQ,[6] answering the most common questions of POSTGRESQL developers. With this information, developers became more productive at fixing bugs and adding features.

Although the source code we inherited from Berkeley was very modular, most Berkeley coders used POSTGRESQL as a test bed for research projects. As a result, improving existing code was not a priority. Their coding styles were also quite varied.

We wrote a tool to reformat the entire source tree in a consistent manner. We wrote a script to find functions that could be marked as *static*[7] or unused functions that could be removed completely. These scripts are run just before each release. A release checklist reminds us of the items to be changed for each release.

As we gained knowledge of the code, we were able to perform more complicated fixes and feature additions. We redesigned poorly structured code. We moved into a mode where each release had major new features, instead of just bug fixes. We improved SQL conformance, added sub-selects, improved locking, and added missing SQL functionality. A company was formed to offer telephone support.

The Usenet discussion group archives started touting us. At one time, we had searched for POSTGRESQL and found that many people were recommending other databases, even though we were addressing user concerns as rapidly as possible. One year later, many people were recommending us to users who needed transaction support, complex queries, commercial-grade SQL support, complex data types, and reliability—clearly our strengths. Other databases were recommended when speed was the overriding concern. Red Hat's shipment of POSTGRESQL as part of its Linux[8] distribution quickly expanded our user base.

Today, every release of POSTGRESQL is a major improvement over the last. Our global

---

[5]All the files mentioned in this chapter are available as part of the POSTGRESQL distribution, or at http://www.postgresql.org/docs.

[6]Frequently Asked Questions

[7]A *static* function is used by only one program file.

[8]Linux is a popular UNIX-like, open source operating system.

development team has mastery of the source code we inherited from Berkeley. In addition, every module is understood by at least one development team member. We are now easily adding major features, thanks to the increasing size and experience of our worldwide development team.

1.5   Open Source Software

POSTGRESQL is *open source software.* The term "open source software" often confuses people. With commercial software, a company hires programmers, develops a product, and sells it to users. With Internet communication, however, new possibilities exist. Open source software has no company. Instead, capable programmers with interest and some free time get together via the Internet and exchange ideas. Someone writes a program and puts it in a place everyone can access. Other programmers join and make changes. When the program is sufficiently functional, the developers advertise the program's availability to other Internet users. Users find bugs and missing features and report them back to the developers, who, in turn, enhance the program.

It sounds like an unworkable cycle, but in fact it has several advantages:

- A company structure is not required, so there is no overhead and no economic restrictions.

- Program development is not limited to a hired programming staff, but taps the capabilities and experience of a large pool of Internet programmers.

- User feedback is facilitated, allowing program testing by a large number of users in a short period of time.

- Program enhancements can be rapidly distributed to users.

1.6   Summary

This chapter has explored the long history of POSTGRESQL, starting with its roots in university research. POSTGRESQL would not have achieved its success without the Internet. The ability to communicate with people around the world has allowed a community of unpaid developers to enhance and support software that rivals commercial database offerings. By allowing everyone to see the source code and contribute to its ongoing development, POSTGRESQL continues to improve every day. The remainder of this book shows how to use this amazing piece of software.

Chapter 2

Issuing Database Commands

In this chapter, you will learn how to connect to the database server and issue simple commands to the POSTGRESQL server.

At this point, the book makes the following assumptions:

- You have installed POSTGRESQL.

- You have a running POSTGRESQL server.

- You are configured as a POSTGRESQL user.   *ecr*

- You have a database called *test*.   *test*

If not, see Appendix B.   *p 256*   *psql createdb test ;   (unit : run as postgres)*

2.1   Starting a Database Session

POSTGRESQL uses a *client/server* model of communication. A POSTGRESQL server is continually running, waiting for client requests. The server processes the request and returns the result to the client.

Choosing an Interface

Because the POSTGRESQL server runs as an independent process on the computer, a user cannot interact with it directly. Instead, client applications have been designed specifically for user interaction. This chapter describes how to interact with POSTGRESQL using the psql client application. Additional interfaces are covered in Chapters 16 and 17.

```
$ psql test
Welcome to psql, the PostgreSQL interactive terminal.

Type:   \copyright for distribution terms
        \h for help with SQL commands
        \? for help on internal slash commands
        \g or terminate with semicolon to execute query
        \q to quit

test=>
```

Figure 2.1: psql session start-up

Choosing a Database

Each POSTGRESQL server controls access to a number of databases. Databases are storage areas used by the server to partition information. For example, a typical installation may have a *production* database, used to keep all information about a company. It may also have a *training* database, used for training and testing purposes. They may have private databases, used by individuals to store personal information. For this exercise, we will assume that you have created an empty database called *test*. If not, see Appendix B.

Starting a Session

To start a psql session and connect to the *test* database, type psql test at the command prompt. Your output should look similar to Figure 2.1. Remember, the operating system command prompt is case-sensitive, so you must type this in all lowercase.[1]

2.2   Controlling a Session

Congratulations. You have successfully connected to the POSTGRESQL server. You can now issue commands and receive replies from the server. Let's try one. Type SELECT CURRENT_USER; and press *Enter* (see Figure 2.2). If you make a mistake, just press *Backspace* and retype the command. It should show your login name underneath the dashed line. This example shows the login name of postgres. The word getpgusername is a column label. The server also reports that it has returned one row of data. The line test=> tells you that the server has finished its current task and is waiting for the next database query.

---

[1]A few operating systems are case-insensitive.

```
test=> SELECT CURRENT_USER;
 getpgusername
---------------
 postgres
(1 row)

test=>
```

Figure 2.2: My first SQL query

```
test=> SELECT
test-> 1 + 3
test-> ;
 ?column?
----------
        4
(1 row)

test=>
```

Figure 2.3: Multiline query

Let's try another one. At the test=> prompt, type SELECT CURRENT_TIMESTAMP; and press *Enter*. You should see the current date and time. Each time you execute the query, the server will report the current time to you.

Typing in the Query Buffer

Typing in the query buffer is similar to typing at an operating system command prompt. However, at an operating system command prompt, *Enter* completes each command. In psql, commands are completed only when you enter a semicolon (;) or *backslash-g* (\g).

As an example, let's do SELECT 1 + 3; but in a different way. See Figure 2.3.[2] Notice that the query is spread over three lines. The prompt changed from => on the first line to -> on the second line to indicate that the query was continued. The semicolon told psql to send the query to the server. We could have easily replaced the semicolon with *backslash-g*. I do not recommend that you type queries as ugly as this one, but longer queries will benefit by being spread over multiple

---

[2]Don't be concerned about ?column?. We will cover that in Section 4.7.

```
test=> SELECT
test-> 2 * 10 + 1
test-> \p
SELECT
2 * 10 + 1
test-> \g
 ?column?
----------
       21
(1 row)

test=>
```

print buffer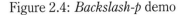

Figure 2.4: *Backslash-p* demo

lines. You might notice that the query is in uppercase. Unless you are typing a string in quotes, the POSTGRESQL server does not care whether words are uppercase or lowercase. For clarity, I recommend you enter words special to POSTGRESQL in uppercase.

Try some queries on your own involving arithmetic. Each computation must start with the word SELECT, then your computation, and finally a semicolon or *backslash-g*. For example, SELECT 4 ^ 10; would return *40*. Addition is performed using a plus symbol (+), subtraction using a minus symbol (-), multiplication using an asterisk (*), and division using a forward slash (/).

If you have *readline*[3] installed, psql will even allow you to use your arrow keys. Your *left* and *right arrow* keys allow you to move around, and the *up* and *down arrows* retrieve previously typed queries.

Displaying the Query Buffer

You can continue typing indefinitely, until you use a semicolon or *backslash-g*. Everything you type will be buffered by psql until you are ready to send the query. If you use *backslash-p* (\p), you will see everything accumulated in the query buffer. In Figure 2.4, three lines of text are accumulated and displayed by the user using *backslash-p*. After display, we use *backslash-g* to execute the query, which returns the value *21*. This ability comes in handy with long queries.

Erasing the Query Buffer

If you do not like what you have typed, use *backslash-r* (\r) to reset or erase the buffer.

---

[3]*Readline* is an open source library that allows powerful command-line editing.

2.3   Getting Help

You might ask, "Are these backslash commands documented anywhere?" If you look at Figure 2.1, you will see that the answer is printed every time psql starts. *Backslash-?* (\?) prints all valid backslash commands. *Backslash-h* displays help for SQL commands. SQL commands are covered in the next chapter.

2.4   Exiting a Session

This chapter would not be complete without showing you how to exit psql. Use *backslash-q* (\q) to quit the session and exit psql. Backslash *g* (go), *p* (print), *r* (reset), and *q* (quit) should be all you need for now.

2.5   Summary

This chapter has introduced the most important features of psql. This knowledge will allow you to try all the examples in this book. In addition, psql has many other features to assist you. Section 16.1 covers psql in detail. You may want to consult that chapter while reading through the book.

Chapter 3

Basic SQL Commands

SQL stands for *Structured Query Language.* It is the most common way to communicate with database servers, and is supported by almost all database systems. In this chapter, you will learn about relational database systems and how to issue the most important SQL commands.

3.1   Relational Databases

As mentioned in Section 1.1, the purpose of a database is rapid data storage and retrieval. Today, most database systems are *relational databases.* While the term "relational database" has a mathematical foundation, in practice it means that all data stored in the database is arranged in a uniform structure.

Figure 3.1 shows a database server with access to three databases: *demo, finance,* and *test.* You could issue the command psql finance and be connected to the *finance* database. You have already dealt with this issue in Chapter 2. Using psql, you chose to connect to database *test* with the command psql test. To see a list of databases available at your site, type psql -l. The first column lists the database names. However, you may not have permission to connect to all of them.

You might ask, "What are those black rectangles in the databases?" They are *tables.* Tables are the foundation of a *relational database management system (*RDBMS*).* They hold the data stored in a database. Each table has a name defined by the person who created it.

Let's look at a single table called *friend* shown in Table 3.1. You can readily see how tables are used to store data. Each *friend* is listed as a separate row in the table. The table records five pieces of information about each friend: *firstname, lastname, city, state,* and *age.* [1]

Each *friend* appears on a separate row; each column contains the same type of information. This is the type of structure that makes relational databases successful. It allows you to select certain rows of data, certain columns of data, or certain cells. You could select the entire row for *Mike*, the entire column for *City,* or a specific cell like *Denver.*

---

[1] In a real-world database, the person's birth date would be stored and not the person's age. The age must be updated each time the person has a birthday. A person's age can be computed when needed from a birth date field.

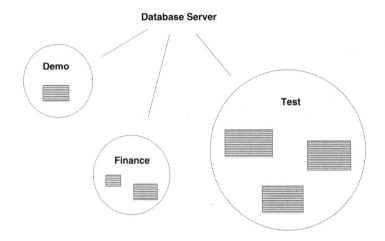

Figure 3.1: Databases

FirstName	LastName	City	State	Age
Mike	Nichols	Tampa	FL	19
Cindy	Anderson	Denver	CO	23
Sam	Jackson	Allentown	PA	22

Table 3.1: Table *friend*

```
test=> CREATE TABLE friend (
test(>              firstname CHAR(15),
test(>              lastname  CHAR(20),
test(>              city      CHAR(15),
test(>              state     CHAR(2),
test(>              age       INTEGER
test(> );
CREATE
```

Figure 3.2: Create table *friend*

Some synonyms exist for the terms "table," "row," and "column." "Table" is more formally referred to as a *relation* or *class,* "row" as *record* or *tuple,* and "column" as *field* or *attribute.*

3.2   Creating Tables

Let's create our own table and call it *friend.* Figure 3.2 shows the psql statement to create this table. You do not have to type the command exactly this way. You can use all lowercase, or you can write it in one long line, and it would work just the same.

Let's look at the statement from the top down. The words CREATE TABLE have special meaning to the database server. They indicate that the next request from the user is to create a table. You will find most SQL requests can be quickly identified by the first few words. The rest of the request has a specific format that is understood by the database server. While capitalization and spacing are optional, the format for a query must be followed exactly. Otherwise, the database server will issue an error such as parser: parse error at or near "pencil", meaning that the database server became confused near the word *pencil.* In such a case, the manual page for the command should be consulted and the query reissued in the proper format. A copy of the POSTGRESQL manual pages appears in Appendix D.

The CREATE TABLE command follows a specific format: first, the two words CREATE TABLE; then the table name; then an opening parenthesis; then a list of column names and their types; followed by a closing parenthesis. The important part of this query appears between the parentheses. You will notice five lines there in Figure 3.2. The first line, firstname CHAR(15), represents the first column of the table to create. This column is named firstname, and the text CHAR(15) indicates the column type and length. The CHAR(15) means the column holds a maximum of 15 characters. The second column is called *lastname* and holds a maximum of 20 characters. Columns of type CHAR() hold characters of a specified length. User-supplied character strings[2] that do not fill the

---

[2]A character string is a group of characters strung together.

✳   *(handwritten: display table defn)*

```
test=> \d friend
        Table "friend"
 Attribute |   Type    | Modifier
-----------+-----------+----------
 firstname | char(15)  |
 lastname  | char(20)  |
 city      | char(15)  |
 state     | char(2)   |
 age       | integer   |
```

Figure 3.3: Example of *backslash-d*

entire length of the field are right-padded with blanks. The columns *city* and *state* are similar. The final column, *age,* is different, however. It is not a CHAR() column, but rather an INTEGER column. It holds whole numbers, not characters. Even if the table contained 5,000 friends, you could be certain that no names appeared in the *age* column, only whole numbers. This consistent structure helps databases to be fast and reliable.

POSTGRESQL supports more column types than just CHAR() and INTEGER. However, in this chapter we will use only these two. Sections 4.1 and 9.2 cover column types in more detail.

Create some tables yourself now. Use only letters for your table and column names. Do not use any numbers, punctuation, or spaces at this time.

The \d command allows you to see information about a specific table or to list all table names in the current database. To see information about a specific table, type \d followed by the name of the table. For example, to see the column names and types of your new *friend* table in psql, type \d friend (Figure 3.3). If you use \d with no table name after it, you will see a list of all table names in the database.

3.3   Adding Data with INSERT

Let's continue toward the goal of making a table exactly like the *friend* table shown in Table 3.1. So far, we have created the table, but it does not contain any friends. You add rows into a table with the INSERT statement. Just as CREATE TABLE has a specific format that must be followed, INSERT also has a specific format. Figure 3.4 shows this format.

You must use single quotes around the character strings. Double quotes will not work. Spacing and capitalization are optional, except inside the single quotes. Inside them, the text is taken literally, so any capitalization will be stored in the database exactly as you specify. If you type too many quotes, you might reach a point where your backslash commands do not work anymore, and your prompt will appear as test'>. Notice the single quote before the greater than symbol. Just

```
test=> INSERT INTO friend VALUES (
test(>                          'Mike',
test(>                          'Nichols',
test(>                          'Tampa',
test(>                          'FL',
test(>                          19
test(> );
INSERT 19053 1
```

Figure 3.4: INSERT into *friend*

type another single quote to get out of this mode, use \r to clear the query buffer, and start again. Notice that the 19 does not have quotes. It does not need them because the column is a numeric column, not a character column. When you do your INSERT operations, be sure to match each piece of data to the receiving column. Figure 3.5 shows the additional INSERT commands needed to make the *friend* table match the three friends shown in Table 3.1.

3.4   Viewing Data with SELECT

You have just seen how to store data in the database. Now, let's retrieve that data. Surprisingly, only one command is provided to get data out of the database—SELECT. You have already used SELECT in your first database query (see Figure 2.2 on page 7). We will now use it to show the rows in the table *friend*. As shown in Figure 3.6, the entire query appears on one line. As queries become longer, breaking them into multiple lines helps make things clearer.

Let's look at this example in detail. First, we have the word SELECT, followed by an asterisk (*), the word FROM, our table name friend, and a semicolon to execute the query. The SELECT starts our command, telling the database server what is coming next. The * tells the server we want all the columns from the table. The FROM friend indicates which table we want to see. Thus, we have said we want all (*) columns from our table *friend*. Indeed, that is what is displayed—the same data as shown in Table 3.1 on page 12.

SELECT has a large number of variations, and we will look at a few of them now. Suppose you want to retrieve only one of the columns from the *friend* table. You might already suspect that the asterisk (*) must be changed in the query. If you replace it with one of the column names, you will see only that column. Try SELECT city FROM friend. You can choose any of the columns. You can even choose multiple columns, by separating the names with a comma. For example, to see first and last names only, use SELECT firstname, lastname FROM friend. Try a few more SELECT commands until you become comfortable.

If you specify a name that is not a valid column name, you will get an error message like ERROR:

```
test=> INSERT INTO friend VALUES (
test(>                           'Cindy',
test(>                           'Anderson',
test(>                           'Denver',
test(>                           'CO',
test(>                           23
test(> );
INSERT 19054 1
test=> INSERT INTO friend VALUES (
test(>                           'Sam',
test(>                           'Jackson',
test(>                           'Allentown',
test(>                           'PA',
test(>                           22
test(> );
INSERT 19055 1
```

Figure 3.5: Additional *friend* INSERT commands

```
test=> SELECT * FROM friend;
    firstname    |      lastname      |      city      | state | age
-----------------+--------------------+----------------+-------+-----
 Mike            | Nichols            | Tampa          | FL    |  19
 Cindy           | Anderson           | Denver         | CO    |  23
 Sam             | Jackson            | Allentown      | PA    |  22
(3 rows)
```

Figure 3.6: My first SELECT

```
test=> SELECT * FROM friend WHERE age = 23;
    firstname    |       lastname       |       city       | state | age
-----------------+----------------------+------------------+-------+-----
   Cindy         | Anderson             | Denver           | CO    | 23
(1 row)
```

Figure 3.7: My first WHERE

```
test=> SELECT * FROM friend WHERE age <= 22;
    firstname    |       lastname       |       city       | state | age
-----------------+----------------------+------------------+-------+-----
   Mike          | Nichols              | Tampa            | FL    | 19
   Sam           | Jackson              | Allentown        | PA    | 22
(2 rows)
```

Figure 3.8: More complex WHERE clause

attribute 'mycolname' not found. If you try selecting from a table that does not exist, you will get an error message like ERROR: Relation 'mytablename' does not exist. POSTGRESQL uses the formal relational database terms *relation* and *attribute* in these error messages.

3.5   Selecting Specific Rows with WHERE

Let's take the next step in controlling the output of SELECT. In the previous section, we showed how to select only certain columns from the table. Now, we will show how to select only certain rows. This operation requires a WHERE clause. Without a WHERE clause, every row is returned.

The WHERE clause goes immediately after the FROM clause. In the WHERE clause, you specify the rows you want returned, as shown in Figure 3.7. The query returns the rows that have an *age* column equal to *23*. Figure 3.8 shows a more complex example that returns two rows.

You can combine the column and row restrictions in a single query, allowing you to select any single cell, or a block of cells. See Figures 3.9 and 3.10.

Up to this point, we have made comparisons only on the *age* column. The *age* column is an INTEGER. The tricky part about the other columns is that they are CHAR() columns, so you must put the comparison value in single quotes. You also have to match the capitalization exactly. See Figure 3.11. If you had compared the *firstname* column to *'SAM'* or *'sam'*, it would have returned no rows. Try a few more comparisons until you are comfortable with this operation.

```
test=> SELECT lastname FROM friend WHERE age = 22;
      lastname
----------------------
 Jackson
(1 row)
```

Figure 3.9: A single cell

```
test=> SELECT city, state FROM friend WHERE age >= 21;
     city        | state
-----------------+-------
 Denver          | CO
 Allentown       | PA
(2 rows)
```

Figure 3.10: A block of cells

```
test=> SELECT * FROM friend WHERE firstname = 'Sam';
    firstname    |       lastname        |      city       | state | age
-----------------+-----------------------+-----------------+-------+-----
 Sam             | Jackson               | Allentown       | PA    | 22
(1 row)
```

Figure 3.11: Comparing string fields

3.6   Removing Data with DELETE

We know how to add data to the database; now we will learn how to remove it. Removal is quite simple. The DELETE command can quickly eliminate any or all rows from a table. The command DELETE FROM friend will delete all rows from the table *friend.* The query DELETE FROM friend WHERE age = 19 will remove only those rows that have an *age* column equal to *19.*

Here is a good exercise. Use INSERT to insert a row into the *friend* table, use SELECT to verify that the row has been properly added, then use DELETE to remove the row. This exercise combines the ideas you learned in the previous sections. Figure 3.12 shows an example.

3.7   Modifying Data with UPDATE

How do you modify data already in the database? You could use DELETE to remove a row and then use INSERT to insert a new row, but that is quite inefficient. The UPDATE command allows you to update data already in the database. It follows a format similar to the previous commands.

Continuing with our *friend* table, suppose Mike had a birthday, so we want to update his age in the table. The example in Figure 3.13 shows the word UPDATE, the table name *friend,* followed by SET, then the column name, the equals sign (=), and the new value. The WHERE clause controls which rows are affected by the UPDATE, just as in a DELETE operation. Without a WHERE clause, all rows are updated.

Notice that the *Mike* row has moved to the end of the list. The next section will explain how to control the order of the display.

3.8   Sorting Data with ORDER BY

In a SELECT query, rows are displayed in an undetermined order. To guarantee that the rows will be returned from SELECT in a specific order, you must add the ORDER BY clause to the end of the SELECT. Figure 3.14 shows the use of ORDER BY. You can reverse the order by adding DESC, as shown in Figure 3.15. If the query also used a WHERE clause, the ORDER BY would appear after the WHERE clause, as in Figure 3.16.

You can ORDER BY more than one column by specifying multiple column names or labels, separated by commas. The command would then sort by the first column specified. For rows with equal values in the first column, it would sort based on the second column specified. Of course, this approach is not useful in the *friend* example because all column values are unique.

3.9   Destroying Tables

This chapter would not be complete without showing you how to remove tables. This task is accomplished using the DROP TABLE command. For example, the command DROP TABLE friend will

```
test=> SELECT * FROM friend;
   firstname    |      lastname      |      city      | state | age
----------------+--------------------+----------------+-------+-----
 Mike           | Nichols            | Tampa          | FL    |  19
 Cindy          | Anderson           | Denver         | CO    |  23
 Sam            | Jackson            | Allentown      | PA    |  22
(3 rows)

test=> INSERT INTO friend VALUES ('Jim', 'Barnes', 'Ocean City','NJ', 25);
INSERT 19056 1
test=> SELECT * FROM friend;
   firstname    |      lastname      |      city      | state | age
----------------+--------------------+----------------+-------+-----
 Mike           | Nichols            | Tampa          | FL    |  19
 Cindy          | Anderson           | Denver         | CO    |  23
 Sam            | Jackson            | Allentown      | PA    |  22
 Jim            | Barnes             | Ocean City     | NJ    |  25
(4 rows)

test=> DELETE FROM friend WHERE lastname = 'Barnes';
DELETE 1
test=> SELECT * FROM friend;
   firstname    |      lastname      |      city      | state | age
----------------+--------------------+----------------+-------+-----
 Mike           | Nichols            | Tampa          | FL    |  19
 Cindy          | Anderson           | Denver         | CO    |  23
 Sam            | Jackson            | Allentown      | PA    |  22
(3 rows)
```

delete

Figure 3.12: DELETE example

```
test=> UPDATE friend SET age = 20 WHERE firstname = 'Mike';
UPDATE 1
test=> SELECT * FROM friend;
   firstname    |      lastname       |      city       | state | age
----------------+---------------------+-----------------+-------+-----
 Cindy          | Anderson            | Denver          | CO    |  23
 Sam            | Jackson             | Allentown       | PA    |  22
 Mike           | Nichols             | Tampa           | FL    |  20
(3 rows)
```

update

Figure 3.13: My first UPDATE

```
test=> SELECT * FROM friend ORDER BY state;
   firstname    |      lastname       |      city       | state | age
----------------+---------------------+-----------------+-------+-----
 Cindy          | Anderson            | Denver          | CO    |  23
 Mike           | Nichols             | Tampa           | FL    |  20
 Sam            | Jackson             | Allentown       | PA    |  22
(3 rows)
```

*Select
with
order by*

Figure 3.14: Use of ORDER BY

```
test=> SELECT * FROM friend ORDER BY age DESC;
   firstname    |      lastname       |      city       | state | age
----------------+---------------------+-----------------+-------+-----
 Cindy          | Anderson            | Denver          | CO    |  23
 Sam            | Jackson             | Allentown       | PA    |  22
 Mike           | Nichols             | Tampa           | FL    |  20
(3 rows)
```

Figure 3.15: Reverse ORDER BY

```
test=> SELECT * FROM friend WHERE age >= 21 ORDER BY firstname;
    firstname    |       lastname        |       city       | state | age
-----------------+-----------------------+------------------+-------+-----
   Cindy         | Anderson              | Denver           | CO    | 23
   Sam           | Jackson               | Allentown        | PA    | 22
(2 rows)
```

Figure 3.16: Use of ORDER BY and WHERE

remove the *friend* table. Both the table structure and the data contained in the table will be erased. We will use the *friend* table in the next chapter, so you should not remove the table at this time. Remember—to remove only the data in the table without removing the table structure itself, use DELETE.

3.10   Summary

This chapter has shown the basic operations of any database:

- Table creation (CREATE TABLE)

- Table destruction (DROP TABLE)

- Displaying (SELECT)

- Adding (INSERT)

- Replacing (UPDATE)

- Removing (DELETE)

This chapter has shown these commands in their simplest forms; real-world queries are much more complex. The next chapters will show how these simple commands can be used to handle some very complicated tasks.

Chapter 4

Customizing Queries

This chapter will illustrate additional capabilities of the basic SQL commands.

4.1 Data Types

Table 4.1 lists the most common column data types. Figure 4.1 shows queries using these types. Notice that numbers do not require quotes, but character strings, dates, and times do require them.

The final SELECT uses psql's \x display mode.[1] Without \x, the SELECT would have displayed too much information to fit on one line. The fields would have wrapped around the edge of the display, making it difficult to read. The columns would still line up, but there would be other data in the way. Of course, another solution to field wrapping is to select fewer columns. Remember, you can select any columns from the table in any order.

Section 9.2 covers column types in more detail.

---

[1]See Section 16.1 for a full list of the psql backslash commands.

p 177

Most common types

Category	Type	Description
character string	CHAR(length)	blank-padded string, fixed storage length
	VARCHAR(length)	variable storage length
number	INTEGER	integer, +/–2 billion range
	FLOAT	floating point number, 15-digit precision
	NUMERIC(precision, decimal)	number with user-defined precision and decimal location
date/time	DATE	date
	TIME	time
	TIMESTAMP	date and time

Table 4.1: Common data types

23

```
test=> CREATE TABLE alltypes (
test(>               state CHAR(2),
test(>               name CHAR(30),
test(>               children INTEGER,
test(>               distance FLOAT,
test(>               budget NUMERIC(16,2),
test(>               born DATE,
test(>               checkin TIME,
test(>               started TIMESTAMP
test(> );
CREATE
test=> INSERT INTO alltypes
test-> VALUES (
test(>        'PA',
test(>        'Hilda Blairwood',
test(>        3,
test(>        10.7,
test(>        4308.20,
test(>        '9/8/1974',
test(>        '9:00',
test(>        '07/03/1996 10:30:00');
INSERT 19073 1
test=> SELECT state, name, children, distance, budget FROM alltypes;
 state |            name             | children | distance | budget
-------+-----------------------------+----------+----------+---------
 PA    | Hilda Blairwood             |        3 |     10.7 | 4308.20
(1 row)


test=> SELECT born, checkin, started FROM alltypes;
    born    | checkin  |        started
------------+----------+-----------------------
 1974-09-08 | 09:00:00 | 1996-07-03 10:30:00-04
(1 row)

test=> \x
Expanded display is on.
test=> SELECT * FROM alltypes;
-[ RECORD 1 ]---------------------------
state    | PA
name     | Hilda Blairwood
children | 3
distance | 10.7
budget   | 4308.20
born     | 1974-09-08
checkin  | 09:00:00
started  | 1996-07-03 10:30:00-04
```

Figure 4.1: Example of common data types

```
test=> INSERT INTO friend (firstname, lastname, city, state)
test-> VALUES ('Mark', 'Middleton', 'Indianapolis', 'IN');
INSERT 19074 1
```

Figure 4.2: Insertion of specific columns

4.2   Quotes Inside Text

Suppose you want to insert the name *O'Donnell*. You might be tempted to enter it in psql as
'O'Donnell', but this approach will not work. The presence of a single quote inside a single-quoted
string generates a parser error. One way to place a single quote inside a single-quoted string is to
use two quotes together—for example, 'O''Donnell'.[2] Two single quotes inside a single-quoted
string causes one single quote to be generated. Another option is to use a backslash—for example,
'O\'Donnell'. The backslash escapes the single quote character.

4.3   Using NULL Values

Let's return to the INSERT statement described in Section 3.3 on page 14. We will continue to
use the *friend* table from the previous chapter. In Figure 3.4, we specified a value for each *friend*
column. Suppose now that we want to insert a new row, but do not want to supply data for all
columns. That is, we want to insert information about *Mark,* but we do not know Mark's age.

Figure 4.2 shows this scenario. After the table name, column names appear in parentheses.
These columns will be assigned, in order, to the supplied data values. If we were supplying data
for all columns, we would not need to name them. In this example, however, we must name the
columns. The table has five columns, but we are supplying only four data values.

The column we did not assign was *age*. The interesting question is, "What is in the *age* cell for
Mark?" The answer is that the age cell contains a NULL value.

NULL is a special value that is valid in any column. You use it when a valid entry for a field is
not known or not applicable. In the previous example, we wanted to add Mark to the database but
did not know his age. It is difficult to imagine what numeric value could be used for Mark's *age*
column. Zero or -1 would be strange age values. Thus, NULL is the appropriate value for his *age*
column.

Suppose we have a *spouse* column. What value should be used if someone is not married?
A NULL value would be the proper value. For a *wedding_anniversary* column, unmarried people
would have a NULL value in that field. NULL values are very useful. Before databases supported
NULL values, users would put special values in columns, such as -1 for unknown numbers and
1/1/1900 for unknown dates. NULL values offer a more consistent way to mark such values.

---

[2]That is not a double qoute between the O and D, but rather two single quotes.

NULL values exhibit special behavior in comparisons. Look at Figure 4.3. First, notice that the *age* column for *Mark* is empty. It is really a NULL. In the next query, because NULL values are unknown, the NULL row does not appear in the output. The third query often confuses people.[3] Why doesn't the *Mark* row appear? The *age* is NULL or unknown, meaning that the database does not know if it equals 99—and does not guess. It refuses to print it. In fact, no comparison exists that will produce the NULL row, except the last query shown.

The tests IS NULL and IS NOT NULL are designed specifically to test for the existence of NULL values. If you are making comparisons on columns that might contain NULL values, you must test for them specifically.

Figure 4.4 shows an example of such a comparison. We have inserted *Jack,* but the *city* and *state* were not known, so they are set to NULL. The next query's WHERE comparison is contrived, but illustrative. Because *city* and *state* are both NULL, you might suspect that the *Jack* row would be returned. However, because NULL means unknown, we have no way to know whether the two NULL values are equal. Again, POSTGRESQL does not guess and does not print the result.

One other issue with NULLs needs clarification. In character columns, a NULL is not the same as a zero-length value. The empty string '' and NULL are different. Figure 4.5 shows an example highlighting this difference. There are no valid numeric and date blank values, but a character string can be blank. When viewed in psql, any blank numeric field must contain a NULL because no blank number exists. However, there are blank strings, so blank strings and NULL values are displayed in the same way in psql. Of course, they are not the same, so be careful not to confuse the meaning of NULL values in character fields.

4.4   Controlling DEFAULT Values

As we learned in the previous section, columns not specified in an INSERT statement are given NULL values. You can change this assignment by using the DEFAULT keyword. When creating a table, the keyword DEFAULT and a value can be used next to each column type. The value will then be used anytime the column value is not supplied in an INSERT. If no DEFAULT is defined, a NULL is used for the column. Figure 4.6 shows a typical use of default values. The default for the *timestamp* column is actually a call to an internal POSTGRESQL variable that returns the current date and time.

4.5   Column Labels

You might have noticed the text that appears at the top of each column in the SELECT output—the *column label.* The label usually is the name of the selected column. However, you can control the text that appears at the top of each column by using the AS keyword. For example, Figure 4.7 replaces the default column label firstname with the column label buddy. You might have noticed

---

[3]The <> means *not equal.*

```
test=> SELECT * FROM friend ORDER BY age DESC;
    firstname    |      lastname        |      city       | state | age
-----------------+----------------------+-----------------+-------+-----
  Cindy          | Anderson             | Denver          | CO    |  23
  Sam            | Jackson              | Allentown       | PA    |  22
  Mike           | Nichols              | Tampa           | FL    |  20
  Mark           | Middleton            | Indianapolis    | IN    |
(4 rows)


test=> SELECT * FROM friend WHERE age > 0 ORDER BY age DESC;
    firstname    |      lastname        |      city       | state | age
-----------------+----------------------+-----------------+-------+-----
  Cindy          | Anderson             | Denver          | CO    |  23
  Sam            | Jackson              | Allentown       | PA    |  22
  Mike           | Nichols              | Tampa           | FL    |  20
(3 rows)


test=> SELECT * FROM friend WHERE age <> 99 ORDER BY age DESC;
    firstname    |      lastname        |      city       | state | age
-----------------+----------------------+-----------------+-------+-----
  Cindy          | Anderson             | Denver          | CO    |  23
  Sam            | Jackson              | Allentown       | PA    |  22
  Mike           | Nichols              | Tampa           | FL    |  20
(3 rows)


test=> SELECT * FROM friend WHERE age IS NULL ORDER BY age DESC;
    firstname    |      lastname        |      city       | state | age
-----------------+----------------------+-----------------+-------+-----
  Mark           | Middleton            | Indianapolis    | IN    |
(1 row)
```

Figure 4.3: NULL handling

```
test=> INSERT INTO friend
test-> VALUES ('Jack', 'Burger', NULL, NULL, 27);
INSERT 19075 1
test=> SELECT * FROM friend WHERE city = state;
 firstname | lastname | city | state | age
-----------+----------+------+-------+-----
(0 rows)
```

Figure 4.4: Comparison of NULL fields

```
test=> CREATE TABLE nulltest (name CHAR(20), spouse CHAR(20));
CREATE
test=> INSERT INTO nulltest VALUES ('Andy', '');
INSERT 19086 1
test=> INSERT INTO nulltest VALUES ('Tom', NULL);
INSERT 19087 1
test=> SELECT * FROM nulltest ORDER BY name;
        name          |        spouse
----------------------+----------------------
 Andy                 |                                ← spouse value is ''
 Tom                  |                                ← spouse value is null
(2 rows)

test=> SELECT * FROM nulltest WHERE spouse = '';
        name          |        spouse
----------------------+----------------------
 Andy                 |
(1 row)

test=> SELECT * FROM nulltest WHERE spouse IS NULL;
        name          | spouse
----------------------+--------
 Tom                  |
(1 row)
```

Figure 4.5: NULL values and blank strings

```
test=> CREATE TABLE account (
test(>          name      CHAR(20),
test(>          balance   NUMERIC(16,2) DEFAULT 0,
test(>          active    CHAR(1) DEFAULT 'Y',
test(>          created   TIMESTAMP DEFAULT CURRENT_TIMESTAMP
test(> );
CREATE
test=> INSERT INTO account (name)
test-> VALUES ('Federated Builders');
INSERT 19103 1
test=> SELECT * FROM account;
         name        | balance | active |        created
---------------------+---------+--------+------------------------
 Federated Builders  |    0.00 | Y      | 1998-05-30 21:37:48-04
(1 row)
```

Using defaults in table creation

yyyy-mm-dd hh:mn:ss-

?

Figure 4.6: Using DEFAULT values

```
test=> SELECT firstname AS buddy FROM friend ORDER BY buddy;
     buddy
-----------------
 Cindy
 Jack
 Mark
 Mike
 Sam
(5 rows)
```

Select field as name

Figure 4.7: Controlling column labels

```
test=> SELECT 1 + 3 AS total;
 total
 -------
      4
(1 row)
```

Figure 4.8: Computation using a column label

hia;
Comments

```
test=> -- a single line comment
test=> /* a multiline
test*>    comment */
```

Figure 4.9: Comment styles

that the query in Figure 2.3 on page 7 has the column label ?column?. The database server returns this label when there is no suitable label. In that case, the result of an addition does not have an appropriate label. Figure 4.8 shows the same query with an appropriate label added using AS.

4.6 Comments

POSTGRESQL allows you to place any text into psql for use as a comment. Two comment styles are possible. The presence of two dashes (--) marks all text to the end of the line as a comment. POSTGRESQL also understands C-style comments, where the comment begins with slash-asterisk (/*) and ends with asterisk-slash (*/). Figure 4.9 shows both comment styles. Notice how the multiline comment is marked by a psql command prompt of *>. It is a reminder that you are in a multiline comment, just as -> is a reminder that you are in a multiline statement, and '> is a reminder that you are in a multiline quoted string.

4.7 AND/OR Usage

Until now, we have used only simple WHERE clause tests. In the following sections, we will demonstrate how to perform more complex WHERE clause testing.

Complex WHERE clause tests are done by connecting simple tests using the words AND and OR. For illustration, new people have been inserted into the *friend* table, as shown in Figure 4.10. Selecting certain rows from the table will require more complex WHERE conditions. For example, if we wanted to select *Sandy Gleason* by name, it would be impossible using only one comparison

```
test=> DELETE FROM friend;
DELETE 6
test=> INSERT INTO friend
test-> VALUES ('Dean', 'Yeager', 'Plymouth', 'MA', 24);
INSERT 19744 1
test=> INSERT INTO friend
test-> VALUES ('Dick', 'Gleason', 'Ocean City', 'NJ', 19);
INSERT 19745 1
test=> INSERT INTO friend
test-> VALUES ('Ned', 'Millstone', 'Cedar Creek', 'MD', 27);
INSERT 19746 1
test=> INSERT INTO friend
test-> VALUES ('Sandy', 'Gleason', 'Ocean City', 'NJ', 25);
INSERT 19747 1
test=> INSERT INTO friend
test-> VALUES ('Sandy', 'Weber', 'Boston', 'MA', 33);
INSERT 19748 1
test=> INSERT INTO friend
test-> VALUES ('Victor', 'Tabor', 'Williamsport', 'PA', 22);
INSERT 19749 1
test=> SELECT * FROM friend ORDER BY firstname;
   firstname    |    lastname    |      city      | state | age
----------------+----------------+----------------+-------+-----
 Dean           | Yeager         | Plymouth       | MA    |  24
 Dick           | Gleason        | Ocean City     | NJ    |  19
 Ned            | Millstone      | Cedar Creek    | MD    |  27
 Sandy          | Gleason        | Ocean City     | NJ    |  25
 Sandy          | Weber          | Boston         | MA    |  33
 Victor         | Tabor          | Williamsport   | PA    |  22
(6 rows)
```

Delete all records

Figure 4.10: New friends

```
test=> SELECT * FROM friend
test-> WHERE firstname = 'Sandy' AND lastname = 'Gleason';
   firstname    |       lastname       |      city       | state | age
----------------+----------------------+-----------------+-------+-----
   Sandy        | Gleason              | Ocean City      | NJ    | 25
(1 row)
```

Figure 4.11: WHERE test for *Sandy Gleason*

```
test=> SELECT * FROM friend
test-> WHERE state = 'NJ' OR state = 'PA'
test-> ORDER BY firstname;
   firstname    |       lastname       |      city       | state | age
----------------+----------------------+-----------------+-------+-----
   Dick         | Gleason              | Ocean City      | NJ    | 19
   Sandy        | Gleason              | Ocean City      | NJ    | 25
   Victor       | Tabor                | Williamsport    | PA    | 22
(3 rows)
```

Figure 4.12: Friends in New Jersey and Pennsylvania

in the WHERE clause. If we tested for firstname = 'Sandy', we would select both *Sandy Gleason* and *Sandy Weber.* If we tested for lastname = 'Gleason', we would get both *Sandy Gleason* and her brother *Dick Gleason.* The proper approach is to use AND to test both *firstname* and *lastname.* This query is shown in Figure 4.11. The AND combines the two needed comparisons.

A similar comparison could be used to select friends living in Cedar Creek, Maryland. Other friends could live in Cedar Creek, Ohio, so the comparison city = 'Cedar Creek' is not enough. The proper test is city = 'Cedar Creek' AND state = 'MD'.

Another complex test would be to select people who live in the state of New Jersey (NJ) or Pennsylvania (PA). Such a comparison requires the use of OR. The test state = 'NJ' OR state = 'PA' would return the desired rows, as shown in Figure 4.12.

An unlimited number of AND and OR clauses can be linked together to perform complex comparisons. When ANDs are linked with other ANDs, there is no possibility for confusion. The same is true of ORs. On the other hand, when ANDs and ORs are both used in the same query, the results can be confusing. Figure 4.13 shows such a case. You might suspect that it would return rows with *firstname* equal to Victor and *state* equal to PA or NJ. In fact, the query returns rows with *firstname* equal to Victor and *state* equal to PA, or *state* equal to NJ. In this case, the AND is

```
test=> SELECT * FROM friend
test-> WHERE firstname = 'Victor' AND state = 'PA' OR state = 'NJ'          No
test-> ORDER BY firstname;
   firstname    |      lastname      |      city       | state | age
----------------+--------------------+-----------------+-------+-----
 Dick           | Gleason            | Ocean City      | NJ    |  19
 Sandy          | Gleason            | Ocean City      | NJ    |  25
 Victor         | Tabor              | Williamsport    | PA    |  22
(3 rows)
```

Figure 4.13: Incorrectly mixing AND and OR clauses

```
test=> SELECT * FROM friend
test-> WHERE firstname = 'Victor' AND (state = 'PA' OR state = 'NJ')       Yes
test-> ORDER BY firstname;
   firstname    |      lastname      |      city       | state | age
----------------+--------------------+-----------------+-------+-----
 Victor         | Tabor              | Williamsport    | PA    |  22
(1 row)
```

Figure 4.14: Correctly mixing AND and OR clauses

evaluated first, then the OR. When mixing ANDs and ORs, it is best to collect the ANDs and ORs into common groups using parentheses. Figure 4.14 shows the proper way to enter this query. Without parentheses, it is very difficult to understand a query with mixed ANDs and ORs.

4.8 Range of Values

Suppose we want to see all friends with ages between 22 and 25. Figure 4.15 shows two queries that produce this result. The first query uses AND to perform two comparisons that *both* must be true. We used <= and >= so the age comparisons included the limiting ages of 22 and 25. If we used < and >, the ages 22 and 25 would not have been included in the output. The second query uses BETWEEN to generate the same comparison. BETWEEN comparisons include the limiting values in the result.

Comparison	Operator
less than	<
less than or equal	<=
equal	=
greater than or equal	>=
greater than	>
not equal	<> or !=

Table 4.2: Comparison operators

```
test=> SELECT *
test-> FROM friend
test-> WHERE age >= 22 AND age <= 25
test-> ORDER BY firstname;
   firstname    |      lastname      |      city      | state | age
----------------+--------------------+----------------+-------+-----
 Dean           | Yeager             | Plymouth       | MA    |  24
 Sandy          | Gleason            | Ocean City     | NJ    |  25
 Victor         | Tabor              | Williamsport   | PA    |  22
(3 rows)

test=> SELECT *
test-> FROM friend
test-> WHERE age BETWEEN 22 AND 25
test-> ORDER BY firstname;
   firstname    |      lastname      |      city      | state | age
----------------+--------------------+----------------+-------+-----
 Dean           | Yeager             | Plymouth       | MA    |  24
 Sandy          | Gleason            | Ocean City     | NJ    |  25
 Victor         | Tabor              | Williamsport   | PA    |  22
(3 rows)
```

Figure 4.15: Selecting a range of values

```
test=> SELECT * FROM friend
test-> WHERE firstname LIKE 'D%'
test-> ORDER BY firstname;
    firstname    |      lastname      |      city      | state | age
-----------------+--------------------+----------------+-------+-----
   Dean          | Yeager             | Plymouth       | MA    | 24
   Dick          | Gleason            | Ocean City     | NJ    | 19
(2 rows)
```

Figure 4.16: *Firstname* begins with D

Comparison	Operation
begins with D	LIKE 'D%'
contains a D	LIKE '%D%'
has D in second position	LIKE '_D%'
begins with D and contains e	LIKE 'D%e%'
begins with D, contains e, then f	LIKE 'D%e%f%'
begins with non-D	NOT LIKE 'D%'

Table 4.3: LIKE comparisons

4.9 LIKE Comparison

Greater than and *less than* comparisons are possible using the operators shown in Table 4.2. Even more complex comparisons can be made. For instance, users often need to compare character strings to see if they match a certain pattern. Sometimes they want only fields that begin with a certain letter or that contain a certain word. The LIKE keyword allows such comparisons. The query in Figure 4.16 returns rows where the *firstname* begins with D. The percent symbol (%) means that any characters can follow the D. Thus the query performs the test firstname LIKE 'D%'.

The test firstname LIKE '%D%' returns those rows where *firstname* contains D anywhere in the field, not just at the beginning. The effect of having a % before and after a character is that the character can appear anywhere in the string.

More complex tests can be performed with LIKE, as shown in Table 4.3. While the percent symbol (%) matches an unlimited number of characters, the underscore (_) matches only a single character. The underscore allows any single character to appear in that position. To test whether a field does *not* match a pattern, use NOT LIKE. To test for an actual percent symbol (%), use backslash-percent (\%). To test for an actual underscore (_), use backslash-underscore (_).

Comparison	Operator
regular expression	~
regular expression, case-insensitive	~*
not equal to regular expression	!~
not equal to regular expression, case-insensitive	!~*

Table 4.4: Regular expression operators

Test	Special Characters
start	^
end	$
any single character	.
set of characters	[ccc]
set of characters not equal	[^ccc]
range of characters	[c-c]
range of characters not equal	[^c-c]
zero or one of previous character	?
zero or multiple of previous characters	*
one or multiple of previous characters	+
OR operator	|

Table 4.5: Regular expression special characters

Attempting to find all character fields that *end* with a certain character can be difficult. For CHAR() columns, like *firstname*, trailing spaces make trailing comparisons difficult with LIKE. Other character column types do not use trailing spaces. Those can, for example, use the test `colname` `LIKE '%g'` to find all rows that end with g. See Section 9.2 for complete coverage of character data types.

4.10   Regular Expressions

Regular expressions allow more powerful comparisons than LIKE and NOT LIKE. Regular expression comparisons are a unique feature of POSTGRESQL. They are very common in Unix, such as in the Unix `grep` command.[4]

Table 4.4 lists the regular expression operators, and Table 4.5 lists the regular expression special characters. Note that the caret (^) has a different meaning outside and inside square brackets ([ ]).

---

[4]Actually, in POSTGRESQL, regular expressions are like `egrep` extended regular expressions.

Test	Operation
begins with D	~ '^D'
contains D	~ 'D'
D in second position	~ '^.D'
begins with D and contains e	~ '^D.*e'
begins with D, contains e, and then f	~ 'D.*e.*f'
contains A, B, C, or D	~ '[A-D]' or ~ '[ABCD]'
contains A or a	~* 'a' or ~ '[Aa]'
does not contain D	!~ 'D'
does not begin with D	!~ '^D' or ~ '^[^D]'
begins with D, with one optional leading space	~ '^ ?D'
begins with D , with optional leading spaces	~ '^ *D'
begins with D, with at least one leading space	~ '^ +D'
ends with G, with optional trailing spaces	~ 'G *$'

'or' not part of re

@ 36

Table 4.6: Examples of regular expressions

*~*u means "case-insensitive," on remaining pattern*

Although regular expressions are powerful, they can be complex to create. Table 4.6 shows some examples, and Figure 4.17 shows selected queries using regular expressions. For a description of each query, see the comment above it.

Figure 4.18 shows two more complex regular expressions. The first query demonstrates how to properly test for a trailing n. Because CHAR() columns contain trailing spaces to fill the column, you must test for possible trailing spaces. (See Section 9.2 for complete coverage on character data types.) The second query might seem surprising. Some might think that it returns rows that do not contain an S. Actually, it returns all rows that have *any* character that is not an S. For example, *Sandy* contains characters that are not S, such as *a, n, d,* and *y,* so that row is returned. The test would prevent rows containing only S's from being printed.

You can also test for the literal characters listed in Table 4.5. Use of a backslash removes any special meaning from the character that follows it. For example, to test for a dollar sign, use \$. To test for an asterisk, use *. To test for a literal backslash, use two backslashes (\\).

Because regular expressions are so powerful, creating them can be challenging. Try some queries on the *friend* table until you are comfortable with regular expression comparisons.

4.11 CASE Clause

Many programming languages have conditional statements, stating *if* condition is true *then* do something, *else* do something else. This kind of structure allows execution of statements based on some condition. Although SQL is not a procedural programming language, it does allow conditional

```
test=> SELECT * FROM friend
test-> ORDER BY firstname;
    firstname    |      lastname       |      city       | state | age
-----------------+---------------------+-----------------+-------+-----
 Dean            | Yeager              | Plymouth        | MA    |  24
 Dick            | Gleason             | Ocean City      | NJ    |  19
 Ned             | Millstone           | Cedar Creek     | MD    |  27
 Sandy           | Gleason             | Ocean City      | NJ    |  25
 Sandy           | Weber               | Boston          | MA    |  33
 Victor          | Tabor               | Williamsport    | PA    |  22
(6 rows)

test=> -- firstname begins with 'S'
test=> SELECT * FROM friend
test-> WHERE firstname ~ '^S'
test-> ORDER BY firstname;
    firstname    |      lastname       |      city       | state | age
-----------------+---------------------+-----------------+-------+-----
 Sandy           | Gleason             | Ocean City      | NJ    |  25
 Sandy           | Weber               | Boston          | MA    |  33
(2 rows)

test=> -- firstname has an e in the second position
test=> SELECT * FROM friend
test-> WHERE firstname ~ '^.e'
test-> ORDER BY firstname;
    firstname    |      lastname       |      city       | state | age
-----------------+---------------------+-----------------+-------+-----
 Dean            | Yeager              | Plymouth        | MA    |  24
 Ned             | Millstone           | Cedar Creek     | MD    |  27
(2 rows)

test=> -- firstname contains b, B, c, or C
test=> SELECT * FROM friend
test-> WHERE firstname ~* '[bc]'
test-> ORDER BY firstname;
    firstname    |      lastname       |      city       | state | age
-----------------+---------------------+-----------------+-------+-----
 Dick            | Gleason             | Ocean City      | NJ    |  19
 Victor          | Tabor               | Williamsport    | PA    |  22
(2 rows)

test=> -- firstname does not contain s or S
test=> SELECT * FROM friend
test-> WHERE firstname !~* 's'
test-> ORDER BY firstname;
    firstname    |      lastname       |      city       | state | age
-----------------+---------------------+-----------------+-------+-----
 Dean            | Yeager              | Plymouth        | MA    |  24
 Dick            | Gleason             | Ocean City      | NJ    |  19
 Ned             | Millstone           | Cedar Creek     | MD    |  27
 Victor          | Tabor               | Williamsport    | PA    |  22
(4 rows)
```

Figure 4.17: Regular expression sample queries

```
test=> -- firstname ends with n
test=> SELECT * FROM friend
test-> WHERE firstname ~ 'n *$'
test-> ORDER BY firstname;
   firstname     |     lastname     |     city     | state | age
-----------------+------------------+--------------+-------+-----
 Dean            | Yeager           | Plymouth     | MA    | 24
(1 row)
```

char cols contain trailing spaces

```
test=> -- firstname contains a non-S character
test=> SELECT * FROM friend
test-> WHERE firstname ~ '[^S]'
test-> ORDER BY firstname;
   firstname     |     lastname     |     city     | state | age
-----------------+------------------+--------------+-------+-----
 Dean            | Yeager           | Plymouth     | MA    | 24
 Dick            | Gleason          | Ocean City   | NJ    | 19
 Ned             | Millstone        | Cedar Creek  | MD    | 27
 Sandy           | Gleason          | Ocean City   | NJ    | 25
 Sandy           | Weber            | Boston       | MA    | 33
 Victor          | Tabor            | Williamsport | PA    | 22
(6 rows)
```

NB match anywhere   *※*

Figure 4.18: Complex regular expression queries

```
test=> SELECT firstname,
test->          age,
test->          CASE
test->              WHEN age >= 21 THEN 'adult'
test->              ELSE 'minor'
test->          END
test-> FROM friend
test-> ORDER BY firstname;
    firstname    | age | case
-----------------+-----+-------
 Dean            |  24 | adult
 Dick            |  19 | minor
 Ned             |  27 | adult
 Sandy           |  25 | adult
 Sandy           |  33 | adult
 Victor          |  22 | adult
(6 rows)
```

Figure 4.19: CASE example

control over the data returned from a query. The WHERE clause uses comparisons to control row selection. The CASE statement allows comparisons in column output. Figure 4.19 shows a query using CASE to create a new output column containing *adult* or *minor* as appropriate, based on the *age* field. Of course, the values *adult* and *minor* do not appear in the table *friend*. The CASE clause allows the creation of those conditional strings.

Figure 4.20 shows a more complex example. It shows a query with multiple WHEN clauses. The AS clause is used to label the column with the word *distance*. Although only SELECT examples are shown, CASE can be used in UPDATE and other complicated situations. CASE allows the creation of conditional values, which can be used for output or for further processing in the same query.

4.12   Distinct Rows

It is often desirable to return the results of a query with no duplicates. The keyword DISTINCT prevents duplicates from being returned. Figure 4.21 shows the use of DISTINCT to prevent duplicate *states* and duplicate *city* and *state* combinations. Notice that DISTINCT operates only on the columns selected in the query. It does not compare nonselected columns when determining uniqueness. Section 5.2 explains how counts can be generated for each of the distinct values.

```
test=> SELECT  firstname,
test->         state,
test->         CASE
test->              WHEN state = 'PA' THEN 'close'
test->              WHEN state = 'NJ' OR state = 'MD' THEN 'far'
test->              ELSE 'very far'
test->         END AS distance
test-> FROM friend
test-> ORDER BY firstname;
    firstname     | state | distance
------------------+-------+----------
 Dean             | MA    | very far
 Dick             | NJ    | far
 Ned              | MD    | far
 Sandy            | NJ    | far
 Sandy            | MA    | very far
 Victor           | PA    | close
(6 rows)
```

Select with Case

CASE
WHEN cond THEN exp
WHEN " " "
ELSE expr
END [AS word]

Figure 4.20: Complex CASE example

```
test=> SELECT state FROM friend ORDER BY state;
 state
-------
 MA
 MA
 MD
 NJ
 NJ
 PA
(6 rows)

test=> SELECT DISTINCT state FROM friend ORDER BY state;
 state
-------
 MA
 MD
 NJ
 PA
(4 rows)
```

only distinct 2-tuples

```
test=> SELECT DISTINCT city, state FROM friend ORDER BY state, city;
      city        | state
------------------+-------
 Boston           | MA
 Plymouth         | MA
 Cedar Creek      | MD
 Ocean City       | NJ
 Williamsport     | PA
(5 rows)
```

Figure 4.21: DISTINCT prevents duplicates

Function	SET option
DATESTYLE	DATESTYLE TO 'ISO' | 'POSTGRES' | 'SQL' | 'US' | 'NONEUROPEAN' | 'EUROPEAN' | 'GERMAN'
TIMEZONE	TIMEZONE TO *'value'*

Table 4.7: SET options

4.13 Functions and Operators

Many functions and operators are available in POSTGRESQL. Function calls can take zero, one, or more arguments and return a single value. You can list all functions and their arguments using psql's \df command. You can use psql's \dd command to display comments about any specific function or group of functions, as shown in Figure 4.22.

Operators differ from functions in the following ways:

- Operators are symbols, not names.

- Operators usually take two arguments.

- Arguments appear to the left and right of the operator symbol.

For example, + is an operator that takes one argument on the left and one on the right, and returns the sum of the arguments. Psql's \do command lists all POSTGRESQL operators and their arguments. Figure 4.23 shows a listing of operators and examples of their use. The standard arithmetic operators—addition (+), subtraction (-), multiplication (*), division (/), modulo/remainder (%), and exponentiation (^)—honor the standard precedence rules. That is, exponentiation is performed first; multiplication, division, and modulo second; and addition and subtraction last. You can use parentheses to alter this precedence. Other operators are evaluated in a left-to-right manner, unless parentheses are present.

4.14 SET, SHOW, and RESET

The SET command allows you to change various POSTGRESQL parameters. The changes remain in effect for the duration of the database connection. Table 4.7 shows two common parameters that can be controlled with SET.

The SET DATESTYLE command controls the appearance of dates when printed in psql, as seen in Table 4.8. It controls the format (slashes, dashes, or year first) and the display of the month first (US) or day first (European). The command SET DATESTYLE TO 'SQL,US' would most likely be selected by users in the United States, while Europeans might prefer SET DATESTYLE TO

```
test=> \df
                        List of functions
    Result   |      Function      |                Arguments
-----------+--------------------+--------------------------------------------
 _bpchar   | _bpchar            | _bpchar int4
 _varchar  | _varchar           | _varchar int4
 float4    | abs                | float4
 float8    | abs                | float8
 ...
```

list all funcs

```
test=> \df int
                     List of functions
    Result  |      Function     |        Arguments
----------+-------------------+------------------------
 int2     | int2              | float4
 int2     | int2              | float8
 int2     | int2              | int2
 int2     | int2              | int4
 ...
```

list group of funcs

```
test=> \df upper
          List of functions
 Result | Function | Arguments
--------+----------+-----------
 text   | upper    | text
(1 row)
```

display a func

```
test=> \dd upper
        Object descriptions
 Name  | Object   | Description
-------+----------+-------------
 upper | function | uppercase
(1 row)
```

display comment about a func

```
test=> SELECT upper('jacket');
 upper
--------
 JACKET
(1 row)
```

```
test=> SELECT sqrt(2.0);   -- square root
      sqrt
-----------------
 1.4142135623731
(1 row)
```

Figure 4.22: Function examples

```
test=> \do
                              List of operators
 Op | Left arg  | Right arg  | Result  |        Description
-----+------------+------------+----------+--------------------------------
  !  | int2       |            | int4     |
  !  | int4       |            | int4     | factorial
  !  | int8       |            | int8     | factorial
  !! |            | int2       | int4     |
 ...
```

list all operators

```
test=> \do /
                         List of operators
 Op | Left arg | Right arg | Result  |           Description
----+----------+----------+----------+----------------------------
  / | box      | point    | box      | divide box by point (scale)
  / | char     | char     | char     | divide
  / | circle   | point    | circle   | divide
  / | float4   | float4   | float4   | divide
 ...
```

Provide info about op "/"

```
test=> \do ^
                       List of operators
 Op | Left arg | Right arg | Result |       Description
----+----------+----------+--------+---------------------
  ^ | float8   | float8   | float8 | exponentiation (x^y)
(1 row)
```

... and "^"

```
test=> \dd ^
            Object descriptions
 Name |  Object  |      Description
------+----------+---------------------
  ^   | operator | exponentiation (x^y)
(1 row)
```

Provide commentary on "^"

```
test=> SELECT 2 + 3 ^ 4;
 ?column?
----------
       83
(1 row)
```

Figure 4.23: Operator examples

Style	Optional Ordering	Output for February 1, 1983
ISO		1983-02-01
POSTGRES	US or NONEUROPEAN	02-01-1983
POSTGRES	EUROPEAN	01-02-1983
SQL	US or NONEUROPEAN	02/01/1983
SQL	EUROPEAN	01/02/1983
German		01.02.1983

mm/dd/yyyy
dd/mm/yyyy

Table 4.8: DATESTYLE output

```
test=> SHOW DATESTYLE;
NOTICE: DateStyle is ISO with US (NonEuropean) conventions
SHOW VARIABLE
test=> SET DATESTYLE TO 'SQL, EUROPEAN';
SET VARIABLE
test=> SHOW DATESTYLE;
NOTICE:  DateStyle is SQL with European conventions
SHOW VARIABLE
test=> RESET DATESTYLE;
RESET VARIABLE
test=> SHOW DATESTYLE;
NOTICE:  DateStyle is ISO with US (NonEuropean) conventions
SHOW VARIABLE
```

ack
ack
ack
ack

Figure 4.24: SHOW and RESET examples

'POSTGRES,EUROPEAN'. The ISO datestyle and GERMAN datestyle are not affected by any of the other options.

The TIMEZONE defaults to the time zone of the server or the PGTZ environment variable. The psql client might be in a different time zone, so SET TIMEZONE allows this parameter to be changed inside psql. See the SET manual page for a full list of SET options.

The SHOW command is used to display the current database session parameters. The RESET command allows a session parameter to be reset to its default value. Figure 4.24 shows examples of these commands.[5]

---
[5]Your site defaults may be different.

4.15 Summary

This chapter has shown how simple commands can be enhanced using features like DISTINCT, CASE, and complex WHERE clauses. These features give users great control over the execution of queries. They were chosen by committees as important features that should be in all SQL databases. Although you may never use all of the features mentioned in this chapter, many of them will prove valuable when solving real-world problems.

Chapter 5

SQL Aggregates

Users often need to summarize database information. Instead of seeing all rows, they want just a count or total. This type of operation is called *aggregation* or gathering together. This chapter focuses on POSTGRESQL's ability to generate summarized database information using aggregates.

5.1 Aggregates

Table 5.1 lists five aggregates. COUNT operates on entire rows; the other four operate on specific columns. Figure 5.1 shows examples of aggregate queries.

Aggregates can be combined with a WHERE clause to produce more complex results. For example, the query SELECT AVG(age) FROM friend WHERE age >= 21 computes the average age of people age 21 or older. This prevents Dick Gleason from being included in the average computation because he is younger than 21. The column label defaults to the name of the aggregate. You can use AS to change it, as described in Section 4.5.

NULL values are not processed by most aggregates, such as MAX(), SUM(), and AVG(); they are simply ignored. However, if a column contains *only* NULL values, the result is NULL, not zero. COUNT(*) is different in this respect. It does count NULL values because it looks at entire rows

Aggregate	Function
COUNT(*)	count of rows
SUM(colname)	total
MAX(colname)	maximum
MIN(colname)	minimum
AVG(colname)	average

COUNT(colname)
COUNT (DISTINCT colname)

Table 5.1: Aggregates

49

```
test=> SELECT * FROM friend ORDER BY firstname;
    firstname     |       lastname       |      city      | state | age
------------------+----------------------+----------------+-------+-----
 Dean             | Yeager               | Plymouth       | MA    |  24
 Dick             | Gleason              | Ocean City     | NJ    |  19
 Ned              | Millstone            | Cedar Creek    | MD    |  27
 Sandy            | Gleason              | Ocean City     | NJ    |  25
 Sandy            | Weber                | Boston         | MA    |  33
 Victor           | Tabor                | Williamsport   | PA    |  22
(6 rows)

test=> SELECT COUNT(*) FROM friend;
 count
-------
     6
(1 row)

test=> SELECT SUM(age) FROM friend;
 sum
-----
 150
(1 row)

test=> SELECT MAX(age) FROM friend;
 max
-----
  33
(1 row)

test=> SELECT MIN(age) FROM friend;
 min
-----
  19
(1 row)

test=> SELECT AVG(age) FROM friend;
 avg
-----
  25
(1 row)
```

Figure 5.1: Examples of Aggregates

using the asterisk(*). It does not examine individual columns like the other aggregates. To find
the COUNT of all non-NULL values in a certain column, use COUNT(*colname*). To find the number of
distinct values in a column, use COUNT(DISTINCT *colname*).

Figure 5.2 illustrates aggregate handling of NULL values. First, a single row containing a NULL
column is used to show aggregates returning NULL results. Two versions of COUNT on a NULL
column are shown. Notice that COUNT never returns a NULL value. Then, a single non-NULL row is
inserted, and the results shown. Notice the AVG() of 3 and NULL is 3, not 1.5, illustrating the NULL
value is not considered in the average computation. Psql's \da command lists all of the aggregates
supported by POSTGRESQL.

5.2   Using GROUP BY

Simple aggregates return one row as a result. It is often desirable, however, to apply an aggregate
to groups of rows. In queries using aggregates with GROUP BY, the aggregate is applied to rows
grouped by another column in the table. For example, SELECT COUNT(*) FROM friend returns the
total number of rows in the table. The query in Figure 5.3 shows the use of GROUP BY to count
the number of people in each state. With GROUP BY, the table is split up into groups by *state*, and
COUNT(*) is applied to each group in turn.

The second query shows the minimum, maximum, and average ages of the people in each state.
It also shows an ORDER BY operation carried out on the aggregate column. Because the column is
the fourth one in the result, you can identify it by the number 4. Using ORDER BY avg would have
worked as well.

You can GROUP BY more than one column, as shown in Figure 5.4. GROUP BY collects all NULL
values into a single group.

5.3   Using HAVING

One more aggregate capability is often overlooked—the HAVING clause. HAVING allows a user to
perform conditional tests on aggregate values. It is often employed in conjunction with GROUP BY.
With HAVING, you can include or exclude groups based on the aggregate value for that group. For
example, suppose you want to know all states in which you have more than one friend. Looking at
the first query in Figure 5.3, you can see exactly which states have more than one friend. HAVING
allows you to test the *count* column, as shown in Figure 5.5. Aggregates cannot be used in a WHERE
clause; they are valid only inside HAVING.

5.4   Query Tips

In Figures 5.3 and 5.5, the queries are spread over several lines. When a query has several
clauses, such as FROM, WHERE, and GROUP BY, it is best to place each clause on a separate

```
test=> CREATE TABLE aggtest (col INTEGER);
CREATE
test=> INSERT INTO aggtest VALUES (NULL);
INSERT 19759 1
test=> SELECT SUM(col) FROM aggtest;
 sum
-----

(1 row)

test=> SELECT MAX(col) FROM aggtest;
 max
-----

(1 row)

test=> SELECT COUNT(*) FROM aggtest;
 count
-------
     1
(1 row)

test=> SELECT COUNT(col) FROM aggtest;
 count
-------
     0
(1 row)

test=> INSERT INTO aggtest VALUES (3);
INSERT 19760 1
test=> SELECT AVG(col) FROM aggtest;
 avg
-----
   3
(1 row)

test=> SELECT COUNT(*) FROM aggtest;
 count
-------
     2
(1 row)

test=> SELECT COUNT(col) FROM aggtest;
 count
-------
     1
(1 row)
```

Figure 5.2: Aggregates and NULL values

```
test=> SELECT state, COUNT(*)
test-> FROM friend
test-> GROUP BY state;
 state | count
-------+-------
 MA    |   2
 MD    |   1
 NJ    |   2
 PA    |   1
(4 rows)
```

SELECT state, COUNT(*)
FROM friend
GROUP BY state
HAVING COUNT(*) > 1;

```
test=> SELECT state, MIN(age), MAX(age), AVG(age)
test-> FROM friend
test-> GROUP BY state
test-> ORDER BY 4 DESC;
 state | min | max | avg
-------+-----+-----+-----
 MA    | 24  | 33  | 28
 MD    | 27  | 27  | 27
 NJ    | 19  | 25  | 22
 PA    | 22  | 22  | 22
(4 rows)
```

or, order by avg DESC

Figure 5.3: Aggregate with GROUP BY

```
test=> SELECT city, state, COUNT(*)
test-> FROM friend
test-> GROUP BY state, city
test-> ORDER BY 1, 2;
      city        | state | count
------------------+-------+-------
 Boston           | MA    |    1
 Cedar Creek      | MD    |    1
 Ocean City       | NJ    |    2
 Plymouth         | MA    |    1
 Williamsport     | PA    |    1
(5 rows)
```

Figure 5.4: GROUP BY with two columns

```
test=> SELECT state, COUNT(*)
test-> FROM friend
test-> GROUP BY state
test-> HAVING COUNT(*) > 1
test-> ORDER BY state;
 state | count
-------+-------
 MA    |    2
 NJ    |    2
(2 rows)
```

Figure 5.5: HAVING

line. This convention makes queries easier to understand. Clear queries also use appropriate capitalization.

In a test database, mistakes do not create a problem. In a live production database, however, one incorrect query can cause great difficulty. It takes five seconds to issue an erroneous query, and sometimes five days to recover from it. Double-check your queries before executing them. This consideration is especially important for UPDATE, DELETE, and INSERT queries, because they modify the database. Also, before performing an UPDATE or DELETE, do a SELECT or SELECT COUNT(*) with the same WHERE clause. Make sure the SELECT result is reasonable before doing the UPDATE or DELETE.

5.5 Summary

Sometimes users want less output rather than more. They want a total, count, average, maximum, or minimum value for a column. Aggregates make this calculation possible. They aggregate data into fewer rows and then send the result to the user.

Chapter 6

Joining Tables

This chapter discusses how to store data using multiple tables. Both multitable storage and multitable queries are fundamental to relational databases.

We start this chapter by examining table and column references, which are important in multitable queries. Then, we cover the advantages of splitting data into multiple tables. Next, we introduce an example based on a mail-order company, showing table creation, insertion, and queries using joins. Finally, we explore a variety of join types.

6.1   Table and Column References

Before dealing with joins, we must mention one important feature. Up to this point, all queries have involved a single table. When a query involves multiple tables, column names can become confusing. Unless you are familiar with each table, it is difficult to know which column names belong to which tables. Sometimes two tables may use the same column name. For these reasons, SQL allows you to fully qualify column names by preceding the column name with the table name. Figure 6.1 shows an example of table name prefixing. In the figure, the first query has unqualified column names. The second query is the same, but with fully qualified column names. A period separates the table name from the column name.

The final query in Figure 6.1 shows another feature. Instead of specifying the table name, you can create a *table alias* to take the place of the table name in the query. The alias name follows the table name in the FROM clause. In this example, *f* is used as an alias for the *friend* table. While these features are not important in single table queries, they are useful in multitable queries.

6.2   Joined Tables

In our *friend* example, splitting data into multiple tables makes little sense. However, in cases where we must record information about a variety of things, multiple tables have benefits. Consider

```
test=> SELECT firstname FROM friend WHERE state = 'PA';
    firstname
-----------------
 Victor
(1 row)

test=> SELECT friend.firstname FROM friend WHERE friend.state = 'PA';
    firstname
-----------------
 Victor
(1 row)

test=> SELECT f.firstname FROM friend f WHERE f.state = 'PA';
    firstname
-----------------
 Victor
(1 row)
```

Figure 6.1: Qualified column names

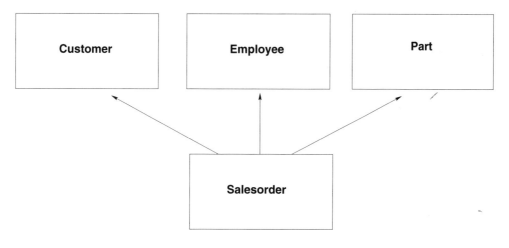

Figure 6.2: Joining tables

a company that sells parts to customers through the mail. Its database has to record information about many things: customers, employees, sales orders, and parts. It is obvious that a single table cannot hold these different types of information in an organized manner. Therefore, we create four tables: *customer, employee, salesorder,* and *part.* Unfortunately, putting information in different tables also causes problems. How do we record which sales orders belong to which customers? How do we record the parts for the sales orders? How do we record which employee received the sales order? The solution is to assign unique numbers to every customer, employee, and part. When we want to record the customer in the *salesorder* table, for example, we put the customer's number in the *salesorder* table. When we want to record which employee took the order, we put the employee's number in the *salesorder* table. When we want to record which part has been ordered, we put the part number in the *salesorder* table.

Breaking up the information into separate tables allows us to keep detailed information about customers, employees, and parts. It also allows us to refer to those specific entries as many times as needed by using a unique number. Figure 6.2 illustrates the joining of the separate tables we will use.

People might question the choice of using separate tables. While not necessary, it is often useful. Without a separate *customer* table, every piece of information about a customer would have to be stored in the *salesorder* table every time a *salesorder* row was added. The customer's name, telephone number, address, and other information would have to be repeated. Any change in customer information, such as a change in telephone number, would have to be performed in all places in which that information is stored. With a *customer* table, the information is stored in one place, and each *salesorder* points to the *customer* table. This approach is more efficient, and it allows for easier administration and data maintenance. The advantages of using multiple tables include the following:

- Easier data modification

- Easier data lookup

- Data stored in only one place

- Less storage space required

The only time duplicate data should *not* be moved to a separate table is when *all* of the following conditions are present:

- The time required to perform a join is prohibitive.

- Data lookup is unnecessary.

- Duplicate data require little storage space.

- Data are very unlikely to change.

The *customer, employee, part,* and *salesorder* example clearly benefits from multiple tables. The process of distributing data across multiple tables to prevent redundancy is called *data normalization.*

6.3   Creating Joined Tables

Figure 6.3 shows the SQL statements needed to create the tables in our mail-order example.[1] The *customer, employee,* and *part* tables all have a column to hold their unique identification numbers. The *salesorder*[2] table includes columns to hold the customer, employee, and part numbers associated with a particular sales order. For the sake of simplicity, we will assume that each *salesorder* entry contains only one part number.

We have used underscore (_) to allow the use of multiple words in column names—for example, customer_id. This is a common practice. You could enter the column as CustomerId, but POST-GRESQL converts all identifiers, such as column and table names, to lowercase; thus the actual column name becomes customerid, which is not very clear. The only way to define nonlowercase column and table names is to use double quotes. Double quotes preserve any capitalization you supply. You can even have spaces in table and column names if you surround the name with double quotes (")—for example, "customer id". If you decide to use this feature, you must put double quotes around the table or column name every time it is referenced. Obviously, this practice can be cumbersome.

---

[1]In the real world, the *name* columns would be much longer, perhaps CHAR(60) or CHAR(180). You should base the length on the longest name you may ever wish to store. Short *names* are used here so they display properly in the examples.

[2]A table cannot be called *order.* The word *order* is a reserved keyword, for use in the ORDER BY clause. Reserved keywords are not available as table or column names.

Upgrage p161

```
test=> CREATE TABLE customer (
test(>                     customer_id INTEGER,
test(>                     name        CHAR(30),
test(>                     telephone   CHAR(20),
test(>                     street      CHAR(40),
test(>                     city        CHAR(25),
test(>                     state       CHAR(2),
test(>                     zipcode     CHAR(10),
test(>                     country     CHAR(20)
test(> );
CREATE
test=> CREATE TABLE employee (
test(>                     employee_id INTEGER,
test(>                     name        CHAR(30),
test(>                     hire_date   DATE
test(> );
CREATE
test=> CREATE TABLE part (
test(>                 part_id     INTEGER,
test(>                 name        CHAR(30),
test(>                 cost        NUMERIC(8,2),
test(>                 weight      FLOAT
test(> );
CREATE
test=> CREATE TABLE salesorder (
test(>                 order_id     INTEGER,
test(>                 customer_id  INTEGER,  -- joins to customer.customer_id
test(>                 employee_id  INTEGER,  -- joins to employee.employee_id
test(>                 part_id      INTEGER,  -- joins to part.part_id
test(>                 order_date   DATE,
test(>                 ship_date    DATE,
test(>                 payment      NUMERIC(8,2)
test(> );
CREATE
```

has fatal flaw (one part_id!)
Fix: p 75

Useful commentary

p 76

Figure 6.3: Creation of company tables

Keep in mind that all table and column names not protected by double quotes should consist of only letters, numbers, and the underscore character. Each name must start with a letter, not a number. Do not use punctuation, except the underscore, in your names. For example, *address, office,* and *zipcode9* are valid names, but *2pair* and *my#* are not.

The example in Figure 6.3 also shows the existence of a column named *customer_id* in two tables. This duplication occurs because the two columns contain the same type of number, a customer identification number. Giving them the same name clearly shows which columns join the tables together. If you wanted to use unique names, you could name the column *salesorder_- customer_id* or *sales_cust_id*. This choice makes the column names unique, but still documents the columns to be joined.

Figure 6.4 shows the insertion of a row into the *customer, employee,* and *part* tables. It also shows the insertion of a row into the *salesorder* table, using the same customer, employee, and part numbers to link the *salesorder* row to the other rows we inserted. For simplicity, we will use only a single row per table.

6.4   Performing Joins

When data are spread across multiple tables, retrieval of that information becomes an important issue. Figure 6.5 indicates how to find the customer name for a given order number. It uses two queries. The first gets the *customer_id* for order number *14673*. The returned customer identification number of *648* then is used in the WHERE clause of the next query. That query finds the customer name record where the *customer_id* equals *648*. We call this two-query approach a *manual join,* because the user manually took the result from the first query and placed that number into the WHERE clause of the second query.

Fortunately, relational databases can perform this type of join automatically. Figure 6.6 shows the same join as in Figure 6.5 but places it in a single query. This query shows all of the elements necessary to perform the join of two tables:

- The two tables involved in the join are specified in the FROM clause.

- The two columns needed to perform the join are specified as equal in the WHERE clause.

- The *salesorder* table's order number is tested in the WHERE clause.

- The *customer* table's customer name is returned from the SELECT.

Internally, the database performs the join by carrying out the following operations:

- `salesorder.order_id = 14673`: Find that row in the *salesorder* table.

- `salesorder.customer_id = customer.customer_id`: From the row just found, get the *customer_id*. Find the equal *customer_id* in the *customer* table.

- `customer.name`: Return *name* from the *customer* table.

```
test=> INSERT INTO customer VALUES (
test(>                                  648,    (customer_id)
test(>                                  'Fleer Gearworks, Inc.',
test(>                                  '1-610-555-7829',
test(>                                  '830 Winding Way',
test(>                                  'Millersville',
test(>                                  'AL',
test(>                                  '35041',
test(>                                  'USA'
test(> );           OID: p79
INSERT 19815 1
test=> INSERT INTO employee VALUES (
test(>                                  24,    (employee_id)
test(>                                  'Lee Meyers',
test(>                                  '10/16/1989'
test(> );
INSERT 19816 1
test=> INSERT INTO part VALUES (
test(>                                  153,    (part_id)
test(>                                  'Garage Door Spring',
test(>                                  6.20    (cost)
test(> );
INSERT 19817 1
test=> INSERT INTO salesorder VALUES(
test(>                                  14673,   (order_id)
test(>                                  648,     (customer_id)
test(>                                  24,      (employee_id)
test(>                                  153,     (part_id)
test(>                                  '7/19/1994',
test(>                                  '7/28/1994',
test(>                                  18.39
test(> );
INSERT 19818 1
```

Figure 6.4: Insertion into company tables

manual join

```
test=> SELECT customer_id FROM salesorder WHERE order_id = 14673;
 customer_id
-------------
         648
(1 row)


test=> SELECT name FROM customer WHERE customer_id = 648;
             name
-------------------------------
 Fleer Gearworks, Inc.
(1 row)
```

Figure 6.5: Finding a customer name using two queries

join

```
test=> SELECT customer.name                  -- query result
test-> FROM   customer, salesorder           -- query tables
test->                                        -- table join
test-> WHERE  customer.customer_id = salesorder.customer_id AND
test->        salesorder.order_id = 14673;   -- query restriction
             name
-------------------------------
 Fleer Gearworks, Inc.
(1 row)
```

Figure 6.6: Finding a customer name using one query

```
test=> SELECT salesorder.order_id
test-> FROM   salesorder, customer
test-> WHERE  customer.name = 'Fleer Gearworks, Inc.' AND
test->        salesorder.customer_id = customer.customer_id;
 order_id
----------
    14673
(1 row)
```

[handwritten annotations: "or, ~ 'fleer'" ; "p 39: matches records w. 'fleer' (case-insensitive) anywhere in customer's name column."]*

Figure 6.7: Finding an order number for a customer name

That is, the database performs the same steps as the manual join, but much faster.

Notice that Figure 6.6 qualifies each column name by prefixing it with the table name, as discussed in Section 6.1. While such prefixing is optional in many cases, it is required in this example because the column *customer_id* exists in both tables mentioned in the FROM clause, *customer* and *salesorder.* Without such prefixing, the query would generate an error: ERROR: Column 'customer_id' is ambiguous.

You can also perform the join in the opposite direction too. In the previous query, the order number was supplied and the customer name returned. In Figure 6.7, the customer name is supplied and the order number returned. The order of items in the FROM and WHERE clauses has also been switched; the ordering of items is not important in these clauses.

6.5   Three- and Four-Table Joins

Figure 6.8 demonstrates a three-table join. In this example, the first printed column is the customer name, and the second column is the employee name. Both columns are labeled *name.* You could use AS to give the columns unique labels. Figure 6.9 shows a four-table join, using AS to make each column label unique. The four-table join matches the arrows in Figure 6.2, with the arrows of the *salesorder* table pointing to the other three tables.

Joins can also be performed among tables that are only indirectly related. Suppose you wish to find employees who have taken orders for each customer. Figure 6.10 shows such a query. Notice that this query displays just the *customer* and *employee* tables. The *salesorder* table is used to join the two tables but does not appear in the result. The DISTINCT keyword is used because multiple orders taken by the same employee for the same customer would make that employee appear more than once, which was not desired. The second query uses an aggregate to return a count for each unique customer/employee pair.

Until now, we have used only a single row in each table. As an exercise, add more *customer,* *employee,* and *part* rows, and add *salesorder* rows that join to these new entries. You can use

```
test=> SELECT customer.name, employee.name
test-> FROM    salesorder, customer, employee
test-> WHERE   salesorder.customer_id = customer.customer_id AND
test->          salesorder.employee_id = employee.employee_id AND
test->          salesorder.order_id = 14673;
          name                  |               name
-------------------------------+-------------------------------
 Fleer Gearworks, Inc.          | Lee Meyers
(1 row)
```

Figure 6.8: Three-table join

```
test=> SELECT customer.name AS customer_name,
test->          employee.name AS employee_name,
test->          part.name AS part_name
test-> FROM    salesorder, customer, employee, part
test-> WHERE   salesorder.customer_id = customer.customer_id AND
test->          salesorder.employee_id = employee.employee_id AND
test->          salesorder.part_id = part.part_id AND
test->          salesorder.order_id = 14673;
        customer_name          |       employee_name        |      part_name
-------------------------------+----------------------------+---------------------
 Fleer Gearworks, Inc.          | Lee Meyers                 | Garage Door Spring
(1 row)
```

Figure 6.9: Four-table join

```
test=> SELECT DISTINCT customer.name, employee.name
test-> FROM   customer, employee, salesorder
test-> WHERE  customer.customer_id = salesorder.customer_id and
test->        salesorder.employee_id = employee.employee_id
test-> ORDER BY customer.name, employee.name;
          name            |            name
--------------------------+-------------------------------
 Fleer Gearworks, Inc.    | Lee Meyers
(1 row)

test=> SELECT DISTINCT customer.name, employee.name, COUNT(*)
test-> FROM   customer, employee, salesorder
test-> WHERE  customer.customer_id = salesorder.customer_id and
test->        salesorder.employee_id = employee.employee_id
test-> GROUP BY customer.name, employee.name
test-> ORDER BY customer.name, employee.name;
          name            |            name                | count
--------------------------+-------------------------------+-------
 Fleer Gearworks, Inc.    | Lee Meyers                     |    1
(1 row)
```

Figure 6.10: Employees who have taken orders for customers

```
     SELECT employee.name
     FROM   customer, employee
@    WHERE  customer.employee_id = employee.employee_id AND
            customer.customer_id = 648;
     -- find customs assigned to employee - id = 24
     SELECT customer.name
     FROM   customer, employee
@    WHERE  customer.employee_id = employee.employee_id AND
            employee.employee_id = 24
     ORDER BY customer.name;
```

Figure 6.11: Joining *customer* and *employee*

Figure 6.4 as an example. Choose any unique identification numbers you like, then try the queries already shown in this chapter with your new data.

6.6 Additional Join Possibilities

So far, all of our example joins have involved the *salesorder* table in some form. Suppose we want to assign an employee to manage each customer account. If we add an *employee_id* column to the *customer* table, the column could store the identification number of the employee assigned to manage the customer's account. Figure 6.11 shows how to perform a join between the *customer* and *employee* tables. The first query finds the employee name assigned to manage customer number *648*. The second query shows the customers managed by employee *24*. Notice that the *salesorder* table is not involved in these queries.

Suppose you want to assign an employee to be responsible for answering detailed questions about parts. You would then add an *employee_id* column to the *part* table, place valid employee identifiers in the column, and perform queries similar to those in Figure 6.12. Adding columns to existing tables is covered in Section 13.2.

In some cases, a join could be performed with the *state* column. For example, to check state mailing codes for validity, a *statecode* table could be created with all valid state codes.[3] An application could check the state code entered by the user and report an error if it is not in the *statecode* table. Another example would be the need to print the full state name in queries. State names could be stored in a separate table and joined when the full state name is desired. Figure 6.13 shows an example of such a *statename* table. Thus we have two more uses for additional tables:

---

[3]The United States Postal Service has assigned a unique two-letter code to each U.S. state.

```
-- find the employee assigned to part number 153
SELECT employee.name
FROM   part, employee
WHERE  part.employee_id = employee.employee_id AND
       part.part_id = 153;


-- find the parts assigned to employee 24
SELECT part.name
FROM   part, employee
WHERE  part.employee_id = employee.employee_id AND
       employee.employee_id = 24
ORDER BY name;
```

part.employee-id : employee
with expertise on that part

Figure 6.12: Joining *part* and *employee*

statename :

Code	name
'AL'	'Alabama'
:	:

```
test=> CREATE TABLE statename (code CHAR(2),
test(>                         name  CHAR(30)
test(> );
CREATE
test=> INSERT INTO statename VALUES ('AL', 'Alabama');
INSERT 20629 1
...


test=> SELECT statename.name AS customer_statename
test-> FROM   customer, statename
test-> WHERE  customer.customer_id = 648 AND
test->        customer.state = statename.code;
```

better : state-code

Figure 6.13: The *statename* table

- Check codes against a list of valid values—that is, allow only valid state codes

- Store code descriptions—that is, state code and state name

6.7   Choosing a Join Key

The join key is the value used to link rows between tables. For example, in Figure 6.4, *648* is the customer key, appearing in the *customer* table to uniquely identify the row, and in the *salesorder* table to refer to that specific *customer* row.

Some people might question whether an identification number is needed. Should the customer name be used as a join key? Using it as the join key is not a good idea for several reasons:

- Numbers are less likely to be entered incorrectly.

- Two customers with the same name would be impossible to distinguish in a join.

- If the customer name changes, all references to that name would have to change.

- Numeric joins are more efficient than joins of long character strings.

- Numbers require less storage space than character strings.

In the *statename* table, the two-letter state code is probably a good join key for the following reasons:

- Two-letter codes are easy for users to remember and enter.

- State codes are always unique.

- State codes do not change.

- Joins of short two-letter codes are not significantly slower than integer joins.

- Two-letter codes do not require significantly more storage space than integers.

Essentially, two choices for join keys exist: identification numbers and short character codes. If an item is referenced repeatedly, it is best to use a short character code as a join key. You can display this key to users and allow them to refer to customers and employees using codes. Users prefer to identify items by short, fixed-length character codes containing numbers and letters. For example, customers might be identified by six-character codes (FLE001), employees by their initials (BAW), and parts by five-character codes (E7245). Codes are easy to use and remember. In many cases, users can choose the codes, as long as they are unique.

It is possible to allow users to enter short character codes and still use identification numbers as join keys. Adding a *code* column to the table accomplishes this goal. For the *customer* table, a new column called *code* can be added to hold the customer code. When the user enters a customer

```
SELECT order_id
FROM   customer, salesorder
WHERE  customer.code = 'FLE001' AND
       customer.customer_id = salesorder.customer_id;
```

(both appear in the table.
The code is for
the user interface)
customer.id customer.code
1 ~ 1
in table

Figure 6.14: Using a customer code

code, the query can find the `customer_id` assigned to the customer code, then use that `customer_id` in joins with other tables. Figure 6.14 shows a query using a customer code to find all order numbers for that customer.

In some cases, identification numbers work well and codes are unnecessary, as in the following cases:

- Items with short lifespans, such as order numbers

- Items without appropriate codes, such as payroll batch numbers

- Items used internally and not referenced by users

Defining codes for such values would be useless. It is better to allow the database to assign a unique number to each item. Chapter 7 discusses database support for assigning unique identifiers.

No universal rule dictates when you should choose codes or identification numbers. U.S. states are clearly better keyed on codes, because only 50 exist. The resulting codes are short, unique, and well known by most users. At the other extreme, order numbers are best used without codes because too many of them are possible and codes would be of little use.

6.8   One-to-Many Joins

Up to this point, when we joined two tables, one row in the first table matched exactly one row in the second table, making the joins *one-to-one joins*. But what if more than one *salesorder* row existed for a customer ID? Multiple order numbers would be printed. In such a *one-to-many* join, one customer row would join to more than one *salesorder* row. Now, suppose no orders were made by a customer. Even though a valid *customer* row would exist, if there were no *salesorder* row for that customer identification number, no rows would be returned. We could call that situation a *one-to-none* join. Section 8.3 covers *outer joins*, which allow unjoined rows to appear in the result.

Consider the example in Figure 6.15. Because the *animal* table's *507 rabbit* row joins to three rows in the *vegetable* table, the *rabbit* row is duplicated three times in the output. This is a one-to-many join. There is no join for the *508 cat* row in the *vegetable* table, so the *508 cat* row does not appear in the output. This is an example of a one-to-none join.

```
test=> SELECT * FROM animal;
 animal_id |       name
-----------+------------------
       507 | rabbit
       508 | cat
(2 rows)


test=> SELECT * FROM vegetable;
 animal_id |       name
-----------+------------------
       507 | lettuce
       507 | carrot
       507 | nut
(3 rows)


test=> SELECT *
test-> FROM animal, vegetable
test-> WHERE animal.animal_id = vegetable.animal_id;
 animal_id |       name       | animal_id |       name
-----------+------------------+-----------+------------------
       507 | rabbit           |       507 | lettuce
       507 | rabbit           |       507 | carrot
       507 | rabbit           |       507 | nut
(3 rows)
```

one to many

Figure 6.15: A one-to-many join

```
test=> SELECT *
test-> FROM animal, vegetable;
 animal_id |       name      | animal_id |      name
-----------+-----------------+-----------+-----------------
       507 | rabbit          |       507 | lettuce
       508 | cat             |       507 | lettuce
       507 | rabbit          |       507 | carrot
       508 | cat             |       507 | carrot
       507 | rabbit          |       507 | nut
       508 | cat             |       507 | nut
(6 rows)
```

Cartesian Product

↳ *First table values vary most rapidly*

Figure 6.16: Unjoined tables

```
SELECT order_id
FROM   customer c, salesorder s
WHERE  c.code = 'FLE001' AND
       c.customer_id = s.customer_id;
```

*select all order ids (from sales order table)
associate with the customer have
customer code of 'FLE001'*

Figure 6.17: Using table aliases

6.9 Unjoined Tables

When joining tables, it is necessary to join each table mentioned in the FROM clause by specifying
joins in the WHERE clause. If you use a table name in the FROM clause but fail to join it in the
WHERE clause, the table is marked as unjoined. It is then paired with every row in the query result.
Figure 6.16 illustrates this effect using the tables from Figure 6.15. The SELECT does not join any
column from *animal* to any column in *vegetable*, causing every value in *animal* to be paired with
every value in *vegetable*. This result, called a *Cartesian product,* is usually not intended. When a
query returns many more rows than expected, look for an unjoined table in the query.

6.10 Table Aliases and Self-joins

In Section 6.1, you saw how to refer to specific tables in the FROM clause using a table alias.
Figure 6.17 shows a rewrite of the query in Figure 6.14 using aliases. A *c* is used as an alias for
the *customer* table, and an *s* is used as an alias for the *salesorder* table. Table aliases are handy in
these cases.

-- all customers in same zip code as customer 648

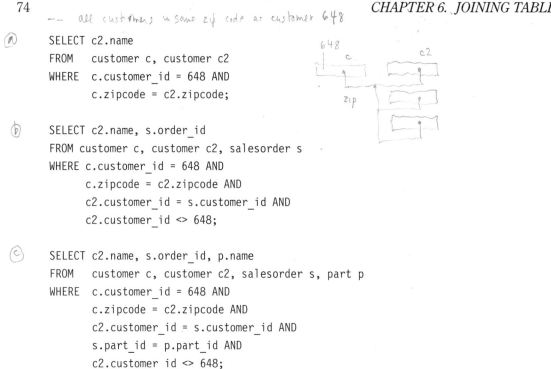

```
(a)   SELECT c2.name
      FROM   customer c, customer c2
      WHERE  c.customer_id = 648 AND
             c.zipcode = c2.zipcode;

(b)   SELECT c2.name, s.order_id
      FROM customer c, customer c2, salesorder s
      WHERE c.customer_id = 648 AND
            c.zipcode = c2.zipcode AND
            c2.customer_id = s.customer_id AND
            c2.customer_id <> 648;

(c)   SELECT c2.name, s.order_id, p.name
      FROM   customer c, customer c2, salesorder s, part p
      WHERE  c.customer_id = 648 AND
             c.zipcode = c2.zipcode AND
             c2.customer_id = s.customer_id AND
             s.part_id = p.part_id AND
             c2.customer_id <> 648;
```

Figure 6.18: Examples of self-joins using table aliases

With table aliases, you can even join a table to itself in a *self-join*. In this case, the same table is given two different alias names. Each alias then represents a different instance of the table. This concept might seem to have questionable utility, but it can prove useful. Figure 6.18 shows practical examples. For simplicity, results are not shown for these queries.

The first query in Figure 6.18 uses *c* as an alias for the *customer* table and *c2* as another alias for *customer*. It finds all customers in the same ZIP code as customer number *648*. The second query finds all customers in the same ZIP code as customer number *648*. It then finds the order numbers placed by those customers. We have restricted the *c2* table's customer identification number to be not equal to *648* because we do not want customer *648* to appear in the result. The third query goes further, retrieving the part numbers associated with those orders.

6.11   Non-equijoins

Equijoins, the most common type of join, use equality (=) to join tables. Figure 6.19 shows our first *non-equijoin*. The first query uses not equal (<>) to perform the join. It returns all customers not in the same country as customer number *648*. The second query uses less than (<) to perform

-- all customers hot in same country as custom 648   ⊕ 74

```
SELECT c2.name
FROM    customer c, customer c2
WHERE   c.customer_id = 648 AND
        c.country <> c2.country
ORDER BY c2.name;
```
-- all employees hired after employee 24   ℯ
```
SELECT e2.name, e2.hire_date
FROM    employee e, employee e2
WHERE   e.employee_id = 24 AND
        e.hire_date < e2.hire_date
ORDER BY e2.hire_date, e2.name;
```
-- all parts that cost less than part 153   ⨍
```
SELECT p2.name, p2.cost
FROM    part p, part p2
WHERE   p.part_id = 153 AND
        p.cost > p2.cost
ORDER BY p2.cost;
```

Figure 6.19: Non-equijoins

the join. Instead of finding equal values to join, it joins all rows later than a specific hire date. The query returns all employees hired after employee number *24*. The third query uses greater than ℯ (>) in a similar way. It returns all parts that cost less than part number *153*. Non-equijoins are not ⨍ used often, but certain queries require them.

6.12   Ordering Multiple Parts

p 61

Our mail-order example has a serious limitation: It allows only one *part_id* per *salesorder*. In the ⟨ real world, this restriction would not be acceptable. Now that we have covered many complex join topics in this chapter, we are ready to create a more complete database layout that allows for multiple parts per order.

Figure 6.20 shows a new version of the *salesorder* table. Notice that the *part_id* column has been removed. The *customer, employee,* and *part* tables remain unchanged.

Figure 6.21 shows a new table, *orderpart*. This table is needed because the original *salesorder* table could hold only one part number per order. Instead of having *part_id* in the *salesorder* table, the *orderpart* table holds one row for each part number ordered. If five part numbers are in order number *15398,* then five rows will appear in the *orderpart* table with *order_id* equal to *15398.*

We also add a *quantity* column. If a customer orders seven of the same part number, we put only one row in the *orderpart* table, but set the *quantity* field equal to *7*. We use DEFAULT to set the quantity to *1* if no quantity is specified.

Notice that the *orderpart* table does not include a *price* field. Instead, the price is stored in the *master table*

```
CREATE TABLE salesorder (
                order_id      INTEGER,
                customer_id   INTEGER,   -- joins to customer.customer_id
                employee_id   INTEGER,   -- joins to employee.employee_id
                order_date    DATE,
                ship_date     DATE,
                payment       NUMERIC(8,2)
);
```

Figure 6.20: New *salesorder* table for multiple parts per order

detail table

```
CREATE TABLE orderpart(
                order_id INTEGER,
                part_id  INTEGER,
                quantity INTEGER DEFAULT 1
);
```

Figure 6.21: The *orderpart* table

See p 61 for customer, employee, part

part table. Whenever the price is needed, a join is performed to get the price. This choice allows us to change a part's price in one place, and all references to it will be updated automatically.[4]

The table layout illustrates the *master/detail* use of tables. The *salesorder* table is the master table, because it holds information common to each order, such as customer and employee identifiers and order date. The *orderpart* table is the detail table, because it contains the specific parts making up the order. Master/detail tables are a common use of multiple tables.

Figure 6.22 shows a variety of queries using the new *orderpart* table. The queries demonstrate increasing complexity. The first query already contains the order number of interest, so there is no reason to use the *salesorder* table. It goes directly to the *orderpart* table to find the parts making up the order, joining to the *part* table to obtain part descriptions. The second query does not have the order number, only the *customer_id* and *order_date*. It must use the *salesorder* table to find the order number, then join to the *orderpart* and *part* tables to get order quantities and part information. The third query does not have the *customer_id,* but instead must join to the customer table to get the *customer_id* for use with the other tables. Notice that each query displays an increasing number of columns to the user. The final query computes the total cost of the order. It uses an aggregate to SUM cost times (*) quantity for each part in the order.

6.13   Primary and Foreign Keys

A join is performed by comparing two columns, like *customer.customer_id* and *salesorder.customer_id*. The *customer.customer_id* is called a *primary key* because it is the unique (primary) identifier for the *customer* table. The *salesorder.customer_id* is called a *foreign key* because it holds a key to another (foreign) table.

6.14   Summary

This chapter dealt with technique—the technique of creating an orderly data layout using multiple tables. Acquiring this skill takes practice. Expect to improve your first table layouts many times.

Good data layout can make your job easier. Bad data layout can turn queries into a nightmare. As you create your first real-world tables, you will learn to identify good and bad data designs. Continually review your table structures and refer to this chapter again for ideas. Do not be afraid to redesign everything. Redesign is hard, but when it is done properly, queries become easier to craft.

Relational databases excel in their ability to relate and compare data. Tables can be joined and analyzed in ways you might never have anticipated. With good data layout and the power of SQL, you can retrieve an unlimited amount of information from your database.

---

[4]In our example, changing *part.price* would change the price on previous orders of the part, which would cause problems. In the real world, we would need a *partprice* table to store the part number, price, and effective date for the price.

```
-- first query :  names of all parts  in order # 15398
SELECT part.name
FROM   orderpart, part
WHERE  orderpart.part_id = part.part_id AND
       orderpart.order_id = 15398;


-- second query  :  names of all parts and assoc'd quantity, for order corresp to
SELECT part.name, orderpart.quantity              customer # 648  on  7/19/1994
FROM salesorder, orderpart, part
WHERE salesorder.customer_id = 648 AND
      salesorder.order_date = '7/19/1994' AND
      salesorder.order_id = orderpart.order_id AND
      orderpart.part_id = part.part_id;


-- third query
SELECT part.name, part.cost, orderpart.quantity
FROM   customer, salesorder, orderpart, part
WHERE  customer.name = 'Fleer Gearworks, Inc.' AND
       salesorder.order_date = '7/19/1994' AND
       salesorder.customer_id = customer.customer_id AND
       salesorder.order_id = orderpart.order_id AND
       orderpart.part_id = part.part_id;


-- fourth query
SELECT SUM(part.cost * orderpart.quantity)
FROM   customer, salesorder, orderpart, part
WHERE  customer.name = 'Fleer Gearworks, Inc.' AND
       salesorder.order_date = '7/19/1994' AND
       salesorder.customer_id = customer.customer_id AND
       salesorder.order_id = orderpart.order_id AND
       orderpart.part_id = part.part_id;
```

Figure 6.22: Queries involving the *orderpart* table

Chapter 7

Numbering Rows

Unique identification numbers and short character codes allow references to specific rows in a table. They were used extensively in Chapter 6. For example, the *customer* table had a *customer_-id* column that held a unique identification number for each customer. The *employee* and *part* tables included similar uniquely numbered columns that were important for joins to those tables.

While unique character codes must be supplied by users, unique row numbers can be generated automatically using two methods. This chapter describes how to use these methods.

7.1 Object Identification Numbers (OIDs) and copy: 175

Every row in POSTGRESQL is assigned a unique, normally invisible number called an *object identification number* (OID). When the software is initialized with initdb,[1] a counter is created and set to approximately seventeen-thousand.[2] The counter is used to uniquely number every row. Although databases may be created and destroyed, the counter continues to increase. It is used by all databases, so identification numbers are always unique. No two rows in any table or in any database will ever have the same object ID.[3]

You have seen object identification numbers already—they are displayed after every INSERT statement. If you look back at Figure 3.4 on page 15, you will see the line INSERT 19053 1. INSERT is the command that was executed, 19053 is the object identification number assigned to the inserted row, and 1 is the number of rows inserted. A similar line appears after every INSERT statement. Figure 6.4 on page 63 shows sequential object identification numbers assigned by consecutive INSERT statements.

Normally, a row's object identification number is displayed only by INSERT queries. However, if the OID is specified by a non-INSERT query, it will be displayed, as shown in Figure 7.1. In that

---

[1] See Appendix B for a description of initdb.

[2] Values less than this are reserved for internal use.

[3] Technically, OID's are unique among all databases sharing a common /data directory tree.

```
test=> CREATE TABLE oidtest(age INTEGER);
CREATE
test=> INSERT INTO oidtest VALUES (7);
INSERT 21515 1
test=> SELECT oid, age FROM oidtest;
  oid  | age
-------+-----
 21515 |   7
(1 row)
```

Figure 7.1: OID test

example, the SELECT has accessed the normally invisible OID column. The OID displayed by the INSERT and the OID displayed by the SELECT are the same.

Even though no OID column is mentioned in CREATE TABLE statements, every POSTGRESQL table includes an invisible column called OID. This column appears only if you specifically access it.[4] The query SELECT * FROM table_name does not display the OID column. However, SELECT oid, * FROM table_name will display it.

Object identification numbers can be used as primary and foreign key values in joins. Since every row has a unique object ID, a separate column is not needed to hold the row's unique number.

For example, in Chapter 6 we used a column called *customer.customer_id*. This column held the customer number and uniquely identified each row. Alternatively, we could have used the row's object identification number as the unique number for each row, eliminating the need to create the column *customer.customer_id*. In that case, *customer.oid* would be the unique customer number.

With this change, a similar change should be made in the *salesorder* table. We could rename *salesorder.customer_id* to *salesorder.customer_oid* because the column now refers to an OID. The column type should be changed as well. The *salesorder.customer_id* was defined as type INTEGER. The new *salesorder.customer_oid* column would hold the OID of the customer who placed the order. For this reason, we should change the column type from INTEGER to OID. Figure 7.2 shows a new version of the *salesorder* table using each row's OID as a join key.

A column of type OID is similar to an INTEGER column, but defining it as a type OID documents that the column holds OID values. Do not confuse a column of type OID with a column named OID. Every row has a column named OID, which is normally invisible. A row can have zero, one, or more user-defined columns of type OID.

A column of type OID is not automatically assigned any special value from the database. Only the column named OID is specially assigned during INSERT.

Also, the *order_id* column in the *salesorder* table could be eliminated. The *salesorder.oid* column would then represent the unique order number.

---

[4]Several other invisible columns exist as well. The POSTGRESQL manuals cover their meaning and use.

```
test=> CREATE TABLE salesorder (
test(>            order_id      INTEGER,
test(>            customer_oid  OID,  -- joins to customer.oid
test(>            employee_oid  OID,  -- joins to employee.oid
test(>            part_oid      OID,  -- joins to part.oid
...
```

Figure 7.2: Columns with OIDs

7.2 Object Identification Number Limitations

This section covers three limitations of object identification numbers.

Nonsequential Numbering

The global nature of object identification assignment means most OIDs in a table are not sequential.
For example, if you insert one customer today, and another one tomorrow, the two customers will
not get sequential OIDs. In fact, their OIDs could differ by thousands because any INSERTs into other
tables between the two customer inserts would increment the object counter. If the OID is not
visible to users, this gap in numbering is not a problem. The nonsequential numbering does not
affect query processing. However, if users can see and enter these numbers, it might seem strange
that customer identification numbers are not sequential and have large gaps between them.

Nonmodifiable

An OID is assigned to every row during INSERT. UPDATE cannot modify the system-generated OID
of a row.

Not Backed Up by Default

During database backups, the system-generated OID of each row is normally not backed up. A flag
must be added to enable the backup of OIDs. See Section 20.5 for details.

7.3 Sequences

POSTGRESQL offers another way of uniquely numbering rows—*sequences*. Sequences are named
counters created by users. After its creation, a sequence can be assigned to a table as a column
DEFAULT. Using sequences, unique numbers can be automatically assigned during INSERT.

Function	Action
nextval('name')	Returns the next available sequence number, and updates the counter
currval('name')	Returns the sequence number from the previous *nextval()* call
setval('name', newval)	Sets the sequence number counter to the specified value

Table 7.1: Sequence number access functions

The advantage of sequences is that they avoid gaps in numeric assignment, as happens with OIDs.[5] Sequences are ideal for use as user-visible identification numbers. If one customer is created today, and another is created tomorrow, then the two customers will have sequential numbers because no other table shares the sequence counter.[6]

Sequence numbers are generally unique only within a single table. For example, if a table has a unique row numbered 937, another table might have a row numbered 937 as well, assigned by a different sequence counter.

7.4   Creating Sequences

Sequences are not created automatically, like OIDs. Instead, you must use the CREATE SEQUENCE command. Three functions control the sequence counter, as shown in Table 7.1.

Figure 7.3 shows an example of sequence creation and sequence function usage. The first command creates the sequence, then various sequence functions are called. Note that the SELECTs do not include a FROM clause. Sequence function calls are not directly tied to any table. In the figure:

- *nextval()* returns ever-increasing values.

- *currval()* returns the previous sequence value without incrementing.

- *setval()* sets the sequence counter to a new value.

Currval() returns the sequence number assigned by a prior *nextval()* call in the current session. It is not affected by the *nextval()* calls of other users, which allows reliable retrieval of *nextval()* assigned values in later queries.

7.5   Using Sequences to Number Rows

Configuring a sequence to uniquely number rows involves several steps:

---

[5]This is not completely accurate. Gaps can occur if a query is assigned a sequence number as part of an aborted transaction. See Section 10.2 for a description of aborted transactions.

[6]Tables can be configured to share sequence counters, if desired.

```
test=> CREATE SEQUENCE functest_seq;
CREATE
test=> SELECT nextval('functest_seq');
 nextval
---------
       1
(1 row)

test=> SELECT nextval('functest_seq');
 nextval
---------
       2
(1 row)

test=> SELECT currval('functest_seq');
 currval
---------
       2
(1 row)

test=> SELECT setval('functest_seq', 100);
 setval
--------
    100
(1 row)

test=> SELECT nextval('functest_seq');
 nextval
---------
     101
(1 row)
```

Figure 7.3: Examples of sequence function use

```
test=> CREATE SEQUENCE customer_seq;
CREATE
test=> CREATE TABLE customer (
test(>              customer_id INTEGER DEFAULT nextval('customer_seq'),
test(>              name CHAR(30)
test(> );
CREATE
test=> INSERT INTO customer VALUES (nextval('customer_seq'), 'Bread Makers');
INSERT 19004 1
test=> INSERT INTO customer (name) VALUES ('Wax Carvers');
INSERT 19005 1
test=> INSERT INTO customer (name) VALUES ('Pipe Fitters');
INSERT 19008 1
test=> SELECT * FROM customer;
 customer_id |               name
-------------+------------------------------
           1 | Bread Makers
           2 | Wax Carvers
           3 | Pipe Fitters
(3 rows)
```

[handwritten annotation: because only (explicitly) supply a name value, not Customer-id]

Figure 7.4: Numbering *customer* rows using a sequence

1. Create the sequence.

2. Create the table, defining *nextval()* as the column default.

3. During the INSERT, do not supply a value for the sequenced column, or use *nextval()*.

Figure 7.4 shows the use of a sequence for unique row numbering in the *customer* table. The first statement creates a sequence counter named *customer_seq*. The second command creates the *customer* table, and defines *nextval('customer_seq')* as the default for the *customer_id* column. The first INSERT manually supplies the sequence value for the column. The *nextval('customer_-seq')* function call will return the next available sequence number, and increment the sequence counter. The second and third INSERTs allow the *nextval('customer_seq')* DEFAULT to be used for the *customer_id* column. Remember, a column's DEFAULT value is used only when a value is not supplied by an INSERT statement. (This is covered in Section 4.4.) The SELECT shows that the *customer* rows have been sequentially numbered.

```
test=> CREATE TABLE customer (
test(>          customer_id SERIAL,
test(>          name CHAR(30)
test(> );
NOTICE:  CREATE TABLE will create implicit sequence 'customer_customer_id_-
seq' for SERIAL column 'customer.customer_id'
NOTICE:  CREATE TABLE/UNIQUE will create implicit index 'customer_customer_id_-
key' for table 'customer'
CREATE
test=> \d customer
                        Table "customer"
  Attribute  |   Type   |                    Extra
-------------+----------+------------------------------------------------------
 customer_id | int4     | not null default nextval('customer_customer_id_seq'::text)
 name        | char(30) |
Index: customer_customer_id_key
test=> INSERT INTO customer (name) VALUES ('Car Wash');
INSERT 19152 1
test=> SELECT * FROM customer;
 customer_id |             name
-------------+-------------------------------
           1 | Car Wash
(1 row)
```

Figure 7.5: The *customer* table using SERIAL

7.6   Serial Column Type

An even easier way to use sequences exists. If you define a column of type SERIAL, a sequence
will be automatically created, and a proper DEFAULT will be assigned to the column. Figure 7.5
shows an example. The first NOTICE line indicates that a sequence was created for the SERIAL
column. Do not be concerned about the second NOTICE line in the figure. (Indexes are covered in
Section 11.1.)

7.7   Manually Numbering Rows

Some people wonder why OIDs and sequences are needed at all. Why can't a database user just
find the highest number in use, add one, and use the result as the new unique row number? In
reality, OIDs and sequences are preferred for several reasons:

- Performance

- Concurrency

- Standardization

First, it is usually a slow process to scan all numbers currently in use to find the next available number. Referring to a counter in a separate location is faster. Second, if one user gets the highest number, and another user is looking for the highest number at the same time, the two users might choose the same next-available highest number. Of course, in this case, the number would not be unique. Such concurrency problems do not occur when using OIDs or sequences. Third, it is more reliable to use database-supplied unique number generation than to generate unique numbers manually.

7.8   Summary

Both OIDs and sequences allow the automatic unique numbering of rows. OIDs are always created and numbered, while sequences require more work to configure. Both are valuable tools for uniquely numbering rows.

Chapter 8

Combining SELECTs

So far, this book has covered topics such as regular expressions, aggregates, and joins. These powerful SQL features allow the construction of complex queries. In some cases, however, even these tools may prove inadequate. This chapter shows how SELECTs can be combined to create even more powerful queries.

8.1 UNION, EXCEPT, and INTERSECT Clauses

Sometimes a single SELECT statement cannot produce the desired result. UNION, EXCEPT, and INTERSECT allow SELECT statements to be chained together, enabling the construction of more complex queries.

For example, suppose we want to output the *friend* table's *firstname* and *lastname* in the same column. Normally, two queries would be required, one for each column. With UNION, however, the output of two SELECTs can be combined in a single query, as shown in Figure 8.1. The query combines two columns into a single output column.

UNION allows an unlimited number of SELECT statements to be combined to produce a single result. Each SELECT must return the same number of columns. If the first SELECT returns two columns, the other SELECTs must return two columns as well. The column types must also be similar. If the first SELECT returns an INTEGER value in the first column, the other SELECTs must return an INTEGER in their first columns, too.

With UNION, an ORDER BY clause can be used only at the end of the last SELECT. The ordering applies to the output of the entire query. In Figure 8.1, the ORDER BY clause specifies the ordering column by number. Instead of a number, we could use ORDER BY firstname because UNION's output labels are the same as the column labels of the first SELECT.

As another example, suppose we have two tables that hold information about various animals. One table holds information about aquatic animals, and the other contains data about terrestrial animals. Two tables are used because each records information specific to one class of animal. The *aquatic_animal* table holds information meaningful only for aquatic animals, like *preferred*

```
test=> SELECT firstname
test-> FROM friend
test-> UNION
test-> SELECT lastname
test-> FROM friend
test-> ORDER BY 1;        -- order by applies to output in entire table
       firstname
---------------------
 Dean
 Dick
 Gleason
 Millstone
 Ned
 Sandy
 Tabor
 Victor
 Weber
 Yeager
(10 rows)
```

Figure 8.1: Combining two columns with UNION

water temperature. The *terrestrial_animal* table holds information meaningful only for terrestrial animals, likc *running speed*. We could have included the animals in the same table, but keeping them separate was clearer. In most cases, we will deal with the animal types separately.

Suppose we need to list all of the animals, both *aquatic* and *terrestrial*. No single SELECT can show the animals from both tables. We cannot join the tables because no join key exists; joining is not desired. Instead, we want rows from the *terrestrial_animal* table and the *aquatic_animal* table output together in a single column. Figure 8.2 shows how these two tables can be combined with UNION.

By default, UNION prevents duplicate rows from being displayed. For example, Figure 8.3 inserts *penguin* into both tables, but *penguin* is not duplicated in the output. To preserve duplicates, you must use UNION ALL, as shown in Figure 8.4.

You can perform more complex operations by chaining SELECTs. EXCEPT allows all rows to be returned from the first SELECT except rows that appear in the second SELECT. Figure 8.5 shows an EXCEPT query. Although the *aquatic_animal* table contains *swordfish* and *penguin,* the query in Figure 8.5 returns only *swordfish*. The *penguin* is excluded from the output because it is returned by the second query. While UNION adds rows to the first SELECT, EXCEPT subtracts rows from it.

INTERSECT returns only rows generated by all SELECTs. Figure 8.6 uses INTERSECT to display only *penguin*. While several animals are returned by the two SELECTs, only *penguin* is returned by both SELECTs.

You can link any number of SELECTs using these methods. The previous examples allowed

```
test=> INSERT INTO terrestrial_animal (name) VALUES ('tiger');
INSERT 19122 1
test=> INSERT INTO aquatic_animal (name) VALUES ('swordfish');
INSERT 19123 1
test=> SELECT name
test-> FROM    aquatic_animal
test-> UNION
test-> SELECT name
test-> FROM    terrestrial_animal;
          name
-------------------------------
 swordfish
 tiger
(2 rows)
```

Figure 8.2: Combining two tables with UNION

```
test=> INSERT INTO aquatic_animal (name) VALUES ('penguin');
INSERT 19124 1
test=> INSERT INTO terrestrial_animal (name) VALUES ('penguin');
INSERT 19125 1
test=> SELECT name
test-> FROM    aquatic_animal
test-> UNION
test-> SELECT name
test-> FROM    terrestrial_animal;
          name
-------------------------------
 penguin
 swordfish
 tiger
(3 rows)
```

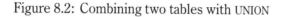

set union

aquatic_animal
swordfish
penguin

terrestrial_animal
tiger
penguin

Figure 8.3: UNION with duplicates

```
test=> SELECT name
test-> FROM    aquatic_animal
test-> UNION ALL
test-> SELECT name
test-> FROM    terrestrial_animal;
              name
---------------------------------
  swordfish
  penguin
  tiger
  penguin
 (4 rows)
```

Figure 8.4: UNION ALL with duplicates

set difference

```
test=> SELECT name
test-> FROM    aquatic_animal
test-> EXCEPT
test-> SELECT name
test-> FROM    terrestrial_animal;
              name
---------------------------------
  swordfish
 (1 row)
```

swordfish
penguin

tiger
penguin

Figure 8.5: EXCEPT restricts output from the first SELECT

```
test=> SELECT name
test-> FROM    aquatic_animal
test-> INTERSECT
test-> SELECT name
test-> FROM    terrestrial_animal;
               name
-------------------------------
 penguin
(1 row)
```

get intersection

Figure 8.6: INTERSECT returns only duplicated rows

multiple columns to occupy a single result column. Without the ability to chain SELECTs using UNION, EXCEPT, and INTERSECT, it would be impossible to generate some of these results. SELECT chaining can enable other sophisticated operations, such as joining a column to one table in the first SELECT, then joining the same column to another table in the second SELECT.

8.2 Subqueries

Subqueries are similar to SELECT chaining. While SELECT chaining combines SELECTs on the same level in a query, however, subqueries allow SELECTs to be embedded *inside* other queries. They can perform several functions:

- They can take the place of a constant.

- They can take the place of a constant yet vary based on the row being processed. *"correlated values"*

- They can return a list of values for use in a comparison.

Subqueries can be quite complicated. If you have trouble understanding this section, skip over it and return to it later.

Subqueries as Constants

A subquery, also called a subselect, can replace a constant in a query. While a constant never changes, a subquery's value is computed every time the query is executed.

As an example, let's use the *friend* table from the previous chapters. Suppose we want to find friends who are not in the same state as Dick Gleason. We could place his state in the query using the constant string 'NJ'. If he moves to another state, however, we would have to change the query. Using the *state* column is more reliable.

Figure 8.7 shows two ways to generate the correct result. One query uses a self-join to do the comparison to Dick Gleason's state. (Self-joins were covered in Section 6.10.) The last query uses a subquery that returns the state as `'NJ'`; this value is used by the upper query. The subquery has taken the place of a constant. Unlike a constant, however, the value is computed every time the query is executed.

Although we have used table aliases in the subquery for clarity, they are not required. A column name with no table specification is automatically paired with a table in the current subquery. If no matching table is found in the current subquery, higher parts of the query are searched for a match. The *state, firstname,* and *lastname* in the subquery refer to the instance of the *friend* table in the subquery. The same column names in the upper query automatically refer to the *friend* instance in that query. If a column name matches two tables in the same subquery, an error is returned, indicating the column is ambiguous.

Subqueries can also eliminate table joins. For example, consider the mail-order parts company used in Figures 6.3 and 6.4 on page 61. To find the customer name for order number 14673, we join the *salesorder* and *customer* tables, as shown in the first query in Figure 8.8. The second query in the figure does not have a join, but instead gets the *customer_id* from a subquery. In general, if a table is involved in only one join, and no columns from the table appear in the query result, the join can be eliminated and the table moved to a subquery.

In this example, we have specified *salesorder.customer_id* and *customer.customer_id* to clearly indicate the tables being referenced. However, this specification is not required. We could have used only *customer_id* in both places. POSTGRESQL finds the first table in the same subquery or higher that contains a matching column name.

Subqueries can be used anywhere a computed value is needed. Each has its own FROM and WHERE clauses. It can also have its own aggregate, GROUP BY, and HAVING clauses. A subquery's only interaction with the upper query is the value it returns. This approach allows sophisticated comparisons that would be difficult if the subquery's clauses had to be combined with those of the upper query.

Subqueries as Correlated Values

In addition to acting as constants in queries, subqueries can act as *correlated values*. Correlated values vary based on the row being processed. A normal subquery is evaluated once and its value used by the upper query. In a *correlated subquery,* the subquery is evaluated repeatedly for every row processed.

For example, suppose you want to find the name of your oldest friend in each state. You can accomplish this task with HAVING and table aliases, as shown in the first query of Figure 8.9. Alternatively, you can execute a subquery for each row that finds the maximum age for that state. If the maximum age equals the age of the current row, the row is output, as shown in the second query. This query references the *friend* table two times, using the aliases *f1* and *f2*. The upper query uses *f1*. The subquery uses *f2*. The correlating specification is WHERE f1.state = f2.state,

```
test=> SELECT * FROM friend ORDER BY firstname;
    firstname    |      lastname      |       city       | state | age
-----------------+--------------------+------------------+-------+-----
 Dean            | Yeager             | Plymouth         | MA    |  24
 Dick            | Gleason            | Ocean City       | NJ    |  19
 Ned             | Millstone          | Cedar Creek      | MD    |  27
 Sandy           | Gleason            | Ocean City       | NJ    |  25
 Sandy           | Weber              | Boston           | MA    |  33
 Victor          | Tabor              | Williamsport     | PA    |  22
(6 rows)

test=> SELECT f1.firstname, f1.lastname, f1.state
test-> FROM   friend f1, friend f2
test-> WHERE  f1.state <> f2.state AND
test->        f2.firstname = 'Dick' AND
test->        f2.lastname = 'Gleason'
test-> ORDER BY firstname, lastname;
    firstname    |      lastname      | state
-----------------+--------------------+-------
 Dean            | Yeager             | MA
 Ned             | Millstone          | MD
 Sandy           | Weber              | MA
 Victor          | Tabor              | PA
(4 rows)

test=> SELECT f1.firstname, f1.lastname, f1.state
test-> FROM   friend f1
test-> WHERE  f1.state <> (
test(>                     SELECT f2.state
test(>                     FROM   friend f2
test(>                     WHERE  f2.firstname = 'Dick' AND
test(>                            f2.lastname = 'Gleason'
test(>                    )
test-> ORDER BY firstname, lastname;
    firstname    |      lastname      | state
-----------------+--------------------+-------
 Dean            | Yeager             | MA
 Ned             | Millstone          | MD
 Sandy           | Weber              | MA
 Victor          | Tabor              | PA
(4 rows)
```

friend table contents

Gleason
Dick
≠
state

(1) self-join equiv to subquery (2)

(2) subquery as stand-in for a constant

Figure 8.7: Friends not in Dick Gleason's state

Task: Find customer name for order-id 14673

Ref tables p 61

salesorder   customer

order-id = customer-id

order-id = 14673

```
test=> SELECT name
test-> FROM    customer, salesorder
test-> WHERE   customer.customer_id = salesorder.customer_id AND
test->         salesorder.order_id = 14673;
          name
--------------------------------
 Fleer Gearworks, Inc.
(1 row)
```

```
test=> SELECT name
test-> FROM    customer
test-> WHERE   customer.customer_id = (
test(>                                 SELECT salesorder.customer_id
test(>                                 FROM salesorder
test(>                                 WHERE order_id = 14673
test(>                                 );
          name
--------------------------------
 Fleer Gearworks, Inc.
(1 row)
```

@ 92   Don't need table qualifier

Figure 8.8: Subqueries can replace some joins

8.2. SUBQUERIES   95

f1   f2

group₀   (handwritten diagram)   state₀

group₁   (handwritten diagram)   state₁

```
test=> SELECT f1.firstname, f1.lastname, f1.age
test-> FROM    friend f1, friend f2
test-> WHERE   f1.state = f2.state
test-> GROUP BY f2.state, f1.firstname, f1.lastname, f1.age
test-> HAVING f1.age = max(f2.age)
test-> ORDER BY firstname, lastname;
  firstname    |      lastname     | age
---------------+-------------------+-----
 Ned           | Millstone         |  27
 Sandy         | Gleason           |  25
 Sandy         | Weber             |  33
 Victor        | Tabor             |  22
(4 rows)

test=> SELECT f1.firstname, f1.lastname, f1.age
test-> FROM    friend f1
test-> WHERE   age = (
test(>              SELECT MAX(f2.age)
test(>              FROM friend f2
test(>              WHERE f1.state = f2.state
test(>         )
test-> ORDER BY firstname, lastname;
  firstname    |      lastname     | age
---------------+-------------------+-----
 Ned           | Millstone         |  27
 Sandy         | Gleason           |  25
 Sandy         | Weber             |  33
 Victor        | Tabor             |  22
(4 rows)
```

(handwritten annotations)

yowzıe

GROUP BY   51

HAVING   51

correlated subquery (b 92)

correlating spec : p 92

easier to understand

Figure 8.9: Correlated subquery

Split the (joined) table into groups by state, firstname, lassname, age

group { state₀ ...
       { state₀ ...
       { state₀ ...
group { state₁ ...

which creates a correlated subquery because the subquery references a column from the upper query. Such a subquery cannot be evaluated once and the same result used for all rows. Instead, it must be evaluated for every row because the upper column value can change.

Subqueries as Lists of Values

The previous subqueries returned one row of data to the upper query. If any of the previous subqueries returned more than one row, an error would be generated: ERROR: More than one tuple returned by a subselect used as an expression. It is possible, however, to have subqueries return multiple rows.

Normal comparison operators like equal and less-than expect a single value on the left and on the right. For example, equality expects one value on the left of the equals sign (=) and one on the right—for example, col = 3. Two special comparisons, IN and NOT IN, allow multiple values to appear on the right side. For example, the test col IN (1,2,3,4) compares col against four values. If col equals any of the four values, the comparison will return true and output the row. The test col NOT IN (1,2,3,4) will return true if col does not equal any of the four values.

You can specify an unlimited number of values on the right side of an IN or NOT IN comparison. More importantly, a subquery (instead of a constant) can be placed on the right side. It can then return multiple rows. The subquery is evaluated, and its output used like a list of constant values.

Suppose we want all employees who took sales orders on a certain date. We could perform this query in two ways. We could join the *employee* and *salesorder* tables, as shown in the first query of Figure 8.10. Alternatively, we could use a subquery, as shown in the second query. In this case, the subquery is evaluated and generates a list of values used by IN to perform the comparison. The subquery is possible because the *salesorder* table is involved in a single join, and the query does not return any columns from the *salesorder* table.

A NOT IN comparison returns true if a column's value is not found. For example, suppose we want to see all customers who have never ordered a product. That is, we need to find the *customers* who have no sales orders. This task cannot be accomplished with a join. We need an *anti-join,* because we want to find all *customer* rows that do not join to any *salesorder* row. Figure 8.11 shows the relevant query. The subquery returns a list of *customer_ids* representing all customers who have placed orders. The upper query returns all customer names where the *customer_id* does not appear in the subquery output.

NOT IN and Subqueries with NULL Values

If a NOT IN subquery returns a NULL value, the NOT IN comparison always returns false. NOT IN requires the upper column to be not equal to every value returned by the subquery. Because all comparisons with NULL return false—even inequality comparisons—NOT IN returns false. NULL comparisons were covered in Section 4.3.

We can prevent NULL values from reaching the upper query by adding IS NOT NULL to the subquery. As an example, in Figure 8.11, if any NULL *customer_id* values existed, the query would

-- all employees who took salesorders on a particular date

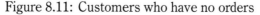

```
test=> SELECT DISTINCT employee.name
test-> FROM    employee, salesorder
test-> WHERE   employee.employee_id = salesorder.employee_id AND
test->         salesorder.order_date = '7/19/1994';
           name
-------------------------------
 Lee Meyers
(1 row)
```

-- all employees who took sales orders on a particular date

```
test=> SELECT name
test-> FROM    employee
test-> WHERE   employee_id IN (
test(>                     SELECT employee_id
test(>                     FROM   salesorder
test(>                     WHERE  order_date = '7/19/1994'
test(>                     );
           name
-------------------------------
 Lee Meyers
(1 row)
```

Figure 8.10: Employees who took orders

-- all customers who have never ordered a product

```
test=> SELECT name
test-> FROM    customer
test-> WHERE   customer_id NOT IN (
test(>                     SELECT customer_id
test(>                     FROM salesorder
test(>                     );
 name
------
(0 rows)
```

< where customer-id is not null

@ 96

NB: otherwise, if any customer-id selected by the subquery is null, the overall SELECT returns no rows

Figure 8.11: Customers who have no orders

return no rows. We can prevent this situation by adding WHERE customer_id IS NOT NULL to the subquery. An IN subquery does not have this problem with NULLs.

Subqueries Returning Multiple Columns

Although most subqueries return a single column to the upper query, it is possible to handle subqueries returning more than one column. For example, the test WHERE (7, 3) IN (SELECT col1, col2 FROM subtable) returns true if the subquery returns a row with 7 in the first column and 3 in the second column. The test WHERE (uppercol1, uppercol2) IN (SELECT col1, col2 FROM subtable) performs equality comparisons between the upper query's two columns and the subquery's two columns. Multiple columns in the upper query can then be compared with multiple columns in the subquery. Of course, the number of values specified on the left of IN or NOT IN must be the same as the number of columns returned by the subquery.

ANY, ALL, and EXISTS Clauses

IN and NOT IN are special cases of the more generic subquery clauses ANY, ALL, and EXISTS. ANY will return true if the comparison operator is true for any value in the subquery. For example, the test col = ANY(5,7,9) returns true if col equals any of the three values. ALL requires all subquery values to compare as true, so col != ALL(5,7,9) returns true if col is not equal to all three values. IN( ) is the same as = ANY( ), and NOT IN( ) is the same as <> ALL( ).

Normally, you can use operators like equal and greater-than only with subqueries returning one row. With ANY and ALL, however, comparisons can be made with subqueries returning multiple rows. They allow you to specify whether any or all of the subquery values, respectively, must compare as true.

EXISTS returns true if the subquery returns any rows, and NOT EXISTS returns true if the subquery returns no rows. By using a correlated subquery, EXISTS permits complex comparisons of upper-query values inside the subquery. For example, two upper-query variables can be compared in the subquery's WHERE clause. EXISTS and NOT EXISTS do not specify anything in the upper query, so it does not matter which columns are returned by the subquery.

Figure 8.12 shows the IN subquery from Figure 8.10, with the query rewritten using ANY and EXISTS. Notice that the EXISTS subquery uses a correlated subquery to join the *employee_id* columns of the two tables. Figure 8.13 shows the NOT IN query from Figure 8.11, with the query rewritten using ALL and NOT EXISTS.

Summary

A subquery can represent a fixed value, a correlated value, or a list of values. You can use any number of subqueries. You can also nest subqueries inside other subqueries.

In some cases, subqueries simply provide an alternative way to phrase a query. In others, a subquery is the only way to produce the desired result.

-- all employees who took sales orders on a particular date

```
SELECT name
FROM    employee
WHERE   employee_id IN (
                  SELECT employee_id
                  FROM    salesorder
                  WHERE   order_date = '7/19/1994'
                );
```

All 3 are equivalent

(1)

```
SELECT name
FROM    employee
WHERE   employee_id = ANY (
                  SELECT employee_id
                  FROM    salesorder
                  WHERE   order_date = '7/19/1994'
                );
```

employees

name employee-id = ANY(...)   (2)

{ list of employee ids

(3)

```
SELECT name
FROM    employee
WHERE   EXISTS (
```

-- correlated query: For a given employee tuple (name, employee-id,...)
correlate its employee-id w. sub-query selected
employee-id

```
                  SELECT employee_id
                  FROM    salesorder
                  WHERE   salesorder.employee_id = employee.employee_id AND
                          order_date = '7/19/1994'
                );
```

Figure 8.12: IN query rewritten using ANY and EXISTS

IN ( )   ←→   = ANY ( )

NOT IN ( )   ←→   <> ALL ( )

-- Customers who have not made an order

```sql
SELECT name
FROM    customer
WHERE   customer_id NOT IN (
                            SELECT customer_id
                            FROM salesorder          ← where customer_id is not NULL;
                            );                                  cf p96


SELECT name
FROM    customer
WHERE   customer_id <> ALL (
                            SELECT customer_id
                            FROM salesorder
                            );


SELECT name
FROM    customer
WHERE NOT EXISTS (
                            SELECT customer_id
                            FROM salesorder
                            WHERE salesorder.customer_id = customer.customer_id
                            );
```

@94

Figure 8.13: NOT IN query rewritten using ALL and EXISTS

```
SELECT name, order_id
FROM    customer, salesorder
WHERE   customer.customer_id = salesorder.customer_id
UNION ALL
SELECT name, NULL
FROM    customer
WHERE   customer.customer_id NOT IN (SELECT customer_id FROM salesorder)
ORDER BY name;
```

Simulate an outer join (not in postgresql 7.0)

Figure 8.14: Simulating outer joins

8.3 Outer Joins

An *outer join* is similar to a normal join, except that it performs special handling to prevent unjoined rows from being suppressed in the result. For example, in the join *customer.customer_id = salesorder.customer_id,* only customers who have sales orders appear in the result. If a customer has no sales orders, he or she is suppressed from the output. If the *salesorder* table is used in an outer join, however, the result will include all customers. The *customer* and *salesorder* tables will then be joined and output, as well as one row for every unjoined *customer.* In the query result, any reference to *salesorder* columns for these unjoined *customers* will return NULL.

POSTGRESQL 7.0 does not support outer joins. You can simulate them using subqueries and UNION ALL, as shown in Figure 8.14. In this example, the first SELECT performs a normal join of the *customer* and *salesorder* tables. The second SELECT displays customers who have no orders, with NULL appearing as their order number.

8.4 Subqueries in Non-SELECT Queries

Subqueries can also be used in UPDATE and DELETE statements. Figure 8.15 shows two examples. The first query deletes all customers with no sales orders. The second query sets the *ship_date* equal to '11/16/96' for all orders made by Fleer Gearworks, Inc. The numbers after DELETE and UPDATE indicate the number of rows affected by the queries.

8.5 UPDATE with FROM

UPDATE can include an optional FROM clause, which permits joins to other tables. The FROM clause also allows the use of columns from other tables in the SET clause. With this capability, columns can be updated with data from other tables.

-- delete customers w. no orders

```
test=> DELETE FROM customer
test-> WHERE customer_id NOT IN (
test(>                                     SELECT customer_id
test(>                                     FROM salesorder
test(>                         );
DELETE 0    -- no. rows affected
test=> UPDATE salesorder
test-> SET     ship_date = '11/16/96'
test-> WHERE   customer_id = (
test(>                         SELECT customer_id
test(>                         FROM    customer
test(>                         WHERE   name = 'Fleer Gearworks, Inc.'
test(>                     );
UPDATE 1
```

Figure 8.15: Subqueries with UPDATE and DELETE

```
UPDATE salesorder            -- table 1
SET    order_date = employee.hire_date
FROM   employee              -- table 2
WHERE  salesorder.employee_id = employee.employee_id AND
       salesorder.order_date < employee.hire_date;
```

Figure 8.16: UPDATE the *order_date*

Suppose we want to update the *salesorder* table's *order_date* column. Some orders have *order_-dates* earlier than the *hire_date* of the employee who recorded the sale. For these rows, we wish to set the *order_date* equal to the employee's *hire_date*. Figure 8.16 shows this query.

The FROM clause allows the use of the *employee* table in the WHERE and SET clauses. While UPDATE can use subqueries to control which rows are updated, the FROM clause allows you to include columns from other tables in the SET clause.

Actually, the FROM clause is not even required. The UPDATE in Figure 8.16 will work in the same way without its FROM clause. POSTGRESQL automatically creates a reference to any table used in a query. That is, the query SELECT salesorder.* automatically adds *salesorder* to the FROM clause and executes the query. Likewise, the query DELETE FROM salesorder WHERE salesorder.order_-date = employee.hire_date AND employee.employee_id = 24 uses the *employee* table. This feature is particularly useful with DELETE because it does not support a FROM clause as SELECT and UPDATE do.

```
test=> INSERT INTO customer (name, city, state, country)
test-> SELECT trim(firstname) || ' ' || lastname, city, state, 'USA'          ⓐ
test-> FROM friend;
INSERT 0 6
```
6 rows inserted so no unique Oid: show 0 instead   ✗

Figure 8.17: Using SELECT with INSERT

8.6 Inserting Data Using SELECT

Up to this point, all of our INSERT statements have inserted a single row. Each INSERT contained a VALUES clause listing the constants to be inserted. Another form of the INSERT statement also   ✳ exists; it allows the output of a SELECT to be used to insert values into a table.

Suppose we wish to add all of our friends from the *friend* table to the *customer* table. As shown in Figure 8.17, instead of a VALUES clause, INSERT can use the output of SELECT to insert data into the table. Each column of the SELECT matches a receiving column in the INSERT. Column names and character string constants can be used in the SELECT output. In the line INSERT 0 6, six rows are inserted into the *customer* table. A zero object identifier is returned because more than one row is inserted.

Inserting into the customer name column presents an interesting challenge. The *friend* table   ⓐ stores first and last names in separate columns. In contrast, the *customer* table has only a single *name* column. The solution is to combine the *firstname* and *lastname* columns, with a space separating them. For example, a *firstname* of 'Dean' and a *lastname* of 'Yeager' must be inserted into *customer.name* as 'Dean Yeager'. This combination becomes possible with *trim()* and the || operator. The *trim()* function removes trailing spaces. The two pipe symbols, ||, allow character strings to be joined together to form a single string, in a process called *concatenation*. In this example, *trim(firstname), space (' '),* and *lastname* are joined using ||.

8.7 Creating Tables Using SELECT

In addition to inserting into existing tables, SELECT can use an INTO clause to create a table and   ✳ place all of its output into the new table. For example, suppose we want to create a new table called *newfriend* that is just like our *friend* table but lacks an *age* column. This task is easily done with the query shown in Figure 8.18. The SELECT...INTO query performs three operations:

1. It creates a table called *newfriend.*

2. It uses SELECT's column labels to name the columns of the new table.

3. It uses SELECT's column types as the column types of the new table.

```
test=> SELECT firstname, lastname, city, state
test-> INTO   newfriend
test-> FROM   friend;
SELECT

test=> \d newfriend
      Table "newfriend"
 Attribute |   Type   | Extra
-----------+----------+-------
 firstname | char(15) |
 lastname  | char(20) |
 city      | char(15) |
 state     | char(2)  |

test=> SELECT * FROM newfriend ORDER BY firstname;
    firstname     |       lastname       |       city       | state
------------------+----------------------+------------------+-------
 Dean             | Yeager               | Plymouth         | MA
 Dick             | Gleason              | Ocean City       | NJ
 Ned              | Millstone            | Cedar Creek      | MD
 Sandy            | Gleason              | Ocean City       | NJ
 Sandy            | Weber                | Boston           | MA
 Victor           | Tabor                | Williamsport     | PA
(6 rows)
```

Figure 8.18: Table creation with SELECT

SELECT...INTO essentially combines CREATE TABLE and SELECT in a single statement. The AS clause can be used to change the column labels and thus control the column names in the new table. The other commands in the figure show the new table's structure and contents.

SELECT...INTO *tablename* can also be written as CREATE TABLE *tablename* AS SELECT.... The preceding query can then be rewritten as CREATE TABLE *newfriend* AS SELECT *firstname, lastname, city, state* FROM *friend*.

8.8 Summary

This chapter has described how to combine queries in ways you probably never anticipated. It showed how queries could be chained and placed inside other queries. In addition, it demonstrated how UPDATE can use FROM, and how SELECT can create tables.

Although these features may seem confusing, they are very powerful. In most cases, you will need only the simplest of these features. However, you may get that rare request that requires one of the more complicated queries covered in this chapter. If you recognize such a query, return to this chapter to refresh your memory.

Chapter 9

Data Types

Data types have been used in previous chapters. This chapter covers them in detail.

9.1 Purpose of Data Types

It is tempting to think that databases would be easier to use if only one data type existed—a type that could hold any type of information, such as numbers, character strings, or dates. Although a single data type would certainly make table creation simpler, having different data types offers definite advantages:

Consistent Results Columns of a uniform type produce consistent results. Displaying, sorting, aggregates, and joins deliver consistent results. No conflict arises over how different types are compared or displayed. For example, selecting from an INTEGER column always yields INTEGER values.

Data Validation Columns of a uniform type accept only properly formated data; invalid data are rejected. For example, a column of type INTEGER will reject a DATE value.

Compact Storage Columns of a uniform type are stored more compactly.

Performance Columns of a uniform type are processed more quickly.

For these reasons, each column in a relational database can hold only one type of data. You cannot mix data types within a column.

This limitation can cause some difficulties. For example, our *friend* table includes an *age* column of type INTEGER. Only whole numbers can be placed in that column. The values "I will ask for his age soon" or "She will not tell me her age" cannot be placed in that column. NULL can represent "I do not know her age." The solution is to create an *age_comments* column of type CHAR() to hold comments that cannot be placed in the *age* field.

Category	Type	Description
Character string	TEXT	variable storage length
	VARCHAR(*length*)	variable storage length with maximum *length*
	CHAR(*length*)	fixed storage length, blank-padded to *length*, internally BPCHAR
Number	INTEGER [INT4]	integer, ±2 billion range, internally INT4
	INT2	integer, ±32 thousand range
	INT8	integer, $\pm 4 \times 10^{18}$ range
	OID	object identifier
	NUMERIC(*precision*, *decimal*)	number, user-defined *precision* and *decimal* location
	FLOAT [FLOAT8]	floating-point number, 15-digit precision, internally FLOAT8
	FLOAT4	floating-point number, 6-digit precision
Temporal	DATE	date
	TIME	time
	TIMESTAMP	date and time
	INTERVAL	interval of time
Logical	BOOL	boolean, *true* or *false*
Geometric	POINT	point
	LSEG	line segment
	PATH	list of points
	BOX	rectangle
	CIRCLE	circle
	POLYGON	polygon
Network	INET	IP address with optional netmask
	CIDR	IP network address
	MACADDR	Ethernet MAC address

Table 9.1: POSTGRESQL data types

9.2 Installed Types

POSTGRESQL supports a large number of data types, as shown in Table 9.1. Except for the number types, all entered values must be surrounded by single quotes.

Character String

Character string types are the most commonly used data types. They can hold any sequence of letters, digits, punctuation, and other valid characters. Typical character strings are names, descriptions, and mailing addresses. You can store any value in a character string. Nevertheless, this type should be used only when other data types are inappropriate, as other types provide better data validation, more compact storage, and better performance.

Three character string data types exist: TEXT, VARCHAR(*length*), and CHAR(*length*). TEXT does not limit the number of characters stored. VARCHAR(*length*) limits the length of the field to *length* characters. Both TEXT and VARCHAR() store only the number of characters in the string. CHAR(*length*) is similar to VARCHAR(), except it always stores exactly *length* characters. This type pads the value with trailing spaces to achieve the specified *length,* and provides slightly faster access than TEXT or VARCHAR().

Understanding why character string types differ from other data types can be difficult. For example, you can store *763* as a character string. In that case, you will store the symbols *7, 6,* and *3,* not the numeric value *763.* Consequently, you cannot add a number to the character string *763,* because it does not make sense to add a number to three symbols. Similarly, the character string *3/8/1992* consists of eight symbols starting with *3* and ending with *2.* If you store this value in a character string data type, it is not a date. You cannot sort the string with other values and expect them to be in chronological order. The string *1/4/1998* is less than *3/8/1992* when both are sorted as character strings because *1* is less than *3.*

These examples illustrate why the other data types are valuable. The other types use predefined formats for their data, and they support more appropriate operations on the stored information.

Nevertheless, there is nothing wrong with storing numbers or dates in character strings when appropriate. The street address *100 Maple Avenue* is best stored in a character string type, even though a number is part of the street address. It makes no sense to store the street number in a separate INTEGER field. Also, part numbers such as *G8223-9* must be stored in character strings because of the *G* and dash. In fact, part numbers that are always five digits, such as *32911* or *00413,* should be stored in character strings as well. They are not real numbers, but symbols. Leading zeros cannot be displayed by INTEGER fields, but are easily displayed in character strings.

Number

Number types allow the storage of numbers. The number types are INTEGER, INT2, INT8, OID, NUMERIC(), FLOAT, and FLOAT4.

INTEGER, INT2, and INT8 store whole numbers of various ranges. Larger ranges require more storage. For example, INT8 requires twice the storage of INTEGER and is slower that INTEGER.

OID is used to store POSTGRESQL object identifiers. Although you could use INTEGER for this purpose, OID better documents the meaning of the value stored in the column.

NUMERIC(*precision, decimal*) allows user-defined digits of *precision*, rounded to *decimal* places. This type is slower than the other number types.

FLOAT and FLOAT4 allow storage of floating-point values. Numbers are stored using 15 (FLOAT) or 6 (FLOAT4) digits of precision. The location of the decimal point is stored separately, so large values such as *4.78145e+32* can be represented. FLOAT and FLOAT4 are fast and have compact storage, but can produce imprecise rounding during computations. When you require complete accuracy of floating-point values, use NUMERIC() instead. For example, store monetary amounts as NUMERIC().

Type	Example	Note
POINT	(2,7)	(*x,y*) coordinates
LSEG	[(0,0),(1,3)]	start and stop points of a line segment
PATH	((0,0),(3,0),(4,5),(1,6))	( ) is a closed path, [ ] is an open path
BOX	(1,1),(3,3)	opposite corner points of a rectangle
CIRCLE	<(1,2),60>	center point and radius
POLYGON	((3,1),(3,3),(1,0))	points form closed polygon

Table 9.2: Geometric types

Temporal

Temporal types allow storage of date, time, and time interval information. Although these data can be stored in character strings, it is better to use temporal types, for the reasons outlined earlier in this chapter.

The four temporal types are DATE, TIME, TIMESTAMP, and INTERVAL. DATE allows storage of a single date consisting of a year, month, and day. The format used to input and display dates is controlled by the DATESTYLE setting (see Section 4.14 on page 43). TIME allows storage of an hour, minute, and second, separated by colons. TIMESTAMP stores both the date and the time—for example, *2000-7-12 17:34:29*. INTERVAL represents an interval of time, like 5 hours or 7 days. INTERVAL values are often generated by subtracting two TIMESTAMP values to find the elapsed time. For example, *1996–12–15 19:00:40* minus *1996–12–8 14:00:10* results in an INTERVAL value of *7 05:00:30*, which is 7 days, 5 hours, and 30 seconds. Temporal types can also handle time zone designations.

Logical

The only logical type is BOOLEAN. A BOOLEAN field can store only true or false, and of course NULL. You can input true as *true, t, yes, y,* or *1*. False can be input as *false, f, no, n,* or *0*. Although true and false can be input in a variety of ways, true is always output as *t* and false as *f.*

Geometric

The geometric types support storage of geometric primitives. They include POINT, LSEG, PATH, BOX, CIRCLE, and POLYGON. Table 9.2 shows the geometric types and typical values for each.

Network

The network types are INET, CIDR, and MACADDR. INET allows storage of an IP address, with or without a netmask. A typical INET value with a netmask is *172.20.90.150 255.255.255.0*. CIDR stores IP network addresses. It allows a subnet mask to specify the size of the network segment. A typical CIDR value is *172.20.90.150/24.* MACADDR stores MAC (Media Access Control) addresses, which are assigned to Ethernet network cards at the time of their manufacture. A typical MACADDR value is *0:50:4:1d:f6:db.*

Internal

A variety of types are used internally. Psql's \dT command shows all data types.

9.3   Type Conversion Using CAST

In most cases, values of one type are converted to another type automatically. In those rare circumstances where you need to explicitly convert one type to another, you can use CAST to perform the conversion. To convert *val* to an INTEGER, use CAST(*val* AS INTEGER). To convert a column *date_col* of type DATE to type TEXT, use CAST(*date_col* AS TEXT). You can also perform type casting using double colons—that is, *date_col::text* or *num_val::numeric(10,2).*

9.4   Support Functions

Functions enable you to access specialized routines from SQL. They take one or more arguments and return a result.

Suppose you want to uppercase a value or column. No command will perform this operation, but a function can handle it. POSTGRESQL has a function called *upper* that takes a single string argument and returns the argument in uppercase. The function call *upper(col)* calls the function *upper* with *col* as its argument and returns it in uppercase. Figure 9.1 shows an example of the use of the *upper* function.

POSTGRESQL provides many functions. Table 9.3 shows the most common ones, organized by the data types supported. Psql's \df shows all defined functions and their arguments. Section 16.1 describes all the psql commands.

If you call a function with a type for which it is not defined, you will get an error message, as shown in the first query of Figure 9.2. In the first query, *5/8/1971* is a character string, not a date. The second query converts *5/8/1971* to a date, so *date_part()* can be used.

9.5   Support Operators

Operators are similar to functions (see Section 4.13 on page 43). Table 9.4 lists the most common operators. Psql's \do command shows all defined operators and their arguments.

```
test=> SELECT * FROM functest;
 name
------
 Judy
(1 row)

test=> SELECT upper(name) FROM functest;
 upper
-------
 JUDY
(1 row)
```

Figure 9.1: Example of a function call

```
test=> SELECT date_part('year', '5/8/1971');          X
ERROR:  Function 'date_part(unknown, unknown)' does not exist
        Unable to identify a function that satisfies the given argument types
        You may need to add explicit typecasts
test=> SELECT date_part('year', CAST('5/8/1971' AS DATE));     OK
 date_part
-----------
      1971
(1 row)
```

Figure 9.2: Error generated by undefined function/type combination.

Type	Function	Example	Returns
Character String	length()	length(*col*)	length of *col*
	character_length()	character_length(*col*)	length of *col*, same as length()
	octet_length()	octet_length(*col*)	length of *col*, including multibyte overhead
	trim()	trim(*col*)	*col* with leading and trailing spaces removed
	trim(BOTH...)	trim(BOTH, *col*)	same as trim()
	trim(LEADING...)	trim(LEADING *col*)	*col* with leading spaces removed
	trim(TRAILING...)	trim(TRAILING *col*)	*col* with trailing spaces removed
	trim(...FROM...)	trim(*str* FROM *col*)	*col* with leading and trailing *str* removed
	rpad()	rpad(*col, len*)	*col* padded on the right to *len* characters
	rpad()	rpad(*col, len, str*)	*col* padded on the right using *str*
	lpad()	lpad(*col, len*)	*col* padded on the left to *len* characters
	lpad()	lpad(*col, len, str*)	*col* padded on the left using *str*
	upper()	upper(*col*)	*col* uppercased
	lower()	lower(*col*)	*col* lowercased
	initcap()	initcap(*col*)	*col* with the first letter capitalized
	strpos()	strpos(*col, str*)	position of *str* in *col*
	position()	position(*str* IN *col*)	same as strpos()
	substr()	substr(*col, pos*)	*col* starting at position *pos*
	substring(...FROM...)	substring(*col* FROM *pos*)	same as substr()
	substr()	substr(*col, pos, len*)	*col* starting at position *pos* for length *len*
	substring(...FROM... FOR...)	substring(*col* FROM pos FOR *len*)	same as substr()
	translate()	translate(*col, from, to*)	*col* with *from* changed to *to*
	to_number()	to_number(*col, mask*)	convert *col* to NUMERIC() based on *mask*
	to_date()	to_date(*col, mask*)	convert *col* to DATE based on *mask*
	to_timestamp()	to_timestamp(*col, mask*)	convert *col* to TIMESTAMP based on *mask*
Number	round()	round(*col*)	round to an integer
	round()	round(*col, len*)	NUMERIC() *col* rounded to *len* decimal places
	trunc()	trunc(*col*)	truncate to an integer
	trunc()	trunc(*col, len*)	NUMERIC() *col* truncated to *len* decimal places
	abs()	abs(*col*)	absolute value
	factorial()	factorial(*col*)	factorial
	sqrt()	sqrt(*col*)	square root
	cbrt()	cbrt(*col*)	cube root
	exp()	exp(*col*)	exponential
	ln()	ln(*col*)	natural logarithm
	log()	log(*log*)	base-10 logarithm
	to_char()	to_char(*col, mask*)	convert *col* to a string based on *mask*
Temporal	date_part()	date_part(*units, col*)	*units* part of *col*
	extract(...FROM...)	extract(*units* FROM *col*)	same as date_part()
	date_trunc()	date_trunc(*units, col*)	*col* rounded to *units*
	isfinite()	isfinite(*col*)	BOOLEAN indicating whether *col* is a valid date
	now()	now()	TIMESTAMP representing current date and time
	timeofday()	timeofday()	string showing date/time in Unix format
	overlaps()	overlaps(*c1, c2, c3, c4*)	BOOLEAN indicating whether *col's* overlap in time
	to_char()	to_char(*col, mask*)	convert *col* to string based on *mask*
Geometric			see psql's \df for a list of geometric functions
Network	broadcast()	broadcast(*col*)	broadcast address of *col*
	host()	host(*col*)	host address of *col*
	netmask()	netmask(*col*)	netmask of *col*
	masklen()	masklen(*col*)	mask length of *col*
	network()	network(*col*)	network address of *col*
NULL	nullif()	nullif(*col1, col2*)	return NULL if *col1* equals *col2*, else return *col1*
	coalesce()	coalesce(*col1, col2,...*)	return first non-NULL argument

[handwritten annotation: units ∈ {year, month, day, ...}*]*

Table 9.3: Common functions *[handwritten annotation:* (only most commonly used!)*]*

Type	Function	Example	Returns
Character	`||`	*col1* `||` *col2*	append *col2* on to the end of *col1*
String	~	*col* ~ *pattern*	BOOLEAN, *col* matches regular expression *pattern*
	!~	*col* !~ *pattern*	BOOLEAN, *col* does not match regular expression *pattern*
	~*	*col* ~* *pattern*	same as ~, but case-insensitive
	!~*	*col* !~* *pattern*	same as !~, but case-insensitive
	~~ [1]	*col* ~~ *pattern*	BOOLEAN, *col* matches LIKE pattern
	LIKE [1]	*col* LIKE *pattern*	same as ~~
	!~~	*col* !~~ *pattern*	BOOLEAN, *col* does not match LIKE pattern
	NOT LIKE	*col* NOT LIKE *pattern*	same as !~~
Number	!	!*col*	factorial
	+	*col1* + *col2*	addition
	−	*col1* − *col2*	subtraction
	*	*col1* * *col2*	multiplication
	/	*col1* / *col2*	division
	%	*col1* % *col2*	remainder/modulo
	^	*col1* ^ *col2*	*col1* raised to the power of *col2*
Temporal	+	*col1* + *col2*	addition of temporal values
	−	*col1* − *col2*	subtraction of temporal values
	(...) OVERLAPS (...)	(*c1, c2*) OVERLAPS (*c3, c4*)	BOOLEAN indicating *cols* overlap in time
Geometric			see psql's \do for a list of geometric operators
Network	<<	*col1* << *col2*	BOOLEAN indicating if *col1* is a subnet of *col2*
	<<=	*col1* <<= *col2*	BOOLEAN indicating if *col1* is equal or a subnet of *col2*
	>>	*col1* >> *col2*	BOOLEAN indicating if *col1* is a supernet of *col2*
	>>=	*col1* >>= *col2*	BOOLEAN indicating if *col1* is equal or a supernet of *col2*

Handwritten annotation (Character/String row): p35

Handwritten annotation (Temporal + row): col 1: date, col 2: interval

Table 9.4: Common operators

Handwritten note at bottom:

1   % matches 0 or more chars
     _ matches 1

```
test=> SELECT CAST('1/1/1992' AS DATE) + CAST('1/1/1993' AS DATE);
ERROR:  Unable to identify an operator '+' for types 'date' and 'date'
        You will have to retype this query using an explicit cast
test=> SELECT CAST('1/1/1992' AS DATE) + CAST('1 year' AS INTERVAL);
        ?column?
------------------------
 1993-01-01 00:00:00-05
(1 row)

test=> SELECT CAST('1/1/1992' AS TIMESTAMP) + '1 year';
        ?column?
------------------------
 1993-01-01 00:00:00-05
(1 row)
```

Figure 9.3: Error generated by undefined operator/type combination

Variable	Meaning
CURRENT_DATE	current date
CURRENT_TIME	current time
CURRENT_TIMESTAMP	current date and time
CURRENT_USER	user connected to the database

Table 9.5: Common variables

All data types support the standard comparison operators <, <=, =, >=, >, and <>. Not all operator/type combinations are defined, however. For example, if you try to add two DATE values, you will get an error, as shown in the first query of Figure 9.3.

9.6 Support Variables

Several variables are defined in POSTGRESQL. These variables are shown in Table 9.5.

```
test=> CREATE TABLE array_test (
test(>                          col1   INTEGER[5],
test(>                          col2   INTEGER[][],
test(>                          col3   INTEGER[2][2][]
test(> );
CREATE
```

Figure 9.4: Creation of array columns

9.7 Arrays

Arrays allow a column to store several simple data values. You can store one-dimensional arrays, two-dimensional arrays, or arrays with any number of dimensions.

You create an array column in the same way as an ordinary column, except that you use brackets to specify the dimensions of the array. The number of dimensions and size of each dimension are for documentation purposes only. Values that do not match the dimensions specified at the time of column creation are not rejected.

Figure 9.4 creates a table with one-, two-, and three-dimensional INTEGER columns. The first and last columns have sizes specified. The first column is a one-dimensional array, also called a list or vector. Values inserted into that column have an appearance like *{3,10,9,32,24}* or *{20,8,9,1,4}*. That is, each value is a list of integers, surrounded by curly braces. The second column, *col2*, is a two-dimensional array. Typical values for this column are *{{2,9,3},{4,3,5}}* or *{{18,6},{32,5}}*. Notice the double braces. The outer brace surrounds two one-dimensional arrays. You can think of this structure as a matrix, with the first one-dimensional array representing the first row of the array, and the second representing the second row of the array. Commas separate the individual elements as well as each pair of braces. The third column of the *array_test* table is a three-dimensional array, holding values like *{{{3,1},{1,9}},{{4,5},{8,2}}}*. This three-dimensional matrix is made up of two 2×2 matrices. Arrays of any size can be constructed.

Figure 9.5 shows a query inserting values into *array_test* plus several queries selecting data from this table. Brackets are used to access individual array elements.

Any data type can be used as an array. If you need to frequently access or update individual elements of the array, use separate columns or tables rather than arrays.

9.8 Large Objects (BLOBs)

POSTGRESQL cannot store values of more than several thousand bytes using the data types discussed so far, nor can binary data be easily entered within single quotes. Instead, large objects—also called Binary Large Objects or BLOBS—are used to store very large values and binary data.

```
test=> INSERT INTO array_test VALUES (
test(>                            '{1,2,3,4,5}',
test(>                            '{{1,2},{3,4}}',
test(>                            '{{{1,2},{3,4}},{{5,6}, {7,8}}}'
test(> );
INSERT 52694 1
test=> SELECT * FROM array_test;
    col1    |     col2     |             col3
------------+--------------+------------------------------
 {1,2,3,4,5} | {{1,2},{3,4}} | {{{1,2},{3,4}},{{5,6},{7,8}}}
(1 row)

test=> SELECT col1[4] FROM array_test;
 col1
------
    4
(1 row)

test=> SELECT col2[2][1] FROM array_test;
 col2
------
    3
(1 row)

test=> SELECT col3[1][2][2] FROM array_test;
 col3
------
    4
(1 row)
```

Figure 9.5: Using arrays

BLOB

```
test=> CREATE TABLE fruit (name CHAR(30), image OID);
CREATE
test=> INSERT INTO fruit
test-> VALUES ('peach', lo_import('/usr/images/peach.jpg'));
INSERT 27111 1
test=> SELECT lo_export(fruit.image, '/tmp/outimage.jpg')
test-> FROM    fruit
test-> WHERE   name = 'peach';
 lo_export
-----------
         1    Means; successful export
(1 row)


test=> SELECT lo_unlink(fruit.image) FROM fruit;
 lo_unlink
-----------
         1
(1 row)
```

Figure 9.6: Using large images

Large objects permit storage of any operating system file, including images or large text files, directly into the database. You load the file into the database using *lo_import()*, and retrieve it from the database using *lo_export()*.

Figure 9.6 shows an example that stores a fruit name and image. The *lo_import()* function stores /usr/images/peach.jpg into the database. The function call returns an OID that is used to refer to the imported large object. This value is stored in *fruit.image*. The *lo_export()* function uses the OID value to find the large object stored in the database, then places the image into the new file /tmp/outimage.jpg. The *1* returned by *lo_export()* indicates a successful export. The *lo_unlink()* function removes large objects.

Full path names must be used with large objects because the database server runs in a different directory than the psql client. Files are imported and exported by the *postgres* user, so *postgres* must have permission to read the file for *lo_import()* and directory write permission for *lo_export()*. Because large objects use the local filesystem, users connecting over a network cannot use *lo_-import* or *lo_export()*. They can, however, use psql's *lo_import* and *lo_export* commands.

9.9 Summary

Use care when choosing your data types. The many data types provide great flexibility. Wise decisions about column names and types will give your database structure and consistency. The appropriate choice also improves performance and allows efficient data storage. Do not choose types hastily—you will regret it later.

Chapter 10

Transactions and Locks

Up to this point, we have used POSTGRESQL as a sophisticated filing cabinet. However, a database is much more. It allows users to view and modify information simultaneously. It helps ensure data integrity. This chapter explores these database capabilities.

10.1 Transactions

Although you may not have heard the term *transaction* before, you have already used transactions. Every SQL query is executed in a transaction. Transactions give databases an all-or-nothing capability when making modifications.

For example, suppose the query UPDATE trans_test SET col = 3 is in the process of modifying 700 rows. After it has modified 200 rows, the user presses *control-C* or hits the computer reset button. When the user looks at *trans_test*, he will see that none of the rows has been updated.

This result might surprise you. Because 200 of the 700 rows had already updated, you might suspect that 200 rows would show as modified. However, POSTGRESQL uses transactions to guarantee that queries are either fully completed or have no effect.

This feature is valuable. Suppose you were executing a query to add $500 to everyone's salary and accidentally kicked the power cord out of the wall during the update procedure. Without transactions, the query may have updated half the salaries, but not the rest. It would be difficult to know where the UPDATE stopped. You would wonder, "Which rows were updated, and which ones were not?" You cannot simply re-execute the query, because some people would have already received their $500 increase. With transactions, you can check to see if any of the rows were updated. If one was updated, then all were updated. If not, you can simply re-execute the query.

```
test=> INSERT INTO trans_test VALUES (1);
INSERT 130057 1
```

Figure 10.1: INSERT with no explicit transaction

```
test=> BEGIN WORK;
BEGIN
test=> INSERT INTO trans_test VALUES (1);
INSERT 130058 1
test=> COMMIT WORK;
COMMIT
```

Figure 10.2: INSERT using an explicit transaction

10.2   Multistatement Transactions

By default, each SQL query runs in its own transaction. Consider Figures 10.1 and 10.2, which show two identical queries. Figure 10.1 is a typical INSERT query. Before POSTGRESQL starts the INSERT, it begins a transaction. It performs the INSERT, then commits the transaction. This step occurs automatically for any query with no explicit transaction. In Figure 10.2, the INSERT uses an explicit transaction. BEGIN WORK starts the transaction, and COMMIT WORK commits the transaction. The only difference between the two queries is that an implied BEGIN WORK...COMMIT WORK surrounds the first INSERT.

Even more valuable is the ability to bind multiple queries into a single transaction. In such a case, either all queries execute to completion or none has any effect. As an example, Figure 10.3 shows two INSERTs in a transaction. PostgreSQL guarantees that either both INSERTs succeed or neither.

As a more complicated example, suppose you have a table of bank account balances, and you wish to transfer $100 from one account to another account. This operation is performed using two queries: an UPDATE to subtract $100 from one account, and an UPDATE to add $100 to another account. The UPDATEs should either both complete or have no effect. If the first UPDATE completes but not the second, the $100 would disappear from the bank records. It would have been subtracted from one account, but never added to the other account. Such errors are very hard to find. Multistatement transactions prevent them from happening. Figure 10.4 shows the two queries bound into a single transaction. The transaction forces POSTGRESQL to perform the queries as a single operation.

When you begin a transaction with BEGIN WORK, you do not have to commit it using COMMIT

```
test=> BEGIN WORK;
BEGIN
test=> INSERT INTO trans_test VALUES (1);
INSERT 130059 1
test=> INSERT INTO trans_test VALUES (2);
INSERT 130060 1
test=> COMMIT WORK;
COMMIT
```

Figure 10.3: Two INSERTs in a single transaction

```
-- transfer $100 from acct 82021 to acct 96814
test=> BEGIN WORK;
BEGIN
test=> UPDATE bankacct SET balance = balance - 100 WHERE acctno = '82021';
UPDATE 1
test=> UPDATE bankacct SET balance = balance + 100 WHERE acctno = '96814';
UPDATE 1
test=> COMMIT WORK;
COMMIT
```

Figure 10.4: Multistatement transaction

```
test=> INSERT INTO rollback_test VALUES (1);
INSERT 19369 1
test=> BEGIN WORK;
BEGIN
test=> DELETE FROM rollback_test;
DELETE 1
test=> ROLLBACK WORK;
ROLLBACK
test=> SELECT * FROM rollback_test;
 x
---
 1
(1 row)
```

Figure 10.5: Transaction rollback

User 1	User 2	Notes
	SELECT (*) FROM *trans_test*	returns 0
INSERT INTO *trans_test* VALUES (1)		add row to *trans_test*
SELECT (*) FROM *trans_test*		returns 1
	SELECT (*) FROM *trans_test*	returns 1

Table 10.1: Visibility of single-query transactions

WORK. Instead, you can close the transaction with ROLLBACK WORK and the transaction will be discarded. The database is left as though the transaction had never been executed. In Figure 10.5, the current transaction is rolled back, causing the DELETE to have no effect. Likewise, if any query inside a multistatement transaction cannot be executed due to an error, the entire transaction is automatically rolled back.

10.3   Visibility of Committed Transactions

Although we have focused on the all-or-nothing nature of transactions, they have other important benefits. Only committed transactions are visible to users. Although the current user sees his changes, other users do not see them until the transaction is committed.

For example, Table 10.1 shows two users issuing queries using the default mode in which every statement is in its own transaction. Table 10.2 shows the same query with user 1 using a

User 1	User 2	Notes
BEGIN WORK		User 1 starts a transaction
	SELECT (*) FROM *trans_test*	returns 0
INSERT INTO *trans_test* VALUES (1)		add row to *trans_test*
SELECT (*) FROM *trans_test*		returns 1　*to User 1*
	SELECT (*) FROM *trans_test*	returns 0　*to User 2*
COMMIT WORK		
	SELECT (*) FROM *trans_test*	returns 1　*to User 2*

Table 10.2: Visibility of multiquery transactions

multiquery transaction. User 1 sees the changes made by his transaction. User 2, however, does not see the changes until user 1 commits the transaction.

This shielding is another advantage of transactions. They insulate users from seeing uncommitted transactions, so that users never see a partially committed view of the database.

As another example, consider the bank account query where we transferred $100 from one bank account to another. Suppose we were calculating the total amount of money in all bank accounts at the same time the $100 was being transferred. If we did not see a consistent view of the database, we might see the $100 removed from the account, but not the $100 added. Our bank account total would then be wrong. A consistent database view means that either we see the $100 in its original account or we see it in its new account. Without this feature, we would have to ensure that no one was making bank account transfers while we were calculating the amount of money in all accounts.

Although this case is a contrived example, real-world database users INSERT, UPDATE, and DELETE data all at the same time, even as others SELECT data. This activity is orchestrated by the database so that each user can operate in a secure manner, knowing that other users will not affect their results in an unpredictable way.

10.4 Read Committed and Serializable Isolation Levels

The previous section illustrated that users see only committed transactions. It did not address what happens if someone commits a transaction *while* you are in your own transaction. In some cases, you need to control whether other transaction commits are seen by your transaction.

POSTGRESQL's default isolation level, READ COMMITTED, allows you to see other transaction commits while your transaction is open. Figure 10.6 illustrates this effect. First, the transaction does a SELECT COUNT(*). Then, while you are sitting at a psql prompt, someone INSERTs into the table. The next SELECT COUNT(*) shows the newly INSERTED row. When another user commits a transaction, it is seen by the current transaction, even if it is committed *after* the current transaction started.

```
test=> BEGIN WORK;
BEGIN
test=> SELECT COUNT(*) FROM trans_test;
 count
-------
     5
(1 row)

test=> --
test=> -- someone commits INSERT INTO trans_test
test=> --
test=> SELECT COUNT(*) FROM trans_test;
 count
-------
     6
(1 row)

test=> COMMIT WORK;
COMMIT
```

ie, "read committeds"

Figure 10.6: Read-committed isolation level

```
test=> BEGIN WORK;
BEGIN
test=> SET TRANSACTION ISOLATION LEVEL SERIALIZABLE;
SET VARIABLE
test=> SELECT COUNT(*) FROM trans_test;
 count
-------
     5
(1 row)

test=> --
test=> -- someone commits INSERT INTO trans_test
test=> --
test=> SELECT COUNT(*) FROM trans_test;
 count
-------
     5
(1 row)

test=> COMMIT WORK;
COMMIT
```

Figure 10.7: Serializable isolation level

You can, however, prevent your transaction from seeing changes made to the database. SET TRANSACTION ISOLATION LEVEL SERIALIZABLE changes the isolation level of the current transaction. SERIALIZABLE isolation prevents the current transaction from seeing commits made by other transactions. Thus, any commit made after the start of the first query of the transaction is not visible. Figure 10.7 shows an example of a SERIALIZABLE transaction.

SERIALIZABLE isolation provides a stable view of the database for SELECT transactions. For transactions containing UPDATE and DELETE queries, SERIALIZABLE mode is more complicated. SERIALIZABLE isolation forces the database to execute all transactions as though they were run *serially* (one after another), even if they are run concurrently. If two concurrent transactions attempt to update the same row, serializability is impossible. In such a case, POSTGRESQL forces one transaction to roll back.

For SELECT-only transactions, use the SERIALIZABLE isolation level when you do not want to see other transaction commits during your transaction. For UPDATE and DELETE transactions, SERIALIZABLE isolation prevents concurrent modification of the same data row; it should therefore be used with caution.

Transaction 1	Transaction 2	Notes
BEGIN WORK	BEGIN WORK	start both transactions
UPDATE row 64		transaction 1 exclusively locks row 64
	UPDATE row 64	transaction 2 must wait to see if transaction 1 commits
COMMIT WORK		transaction 1 commits; transaction 2 returns from UPDATE
	COMMIT WORK	transaction 2 commits

Table 10.3: Waiting for a lock

10.5   Locking

Exclusive locks, also called *write locks,* prevent other users from modifying a row or an entire table. Rows modified by UPDATE and DELETE are then exclusively locked automatically for the duration of the transaction. This approach prevents other users from changing the row until the transaction is either committed or rolled back.

Table 10.3 shows two simultaneous UPDATE transactions affecting the same row. The first transaction must wait to see whether the second transaction commits or rolls back. If SERIALIZABLE isolation level had been used, transaction 2 would have been rolled back automatically if transaction 1 committed.

The only time when users must wait for other users is when they are trying to modify the same row. If they modify different rows, no waiting is necessary. SELECT queries never have to wait.

The database performs locking automatically. In certain cases, however, locking must be controlled manually. As an example, Figure 10.8 shows a query that first SELECTs a row, then performs an UPDATE. The problem arises because another user can modify the *James* row between the SELECT and UPDATE. To prevent this problem, you can use SERIALIZABLE isolation. In this mode, however, one of the UPDATEs would fail.

A better solution is to use SELECT...FOR UPDATE to lock the selected rows. Figure 10.9 shows the same query using SELECT...FOR UPDATE. Another user cannot modify the *James* row between the SELECT...FOR UPDATE and UPDATE. In fact, the row remains locked until the transaction ends.

You can also manually control locking by using the LOCK command. It allows specification of a transaction's lock type and scope. See the LOCK manual page for more information.

10.6   Deadlocks

It is possible to create an unrecoverable lock condition, called a *deadlock*. Table 10.4 illustrates how two transactions might become deadlocked. In this example, each transaction holds a lock and is waiting for the other transaction's lock to be released. POSTGRESQL must roll back one transaction because otherwise the two transactions will wait forever. Obviously, if they had acquired locks in the same order, no deadlock would occur.

```
test=> BEGIN WORK;
BEGIN
test=> SELECT *                                        -- select row
test-> FROM lock_test
test-> WHERE name = 'James';
 id |              name
-----+-------------------------------
 521 | James
(1 row)

test=> --
test=> -- the SELECTed row is not locked
test=> --
test=> UPDATE lock_test                                -- update row
test-> SET name = 'Jim'
test-> WHERE name = 'James';
UPDATE 1
test=> COMMIT WORK;
COMMIT
```

Figure 10.8: SELECT with no locking

Transaction 1	Transaction2	Notes
BEGIN WORK	BEGIN WORK	start both transactions
UPDATE row 64	UPDATE row 83	independent rows write-locked
UPDATE row 83		holds waiting for transaction 2 to release write lock
	UPDATE row 64	attempt to get write lock held by transaction 1
	auto-ROLLBACK WORK	deadlock detected—transaction 2 is rolled back
COMMIT WORK		transaction 1 returns from UPDATE and commits

Table 10.4: Deadlock

```
test=> BEGIN WORK;
BEGIN
test=> SELECT *
test-> FROM lock_test
test-> WHERE name = 'James'
test-> FOR UPDATE;
 id  |               name
-----+-------------------------------
 521 | James
(1 row)

test=> --
test=> -- the SELECTed row is locked
test=> --
test=> UPDATE lock_test
test-> SET name = 'Jim'
test-> WHERE name = 'James';
UPDATE 1
test=> COMMIT WORK;
COMMIT
```

Figure 10.9: SELECT...FOR UPDATE

10.7 Summary

Single-user database queries are concerned with *getting the job done.* Multiuser queries must be designed to gracefully handle multiple users accessing the same data.

Multiuser interaction can be very confusing, because the database is constantly changing. In a multiuser environment, improperly constructed queries can randomly fail when users perform simultaneous operations. Queries cannot assume that rows from previous transactions still exist.

By learning about POSTGRESQL'S multiuser behavior, you are now prepared to create robust queries. POSTGRESQL has the features necessary to construct reliable multiuser queries.

Chapter 11

Performance

In an ideal world, users would never need to be concerned about performance. The system would tune itself. Unfortunately, we do not live in an ideal world. An untuned database can be thousands of times slower than a tuned one, so it pays to take steps to improve performance. This chapter shows you how to get the optimal performance from your database.

11.1   Indexes

When accessing a table, POSTGRESQL normally reads from the beginning of the table to the end, looking for relevant rows. With an index, it can quickly find specific values in the index, then go directly to matching rows. In this way, indexes allow fast retrieval of specific rows from a table.

For example, consider the query SELECT * FROM customer WHERE col = 43. Without an index, POSTGRESQL must scan the entire table looking for rows where *col* equals *43*. With an index on *col*, POSTGRESQL can go directly to rows where *col* equals *43*, bypassing all other rows.

For a large table, it can take minutes to check every row. Using an index, finding a specific row takes fractions of a second.

Internally, POSTGRESQL stores data in operating system files. Each table has its own file, and data rows are stored one after another in the file. An index is a separate file that is sorted by one or more columns. It contains pointers into the table file, allowing rapid access to specific values in the table.

POSTGRESQL does not create indexes automatically. Instead, users should create them for columns frequently used in WHERE clauses.

To create an index, use the CREATE INDEX command, as shown in Figure 11.1. In this example, *customer_custid_idx* is the name of the index, *customer* is the table being indexed, and *customer_id* is the column being indexed. Although you can use any name for the index, it is good practice to use the table and column names as part of the index name—for example, *customer_customer_id_idx* or *i_customer_custid*. This index is useful only for finding rows in *customer* for specific *customer_ids*.

```
test=> CREATE INDEX customer_custid_idx ON customer (customer_id);
CREATE
```

Figure 11.1: Example of CREATE INDEX

It cannot help when you are accessing other columns, because indexes are sorted by a specific column.

You can create as many indexes as you wish. Of course, an index on a seldom-used column is a waste of disk space. Also, performance can suffer if too many indexes exist, because row changes require an update to each index.

It is possible to create an index spanning multiple columns. Multicolumn indexes are sorted by the first indexed column. When the first column contains several equal values, sorting continues using the second indexed column. Multicolumn indexes are useful only on columns with many duplicate values.

The command CREATE INDEX customer_age_gender_idx ON customer (age, gender) creates an index that is sorted by *age* and, when several *age* rows have the same value, then sorted on *gender*. This index can be used by the query SELECT * FROM customer WHERE age = 36 AND gender = 'F' and the query SELECT * FROM customer WHERE age = 36.

The index *customer_age_gender_idx* is useless if you wish to find rows based only on *gender*, however. The *gender* component of the index can be used only after the *age* value has been specified. Thus, the query SELECT * FROM customer WHERE gender = 'F' cannot use the index because it does not place a restriction on *age*, which is the first part of the index.

Indexes can be useful for columns involved in joins, too. They can even be employed to speed up some ORDER BY clauses.

To remove an index, use the DROP INDEX command. See the CREATE_INDEX and DROP_INDEX manual pages for more information.

11.2   Unique Indexes

Unique indexes resemble ordinary indexes, except that they prevent duplicate values from occurring in the table. Figure 11.2 shows the creation of one table and a unique index. The index is unique because of the keyword UNIQUE. The remaining queries try to insert a duplicate value, but the unique index prevents this and displays an appropriate error message.

Sometimes unique indexes are created only to prevent duplicate values, not for performance reasons. Multicolumn unique indexes ensure that the combination of indexed columns remains unique. Unique indexes do allow multiple NULL values, however. Unique indexes both speed data access and prevent duplicates.

```
test=> CREATE TABLE duptest (channel INTEGER);
CREATE
test=> CREATE UNIQUE INDEX duptest_channel_idx ON duptest (channel);
CREATE
test=> INSERT INTO duptest VALUES (1);
INSERT 130220 1
test=> INSERT INTO duptest VALUES (1);
ERROR:  Cannot insert a duplicate key into unique index duptest_channel_idx
```

Figure 11.2: Example of a unique index

11.3 CLUSTER

The CLUSTER command reorders the table file to match the ordering of an index. This specialized command is valuable when performance is critical and the indexed column has many duplicate values.

For example, suppose the column *customer.age* has many duplicate values, and the query SELECT * FROM customer WHERE age = 98 is executed. An index on *age* allows rapid retrieval of the row locations from the index. If thousands of matching rows exist, however, they may be scattered in the table file, requiring many disk accesses to retrieve them. CLUSTER reorders the table, placing duplicate values next to each other. This speeds access for large queries accessing many duplicate values.

CLUSTER even helps with range queries like *col >= 3* AND *col <= 5*. The command places these rows next to each other on disk, speeding indexed lookups.

In addition, CLUSTER can also speed ORDER BY processing. See the CLUSTER manual page for more information.

11.4 VACUUM

When POSTGRESQL updates a row, it keeps the original copy of the row in the table file and writes a new one. The original row, marked as expired, is used by other transactions still viewing the database in its prior state. Deletions are similarly marked as expired, but not removed from the table file.

The VACUUM command removes expired rows from the file. In the process, it moves rows from the end of the table into the expired spots, thereby compacting the table file.

You should run VACUUM periodically to clean out expired rows. For tables that are heavily modified, it is useful to run VACUUM every night in an automated manner. For tables with few

```
test=> EXPLAIN SELECT customer_id FROM customer;
NOTICE:   QUERY PLAN:

Seq Scan on customer  (cost=0.00..15.00 rows=1000 width=4)

EXPLAIN
```

Figure 11.3: Using EXPLAIN

modifications, VACUUM should be run less frequently. The command exclusively locks the table while processing.

You can run VACUUM in two ways. Using VACUUM alone vacuums all tables in the database. Using VACUUM *tablename* vacuums a single table.

11.5   VACUUM ANALYZE

The VACUUM ANALYZE command resembles VACUUM, but also collects statistics about each column's proportion of duplicate values and the maximum and minimum values. POSTGRESQL uses this information when deciding how to efficiently execute complex queries. You should run VACUUM ANALYZE when a table is initially loaded and when a table's data changes dramatically.

The VACUUM manual page shows all of the VACUUM options.

11.6   EXPLAIN

EXPLAIN causes POSTGRESQL to display how a query will be executed, rather than executing it. As an example, Figure 11.3 shows a SELECT query preceeded by the word EXPLAIN. In the figure, POSTGRESQL reports a *sequential scan* will be used on *customer,* meaning it will read the entire table. The *cost* is an estimate of the work required to execute the query (the numbers are only meaningful for comparison). The *rows* indicates the number of result rows expected. The *width* is the number of bytes per row.

Figure 11.4 shows more interesting examples of EXPLAIN. The first EXPLAIN shows a SELECT with the restriction *customer_id = 55*. The command reports another sequential scan, but the restriction causes POSTGRESQL to estimate that ten rows will be returned. A VACUUM ANALYZE command is then run, causing the next query to properly estimate that one row will be returned instead of ten. An index is created, and the query rerun. This time, an *index scan* is used, allowing POSTGRESQL to go directly to the rows where *customer_id* equals *55*. The next EXPLAIN shows a query with no WHERE restriction. POSTGRESQL realizes that the index is useless and performs a

```
test=> EXPLAIN SELECT customer_id FROM customer WHERE customer_id = 55;
NOTICE:  QUERY PLAN:


Seq Scan on customer  (cost=0.00..22.50 rows=10 width=4)
```
@ 134

```
EXPLAIN
test=> VACUUM ANALYZE customer;
VACUUM
test=> EXPLAIN SELECT customer_id FROM customer WHERE customer_id = 55;
NOTICE:  QUERY PLAN:


Seq Scan on customer  (cost=0.00..17.50 rows=1 width=4)


EXPLAIN
test=> CREATE UNIQUE INDEX customer_custid_idx ON customer (customer_id);
CREATE
test=> EXPLAIN SELECT customer_id FROM customer WHERE customer_id = 55;
NOTICE:  QUERY PLAN:


Index Scan using customer_custid_-
idx on customer  (cost=0.00..2.01 rows=1 width=4)


EXPLAIN
test=> EXPLAIN SELECT customer_id FROM customer;
NOTICE:  QUERY PLAN:


Seq Scan on customer  (cost=0.00..15.00 rows=1000 width=4)


EXPLAIN
test=> EXPLAIN SELECT * FROM customer ORDER BY customer_id;
NOTICE:  QUERY PLAN:


Index Scan using customer_custid_-
idx on customer  (cost=0.00..42.00 rows=1000 width=4)


EXPLAIN
```

Figure 11.4: More complex EXPLAIN examples

```
test=> EXPLAIN SELECT * FROM tab1, tab2 WHERE col1 = col2;
NOTICE:  QUERY PLAN:

Merge Join  (cost=139.66..164.66 rows=10000 width=8)
   -> Sort  (cost=69.83..69.83 rows=1000 width=4)
        -> Seq Scan on tab2  (cost=0.00..20.00 rows=1000 width=4)
   -> Sort  (cost=69.83..69.83 rows=1000 width=4)
        -> Seq Scan on tab1  (cost=0.00..20.00 rows=1000 width=4)

EXPLAIN
```

Figure 11.5: EXPLAIN example using joins

sequential scan. The last query has an ORDER BY that matches an index, so POSTGRESQL uses an index scan.

Even more complex queries can be studied using EXPLAIN, as shown in Figure 11.5. In this example, *tab1* and *tab2* are joined on *col1* and *col2*. Each table is sequentially scanned, and the result sorted. The two results are then *merge joined* to produce output. It also supports *hash join* and *nested loop* join methods. It chooses the join method it believes to be the fastest.

11.7 Summary

A variety of tools are available to speed up POSTGRESQL queries. Although their use is not required, they can produce huge improvements in query speed. Section 20.8 outlines more steps that database administrators can take to improve performance.

Chapter 12

Controlling Results

When a SELECT query is issued in psql, it travels to the POSTGRESQL server, is executed, and the result then sent back to psql to be displayed. POSTGRESQL allows you to exert fine-grained control over which rows are returned. This chapter explores the methods available to achieve this goal.

12.1 LIMIT

The LIMIT and OFFSET clauses of SELECT allow the user to specify which rows to return. For example, suppose *customer* has 1,000 rows with *customer_id* values ranging from 1 to 1,000. Figure 12.1 shows queries using LIMIT and LIMIT...OFFSET. The first query sorts the table by *customer_id* and uses LIMIT to return the first three rows. The second query is similar, except that it skips to the 997th row before returning three rows.

Notice that each query uses ORDER BY. Although this clause is not required, LIMIT without ORDER BY returns random rows from the query, which would be useless.

LIMIT improves performance by reducing the number of rows returned to the client. If an index matches the ORDER BY, sometimes LIMIT can even produce results without executing the entire query.

12.2 Cursors

Ordinarily, all rows generated by a SELECT are returned to the client. Cursors allow a SELECT query to be named, and individual result rows retrieved as needed by the client.

Figure 12.2 shows an example of cursor usage. Note that cursor activity must take place inside a transaction. To declare cursors, you use DECLARE...CURSOR FOR SELECT.... The result rows are retrieved using FETCH. MOVE allows the user to move the cursor position. CLOSE releases all

```
test=> SELECT customer_id FROM customer ORDER BY customer_id LIMIT 3;
  customer_id
-------------
            1
            2
            3
(3 rows)

test=> SELECT customer_id FROM customer ORDER BY customer_-
id LIMIT 3 OFFSET 997;
  customer_id
-------------
          998
          999
         1000
(3 rows)
```

Figure 12.1: Examples of LIMIT and LIMIT/OFFSET

rows stored in the cursor. See the DECLARE, FETCH, MOVE, and CLOSE manual pages for more information.

12.3   Summary

LIMIT specifies which rows to return in the result. Cursors allow dynamic row retrieval. The difference between LIMIT and cursors is that LIMIT specifies the rows as part of the SELECT, while cursors allow dynamic fetching of rows. Both LIMIT and cursors offer new ways to tailor your queries so that you obtain exactly the desired results.

```
test=> BEGIN WORK;
BEGIN
test=> DECLARE customer_cursor CURSOR FOR
test-> SELECT customer_id FROM customer;
SELECT
test=> FETCH 1 FROM customer_cursor;
 customer_id
-------------
          1
(1 row)

test=> FETCH 1 FROM customer_cursor;
 customer_id
-------------
          2
(1 row)

test=> FETCH 2 FROM customer_cursor;
 customer_id
-------------
          3
          4
(2 rows)

test=> FETCH -1 FROM customer_cursor;
 customer_id
-------------
          3
(1 row)

test=> FETCH -1 FROM customer_cursor;
 customer_id
-------------
          2
(1 row)

test=> MOVE 10 FROM customer_cursor;
MOVE
test=> FETCH 1 FROM customer_cursor;
 customer_id
-------------
         13
(1 row)
test=> CLOSE customer_cursor;
CLOSE
test=> COMMIT WORK;
COMMIT
```

Figure 12.2: Cursor usage

Chapter 13

Table Management

This chapter covers a variety of topics involved in managing SQL tables.

13.1   Temporary Tables

Temporary tables are short-lived tables—they exist only for the duration of a database session. When a database session terminates, its temporary tables are automatically destroyed. Figure 13.1 illustrates this concept. In the figure, CREATE TEMPORARY TABLE creates a temporary table. On psql exit, the temporary table is destroyed. Restarting psql reveals that the temporary table no longer exists.

Temporary tables are visible only to the session that creates them; they remain invisible to other users. In fact, several users can create temporary tables with the same name, and each user will see only his version of the table. (See Table 13.1 for an example.) Temporary tables even mask ordinary tables with the same name.

Temporary tables are ideal for holding intermediate data used by the current SQL session. For example, suppose you need to do many SELECTs on the result of a complex query. An efficient strategy is to execute the complex query once, then store the result in a temporary table.

As an example, Figure 13.2 uses SELECT ... INTO TEMPORARY TABLE to collect all Pennsylvania customers into a temporary table. It also creates a temporary index on the temporary table. The

User 1	User 2
CREATE TEMPORARY TABLE *temptest* (*col* INTEGER)	CREATE TEMPORARY TABLE *temptest* (*col* INTEGER)
INSERT INTO *temptest* VALUES (1)	INSERT INTO *temptest* VALUES (2)
SELECT *col* FROM *temptest* returns 1	SELECT *col* FROM *temptest* returns 2

Table 13.1: Temporary table isolation

```
$ psql test
Welcome to psql, the PostgreSQL interactive terminal.

Type:  \copyright for distribution terms
       \h for help with SQL commands
       \? for help on internal slash commands
       \g or terminate with semicolon to execute query
       \q to quit

test=> CREATE TEMPORARY TABLE temptest(col INTEGER);
CREATE
test=> SELECT * FROM temptest;
 col
-----
(0 rows)

test=> \q
$ psql test
Welcome to psql, the PostgreSQL interactive terminal.

Type:  \copyright for distribution terms
       \h for help with SQL commands
       \? for help on internal slash commands
       \g or terminate with semicolon to execute query
       \q to quit

test=> SELECT * FROM temptest;
ERROR:  Relation 'temptest' does not exist
```

Figure 13.1: Temporary table auto-destruction

```
test=> SELECT *
test-> INTO TEMPORARY customer_pennsylvania
test-> FROM customer
test-> WHERE state = 'PA';
SELECT
test=> CREATE index customer_penna_custid_idx ON customer_-
pennsylvania (customer_id);
CREATE
```

✗ select into a temporary table

Figure 13.2: Example of temporary table use

customer_pennsylvania table can then be used in subsequent SELECT queries. Multiple users can perform this operation at the same time with the same temporary names without fear of collision.

13.2 ALTER TABLE

ALTER TABLE allows the following operations:

- Rename tables   *alter table <tabname> rename to <new tabname>*

- Rename columns   *"   "   "   rename column <oldcolname> to <new colname>*

- Add columns   *"   "   "   add column <colname> <type>*

- Add column defaults *"   "   "   alter column <colname> set default <defval>*

- Remove column defaults *"   "   "   alter column <colname> drop default*

Figure 13.3 shows examples of these options.

13.3 GRANT and REVOKE

When a table is created, only its owner can access it. If the owner wants others to have access, he must change the table's permissions using the GRANT command. Figure 13.4 shows some *✗* examples of the use of GRANT. Available privileges are SELECT, UPDATE, DELETE, RULE, and ALL. Access can be granted to individual users, groups, or everyone (PUBLIC). The rules for granting access are covered in Section 13.6. *p 149*

REVOKE removes permissions from a table. See the GRANT and REVOKE manual pages for more *✗* information.   *365   424*

```
test=> CREATE TABLE altertest (col1 INTEGER);
CREATE
test=> ALTER TABLE altertest RENAME TO alterdemo;
ALTER
test=> ALTER TABLE alterdemo RENAME COLUMN col1 TO democol;
ALTER
test=> ALTER TABLE alterdemo ADD COLUMN col2 INTEGER;
ALTER
test=> -- show renamed table, renamed column, and new column
test=> \d alterdemo
        Table "alterdemo"
 Attribute |  Type   | Modifier
-----------+---------+----------
 democol   | integer |
 col2      | integer |

test=> ALTER TABLE alterdemo ALTER COLUMN col2 SET DEFAULT 0;
ALTER
test=> -- show new default value
test=> \d alterdemo
        Table "alterdemo"
 Attribute |  Type   | Modifier
-----------+---------+-----------
 democol   | integer |
 col2      | integer | default 0
test=> ALTER TABLE alterdemo ALTER COLUMN col2 DROP DEFAULT;
ALTER
```

Figure 13.3: ALTER TABLE examples

```
test=> CREATE TABLE permtest (col INTEGER);
CREATE
test=> -- now only the owner can use permtest
test->
test=> GRANT SELECT ON permtest TO meyers;
CHANGE
test=> -- now user 'meyers' can do SELECTs on permtest
test=>
test=> GRANT ALL ON permtest TO PUBLIC;
CHANGE
test=> -- now all users can perform all operations on permtest
test=>
```

(handwritten annotation:)

grant ⎰ Select
       ⎱ update
         delete on ⎰ <tabname>
         rule   ⎱ <viewname>
         all   <seqname>

to ⎰ <usr>
   ⎱ group <grp>.
     public

(handwritten:) undo: REVOKE ALL ON permtest FROM PUBLIC;

Figure 13.4: Examples of the GRANT command

13.4 Inheritance

Inheritance allows the creation of a new table related to an existing table. Figure 13.5 shows the creation of an inherited table. With inheritance, the child table receives all of the columns of its parent, plus the additional columns it defines. In the example, *child_test* gets *col1* from *parent_test*, plus the column *col2*.

Inheritance also links rows in parent and child tables. If the parent table is referenced with an asterisk suffix, rows from the parent and all children are accessed. Figure 13.6 shows insertion into two tables related by inheritance. In the figure, *parent_test* accesses only the *parent_test* rows, but *parent_test** accesses both *parent_test* and *child_test* rows. That is, *parent_test** accesses only columns common to all tables. Because *child_test.col2* is not in the parent table, it is not displayed. Figure 13.7 shows that inherited tables can be layered on top of one another.

Consider a practical example that records information about employees and managers. The table *employee* can hold information about nonmanagerial employees; the table *manager* can hold information about managers. The *manager* table can inherit all the columns from *employee* and have additional columns as well. You can then access nonmanagerial employees using *employee*, managers using *manager*, and all employees including managers using *employee**.

POSTGRESQL release 7.1 and later automatically accesses any inherited tables. An asterisk is not needed after the table name. The keyword ONLY is used to prevent inherited table access.

(handwritten:) select ... from <tabname> only

(handwritten:)
employee   (non mgr)
   ↑
manager

```
test=> CREATE TABLE parent_test (col1 INTEGER);
CREATE
test=> CREATE TABLE child_test (col2 INTEGER) INHERITS (parent_test);
CREATE
test=> \d parent_test
         Table "parent_test"
 Attribute |  Type  | Modifier
-----------+--------+----------
 col1      | integer |

test=> \d child_test
          Table "child_test"
 Attribute |  Type  | Modifier
-----------+--------+----------
 col1      | integer |
 col2      | integer |
```

like "extends"

Figure 13.5: Creation of inherited tables

```
test=> INSERT INTO parent_test VALUES (1);
INSERT 18837 1
test=> INSERT INTO child_test VALUES (2,3);
INSERT 18838 1
test=> SELECT * FROM parent_test;
 col1
------
    1
(1 row)

test=> SELECT * FROM child_test;
 col1 | col2
------+------
    2 |    3
(1 row)

test=> SELECT * FROM parent_test*;
 col1
------
    1
    2
(2 rows)
```

col 1 is common to parent_test, child_test

Figure 13.6: Accessing inherited tables

```
test=> CREATE TABLE grandchild_test (col3 INTEGER) INHERITS (child_test);
CREATE
test=> INSERT INTO grandchild_test VALUES (4, 5, 6);
INSERT 18853 1
test=> SELECT * FROM parent_test*;
 col1
------
    1
    2
    4
(3 rows)

test=> SELECT * FROM child_test*;
 col1 | col2
------+------
    2 |    3
    4 |    5
(2 rows)
```

parent_test

col1
1

col1 is common to parent_test, child_test, grandchild_test

child_test

col1	col2
2	3

col2 and col3 are common to child_test, grandchild_test

Figure 13.7: Inheritance in layers

grandchild_test

col1	col2	col3
4	5	6

-- create view to show only certain rows

```
test=> CREATE VIEW customer_ohio AS
test-> SELECT *
test-> FROM customer
test-> WHERE state = 'OH';
CREATE 18908 1
test=>
test=> -- let sanders see only Ohio customers
test=> GRANT SELECT ON customer_ohio TO sanders;
CHANGE
test=>
test=> -- create view to show only certain columns
test=> CREATE VIEW customer_address AS
test-> SELECT customer_id, name, street, city, state, zipcode, country
test-> FROM customer;
CREATE 18909 1
test=>
test=> -- create view that combines fields from two tables
test=> CREATE VIEW customer_finance AS
test-> SELECT customer.customer_id, customer.name, finance.credit_limit
test-> FROM customer, finance
test-> WHERE customer.customer_id = finance.customer_id;
CREATE 18910 1
```

Figure 13.8: Examples of views

13.5 Views   327   CREATE VIEW

Views are pseudo-tables. That is, they are not real tables, but nevertheless appear as ordinary tables to SELECT. A view can represent a subset of a real table, selecting certain columns or certain rows from an ordinary table. A view can even represent joined tables. Because views are assigned separate permissions, you can use them to restrict table access so that users see only specific rows or columns of a table.

Views are created using the CREATE VIEW command. Figure 13.8 shows the creation of several views. The view *customer_ohio* selects only customers from Ohio. SELECTs on it will therefore show only Ohio customers. The user *sanders* is then given SELECT access to the view. The *customer_address* will show only address information. The *customer_finance* view is a join of *customer* and *finance,* showing columns from both tables.

DROP VIEW removes a view. Because views are not ordinary tables, INSERTs, UPDATEs, and DELETEs on views have no effect. The next section shows how rules can correct this problem.

```
test=> CREATE TABLE ruletest (col INTEGER);
CREATE
test=> CREATE RULE ruletest_insert AS      -- rule name          Rule to prevent insert
test-> ON INSERT TO ruletest               -- INSERT rule
test-> DO INSTEAD                           -- DO INSTEAD-type rule
test->      NOTHING;                        -- ACTION is NOTHING
CREATE 18932 1
test=> INSERT INTO ruletest VALUES (1);
test=> SELECT * FROM ruletest;
 col
-----
(0 rows)
```

Figure 13.9: Rule to prevent an INSERT

13.6 Rules

Rules allow actions to take place when a table is accessed. In this way, they can modify the effects
of SELECT, INSERT, UPDATE, and DELETE.

Figure 13.9 shows a rule that prevents INSERTs into a table. The INSERT rule is named *ruletest_-
insert* and the action is NOTHING. NOTHING is a special rule keyword that does nothing.

Two types of rules exist. Do rules perform SQL commands in addition to the submitted query.
DO INSTEAD rules replace the user query with the rule action.

Figure 13.10 shows how rules can track table changes. In the figure, *service_request* holds
current service requests, and *service_request_log* records changes in the *service_request* table. The
figure also creates two DO rules on *service_request*. The rule *service_request_update* causes an
INSERT into *service_request_log* each time that *service_request* is updated. The special keyword
old is used to insert the pre-UPDATE column values into *service_request_log*; the keyword *new*
would refer to the new query values. The second rule, *service_request_delete*, tracks deletions
to *service_request* by inserting into *service_request_log*. To distinguish updates from deletes in
service_request_log, updates are inserted with a *mod_type* of 'U' and deletes with a *mod_type* of 'D'.

In figure 13.10, DEFAULT was used for the user name and timestamp fields. A column's default
value is used when an INSERT does not supply a value for the column. In this example, defaults
allow auto-assignment of these values on INSERT to *service_request*, and on rule INSERTs to *service_-
request_log*.

Figure 13.11 demonstrates the use of these rules. A row is inserted, updated, and deleted from
service_request. A SELECT on *service_request_log* shows the UPDATE rule recorded the pre-UPDATE
values, a *U* in *mod_type*, and the user, date, and time of the UPDATE. The DELETE rule follows a
similar pattern.

```
test=> CREATE TABLE service_request (
test->                    customer_id INTEGER,
test->                    description text,
test->                    cre_user text DEFAULT CURRENT_USER,
test->                    cre_timestamp timestamp DEFAULT CURRENT_TIMESTAMP);
CREATE
test=> CREATE TABLE service_request_log (
test->                    customer_id INTEGER,
test->                    description text,
test->                    mod_type char(1),
test->                    mod_user text DEFAULT CURRENT_USER,
test->                    mod_timestamp timestamp DEFAULT CURRENT_TIMESTAMP);
CREATE
test=> CREATE RULE service_request_update AS      -- UPDATE rule
test-> ON UPDATE TO service_request
test-> DO
test->     INSERT INTO service_request_log (customer_id, description, mod_type)
test->     VALUES (old.customer_id, old.description, 'U');
CREATE 19670 1
test=> CREATE RULE service_request_delete AS      -- DELETE rule
test-> ON DELETE TO service_request
test-> DO
test->     INSERT INTO service_request_log (customer_id, description, mod_type)
test->     VALUES (old.customer_id, old.description, 'D');
CREATE 19671 1
```

Figure 13.10: Rules to log table changes

```
test=> INSERT INTO service_request (customer_id, description)        -- No rule for inserts
test-> VALUES (72321, 'Fix printing press');
INSERT 18808 1
test=> UPDATE service_request
test-> SET description = 'Fix large printing press'
test-> WHERE customer_id = 72321;
UPDATE 1
test=> DELETE FROM service_request
test-> WHERE customer_id = 72321;
DELETE 1
test=> SELECT *
test-> FROM service_request_log
test-> WHERE customer_id = 72321;
 customer_id |        description        | mod_type | mod_user |     mod_timestamp
-------------+---------------------------+----------+----------+------------------------
       72321 | Fix printing press        | U        | williams | 2000-04-09 07:13:07-04      updated info
       72321 | Fix large printing press  | D        | matheson | 2000-04-10 12:47:20-04      deleted info
(2 rows)
```

Figure 13.11: Use of rules to log table changes

Although views ignore INSERT, UPDATE, and DELETE, rules can be used to properly handle them.
Figure 13.12 shows the creation of a table and a view on the table. In the figure, INSERTs into a
view are ignored, as are UPDATEs and DELETEs.

Figure 13.13 shows the creation of DO INSTEAD rules to properly handle INSERT, UPDATE, and
DELETE. This procedure involves changing INSERT, UPDATE, and DELETE queries on the view
to queries on *realtable*. Notice that the INSERT rule uses *new* to reference the new value to be
inserted. In contrast, UPDATE and DELETE use *old* to reference old values. Figure 13.14 shows
how the view properly handles modifications. It would be wise to add an index on *col* because the
rules do lookups on that column.

You can also create SELECT rules. In fact, views are implemented internally as SELECT rules.
Rules can even be applied to only certain rows. To remove them, use DROP RULE command. See
the CREATE_RULE and DROP_RULE manual pages for more information.   296, 345

Creating a rule whose action performs the same command on the same table causes an infinite
loop. That is, POSTGRESQL will call the rule again and again from the rule action. For example, if
an UPDATE rule on *ruletest* has a rule action that also performs an UPDATE on *ruletest,* it will cause
an infinite loop. POSTGRESQL will detect the infinite loop and return an error.

Fortunately, POSTGRESQL also supports triggers. Triggers allow actions to be performed when
a table is modified. In this way, they can perform actions that cannot be implemented using rules.
See Section 18.4 for information on the use of triggers.

```
test=> CREATE TABLE realtable (col INTEGER);
CREATE
test=> CREATE VIEW view_realtable AS SELECT * FROM realtable;
CREATE 407890 1
test=> INSERT INTO realtable VALUES (1);
INSERT 407891 1
test=> INSERT INTO view_realtable VALUES (2);
INSERT 407893 1
test=> SELECT * FROM realtable;
 col
-----
   1
(1 row)

test=> SELECT * FROM view_realtable;
 col
-----
   1
(1 row)
```

Figure 13.12: Views ignore table modifications

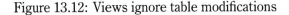

```
test=> CREATE RULE view_realtable_insert AS      -- INSERT rule
test-> ON INSERT TO view_realtable
test-> DO INSTEAD
test->      INSERT INTO realtable
test->      VALUES (new.col);
CREATE 407894 1
test=>
test=> CREATE RULE view_realtable_update AS      -- UPDATE rule
test-> ON UPDATE TO view_realtable
test-> DO INSTEAD
test->      UPDATE realtable
test->      SET col = new.col
test->      WHERE col = old.col;
CREATE 407901 1
test=>
test=> CREATE RULE view_realtable_delete AS      -- DELETE rule
test-> ON DELETE TO view_realtable
test-> DO INSTEAD
test->      DELETE FROM realtable
test->      WHERE col = old.col;
CREATE 407902 1
```

Figure 13.13: Rules to handle view modifications

```
test=> INSERT INTO view_realtable VALUES (3);
INSERT 407895 1
test=> SELECT * FROM view_realtable;
 col
-----
   1
   3
(2 rows)

test=> UPDATE view_realtable
test-> SET col = 4;
UPDATE 2
test=> SELECT * FROM view_realtable;
 col
-----
   4
   4
(2 rows)

test=> DELETE FROM view_realtable;
DELETE 2
test=> SELECT * FROM view_realtable;
 col
-----
(0 rows)
```

Figure 13.14: Example of rules that handle view modifications

373   380

13.7 LISTEN and NOTIFY

POSTGRESQL allows users to send signals to one another using LISTEN and NOTIFY. For example, suppose a user wants to receive notification when a table is updated. He can register the table name using the LISTEN command. If someone updates the table and then issues a NOTIFY command, all registered listeners will be informed of the change. For more information, see the LISTEN and NOTIFY manual pages.

13.8 Summary

This chapter has covered features that give administrators and users new capabilities in managing database tables. Chapter 14 turns to restrictions that can be placed on table columns to improve data management.

Chapter 14

Constraints

Constraints keep user data *constrained*, thereby helping to prevent invalid data from being entered into the database. Defining a data type for a column is a constraint in itself. For example, a column of type DATE constrains the column to valid dates.

This chapter covers a variety of constraints. We have already shown DEFAULT can be specified at table creation. Constraints are defined at table creation in a similar way.

14.1 NOT NULL

The constraint NOT NULL prevents NULL values from appearing in a column. Figure 14.1 shows the creation of a table with a NOT NULL constraint. Insertion of a NULL value, or an INSERT that would set *col2* to NULL, causes the INSERT to fail. As shown in the figure, an UPDATE of a NULL value also fails.

Figure 14.2 adds a DEFAULT value for *col2*. This addition permits INSERTs that do not specify a value for *col2*.

14.2 UNIQUE

The UNIQUE constraint prevents duplicate values from appearing in the column. It is implemented by creating a unique index on a column. As indicated in Figure 14.3, UNIQUE prevents duplicates. CREATE TABLE displays the name of the unique index created. The figure also shows that multiple NULL values can be inserted into a UNIQUE column.

If a UNIQUE constraint consists of more than one column, UNIQUE cannot be used as a column constraint. Instead, you must use a separate UNIQUE line to specify the columns that make up the constraint. This approach creates a UNIQUE *table constraint*.

Figure 14.4 shows a multicolumn UNIQUE constraint. While *col1* or *col2* themselves may not be unique, the constraint requires the combination of *col1* and *col2* to be unique. For example, in a

155

```
test=> CREATE TABLE not_null_test (
test(>                              col1 INTEGER,
test(>                              col2 INTEGER NOT NULL
test(>                              );
CREATE
test=> INSERT INTO not_null_test
test-> VALUES (1, NULL);
ERROR:  ExecAppend: Fail to add null value in not null attribute col2
test=> INSERT INTO not_null_test (col1)
test-> VALUES (1);
ERROR:  ExecAppend: Fail to add null value in not null attribute col2
test=> INSERT INTO not_null_test VALUES (1, 1);
INSERT 174368 1
test=> UPDATE  not_null_test SET col2 = NULL;
ERROR:  ExecReplace: Fail to add null value in not null attribute col2
```

Figure 14.1: NOT NULL constraint

```
test=> CREATE TABLE not_null_with_default_test (
test(>                                      col1 INTEGER,
test(>                                      col2 INTEGER NOT NULL DEFAULT 5
test(>                                      );
CREATE
test=> INSERT INTO not_null_with_default_test (col1)
test-> VALUES (1);
INSERT 148520 1
test=> SELECT *
test-> FROM not_null_with_default_test;
 col1 | col2
------+------
    1 |    5
(1 row)
```

Figure 14.2: NOT NULL with DEFAULT constraint

```
test=> CREATE TABLE uniquetest (col1 INTEGER UNIQUE);
NOTICE:  CREATE TABLE/UNIQUE will create implicit index 'uniquetest_col1_-
key' for table 'uniquetest'
CREATE
test=> \d uniquetest
        Table "uniquetest"
 Attribute |  Type   | Modifier
-----------+---------+----------
 col1      | integer |
Index: uniquetest_col1_key

test=> INSERT INTO uniquetest VALUES (1);
INSERT 148620 1
test=> INSERT INTO uniquetest VALUES (1);
ERROR:  Cannot insert a duplicate key into unique index uniquetest_col1_key
test=> INSERT INTO uniquetest VALUES (NULL);
INSERT 148622 1
test=> INSERT INTO uniquetest VALUES (NULL);
INSERT
```

multiple null values may go into UNIQUE column

Figure 14.3: UNIQUE column constraint

```
test=> CREATE TABLE uniquetest2 (
test(>                          col1 INTEGER,
test(>                          col2 INTEGER,
test(>                          UNIQUE (col1, col2)
test(>                          );
NOTICE:  CREATE TABLE/UNIQUE will create implicit index 'uniquetest2_col1_-
key' for table 'uniquetest2'
```

Handle uniqueness involving 2 cols

Figure 14.4: Multicolumn UNIQUE constraint

```
test=> CREATE TABLE primarytest (col INTEGER PRIMARY KEY);
NOTICE:  CREATE TABLE/PRIMARY KEY will create implicit index 'primarytest_-
pkey' for table 'primarytest'
CREATE
test=> \d primarytest
         Table "primarytest"
 Attribute |  Type  | Modifier
-----------+--------+----------
 col       | integer | not null
Index: primarytest_pkey
```

Figure 14.5: Creation of a PRIMARY KEY column

table that contains the driver's license numbers of people in various states, two people in different states might have the same license number, but the combination of their state and license number should always be unique.

14.3 PRIMARY KEY

The PRIMARY KEY constraint, which marks the column that uniquely identifies each row, is a combination of UNIQUE and NOT NULL constraints. With this type of constraint, UNIQUE prevents duplicates, and NOT NULL prevents NULL values in the column. Figure 14.5 shows the creation of a PRIMARY KEY column. Notice that an index is created automatically, and the column is defined as NOT NULL.

Just as with UNIQUE, a multicolumn PRIMARY KEY constraint must be specified on a separate line. In Figure 14.6, *col1* and *col2* are combined to form the primary key.

A table cannot have more than one PRIMARY KEY specification. Primary keys have special meaning when using foreign keys, which are covered in the next section.

14.4 Foreign Key/REFERENCES

Foreign keys are more complex than primary keys. Primary keys make a column UNIQUE and NOT NULL. Foreign keys, on the other hand, constrain data based on columns in other tables. They are called *foreign keys* because the constraints are foreign—that is, outside the table.

For example, suppose a table contains customer addresses, and part of each address is a United States two-character state code. If a table held all valid state codes, a foreign key constraint could be created to prevent a user from entering invalid state codes.

```
test=> CREATE TABLE primarytest2 (
test(>                            col1 INTEGER,
test(>                            col2 INTEGER,
test(>                            PRIMARY KEY(col1, col2)
test(>                            );
NOTICE:  CREATE TABLE/PRIMARY KEY will create implicit index 'primarytest2_-
pkey' for table 'primarytest2'
CREATE
```

Figure 14.6: Example of a multicolumn PRIMARY KEY

Figure 14.7 shows the creation of a primary key/foreign key relationship. Foreign key constraints are created by using REFERENCES to refer to the primary key of another table. Foreign keys link the tables together and prevent the insertion or updating of invalid data.

Figure 14.8 shows how foreign keys constrain column values. Here *AL* is a primary key value in *statename,* so the INSERT is accepted. *XX* is not a primary key value in *statename,* so the INSERT is rejected by the foreign key constraint.

Figure 14.9 shows the creation of the company tables from Figure 6.3, page 61, using primary and foreign keys.

A variety of foreign key options are discussed next that make foreign keys even more powerful.

Modification of Primary Key Row

If a foreign key constraint references a row as its primary key, and the primary key row is updated or deleted, then the default foreign key action is to prevent the operation. The foreign key options ON UPDATE and ON DELETE, however, allow a different action to be taken. Figure 14.10 shows how these options work. The new *customer* table's ON UPDATE CASCADE specifies that if *statename's* primary key is updated, *customer.state* should be updated with the new value as well. The foreign key ON DELETE SET NULL option specifies that if someone tries to delete a *statename* row that is referenced by another table, the delete operation should set the foreign key to NULL.

The ON UPDATE and ON DELETE options can have the following actions:

NO ACTION UPDATEs and DELETEs to the primary key are prohibited if referenced by a foreign key row. This is the default.

CASCADE UPDATEs to the primary key update all foreign key columns that reference it. DELETEs on the primary key cause the deletion of all foreign key rows that reference it.

SET NULL UPDATEs and DELETEs to the primary key row cause the foreign key to be set to NULL.

```
test=>  CREATE TABLE statename (code CHAR(2) PRIMARY KEY,
test(>                          name   CHAR(30)
test(> );
CREATE
test=> INSERT INTO statename VALUES ('AL', 'Alabama');
INSERT 18934 1

...

test=> CREATE TABLE customer (
test(>                        customer_id INTEGER,
test(>                        name        CHAR(30),
test(>                        telephone   CHAR(20),
test(>                        street      CHAR(40),
test(>                        city        CHAR(25),
test(>                        state       CHAR(2) REFERENCES statename,
test(>                        zipcode     CHAR(10),
test(>                        country     CHAR(20)
test(> );
CREATE
```

Figure 14.7: Foreign key creation

```
test=> INSERT INTO customer (state)
test-> VALUES ('AL');
INSERT 148732 1
test=> INSERT INTO customer (state)
test-> VALUES ('XX');
ERROR:  <unnamed> referential integrity violation -
key referenced from customer not found in statename
```

Figure 14.8: Foreign key constraints

```
test=> CREATE TABLE customer (
test(>                    customer_id INTEGER PRIMARY KEY,
test(>                    name        CHAR(30),
test(>                    telephone   CHAR(20),
test(>                    street      CHAR(40),
test(>                    city        CHAR(25),
test(>                    state       CHAR(2),
test(>                    zipcode     CHAR(10),
test(>                    country     CHAR(20)
test(> );
CREATE
test=> CREATE TABLE employee (
test(>                    employee_id INTEGER PRIMARY KEY,
test(>                    name        CHAR(30),
test(>                    hire_date   DATE
test(> );
CREATE
test=> CREATE TABLE part (
test(>                part_id   INTEGER PRIMARY KEY,
test(>                name      CHAR(30),
test(>                cost      NUMERIC(8,2),
test(>                weight    FLOAT
test(> );
CREATE
test=> CREATE TABLE salesorder (
test(>                    order_id     INTEGER,
test(>                    customer_id  INTEGER REFERENCES customer,     fk  Constraint
test(>                    employee_id  INTEGER REFERENCES employee,     fk    "
test(>                    part_id      INTEGER REFERENCES part,         fk    "
test(>                    order_date   DATE,
test(>                    ship_date    DATE,
test(>                    payment      NUMERIC(8,2)
test(> );
CREATE
```

Figure 14.9: Creation of company tables using primary and foreign keys

```
test=> CREATE TABLE customer (
test(>                     customer_id INTEGER,
test(>                     name        CHAR(30),
test(>                     telephone   CHAR(20),
test(>                     street      CHAR(40),
test(>                     city        CHAR(25),
test(>                     state       CHAR(2) REFERENCES statename
test(>                                         ON UPDATE CASCADE
test(>                                         ON DELETE SET NULL,
test(>                     zipcode     CHAR(10),
test(>                     country     CHAR(20)
test(> );
CREATE
```

Figure 14.10: *Customer* table with foreign key actions

SET DEFAULT   UPDATEs and DELETEs to the primary key row cause the foreign key to be set to its DEFAULT.

Figure 14.11 illustrates the use of the CASCADE and NO ACTION rules. First, *primarytest,* which was used in Figure 14.5, is created. Then a *foreigntest* table with ON UPDATE CASCADE and ON DELETE NO ACTION is created. NO ACTION is the default, so ON DELETE NO ACTION was not required. Next, a single row is inserted into each table, and an UPDATE on *primarytest* cascades to UPDATE *foreigntest.* The *primarytest* row cannot be deleted unless the foreign key row is deleted first. Foreign key actions offer you great flexibility in controlling how primary key changes affect foreign key rows.

Multicolumn Primary Keys

To specify a multicolumn primary key, it was necessary to use PRIMARY KEY on a separate line in the CREATE TABLE statement. Multicolumn foreign keys have the same requirement. Using *primarytest2* from Figure 14.6, Figure 14.12 shows how to create a multicolumn foreign key. FOREIGN KEY (*col, ...)* must be used to label any multicolumn foreign key table constraints.

Handling NULL Values in the Foreign Key

A NULL value cannot reference a primary key. A single-column foreign key is either NULL or matches a primary key. In a multicolumn foreign key, sometimes only part of a foreign key can be NULL. The default behavior allows some columns in a multicolumn foreign key to be NULL and others to be not NULL.

```
test=> CREATE TABLE primarytest (col INTEGER PRIMARY KEY);
NOTICE:  CREATE TABLE/PRIMARY KEY will create implicit index 'primarytest_-
pkey' for table 'primarytest'
CREATE
test=> CREATE TABLE foreigntest (
test(>                         col2 INTEGER REFERENCES primarytest
test(>                         ON UPDATE CASCADE
test(>                         ON DELETE NO ACTION
test(>                         );
NOTICE:  CREATE TABLE will create implicit trigger(s) for FOREIGN KEY check(s)
CREATE
test=> INSERT INTO primarytest values (1);
INSERT 148835 1
test=> INSERT INTO foreigntest values (1);
INSERT 148836 1
test=>
test=> -- CASCADE UPDATE is performed
test=>
test=> UPDATE primarytest SET col = 2;
UPDATE 1
test=> SELECT * FROM foreigntest;
 col2
------
    2
(1 row)

test=>
test=> -- NO ACTION prevents deletion
test=>
test=> DELETE FROM primarytest;
ERROR:  <unnamed> referential integrity violation -
key in primarytest still referenced from foreigntest
test=>
test=> -- By deleting the foreign key first, the DELETE succeeds
test=>
test=> DELETE FROM foreigntest;
DELETE 1
test=> DELETE FROM primarytest;
DELETE 1
```

[handwritten annotation: default... deletes of row w pk that is ref'd by another table as fk are prohibited]

Figure 14.11: Foreign key actions

```
test=> CREATE TABLE primarytest2 (
test(>                            col1 INTEGER,
test(>                            col2 INTEGER,
test(>                            PRIMARY KEY(col1, col2)
test(>                            );
NOTICE:  CREATE TABLE/PRIMARY KEY will create implicit index 'primarytest2_-
pkey' for table 'primarytest2'
CREATE
test=> CREATE TABLE foreigntest2 (col3 INTEGER,
test(>                            col4 INTEGER,
test(>                            FOREIGN KEY (col3, col4) REFERENCES primary-
test2
test->                            );
NOTICE:  CREATE TABLE will create implicit trigger(s) for FOREIGN KEY check(s)
CREATE
```

Figure 14.12: Example of a multicolumn foreign key

Using MATCH FULL in a multicolumn foreign key constraint requires all columns in the key to be NULL or all columns to be not NULL. Figure 14.13 illustrates this case. First, the tables from Figure 14.12 are used to show that the default allows one column of a foreign key to be set to NULL. Next, the table *matchtest* is created with the MATCH FULL foreign key constraint option. MATCH FULL allows all key columns to be set to NULL, but rejects the setting of only some multicolumn key values to NULL.

Frequency of Foreign Key Checking

By default, foreign key constraints are checked at the end of each INSERT, UPDATE, and DELETE query. Thus, if you perform a set of complex table modifications, the foreign key constraints must remain valid at all times. For example, using the tables in Figure 14.7, if a new state is added and then a new customer in the new state is inserted, the new state must be added to *statename* before the customer is added to *customer.*

In some cases, it may not be possible to keep foreign key constraints valid between queries. For example, if two tables are foreign keys for each other, it may not be possible to INSERT into one table without having the other table row already present. A solution is to use the DEFERRABLE foreign key option and SET CONSTRAINTS so that foreign key constraints are checked only at transaction commit. With this approach, a multiquery transaction can make table modifications that violate foreign key constraints inside the transaction as long as the foreign key constraints are met at

```
test=> INSERT INTO primarytest2
test-> VALUES (1,2);
INSERT 148816 1
test=> INSERT INTO foreigntest2
test-> VALUES (1,2);
INSERT 148817 1
test=> UPDATE foreigntest2
test-> SET col4 = NULL;
UPDATE 1
test=> CREATE TABLE matchtest (
test(>                 col3 INTEGER,
test(>                 col4 INTEGER,
test(>                 FOREIGN KEY (col3, col4) REFERENCES primarytest2
test(>                         MATCH FULL
test(>                     );
NOTICE:  CREATE TABLE will create implicit trigger(s) for FOREIGN KEY check(s)
CREATE
test=> UPDATE matchtest
test-> SET col3 = NULL, col4 = NULL;
UPDATE 1
test=> UPDATE matchtest
test-> SET col4 = NULL;
ERROR:  <unnamed> referential integrity violation -
MATCH FULL doesn't allow mixing of NULL and NON-NULL key values
```

[handwritten annotations:] primary test has col1 col2 / 1 2 ; foreigntest2 has col3 col4 / 1 NULL ; OK, unless specify MATCH FULL

Figure 14.13: MATCH FULL foreign key

transactions commit. Figure 14.14 is a contrived example of this case; the proper way to perform this query is to INSERT into *primarytest* first, then INSERT into *defertest*. In complex situations, such reordering might not be possible, so DEFERRABLE and SET CONSTRAINTS should be used to defer foreign key constraints. A foreign key may also be configured as INITIALLY DEFERRED, causing the constraint to be checked only at transaction commit by default.

You can name constraints if desired. The constraint names will appear in constraint violation messages and can be used by SET CONSTRAINTS. See the CREATE_TABLE and SET manual pages for more information.

14.5 CHECK

The CHECK constraint enforces column value restrictions. Such constraints can restrict a column, for example, to a set of values, only positive numbers, or reasonable dates. Figure 14.15 shows an example of CHECK constraints using a modified version of the *friend* table from Figure 3.2, page 13. This figure has many CHECK clauses:

state Forces the column to be two characters long. CHAR() pads the field with spaces, so *state* must be *trim()*-ed of trailing spaces before *length()* is computed. *(else a 1char val would look ok)*

age Forces the column to hold only positive values.

gender Forces the column to hold either *M* or *F*.

last_met Forces the column to include dates between January 1, 1950, and the current date.

table Forces the table to accept only rows where *firstname* is not *ED* or *lastname* is not *RIVERS*. The effect is to prevent *Ed Rivers* from being entered into the table. His name will be rejected if it is in uppercase, lowercase, or mixed case. This restriction must be implemented as a table-level CHECK constraint. Comparing *firstname* to *ED* at the column level would have prevented all *EDs* from being entered, which was not desired. Instead, the desired restriction is a combination of *firstname* and *lastname*.

Next, the example tries to INSERT a row that violates all CHECK constraints. Although the CHECK failed on the *friend2_last_met* constraint, if that were corrected, the other constraints would prevent the insertion. By default, CHECK allows NULL values.

14.6 Summary

This chapter covered a variety of constraints that help restrict user data within specified limits. With small databases, constraints are of marginal benefit. With databases holding millions of rows, however, they help keep database information organized and complete.

CREATE TABLE primarytest (col2 INTEGER PRIMAY KEY);

```
test=> CREATE TABLE defertest(
test(>                         col2 INTEGER REFERENCES primarytest
test(>                                   DEFERRABLE
test(> );
NOTICE:  CREATE TABLE will create implicit trigger(s) for FOREIGN KEY check(s)
CREATE
test=> BEGIN;
BEGIN
test=> -- INSERT is attempted in non-DEFERRABLE mode
test=>
test=> INSERT INTO defertest VALUES (5);
ERROR:  <unnamed> referential integrity violation -
key referenced from defertest not found in primarytest
test=> COMMIT;
COMMIT
test=> BEGIN;
BEGIN
test=> -- all foreign key constraints are set to DEFERRED
test=>
test=> SET CONSTRAINTS ALL DEFERRED;
SET CONSTRAINTS
test=> INSERT INTO defertest VALUES (5);
INSERT 148946 1
test=> INSERT INTO primarytest VALUES (5);
INSERT 148947 1
test=> COMMIT;
COMMIT
```

Is this example correct?

Figure 14.14: DEFERRABLE foreign key constraint

```
test=> CREATE TABLE friend2 (
test(>            firstname  CHAR(15),
test(>            lastname   CHAR(20),
test(>            city       CHAR(15),
test(>            state      CHAR(2)     CHECK (length(trim(state)) = 2),
test(>            age        INTEGER     CHECK (age >= 0),
test(>            gender     CHAR(1)     CHECK (gender IN ('M','F')),
test(>            last_met   DATE        CHECK (last_met BETWEEN '1950-01-01'
test(>                                         AND CURRENT_DATE),
test(>            CHECK (upper(trim(firstname)) != 'ED' OR
test(>                   upper(trim(lastname)) != 'RIVERS')
test(> );
CREATE
test=> INSERT INTO friend2
test-> VALUES ('Ed', 'Rivers', 'Wibbleville', 'J', -35, 'S', '1931-09-23');
ERROR:  ExecAppend: rejected due to CHECK constraint friend2_last_met
```

Figure 14.15: CHECK constraints

CHECK (not (upper (trim (firstname)) = 'ED' and
               upper (trim (lastname)) = 'RIVERS'))

Chapter 15

Importing and Exporting Data

COPY allows rapid loading and unloading of user tables. This command can write the contents of a table to an ASCII file or load a table from an ASCII file. These files can be used for backup purposes or to transfer data between POSTGRESQL and other applications.

The first section of this chapter describes the use of COPY to unload and load database tables. The next part of the chapter shows how to use COPY to share data with other applications. The final section contains tips for using COPY.

15.1 Using COPY

COPY...TO allows you to copy the contents of a table to a file. The file can later be read using COPY...FROM.

Figure 15.1 shows the creation of a table with columns of various types. Two rows are then inserted into *copytest*. SELECT shows the contents of the table, and COPY...TO writes the table to the file /tmp/copytest.out. The rows are then deleted. Finally, COPY...FROM reloads the table, as shown by the last SELECT.

COPY provides a quick way to load and unload tables. It is used for database backup (see Section 20.5). The following sections cover various COPY features that are important when reading or writing COPY files in other applications.

227

15.2 COPY File Format

COPY...TO can export data to be loaded into other applications, and COPY...FROM can import data from other applications. If you are constructing a file for use with the COPY command or are reading a COPY file in another application, it is important to understand COPY's file format.

Figure 15.2 shows the contents of the COPY file from Figure 15.1. First, \q exits psql to an

```
test=> CREATE TABLE copytest (
test(>                      intcol  INTEGER,
test(>                      numcol  NUMERIC(16,2),
test(>                      textcol TEXT,
test(>                      boolcol BOOLEAN
test(> );
CREATE
test=> INSERT INTO copytest
test-> VALUES (1, 23.99, 'fresh spring water', 't');
INSERT 174656 1
test=> INSERT INTO copytest
test-> VALUES (2, 55.23, 'bottled soda', 't');
INSERT 174657 1
test=> SELECT * FROM copytest;
 intcol | numcol |      textcol       | boolcol
--------+--------+--------------------+---------
      1 |  23.99 | fresh spring water | t
      2 |  55.23 | bottled soda       | t
(2 rows)

test=> COPY copytest TO '/tmp/copytest.out';
COPY
test=> DELETE FROM copytest;     # empties but does not drop the table
DELETE 2
test=> COPY copytest FROM '/tmp/copytest.out';
COPY
test=> SELECT * FROM copytest;
 intcol | numcol |      textcol       | boolcol
--------+--------+--------------------+---------
      1 |  23.99 | fresh spring water | t
      2 |  55.23 | bottled soda       | t
(2 rows)
```

Figure 15.1: Example of COPY...TO and COPY...FROM

```
test=> \q
$ cat /tmp/copytest.out
1       23.99   fresh spring water      t
2       55.23   bottled soda    t

$ sed 's/        /<TAB>/g' /tmp/copytest.out  # the gap between /  / is a TAB
1<TAB>23.99<TAB>fresh spring water<TAB>t
2<TAB>55.23<TAB>bottled soda<TAB>t
```

Figure 15.2: Example of COPY...FROM

operating system prompt. Then, the Unix cat[1] command displays the file /tmp/copytest.out. This file contains one line for every row in the table. Columns in the file are separated by tabs. These tabs are called *delimiters* because they delimit (that is, separate) columns.

Tabs are difficult to see because they look like multiple spaces. The next command processes the file using sed [2] to display tabs as <TAB>. This option clearly shows the tabs in the file, which differ from spaces.

The columns in Figure 15.2 do not line up as they do in psql, because they are of different lengths. The value of *textcol* in the first line is longer than the value in the second line. The lack of alignment is expected because the COPY file is designed for easy processing, with one tab between each column. It is not designed for display purposes.

15.3 DELIMITERS

You can easily change the default tab column delimiter. COPY's USING DELIMITERS option allows you to set the column delimiter. In Figure 15.3, setting the delimiter to a pipe symbol (|) causes the output file to use pipes to separate columns.

If a COPY file does not use the default tab column delimiter, COPY...FROM must employ the proper USING DELIMITERS option. As shown in Figure 15.4, if a file uses pipes rather than tabs as column delimiters, COPY...FROM must specify pipes as delimiters. The first COPY...FROM fails because it cannot find a tab to separate the columns. The second COPY...FROM succeeds because the proper delimiter for the file was used.

---

[1]Non-Unix operating system users would use the *type* command.

[2]The sed operating system command replaces one string with another. See the sed(1) manual page for more information.

✳

```
test=> COPY copytest TO '/tmp/copytest.out' USING DELIMITERS '|';
COPY
test=> \q
$ cat /tmp/copytest.out
1|23.99|fresh spring water|t
2|55.23|bottled soda|t
```

Figure 15.3: Example of COPY...TO...USING DELIMITERS

NB   If use certain delimiter to create file, need
      same delimiter to read it in.

```
test=> DELETE FROM copytest;
DELETE 2
test=>
test=> COPY copytest FROM '/tmp/copytest.out';
ERROR:  copy: line 1, pg_atoi: error in "1|23.99|fresh spring water|t": can-
not parse "|23.99|fresh spring water|t"
test=>
test=> COPY copytest FROM '/tmp/copytest.out' USING DELIMITERS '|';
COPY
```

Figure 15.4: Example of COPY...FROM...USING DELIMITERS

```
test=> COPY copytest FROM stdin;
Enter data to be copied followed by a newline.
End with a backslash and a period on a line by itself.
test> 3 77.43   coffee  f          (tab-separated)
test> \.
test=> COPY copytest TO stdout;
1       23.99    fresh spring water       t
2       55.23    bottled soda     t
3       77.43    coffee  f
test=>
```

Figure 15.5: COPY using *stdin* and *stdout*

15.4   COPY Without Files

COPY can also be used without files. The command can, for example, use the same input and output
locations used by psql. The special name *stdin* represents the psql input, and *stdout* represents
the psql output. Figure 15.5 shows how you can use *stdin* to supply COPY input directly from
your keyboard. For clarity, text typed by the user appears in bold. The gaps in the second typed
line were generated by pressing the tab key. The user typed \. to exit COPY...FROM. A COPY to
stdout operation displays the COPY output on your screen, which can be useful when using psql in
automated scripts.

15.5   Backslashes and NULL Values

There is potential for confusion if the character used as a column delimiter also exists in user data.
If both appear the same way in the file, COPY...FROM would be unable to determine whether the
character is a delimiter or user data.

COPY avoids any confusion by specially marking delimiters appearing in user data. It precedes
them with a backslash (\). If a pipe is the delimiter, COPY...TO uses pipes (|) for delimiters, and
backslash-pipes (\|) for pipes in user data. In Figure 15.6, for example, each column is separated
by a pipe, but the pipe that appears in user data is output as *abc \ | def.*

Use of a backslash causes any character that follows it to be treated specially. As a result, a
backslash in user data is output as two backslashes (\\).

Another special backslash used in Figure 15.6 is \N, which represents NULL. It prevents NULL
values from being confused with user values.

To change the default NULL representation, you use WITH NULL AS. For example, the command COPY copytest TO '/tmp/copytest.out' WITH NULL AS '?' will output NULL values as ques-

```
test=> DELETE FROM copytest;
DELETE 3
test=> INSERT INTO copytest
test-> VALUES (4, 837.20, 'abc|def', NULL);
INSERT 174786 1
test=> COPY copytest TO stdout USING DELIMITERS '|';
4|837.20|abc\|def|\N
```

Figure 15.6: COPY backslash handling

Backslash String	Meaning
\ TAB	tab if using default delimiter tab
\\|	*pipe* if using *pipe* as the delimiter
\N	NULL if using the default NULL output
\b	backspace
\f	form feed
\n	newline
\r	carriage return
\t	tab
\v	vertical tab
\###	character represented by octal number ###
\\	backslash

Table 15.1: Backslashes understood by COPY

tion marks. Unfortunately, it will make a user column containing a single question mark indistinguishable from a NULL in the file. To output NULL values as blank columns, use the command COPY copytest TO '/tmp/copytest.out' WITH NULL AS '\,'. To treat empty columns as NULL values on input, use COPY copytest FROM '/tmp/copytest.out' WITH NULL AS '\,'.

Table 15.1 summarizes the delimiter, NULL, and backslash handling of COPY. The first two lines in the table show that preceding a character with a backslash prevents the character from being interpreted as a delimiter. The next line shows that $\backslash N$ means NULL under the default representation. The other backslash entries show simple representations for common characters. The last line shows that a double-backslash is required to represent a literal backslash.

15.6 COPY Tips

You must use full path names with the COPY command because the database server runs in a different directory than the psql client. Files are read and written by the *postgres* user, so *postgres* must have permission to read the file for COPY...FROM and directory write permission for COPY...TO. Because COPY uses the local file system, users connecting over a network cannot use file names. They can use *stdin* and *stdout,* or psql's \copy command.

By default, the system-generated OID column is not written out, and loaded rows receive new OIDs. COPY...WITH OIDS allows OIDs to be written and read.

COPY writes only entire tables. To COPY only part of a table, use SELECT...INTO TEMPORARY TABLE with an appropriate WHERE clause and then COPY the temporary table to a file.

See the COPY manual page for more detailed information.

15.7 Summary

COPY can be thought of as a crude INSERT and SELECT command. It imports and exports data in a very generic format, which makes it ideal for use by other applications and for backup purposes.

Chapter 16

Database Query Tools

This chapter covers two popular POSTGRESQL database query tools: psql and pgaccess.

16.1 Psql

This section summarize the capabilities of psql. The psql manual has detailed information about each item. See Chapter 2 for an introduction to psql.

Query Buffer Commands

Table 16.1 shows the commands used to control psql's query buffer. There is one item of particular interest, *edit* (*\e*), which allows editing of the query buffer. The *\e* command loads the contents of   \e
the query buffer into the default editor. When the user exits the editor, the editor's contents are reloaded into the query buffer, ready for execution. The environment variable EDITOR specifies the default editor.

General Commands

Table 16.2 lists psql's general commands. Psql's local *copy* interface allows copy operations using files local to the computer running psql, rather than local to the computer running the database server. Later sections in this chapter cover the use of the *\set, \unset,* and *\pset* commands.

Output Format Options

The *\pset* command controls the output format used by psql. Table 16.3 lists the available formatting   \pset
commands, and Figure 16.1 shows examples of their use. In the figure, *\pset tuples_only* causes psql to show only data rows, suppressing table headings and row counts. The *tuples_only* does not

Function	Command	Argument
Print	\p	
Execute	\g or ;	*file* or |*command*
Quit	\q	
Clear	\r	
Edit	\e	*file* or ; by itself
Backslash help	\?	
SQL help	\h	*topic*
Include file	\i	*file*
Output to file/command	\o	*file* or |*command*
Write buffer to file	\w	*file* [1]
Show/save query history	\s	*file*
Run subshell	\!	*command*

Table 16.1: `psql`'s query buffer commands

Operation	Command
Connect to another database	\connect *dbname*
Copy table file to/from database	\copy *tablename* to|from *filename*
Set a variable	\set *variable* or \set *variable value*
Unset a variable	\unset *variable*
Set output format	\pset *option* or \pset *option value*
Echo	\echo *string* or \echo `command`
Echo to \o output	\qecho *string* or \qecho `command`
Copyright	\copyright
Change character encoding	\encoding *newencoding*

Table 16.2: `psql`'s general commands

1 Eg: buffer still full after \g ; if successful, then \w file (say)

Format	Parameter	Options
Field alignment	format	unaligned, aligned, html, or latex
Field separator	fieldsep	*separator*
One field per line	expanded	
Rows only	tuples_only	*(toggle)*
Row separator	recordsep	*separator*
Table title	title	*title*
Table border	border	0, 1, or 2
Display NULL values	null	*null_string*
HTML table tags	tableattr	*tags*
Page output	pager	*command*

Table 16.3: psql's \pset options

\pset parm

NB: no \g or ;
after \pset commands
(like \r, \e, etc)

```
test=> SELECT NULL;
 ?column?
----------

(1 row)
```

```
test=> \pset tuples_only
Showing only tuples.
test=> SELECT NULL;

```

```
test=> \pset null '(null)'
Null display is '(null)'.
test=> SELECT NULL;
 (null)
```

Figure 16.1: Example of *\pset*

Modifies	Command	Argument
Field alignment	\a	
Field separator	\f	*separator*
One field per line	\x	
Rows only	\t	
Table title	\C	*title*
Enable HTML	\H	
HTML table tags	\T	*tags*

\pset Fieldsep sep

Table 16.4: psql's output format shortcuts

take a second argument, as it is an *on/off* parameter. The first *pset tuples_only* turns it on, and the second one turns it off. The second *pset* in the figure causes psql to display NULL as *(null)*.

Output Format Shortcuts

In addition to using *pset*, some output format options have shortcuts, as shown in Table 16.4.

Variables

The *set* command sets a variable, and *unset* removes a variable. To access a variable you precede its name with a colon. The *set* command used alone lists all defined variables.

Figure 16.2 shows the use of psql variables. The first variable assigned, *num_var*, is accessed in the SELECT query by preceding the variable name with a colon. The second *set* command places the word SELECT into a variable, then uses that variable to perform a SELECT query. The next example uses backslash-quotes (\') to create a string that contains single quotes. This variable then replaces a quoted string in a query. With *date_var,* grave accents (`) allow a command to be run and the result placed into a variable. In this case, the output of the Unix date command is captured and placed into a variable. The assignment to *date_var2* combines the use of backslash-quotes and grave accents to run the date command and surround it with single quotes. The final SELECT shows that *date_var2* holds a quoted date string that can be used in queries.

Psql includes a number of predefined variables, as listed in Table 16.5. The variables in the first group contain useful information; the others affect psql's behavior. Some of the predefined variables do not take an argument but are activated using *set,* and deactivated using *unset.*

Listing Commands

You can find a great deal of information about the current database by using psql's listing commands, as shown in Table 16.6.   They provide information about tables, indexes, functions, and other objects defined in the database.

```
test=> \set num_var 4
test=> SELECT :num_var;
 ?column?
----------
        4
(1 row)
```

-- interpolate the value

note: nothing special about 'operation': just var

```
test=> \set operation SELECT
test=> :operation :num_var;
 ?column?
----------
        4
(1 row)


test=> \set str_var '\'My long string\''
test=> \echo :str_var
'My long string'
test=> SELECT :str_var;
    ?column?
----------------
 My long string
(1 row)
```

✳

```
test=> \set date_var `date`
test=> \echo :date_var
Thu Aug 11 20:54:21 EDT 1994
```

static

✳

```
test=> \set date_var2 '\'' `date` '\''
test=> \echo :date_var2
'Thu Aug 11 20:54:24 EDT 1994'
test=> SELECT :date_var2;
          ?column?
------------------------------
 Thu Aug 11 20:54:24 EDT 1994
(1 row)
```

dynamic

← what is date and what else is like it?

Figure 16.2: psql variables

Meaning	Variable Name	Argument
Database	DBNAME	
Multibyte encoding	ENCODING	
Host	HOST	
Previously assigned OID	LASTOID	
Port	PORT	
User	USER	
Echo queries	ECHO	all
Echo \d* queries	ECHO_HIDDEN	noexec
History control	HISTCONTROL	ignorespace, ignoredups, or ignoreboth
History size	HISTSIZE	*command_count*
Terminate on end of file	IGNOREEOF	*eof_count*
\lobject transactions	LO_TRANSACTION	rollback, commit, nothing
Stop on query errors	ON_ERROR_STOP	
Command prompt	PROMPT1, PROMPT2, PROMPT3	*string*
Suppress output	QUIET	
Single-line mode	SINGLELINE	
Single-step mode	SINGLESTEP	

Table 16.5: `psql`'s predefined variables

Listing	Command	Argument
Table, index, view, or sequence	\d	*name*
Tables	\dt	*name*
Indexes	\di	*name*
Sequences	\ds	*name*
Views	\dv	*name*
Permissions	\z or \dp	*name*
System tables	\dS	*name*
Large objects	\dl	*name*
Types	\dT	*name*
Functions	\df	*name*
Operators	\do	*name*
Aggregates	\da	*name*
Comments	\dd	*name*
Databases	\l	

Table 16.6: psql's listing commands

Most listing commands take an optional *name* parameter, which can be specified as a regular expression. For example, \dt sec displays all table names beginning with *sec,* and \dt .*x.* shows all table names containing an *x.* Regular expressions were covered in Section 4.10.

When you are using listing commands, the descriptions of the various data types and functions are called *comments.* POSTGRESQL predefines many comments, and the COMMENT command allows users to define their own as well. The \dd command and others then display these comments. See the COMMENT manual page for more information.

Many commands support the use of an optional plus sign, which shows additional information. For example, \dT lists all data types, \dT+ includes the size of each type, and \df+ shows additional information about functions. With the other commands, a plus sign causes the comments for the object to be displayed.

Large Object Commands

Psql has a local large object interface that supports large object operations using files local to the computer running psql, rather than local to the computer running the database server. Table 16.7 shows the local large object commands supported.

Large Objects	Command	Argument
Import	\lo_import	*file*
Export	\lo_export	*oid file*
Unlink	\lo_unlink	*oid*
List	\lo_list	

Table 16.7: psql's large object commands

Psql Command-line Arguments and Start-up File

You can change the behavior of psql when starting a new session. Psql is normally started from the command line by typing psql followed by the database name. However, psql accepts extra arguments between psql and the database name, which modify psql's behavior. For example, psql -f file test will read commands from file, rather than from the keyboard. Table 16.8 summarizes psql's command-line options. Consult the psql manual page for more detailed information.

Another way to change the behavior of psql on start-up is to create a file called .psqlrc in your home directory. Each time psql starts, it executes any backslash or SQL commands in that file.

16.2   Pgaccess

Pgaccess is a graphical database tool that is used for accessing tables, queries, views, sequences, functions, reports, forms, scripts, users, and schemas. It is written using the POSTGRESQL TCL/TK interface. Its source code appears in pgsql/src/bin/pgaccess.

Figure 16.3 shows the opening window of pgaccess. The tabs on the left show the items that can be accessed. The menu at the top permits database actions, table import/export, and object creation, deletion, and renaming.

Figure 16.4 shows the *table* window. This window allows table rows to be viewed and modified. The pgaccess manual page and help screens cover its capabilities in more detail.

16.3   Summary

This chapter covered psql and pgaccess, the most popular POSTGRESQL query tools. They are valuable tools for accessing POSTGRESQL.

Option	Capability	Argument	Additional Argument
Connection	Database (optional)	-d	*database*
	Host name	-h	*hostname*
	Port	-p	*port*
	User	-U	*user*
	Force password prompt	-W	
	Version	-V	
Controlling Output	Field alignment	-A	
	Field separator	-F	*separator*
	Record separator	-R	*separator*
	Rows only	-t	
	Extended output format	-x	
	Echo \d* queries	-E	
	Quiet mode	-q	
	HTML output	-H	
	HTML table tags	-T	*tags*
	Set \pset options	-P	*option* or *option=value*
	List databases	-l	
	Disable *readline*	-n	
Automation	Echo all queries from scripts	-a	
	Echo queries	-e	
	Execute query	-c	*query*
	Get queries from file	-f	*file*
	Output to file	-o	*file*
	Single-step mode	-s	
	Single-line mode	-S	
	Suppress reading ~/.psqlrc	-X	
	Set variable	-v	*var* or *var=value*

Table 16.8: `psql`'s command-line arguments

Figure 16.3: Pgaccess's opening window

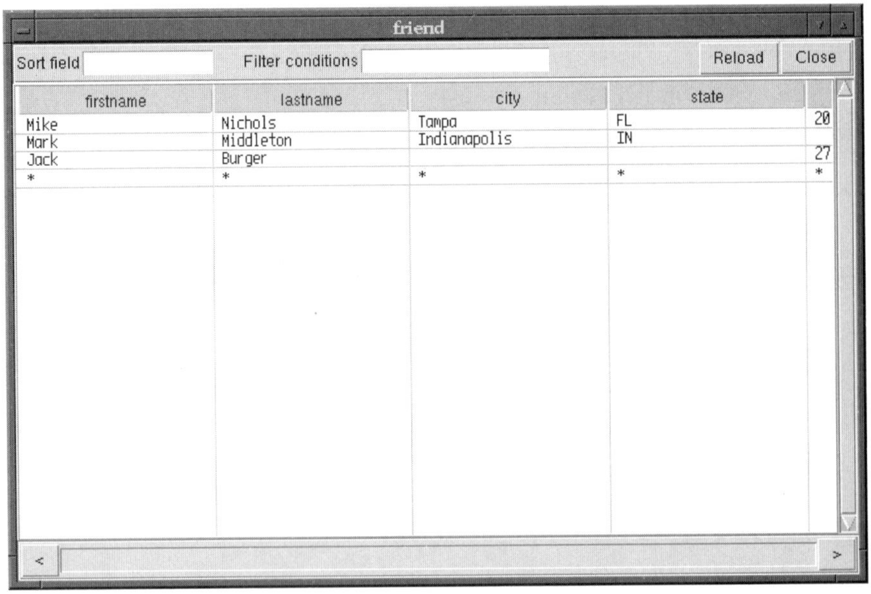

Figure 16.4: Pgaccess's table window

Chapter 17

Programming Interfaces

Psql is ideal for interactively entering SQL commands and for running automated scripts, but it is not ideal for writing applications. Fortunately, POSTGRESQL has interfaces for many programming languages. Programming languages include variables, functions, conditional evaluation, looping, and complex input/output routines, all of which are required for writing good applications.

Table 17.1 shows the supported programming interfaces. These language interfaces allow applications to pass queries to POSTGRESQL and receive results. The compiled languages execute more quickly, but are more difficult to program than the interpreted ones.

This chapter will show the same application using each of the interfaces listed in Figure 17.1. The application is a very simple one that prompts the user for a United States state code and outputs the state name that goes with the code. Figure 17.1 shows the sample application being run. For clarity, the text typed by the user appears in bold. The program displays a prompt, the user types *AL,* and the program displays *Alabama.* Although state codes are unique, the application is written to allow multiple query return values. The application uses the *statename* table, which is recreated in Figure 17.2.

Additional information about POSTGRESQL interfaces is available in the *Programmer's Manual* mentioned in Appendix A.2.   233

```
Enter a state code:  AL
Alabama
```

Figure 17.1: Sample application being run

Interface	Language	Processing	Advantages
LIBPQ	C	compiled	native interface
LIBPGEASY	C	compiled	simplified C
ECPG	C	compiled	ANSI embedded SQL C
LIBPQ++	C++	compiled	object-oriented C
ODBC	ODBC	compiled	application connectivity
JDBC	Java	both	portability
PERL	Perl	interpreted	text processing
PGTCLSH	TCL/TK	interpreted	interfacing, windowing
PYTHON	Python	interpreted	object-oriented
PHP	HTML	interpreted	dynamic Web pages

Table 17.1: Interface summary

```
test=>  CREATE TABLE statename (code CHAR(2) PRIMARY KEY,
test(>                          name  CHAR(30)
test(> );
CREATE
test=> INSERT INTO statename VALUES ('AL', 'Alabama');
INSERT 18934 1
test=> INSERT INTO statename VALUES ('AK', 'Alaska');
INSERT 18934 1
...
```

Figure 17.2: *Statename* table

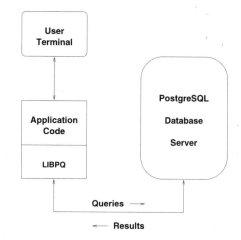

Figure 17.3: LIBPQ data flow

17.1 C Language Interface (LIBPQ)

LIBPQ is the native C interface to POSTGRESQL. Psql and most other interfaces use it internally for database access.

Figure 17.3 shows how LIBPQ is used. The application code communicates with the user's terminal and uses LIBPQ for database access. It turn, LIBPQ sends queries to the database server and retrieves results.

Figure 17.4 shows the sample program using LIBPQ to access POSTGRESQL. The sample program performs the following tasks:

- Establish a database connection

- Prompt for and read the state code

- Form an appropriate SQL query

- Pass the SQL query to LIBPQ

- Have POSTGRESQL execute the query

- Retrieve the query results from LIBPQ

- Display the results to the user

- Terminate the database connection

All interactions with the database are accomplished via LIBPQ functions. The following LIBPQ functions are called by the sample program:

```c
/*
 *  libpq sample program
 */

#include <stdio.h>
#include <stdlib.h>
#include "libpq-fe.h"                           /* libpq header file */

int
main()
{
    char        state_code[3];                  /* holds state code entered by user */
    char        query_string[256];              /* holds constructed SQL query */
    PGconn      *conn;                           /* holds database connection */
    PGresult    *res;                           /* holds query result */
    int         i;

    conn = PQconnectdb("dbname=test");          /* connect to the database */

    if (PQstatus(conn) == CONNECTION_BAD)       /* did the database connection fail? */
    {
        fprintf(stderr, "Connection to database failed.\n");
        fprintf(stderr, "%s", PQerrorMessage(conn));
        exit(1);
    }

    printf("Enter a state code:  ");            /* prompt user for a state code */
    scanf("%2s", state_code);

    sprintf(query_string,                       /* create an SQL query string */
            "SELECT name \
             FROM statename \
             WHERE code = '%s'", state_code);

    res = PQexec(conn, query_string);           /* send the query */

    if (PQresultStatus(res) != PGRES_TUPLES_OK) /* did the query fail? */
    {
        fprintf(stderr, "SELECT query failed.\n");
        PQclear(res);
        PQfinish(conn);
        exit(1);
    }

    for (i = 0; i < PQntuples(res); i++)        /* loop through all rows returned */
        printf("%s\n", PQgetvalue(res, i, 0));  /* print the value returned */

    PQclear(res);                               /* free result */

    PQfinish(conn);                             /* disconnect from the database */

    return 0;
}
```

Figure 17.4: LIBPQ sample program

PQconnectdb() Connect to the database.

PQexec() Send the query to the database.

PQntuples() Return the number of rows (tuples) in the result.

PQgetvalue() Return a specific row and column of the result.

PQclear() Free resources used by the result.

PQfinish() Close the database connection.

These functions are the most common LIBPQ functions. The *Programmer's Manual* covers all of this interface's functions and shows additional examples.

17.2 Pgeasy (LIBPGEASY)

LIBPGEASY is a simplified C interface that hides some of the complexity of LIBPQ. Figure 17.5 shows a LIBPGEASY version of our state code application. No error checking is required because LIBPGEASY automatically terminates the program if an error occurs. You can change this default using *on_error_continue()*.

17.3 Embedded C (ECPG)

Rather than using function calls to perform SQL queries, ECPG allows SQL commands to be embedded in a C program. The ECPG preprocessor converts lines marked by EXEC SQL to native SQL calls. The resulting file is then compiled as a C program.

Figure 17.6 shows an ECPG version of our application. The interface implements the ANSI embedded SQL C standard, which is supported by many database systems.

17.4 C++ (LIBPQ++)

LIBPQ++ is POSTGRESQL's C++ interface. Figure 17.7 shows our application using this interface. LIBPQ++ allows database access using object methods rather than function calls.

17.5 Compiling Programs

The interfaces discussed so far have been based on C or C++. Each interface requires certain *include* and *library* files to generate an executable version of the program.

```
/*
 * libpgeasy sample program
 */

#include <stdio.h>
#include <libpq-fe.h>
#include <libpgeasy.h>                          /* libpgeasy header file */

int
main()
{
    char        state_code[3];                  /* holds state code entered by user */
    char        query_string[256];              /* holds constructed SQL query */
    char        state_name[31];                 /* holds returned state name */

    connectdb("dbname=test");                   /* connect to the database */

    printf("Enter a state code:  ");            /* prompt user for a state code */
    scanf("%2s", state_code);

    sprintf(query_string,                       /* create an SQL query string */
            "SELECT name \
             FROM statename \
             WHERE code = '%s'", state_code);

    doquery(query_string);                      /* send the query */

    while (fetch(state_name) != END_OF_TUPLES)  /* loop through all rows returned */
        printf("%s\n", state_name);             /* print the value returned */

    disconnectdb();                             /* disconnect from the database */

    return 0;
}
```

Figure 17.5: LIBPGEASY sample program

```
/*
 *  ecpg sample program
 */

#include <stdio.h>

EXEC SQL INCLUDE sqlca;                          /* ecpg header file */

EXEC SQL WHENEVER SQLERROR sqlprint;

int
main()
{
EXEC SQL BEGIN DECLARE SECTION;
    char       state_code[3];                    /* holds state code entered by user */
    char      *state_name = NULL;                /* holds value returned by query */
    char       query_string[256];                /* holds constructed SQL query */
EXEC SQL END DECLARE SECTION;

    EXEC SQL CONNECT TO test;                     /* connect to the database */

    printf("Enter a state code:  ");              /* prompt user for a state code */
    scanf("%2s", state_code);

    sprintf(query_string,                         /* create an SQL query string */
            "SELECT name \
             FROM statename \
             WHERE code = '%s'", state_code);

    EXEC SQL PREPARE s_statename FROM :query_string;
    EXEC SQL DECLARE c_statename CURSOR FOR s_statename;/* DECLARE a cursor */

    EXEC SQL OPEN c_statename;                     /* send the query */

    EXEC SQL WHENEVER NOT FOUND DO BREAK;

    while (1)                                      /* loop through all rows returned */
    {
        EXEC SQL FETCH IN c_statename INTO :state_name;
        printf("%s\n", state_name);                /* print the value returned */
        state_name = NULL;
    }

    free(state_name);                              /* free result */

    EXEC SQL CLOSE c_statename;                    /* CLOSE the cursor */

    EXEC SQL COMMIT;

    EXEC SQL DISCONNECT;                           /* disconnect from the database */

    return 0;
}
```

Figure 17.6: ECPG sample program

```
/*
 *  libpq++ sample program
 */

#include <iostream.h>
#include <libpq++.h>                              // libpq++ header file

int main()
{
    char       state_code[3];                     // holds state code entered by user
    char       query_string[256];                 // holds constructed SQL query
    PgDatabase data("dbname=test");               // connects to the database

    if ( data.ConnectionBad() )                   // did the database connection fail?
    {
        cerr << "Connection to database failed." << endl
             << "Error returned: " << data.ErrorMessage() << endl;
        exit(1);
    }

    cout << "Enter a state code:  ";              // prompt user for a state code
    cin.get(state_code, 3, '\n');

    sprintf(query_string,                         // create an SQL query string
            "SELECT name \
            FROM statename \
            WHERE code = '%s'", state_code);

    if ( !data.ExecTuplesOk(query_string) )       // send the query
    {
        cerr << "SELECT query failed." << endl;
        exit(1);
    }

    for (int i=0; i < data.Tuples(); i++)         // loop through all rows returned
            cout << data.GetValue(i,0) << endl;   // print the value returned

    return 0;
}
```

Figure 17.7: Libpq++ sample program

/usr/include/pgsql , /usr/lib/libpg.so, etc

Interface include files are typically installed in `/usr/local/pgsql/include`. The compiler flag *-I* is needed to ensure that the compiler searches the specified directory for include files—for example, `-I/usr/local/pgsql/include`.

Interface libraries are typically installed in `/usr/local/pgsql/lib`. The compiler flag *-L* is needed to ensure that the compiler searches the directory for library files—for example, `-L/usr/local/pgsql/lib`.

The compiler flag *-l* is needed for the compiler to link to a specific library file. To link to `libpq.a` or `libpq.so`, the flag `-lpq` is needed. Because the *-l* flag knows that the file begins with *lib*, `-llibpq` is not correct—just `-lpq`.

The commands to compile *myapp* for various interfaces are listed below:

LIBPQ `cc -I/usr/local/pgsql/include -o myapp myapp.c -L/usr/local/pgsql/lib -lpq`

LIBPGEASY `cc -I/usr/local/pgsql/include -o myapp myapp.c -L/usr/local/pgsql/lib -lpgeasy`

ECPG `ecpg myapp.pgc`
     `cc -I/usr/local/pgsql/include -o myapp myapp.c -L/usr/local/pgsql/lib -lecpg`

LIBPQ++ `cc++ -I/usr/local/pgsql/include -o myapp myapp.cpp -L/usr/local/pgsql/lib -lpq++`

Notice that each interface has its own library. ECPG requires the `ecpg` preprocessor to be run before compilation. LIBPQ++ requires the use of a different compiler.

17.6 Assignment to Program Variables

POSTGRESQL is a network-capable database. That is, the database server and user application can be run on different computers. Because character strings have the same representation on all computers, they are used for communication between the user program and database server. Queries are submitted as character strings, and results are passed back as character strings. This approach provides reliable communication even when the two computers involved are quite different.

The sample programs in this chapter perform SELECTs on a CHAR(30) column. Because query results are returned as character strings, returned values can be assigned directly to program variables. In contrast, noncharacter string columns, like INTEGER and FLOAT, cannot be assigned directly to integer or floating-point variables. A conversion might be required instead.

For example, when you are using LIBPQ or LIBPQ++, a SELECT on an INTEGER column does not return an integer from the database, but rather a character string that must be converted to an integer by the application. An INTEGER is returned as the string *'983'* rather than the integer value *983*. To assign this value to an integer variable, you use the C library function *atoi()*—for example, `var = atoi(colval)`.

One exception involves BINARY cursors, which return binary representations of column values. You can assign results from BINARY cursors directly to program variables. However, because they return column values in binary format, both the application and the database server must be running on the same computer or at least on computers with the same CPU architecture. See the DECLARE manual page for more information on BINARY cursors.

LIBPGEASY uses *fetch()* to return values directly into program variables. This function should place results into character string variables or use BINARY cursors if possible.

ECPG automatically converts data returned by POSTGRESQL to the proper format before assignment to program variables.

The interpreted languages covered later in this chapter have type-less variables, so they do not have this problem.

17.7 ODBC

ODBC (Open Database Connectivity) is an interface used by some applications and application-building tools to access SQL databases. This middleware layer is not meant for programming directly, but rather for communicating with other applications.

The ODBC source code is located in `pgsql/src/interfaces/odbc`. It can be compiled on both Unix and non-Unix operating systems.

17.8 Java (JDBC)

Figure 17.8 shows a Java version of the same application.

The interface's source code is located in `pgsql/src/interfaces/jdbc`. Once the interface is compiled, the file `postgresql.jar` should be copied to the directory containing the other `jar` files. The full path name of `postgresql.jar` must then be added to the CLASSPATH environment variable.

Java programs are compiled using `javac` and run using `java`. Java is both a compiled and interpreted language. It is compiled for speed, but interpreted when executed so that any computer can run the compiled program.

17.9 Scripting Languages

Up to this point, the interfaces discussed have used compiled languages. Compiled languages require user programs to be *compiled* into CPU instructions.

The remaining interfaces are scripting languages. Scripting languages execute more slowly than compiled languages, but offer several benefits:

```
/*
 *  Java sample program
 */

import java.io.*;
import java.sql.*;

public class sample
{
    Connection  conn;                           // holds database connection
    Statement   stmt;                           // holds SQL statement
    String      state_code;                     // holds state code entered by user

    public sample() throws ClassNotFoundException, FileNotFoundException, IOException, SQLException
    {
        Class.forName("org.postgresql.Driver");     // load database interface
                                                    // connect to the database
        conn = DriverManager.getConnection("jdbc:postgresql:test", "testuser", "");
        stmt = conn.createStatement();

        System.out.print("Enter a state code: ");   // prompt user for a state code
        System.out.flush();
        BufferedReader r = new BufferedReader(new InputStreamReader(System.in));
        state_code = r.readLine();

        ResultSet res = stmt.executeQuery(          // send the query
            "SELECT name " +
            "FROM statename " +
            "WHERE code = '" + state_code + "'");

        if (res != null)
            while(res.next())
            {
                String state_name = res.getString(1);
                System.out.println(state_name);
            }

        res.close();
        stmt.close();
        conn.close();
    }

    public static void main(String args[])
    {
        try {
            sample test = new sample();
        } catch(Exception exc)
        {
            System.err.println("Exception caught.\n" + exc);
            exc.printStackTrace();
        }
    }
}
```

Figure 17.8: Java sample program

```perl
#!/usr/local/bin/perl
#
#   Perl sample program
#

use Pg;                                          # load database routines

$conn = Pg::connectdb("dbname=test");            # connect to the database
                                                 # did the database connection fail?
die $conn->errorMessage unless PGRES_CONNECTION_OK eq $conn->status;

print "Enter a state code: ";                    # prompt user for a state code
$state_code = <STDIN>;
chomp $state_code;

$result = $conn->exec(                           # send the query
        "SELECT name \
         FROM statename \
         WHERE code = '$state_code'");
                                                 # did the query fail?
die $conn->errorMessage unless PGRES_TUPLES_OK eq $result->resultStatus;

while (@row = $result->fetchrow) {               # loop through all rows returned
        print @row, "\n";                        # print the value returned
}
```

Figure 17.9: Perl sample program

- No compilation required

- More powerful commands

- Automatic creation of variables

- Variables that can hold any type of data

17.10   Perl

Figure 17.9 shows our state code application in Perl. Perl is a good choice for writing scripts and small applications. It is popular for processing text files and generating dynamic Web pages using CGI (Common Gateway Interface). A Perl/DBI interface is also available.

```
#!/usr/local/pgsql/bin/pgtclsh
#
#    pgtclsh sample program
#

set conn [pg_connect test]                         ;# connect to the database

puts -nonewline "Enter a state code:  "            ;# prompt user for a state code
flush stdout
gets stdin state_code
                                                   ;# send the query
set res [pg_exec $conn \
        "SELECT name \
         FROM statename \
         WHERE code = '$state_code'"]

set ntups [pg_result $res -numTuples]

for {set i 0} {$i < $ntups} {incr i} {             ;# loop through all rows returned
        puts stdout [lindex [pg_result $res -getTuple $i] 0]   ;# print the value returned

}
pg_disconnect $conn                                ;# disconnect from the database
```

Figure 17.10: TCL sample program

17.11 TCL/TK (PGTCLSH/PGTKSH)

Figure 17.10 shows a TCL version of our application. This interface's specialty is accessing other toolkits and applications. The TK graphical interface toolkit is one example. TCL uses it for graphical applications. The TK toolkit has become so popular that several other scripting languages also use it as their graphical interface library.

17.12 Python

Python, an object-oriented scripting language, is considered to be a well-designed language, with code that is easy to read and maintain. Figure 17.11 shows the state code application written in Python. This interface's source code is located in pgsql/src/interfaces/python.

```
#! /usr/local/bin/python
#
#   Python sample program
#

import sys

from pg import DB                                # load database routines

conn = DB('test')                                # connect to the database

sys.stdout.write('Enter a state code:  ')        # prompt user for a state code
state_code = sys.stdin.readline()
state_code = state_code[:-1]

for name in conn.query(                          # send the query
        "SELECT name \
         FROM statename \
         WHERE code = '"+state_code+"'").getresult():
        sys.stdout.write('%s\n' % name)          # print the value returned
```

Figure 17.11: Python sample program

17.13 PHP

PHP is used for Web browser access to POSTGRESQL. With PHP, database commands can be embedded in Web pages.

Two Web pages are required for our state code application: one for data entry and another for display. Figure 17.12 shows a Web page that allows entry of a state code. Figure 17.13 shows a second Web page that performs a SELECT and displays the results. Normal Web page commands (HTML tags) begin with < and end with >. By contrast, PHP code begins with <? and ends with ?>. The PHP interface does not ship with POSTGRESQL, but can be downloaded from http://www.php.net.

17.14 Installing Scripting Languages

The interpreted languages described in this chapter all require a database interface to be installed into the language. This task is done by either recompiling the language or dynamically loading the interface into the language. The following list gives details about each interface:

Perl *Use* loads the POSTGRESQL interface into the Perl interpreter.

TCL/TK TCL/TK offers three interface options:

```
<!--
 -- PHP sample program -- input
 -->

<HTML>
<BODY>
<!-- prompt user for a state code -->
<FORM ACTION="<? echo $SCRIPT_NAME ?>/pg/sample2.phtml?state_code" method="POST">
Client Number:
<INPUT TYPE="text" name="state_code" value="<? echo $state_code ?>"
        maxlength=2 size=2>
<BR>
<INPUT TYPE="submit" value="Continue">
</FORM>
</BODY>
</HTML>
```

Figure 17.12: PHP sample program—input

- A prebuilt TCL interpreter called `pgtclsh`
- A prebuilt TCL/TK interpreter called `pgtksh`, like TCL/TK's `wish`
- A loadable library called `libpgtcl`

Python *Import* loads the POSTGRESQL interface into the Python interpreter.

PHP PHP must be recompiled to access POSTGRESQL.

17.15 Summary

All interface source code is located in `pgsql/src/interfaces`. Each interface includes sample source code for use in writing your own programs.

These interfaces allow the creation of professional database applications. Each interface has certain advantages. Some are easier, some are faster, some are more popular, and some work better in certain environments. Choosing an interface is often a difficult task. The information in this chapter should make that choice easier.

```
<!--
 -- PHP sample program -- output
 -->

<HTML>
<BODY>
<?
        $database = pg_Connect("", "", "", "", "test"); # connect to the database

        if (!$database)                               # did the database connection fail?
        {
                echo "Connection to database failed.";
                exit;
        }

        $result = pg_Exec($database,                  # send the query
                "SELECT name " .
                "FROM statename " .
                "WHERE code = '$state_code'");


        for ($i = 0; $i < pg_NumRows($result); $i++)  # loop through all rows returned
        {
                echo pg_Result($result,$i,0);         # print the value returned
                echo "<BR>";
        }
?>
</BODY>
</HTML>
```

Figure 17.13: PHP sample program—output

Chapter 18

Functions and Triggers

Chapter 17 focused on client-side programming—programs that run on the user's computer and interact with the POSTGRESQL database. Server-side functions, sometimes called *stored procedures*, run inside the database server rather than in the client application.

Several good uses for server-side functions exist. For example, if a function is used by many applications, it can be embedded into the database server. With this approach, each application no longer needs a copy of the function. Whenever the function is needed, the client can simply call it. Unlike client-side functions, server-side functions can be called within SQL queries. Also, functions centrally installed in the server are easily modified. When a function is changed, all client applications immediately start using the new version.

Table 9.3 on page 113 lists many preinstalled server-side functions, like *upper()* and *date_part()*. This chapter shows how to create your own functions. It also covers special server-side functions called triggers, which are called automatically when a table is modified.

18.1 Functions

Server-side functions can be written in several languages:

- SQL

- PL/PGSQL

- PL/TCL

- PL/Perl

- C

SQL and PL/PGSQL functions are covered in this chapter. C functions are more complex and are covered in Chapter 19.

```
test=> CREATE FUNCTION ftoc(float)
test-> RETURNS float
test-> AS 'SELECT ($1 - 32.0) * 5.0 / 9.0;'
test-> LANGUAGE 'sql';
CREATE
test=> SELECT ftoc(68);
 ftoc
------
   20
(1 row)
```

Figure 18.1: SQL *ftoc* function

18.2   SQL Functions

SQL functions allow you to name queries and store them in the database for later access. This section describes a variety of SQL functions of increasing complexity.

Functions are created with the CREATE FUNCTION command and removed with DROP FUNCTION. CREATE FUNCTION requires the following information:

- Function name

- Number of function arguments

- Data type of each argument

- Function return type

- Function action

- Language used by the function action

Figure 18.1 shows the creation of a simple SQL function to convert a temperature from Fahrenheit to centigrade degrees. It supplies the following information to CREATE FUNCTION:

- Function name is *ftoc*

- Function takes one argument of type *float*

- Function returns a *float*

- Function action is SELECT *($1 - 32.0) * 5.0 / 9.0;*

- Function language is SQL

```
test=> CREATE FUNCTION tax(numeric)
test-> RETURNS numeric
test-> AS 'SELECT ($1 * 0.06::numeric(8,2))::numeric(8,2);'
test-> LANGUAGE 'sql';
CREATE
test=> SELECT tax(100);
 tax
------
 6.00
(1 row)
```

Figure 18.2: SQL *tax* function

Although most functions return only one value, SQL functions can return multiple values using SETOF. Function actions can also contain INSERTs, UPDATEs, and DELETEs as well as multiple queries separated by semicolons.

The function action in *ftoc()* uses SELECT to perform a computation. It does not access any tables. The *$1* in the SELECT is automatically replaced by the first argument of the function call. If a second argument were present, it would be represented as *$2*.

When the query SELECT ftoc(68) is executed, it calls *ftoc()*. This function replaces *$1* with *68* and then makes the computation. In a sense, it executes a SELECT inside a SELECT. The outer SELECT calls *ftoc()*, and *ftoc()* uses its own SELECT to perform the computation.

Constants in the function contain decimal points, so floating-point computations are performed. Without them, division would be performed using integers. For example, the query SELECT 1/4 returns *0*, whereas SELECT 1.0/4.0 returns *0.25*.

Figure 18.2 shows an SQL server-side function to compute a tax. The casts to NUMERIC(8,2) are required because the result of the computation must be rounded to two decimal places. This function uses the more compact double-colon form of type casting, rather than CAST. Section 9.3 provides more information about type casting. SELECT tax(100) performs a simple computation, similar to *ftoc()*.

One powerful use of server-side functions is their use in SQL queries. Figure 18.3 shows the use of *tax()* with the *part* table from Figure 6.3. In this figure, three rows are inserted into the table, then a SELECT displays columns from the *part* table with additional computed columns showing the tax and the cost plus tax.

Figure 18.4 shows a more complex function that computes shipping charges. This function uses CASE to compute shipping charges based on weight. It calls *shipping()* to generate a detailed analysis of the tax and shipping charges associated with each part. It prints the part number, name, cost, tax, subtotal of cost plus tax, shipping charge, and total of cost, tax, and shipping charge. The SELECT uses *trim()* to remove trailing spaces and narrow the displayed result.

```
test=> CREATE TABLE part (
test(>                    part_id      INTEGER,
test(>                    name         CHAR(30),
test(>                    cost         NUMERIC(8,2),
test(>                    weight       FLOAT
test(> );
CREATE
test=> INSERT INTO part VALUES (637, 'cable', 14.29, 5);
INSERT 20867 1
test=> INSERT INTO part VALUES (638, 'sticker', 0.84, 1);
INSERT 20868 1
test=> INSERT INTO part VALUES (639, 'bulb', 3.68, 3);
INSERT 20869 1
test=> SELECT part_id,
test->        name,
test->        cost,
test->        tax(cost),
test->        cost + tax(cost) AS total
test-> FROM part
test-> ORDER BY part_id;
 part_id |            name             | cost  | tax  | total
---------+-----------------------------+-------+------+-------
     637 | cable                       | 14.29 | 0.86 | 15.15
     638 | sticker                     |  0.84 | 0.05 |  0.89
     639 | bulb                        |  3.68 | 0.22 |  3.90
(3 rows)
```

Figure 18.3: Recreation of the *part* table

```
test=> CREATE FUNCTION shipping(numeric)
test-> RETURNS numeric
test-> AS 'SELECT CASE
test'>                WHEN $1 < 2            THEN CAST(3.00 AS numeric(8,2))
test'>                WHEN $1 >= 2 AND $1 < 4 THEN CAST(5.00 AS numeric(8,2))
test'>                WHEN $1 >= 4           THEN CAST(6.00 AS numeric(8,2))
test'>            END;'
test-> LANGUAGE 'sql';
CREATE

test=> SELECT part_id,
test->          trim(name) AS name,
test->          cost,
test->          tax(cost),
test->          cost + tax(cost) AS subtotal,
test->          shipping(weight),
test->          cost + tax(cost) + shipping(weight) AS total
test-> FROM part
test-> ORDER BY part_id;
 part_id |  name    | cost  | tax  | subtotal | shipping | total
---------+---------+-------+------+----------+----------+-------
     637 | cable   | 14.29 | 0.86 |   15.15  |   6.00   | 21.15
     638 | sticker |  0.84 | 0.05 |    0.89  |   3.00   |  3.89
     639 | bulb    |  3.68 | 0.22 |    3.90  |   5.00   |  8.90
(3 rows)
```

Figure 18.4: SQL *shipping* function

```
test=> CREATE FUNCTION getstatename(text)
test-> RETURNS text
test-> AS 'SELECT CAST(name AS TEXT)
test->     FROM  statename
test->     WHERE code = $1;'
test-> LANGUAGE 'sql';
CREATE
test=> SELECT getstatename('AL');
        getstatename
--------------------------------
 Alabama
(1 row)
```

Figure 18.5: SQL *getstatename* function

If the tax rate or shipping charges change, you can easily modify the function to reflect the new rates. Simply use DROP FUNCTION to remove the function and then recreate it with new values. All user applications will automatically begin using the new version because the computations are embedded in the database, not in the user applications.

Server-side functions can also access database tables. Figure 18.5 shows an SQL function that internally accesses the *statename* table. It looks up the proper state name for the state code supplied to the function.

Figure 18.6 shows two queries which yield identical results, though using different approaches. The first query joins the *customer* and *statename* tables. The second query does a SELECT on *customer;* for each row, *getstatename()* is then called to find the customer's state name. The two queries yield the same result only if each customer row joins to exactly one *statename* row. If any *customer* rows did not join to a *statename* row or joined to many *statename* rows, the results would be different. Also, because the second query executes the SQL function for every row in *customer,* it works more slowly than the first query.

18.3 PL/PGSQL Functions

PL/PGSQL is another language intended for server-side functions. It is a true programming language. While SQL functions allow only argument substitution, PL/PGSQL includes features such as variables, conditional evaluation, and looping.

PL/PGSQL is not installed in each database by default. To use it in database *test*, you must install it by running `createlang plpgsql test` from the operating system prompt.

Figure 18.7 shows a PL/PGSQL version of the SQL function *getstatename* from Figure 18.5. It illustrates several PL/PGSQL features:

```
test=> SELECT customer.name, statename.name
test-> FROM   customer, statename
test-> WHERE  customer.state = statename.code
test-> ORDER BY customer.name;
            name            |            name
----------------------------+----------------------------
 Fleer Gearworks, Inc.      | Alabama
 Mark Middleton             | Indiana
 Mike Nichols               | Florida
(3 rows)


test=> SELECT customer.name, getstatename(customer.state)
test-> FROM   customer
test-> ORDER BY customer.name;
            name            |          getstatename
----------------------------+----------------------------
 Fleer Gearworks, Inc.      | Alabama
 Mark Middleton             | Indiana
 Mike Nichols               | Florida
(3 rows)
```

Figure 18.6: Getting state name using a join and a function

```
test=> CREATE FUNCTION getstatename2(text)
test-> RETURNS text
test-> AS 'DECLARE ret TEXT;
test'>     BEGIN
test'>         SELECT INTO ret CAST(name AS TEXT)
test'>         FROM   statename
test'>         WHERE code = $1;
test'>         RETURN ret;
test'>     END;'
test'> LANGUAGE 'plpgsql';
CREATE
```

Figure 18.7: PL/PGSQL version of *getstatename*

DECLARE Defines variables used in the function.

SELECT INTO A special form of SELECT that allows query results to be placed into variables. It should not be confused with SELECT * INTO.

RETURN Exits and returns a value from the function.

Figure 18.8 shows a more complicated PL/PGSQL function. It accepts a *text* argument and returns the argument in uppercase, with a space between each character. The next SELECT uses this result to display a report heading. This function illustrates the use of variables and WHILE loops in PL/PGSQL.

Figure 18.9 shows an even more complicated PL/PGSQL function. It takes a state name as a parameter and finds the proper state code. Because state names are longer than state codes, they are often misspelled. This function deals with misspellings by performing lookups in several ways. First, it attempts to find an exact match. If that attempt fails, it searches for a unique state name that matches the first 2, 4, or 6 characters, up to the length of the supplied string. If a unique state is not found, the function returns an empty string *('')*. Figure 18.10 shows several *getstatecode()* function calls. The *getstatecode()* function illustrates three new PL/PGSQL features:

%TYPE Data type that matches a database column.

RECORD Data type that stores the result of a SELECT.

FOUND A predefined BOOLEAN variable that represents the status of the previous SELECT INTO.

Many other PL/PGSQL features are covered in the *User's Manual* mentioned in Appendix A.2.

Figure 18.11 shows a PL/PGSQL function that provides a server-side interface for maintaining the *statename* table. The function *change_statename* performs INSERT, UPDATE, and DELETE operations on the *statename* table. The function is called with a state code and state name. If the state code is not in the table, it is inserted. If it already exists, the state name is updated. If the function is called with an empty state name *('')*, the state is deleted from the table. The function returns true *('t')* if *statename* was changed, and false *('f')* if *statename* was unmodified. Figure 18.12 shows examples of its use.

18.4 Triggers

Rules allow SQL queries to be executed when a table is accessed (see Section 13.6). Triggers offer an alternative way to perform actions on INSERT, UPDATE, or DELETE. They are ideal for checking or modifying a column value before it is added to the database.

Triggers and rules are implemented differently, however. Triggers call server-side functions for each modified row, whereas rules rewrite user queries or add queries. The former are ideal for checking or modifying a row before it is added to the database. The latter are ideal when the action affects other tables.

```
test=> CREATE FUNCTION spread(text)
test-> RETURNS text
test-> AS 'DECLARE
test'>         str text;
test'>         ret text;
test'>         i   integer;
test'>         len integer;
test'>
test'>     BEGIN
test'>         str := upper($1);
test'>         ret := '''';            -- start with zero length
test'>         i   := 1;
test'>         len := length(str);
test'>         WHILE i <= len LOOP
test'>             ret := ret || substr(str, i, 1) || '' '';
test'>             i := i + 1;
test'>         END LOOP;
test'>         RETURN ret;
test'>     END;'
test-> LANGUAGE 'plpgsql';
CREATE
test=> SELECT spread('Major Financial Report');
                  spread
-----------------------------------------------
 M A J O R   F I N A N C I A L   R E P O R T
(1 row)
```

Figure 18.8: PL/PGSQL *spread* function

```
test=> CREATE FUNCTION getstatecode(text)
test-> RETURNS text
test-> AS 'DECLARE
test'>        state_str   statename.name%TYPE;
test'>        statename_rec record;
test'>        i          integer;
test'>        len        integer;
test'>        matches     record;
test'>        search_str text;
test'>
test'>    BEGIN
test'>        state_str := initcap($1);              -- capitalization match column
test'>        len := length(trim($1));
test'>        i   := 2;
test'>
test'>        SELECT INTO statename_rec *            -- first try for an exact match
test'>        FROM    statename
test'>        WHERE   name = state_str;
test'>        IF FOUND
test'>        THEN    RETURN statename_rec.code;
test'>        END IF;
test'>
test'>        WHILE i <= len LOOP                    -- test 2,4,6,... chars for match
test'>            search_str = trim(substr(state_str, 1, i)) || ''%'';
test'>            SELECT INTO matches COUNT(*)
test'>            FROM    statename
test'>            WHERE   name LIKE search_str;
test'>
test'>            IF matches.count = 0              -- no matches, failure
test'>            THEN    RETURN NULL;
test'>            END IF;
test'>            IF matches.count = 1             -- exactly one match, return it
test'>            THEN
test'>                SELECT INTO statename_rec *
test'>                FROM    statename
test'>                WHERE   name LIKE search_str;
test'>                IF FOUND
test'>                THEN    RETURN statename_rec.code;
test'>                END IF;
test'>            END IF;
test'>            i := i + 2;                       -- >1 match, try 2 more chars
test'>        END LOOP;
test'>        RETURN '''' ;
test'>    END;'
test-> LANGUAGE 'plpgsql';
```

Figure 18.9: PL/PGSQL *getstatecode* function

```
test=> SELECT getstatecode('Alabama');
 getstatecode
--------------
 AL
(1 row)

test=> SELECT getstatecode('ALAB');
 getstatecode
--------------
 AL
(1 row)

test=> SELECT getstatecode('Al');
 getstatecode
--------------
 AL
(1 row)

test=> SELECT getstatecode('Ail');
 getstatecode
--------------

(1 row)
```

Figure 18.10: Calls to *getstatecode* function

```
test=> CREATE FUNCTION change_statename(char(2), char(30))
test-> RETURNS boolean
test-> AS 'DECLARE
test'>     state_code ALIAS FOR $1;
test'>     state_name ALIAS FOR $2;
test'>     statename_rec RECORD;
test'>
test'>     BEGIN
test'>         IF length(state_code) = 0                 -- no state code, failure
test'>         THEN    RETURN ''f'';
test'>         ELSE
test'>             IF length(state_name) != 0            -- is INSERT or UPDATE?
test'>             THEN
test'>                 SELECT INTO statename_rec *
test'>                 FROM    statename
test'>                 WHERE   code = state_code;
test'>                 IF NOT FOUND                       -- is state not in table?
test'>                 THEN    INSERT INTO statename
test'>                         VALUES (state_code, state_name);
test'>                 ELSE    UPDATE statename
test'>                         SET     name = state_name
test'>                         WHERE   code = state_code;
test'>                 END IF;
test'>                 RETURN ''t'';
test'>             ELSE                                   -- is DELETE
test'>                 SELECT INTO statename_rec *
test'>                 FROM    statename
test'>                 WHERE   code = state_code;
test'>                 IF FOUND
test'>                 THEN    DELETE FROM statename
test'>                         WHERE code = state_code;
test'>                         RETURN ''t'';
test'>                 ELSE    RETURN ''f'';
test'>                 END IF;
test'>             END IF;
test'>         END IF;
test'>     END;'
test-> LANGUAGE 'plpgsql';
```

Figure 18.11: PL/PGSQL *change_statename* function

```
test=> DELETE FROM statename;
DELETE 1
test=> SELECT change_statename('AL','Alabama');
 change_statename
------------------
 t
(1 row)


test=> SELECT * FROM statename;
 code |              name
------+-------------------------------
 AL   | Alabama
(1 row)


test=> SELECT change_statename('AL','Bermuda');
 change_statename
------------------
 t
(1 row)


test=> SELECT * FROM statename;
 code |              name
------+-------------------------------
 AL   | Bermuda
(1 row)


test=> SELECT change_statename('AL','');
 change_statename
------------------
 t
(1 row)


test=> SELECT change_statename('AL','');    -- row was already deleted
 change_statename
------------------
 f
(1 row)
```

Figure 18.12: Examples using *change_statename()*

With triggers, special server-side functions can be called every time a row is modified. These special functions can be written in any server-side language except SQL. They control the action taken by the query. For example, they can reject certain values or modify values before they are added to the database. Triggers that return NULL cause the operation that caused the trigger to be ignored.

Server-side trigger functions are special because they have predefined variables to access the row that caused the trigger. For INSERT triggers, the variable *new* represents the row being inserted. For DELETE, the variable *old* represents the row being deleted. For UPDATE, triggers can access the pre-UPDATE row using *old* and the post-UPDATE row using *new*. These variables are the same as the *old* and *new* variables employed in rules.

Figure 18.13 shows the creation of a special server-side trigger function called *trigger_insert_-update_statename*. This function uses the *new* RECORD variable to perform the following actions:

- Reject a state code that is not exactly two alphabetic characters

- Reject a state name that contains nonalphabetic characters

- Reject a state name less than three characters in length

- Uppercase the state code

- Capitalize the state name

If a user enters invalid data, RAISE EXCEPTION aborts the current query and displays an appropriate error message. Validity checks can also be performed using CHECK constraints (see Section 14.5).

Uppercase and capitalization occur by simply assigning values to the *new* variable. The function return type is *opaque* because *new* is returned by the function.

CREATE TRIGGER causes *trigger_insert_update_statename()* to be called every time a row is inserted or updated in *statename*. The remaining queries in Figure 18.13 show three rejected INSERTs as well as a successful INSERT that is properly uppercased and capitalized by the function.

Trigger functions can be quite complicated. They can perform loops, SQL queries, and any operation supported in server-side functions. See the CREATE_TRIGGER and DROP_TRIGGER manual pages for additional information.

18.5   Summary

Server-side functions allow programs to be embedded into the database. These programs can be accessed from client applications and used in database queries. Moving code *into the server* allows for increased efficiency, maintainability, and consistency. Triggers are special server-side functions that are called when a table is modified.

```
test=> CREATE FUNCTION trigger_insert_update_statename()
test-> RETURNS opaque
test-> AS 'BEGIN
test'>        IF new.code !~ ''^[A-Za-z][A-Za-z]$''
test'>        THEN    RAISE EXCEPTION ''State code must be two alphabetic characters.'';
test'>        END IF;
test'>        IF new.name !~ ''^[A-Za-z ]*$''
test'>        THEN    RAISE EXCEPTION ''State name must be only alphabetic characters.'';
test'>        END IF;
test'>        IF length(trim(new.name)) < 3
test'>        THEN    RAISE EXCEPTION ''State name must longer than two characters.'';
test'>        END IF;
test'>        new.code = upper(new.code);            -- uppercase statename.code
test'>        new.name = initcap(new.name);          -- capitalize statename.name
test'>        RETURN new;
test'>    END;'
test-> LANGUAGE 'plpgsql';
CREATE

test=> CREATE TRIGGER trigger_statename
test-> BEFORE INSERT OR UPDATE
test-> ON statename
test-> FOR EACH ROW
test-> EXECUTE PROCEDURE trigger_insert_update_statename();
CREATE

test=> DELETE FROM statename;
DELETE 1
test=> INSERT INTO statename VALUES ('a', 'alabama');
ERROR:  State code must be two alphabetic characters.
test=> INSERT INTO statename VALUES ('al', 'alabama2');
ERROR:  State name must be only alphabetic characters.
test=> INSERT INTO statename VALUES ('al', 'al');
ERROR:  State name must longer than two characters.
test=> INSERT INTO statename VALUES ('al', 'alabama');
INSERT 292898 1
test=> SELECT * FROM statename;
 code |            name
------+-------------------------------
 AL   | Alabama
(1 row)
```

Figure 18.13: Trigger creation

Chapter 19

Extending POSTGRESQL Using C

Although POSTGRESQL offers a large number of functions, operators, data types, and aggregates, sometimes users may still need to create their own. Chapter 18 showed how to create functions in languages other than C. This chapter covers C functions and the creation of custom operators, data types, and aggregates that behave just like the ones already present in POSTGRESQL.

Extending POSTGRESQL in this way involves several steps:

1. Write C code to implement the new functionality.

2. Compile the C code into an object file that contains CPU instructions.

3. Issue CREATE FUNCTION commands to register the new functions.

4. Issue the proper commands if creating operators, data types, or aggregates:

   - CREATE OPERATOR
   - CREATE TYPE
   - CREATE AGGREGATE

The full details of extending POSTGRESQL are beyond the scope of this book. This chapter will therefore provide just an overview of this topic. The *Programmer's Manual* mentioned in Appendix A.2 has more detailed information.

19.1   Write the C Code

The best way to add a new function, operator, data type, or aggregate is to start with a copy of a file from the POSTGRESQL source directory pgsql/src/backend/utils/adt. Start with a file that contains functions similar to the ones you need, but make sure that your new function names are unique.

```
#include "postgres.h"
double *ctof(double *deg)
{
    double *ret = palloc(sizeof(double));

    *ret = (*deg * 9.0 / 5.0) + 32.0;
    return ret;
}
```

Figure 19.1: C *ctof* function

For example, Chapter 18 included a *ftoc()* SQL function that converted a temperature from Fahrenheit to centigrade degrees. Figure 19.1 shows a C function that converts from centigrade to Fahrenheit.

While writing C functions, you may find it necessary to execute SQL queries from inside the function. The server programming interface (SPI) allows C functions to execute SQL queries and process results from within these functions.

19.2   Compile the C Code

The next step is to compile the C file into an object file that contains CPU instructions. As part of this step, you must create a special object file that can be *dynamically linked* into the POSTGRESQL server. Many operating systems require special flags to create an object file that can be dynamically linked. The best way to find the required flags is to go to pgsql/src/test/regress and type make clean and then make regress.so.[1] This command will display the compile commands used to generate the dynamically linkable object file regress.so. The -*I* compile flags allow searching for include files. Other flags are used for generating dynamic object files; use them to compile your C code into a dynamically linkable object file. You may need to consult your operating system documentation for assistance in locating the proper flags.

19.3   Register the New Functions

Now that you have created a dynamically linkable object file, you must register its functions with POSTGRESQL. The CREATE FUNCTION command registers a new function by storing information in the database. Figure 19.2 shows the CREATE FUNCTION command for *ctof.* The function *ctof* takes

---

[1]Some operating systems may use gmake rather than make. Also, some operating systems will use regress.o rather than regress.so.

```
test=> CREATE FUNCTION ctof(float)
test-> RETURNS float
test-> AS '/users/pgman/sample/ctof.so'
test-> LANGUAGE 'C';
CREATE
```

Figure 19.2: Create function *ctof*

```
test=> SELECT ctof(20);
 ctof
------
   68
(1 row)
```

Figure 19.3: Calling function *ctof*

a *float* argument and returns a *float*. The SQL data type *float* is the same as the C type *double* used in *ctof()*. The dynamically linkable object file is specified as /users/pgman/sample/ctof.so and is written in the C language.

A single object file can contain many functions. You must use CREATE FUNCTION to register each function you want to access from POSTGRESQL. CREATE FUNCTION also allows nonobject files to be used as functions (see Chapter 18).

Once the functions are registered, they can be called just like POSTGRESQL internal functions. Figure 19.3 shows the *ctof()* function used in a SELECT statement. See CREATE_FUNCTION for more information.

19.4 Create Operators, Types, and Aggregates

Optionally, you can build operators, types, and aggregates using functions. CREATE OPERATOR, CREATE TYPE, and CREATE AGGREGATE register that a set of functions should behave as an operator, type, or aggregate. They name the new operator, type, or aggregate, and then call the supplied function whenever its name is accessed. See CREATE_OPERATOR, CREATE_TYPE, and CREATE_-AGGREGATE for more information.

19.5 Summary

Extending POSTGRESQL is a complicated process. This chapter has covered only the basic concepts. Refer to the *Programmer's Manual* for more detailed information.

Chapter 20

Administration

This chapter covers a variety of administrative tasks. The chapter assumes POSTGRESQL is installed and running. If it is not, see Appendix B.

20.1 Files

/var/lib/pgsql

When POSTGRESQL is installed, it creates files in its home directory, typically /usr/local/pgsql. This directory holds all the files needed by POSTGRESQL in various subdirectories:

/bin POSTGRESQL command-line programs, such as psql.

/data Configuration files and tables shared by all databases. For example, *pg_shadow* is a table shared by all databases.

/data/base A subdirectory for each database. Using the du and ls commands, administrators can display the amount of disk space used by each database, table, or index.

/doc POSTGRESQL documentation.

/include Include files used by various programming languages.

/lib Libraries used by various programming languages. This subdirectory also contains files used during initialization and sample configuration files that can be copied to /data and modified.

/man POSTGRESQL manual pages.

var
|
lib
backups/ data/   initdb.i18n

20.2 Creating Users

To create new users, you run createuser from an operating system prompt. Initially, only the POSTGRESQL superuser, typically *postgres*, can create new users. Other users can be given permission to create new users and databases.

223

```
$ createuser demouser1          -- ① Method to create a user
Shall the new user be allowed to create databases? (y/n) n
Shall the new user be allowed to create more new users? (y/n) n
CREATE USER
$ psql test
Welcome to psql, the PostgreSQL interactive terminal.

Type:  \copyright for distribution terms
       \h for help with SQL commands
       \? for help on internal slash commands
       \g or terminate with semicolon to execute query
       \q to quit

test=> CREATE USER demouser2;     -- ② method to create a user
CREATE USER
test=> ALTER USER demouser2 CREATEDB;
ALTER USER
test=> CREATE GROUP demogroup WITH USER demouser1, demouser2;
CREATE GROUP
test=> CREATE TABLE grouptest (col INTEGER);
CREATE
test=> GRANT ALL on grouptest TO GROUP demogroup;
CHANGE
test=> \connect test demouser2
You are now connected to database test as user demouser2.
test=> \q
```

Figure 20.1: Examples of user administration

POSTGRESQL user names do not have to be operating system users. For installations using database password authentication, a `createuser` flag allows passwords to be assigned.

Users are removed with `dropuser`. The CREATE USER, ALTER USER, and DROP USER commands are available in SQL.

POSTGRESQL also supports the creation of groups using CREATE GROUP in SQL. GRANT permissions can be specified using these groups.

Figure 20.1 shows examples of user administration commands. In the figure, one user is created from the command line, a second user is created in `psql`, and a user is modified. Next, a group is created and given table permissions. Finally, the program reconnects to the database as a different user, which is possible because the site has local users configured with *trust* access. This issue is covered in Section 20.4.

These commands can be performed only by a user with *create user* privileges. More information about each command can be found in the manual pages.

```
$ createdb demodb1
CREATE DATABASE
$ psql test
Welcome to psql, the PostgreSQL interactive terminal.

Type:  \copyright for distribution terms
       \h for help with SQL commands
       \? for help on internal slash commands
       \g or terminate with semicolon to execute query
       \q to quit

test=> CREATE DATABASE demodb2;
CREATE DATABASE
test=> DROP DATABASE demodb1;
DROP DATABASE
test=> \connect demodb2
You are now connected to database demodb2.
demodb2=> \q
```

Figure 20.2: Examples of database creation and removal

20.3 Creating Databases

To create new databases, you run createdb from an operating system prompt. Initially, only the POSTGRESQL superuser can create new databases. Other users can be given permission to create new databases.

The createdb program creates a new database by making a copy of the *template1* database. This database is created when POSTGRESQL is first initialized. Any modifications to *template1* will appear in subsequently created databases.

Databases are removed with dropdb. The CREATE DATABASE and DROP DATABASE commands are also available in SQL.

Figure 20.2 shows one database created from the command line and another one created through psql. A database is then destroyed, and a connection made to a new database. Additional information about each command can be found in the manual pages.

20.4 Access Configuration

POSTGRESQL allows administrators to control database access. Access can be granted based on the database, user, or TCP/IP network address. By default, POSTGRESQL allows database access only to users logged into the computer running the database server. To enable network access, the postmaster must be started with the *-i* flag.

Database access is controlled via the `data/pg_hba.conf` file, which is located in the POSTGRESQL home directory. It contains several types of configuration entries:

Local

Local entries control access by users logged into the same computer as the database server. *Local* connections use Unix domain sockets. The following per-database authentication options are available:

- *trust*—Trust users connecting to this database.

- *password*—Require a password of users connecting to this database.

- *crypt*—Like *password,* except send the password in an encrypted manner. This method is more secure than *password.*

- *reject*—Reject all connection requests for this database.

Host and Hostssl

Host and *hostssl* entries control TCP/IP network access. They include host and netmask fields. These entries support all of the *local* options, plus the following:

- *ident*—Use a remote `ident` server for authentication.

- *krb4*—Use Kerberos IV authentication.

- *krb5*—Use Kerberos V authentication.

These entries are effective only if the `postmaster` uses the *-i* option. *Hostssl* controls access via the Secure Socket Layer (SSL) if enabled in the server.

User Mappings

By default, passwords used by *password* and *crypt* appear in the *pg_shadow* table. This table is managed by `createuser` and ALTER USER.

In addition, *password* takes an optional argument that specifies a secondary password file which overrides *pg_shadow.* This file contains user names and passwords of people who are allowed to connect. Using this method, a set of users can be given access to certain databases. See the `pg_passwd` manual page for more information on creating secondary password files. Currently, *crypt* does not support secondary password files.

The *ident* entry also takes an optional argument that specifies a special map name to map *ident* user names to database user names. The file `data/pg_ident.conf` records these mappings.

Examples

Local entries are configured on per-database hosts. A database entry of *all* applies to all databases. In data/pg_hba.conf, the lines

```
local      all                                       trust
host       all        127.0.0.1      255.255.255.255  trust
```

cause all local users to be trusted. The first line affects users connecting via Unix domain sockets; the second line controls local users connecting to the same machine by TCP/IP. The local machine is accessed as TCP/IP address *127.0.0.1 (localhost)*.

Both *host* and *hostssl* entries require the additional specification of host addresses and network masks. The lines

```
host       all        192.168.34.0   255.255.255.255  crypt
host       all        192.168.90.0   255.255.255.0    password
```

force all users from host *192.168.34.0* and network *192.168.90.0* to provide passwords. *Crypt* encrypts the passwords that are sent; *password* sends passwords over the network without encryption. The line

```
host       all        192.168.98.0   255.255.255.255  password finance
```

is similar to the previous entries, except that it uses the user names/passwords stored in *finance* to authenticate users.

The lines

```
host       sales      192.168.7.12   255.255.255.255  ident
host       sales      192.168.7.64   255.255.255.255  ident support
```

use ident on the remote machine to verify the users connecting to database *sales* from the hosts *192.168.7.12* and *192.168.7.64*. The second entry uses the *support* user name mapping in data/pg_- ident.conf.

Connections from hosts and networks not appearing in the file are rejected. For more information, see the file data/pg_hba.conf and the *Administrator's Guide* discussed in Appendix A.2.

For database client applications, the environment variables PGHOST, PGPORT, PGUSER, PGPASS- WORD, PGDATESTYLE, PGTZ, PGCLIENTENCODING, and PGDATABASE are helpful for setting default connection parameters and options. The POSTGRESQL documentation provides more information about them.

20.5   Backup and Restore

Database backups allow databases to be restored if a disk drive fails, a table is accidentally dropped, or a database file is accidentally deleted. If the databases are idle, a standard file system backup

```
$ pg_dump test > /tmp/test.dump
$ createdb newtest
CREATE DATABASE
$ psql newtest < /tmp/test.dump
```

Figure 20.3: Making a new copy of database *test*

will suffice as a POSTGRESQL backup. If the databases are active, you must use the pg_dumpall utility to create a reliable backup. This utility outputs a consistent snapshot of all databases into a file that can be included in a file system backup. In fact, once a pg_dumpall file has been created, you do not need to back up the /data/base database files. A few configuration files in /data, such as data/pg_hba.conf, should be included in a file system backup because they do not appear in the pg_dumpall file. The pg_dump utility can dump a single POSTGRESQL database.

To restore from a backup using a pg_dumpall file, POSTGRESQL must be initialized, any manually edited configuration files restored to /data, and the database dump file run by psql. This action will recreate and reload all databases.

Individual databases can be reloaded from pg_dump files by creating a new database and loading it using psql. For example, Figure 20.3 creates an exact copy of the *test* database. It dumps the contents of the database into the file /tmp/test.dump. A new database called *newtest* is created, then the dump file is loaded into the new database.

Dump files contain ordinary SQL queries and COPY commands. Because the files contain database information, they should be created so that only authorized users have permission to read them. See the pg_dump and pg_dumpall manual pages for more information about these commands.

20.6   Server Start-up and Shutdown

The POSTGRESQL server uses two distinct programs: postmaster and postgres. The postmaster process accepts all requests for database access. It does authentication and starts a postgres process to handle the connection. The postgres process executes user queries and returns results. Figure 20.4 illustrates this relationship.

POSTGRESQL sites normally have many postgres processes, but only one postmaster process. One postgres process exists for every open database session.

Once administrators start the postmaster, the postmaster will start postgres backends as connection requests arrive. The postmaster can be started from either the command line or a script. The operating system start-up scripts can even be modified to start the postmaster automatically.

A third way to start the postmaster is using pg_ctl. This utility allows easy starting and stopping of the postmaster. See the pg_ctl manual page for more information.

To stop the postmaster, you can send the process a signal using kill, or use pg_ctl.

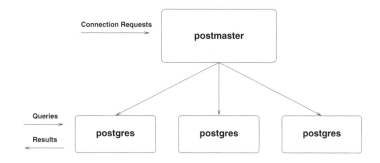

Figure 20.4: Postmaster and postgres processes

20.7 Monitoring

Both postmaster and postgres produce useful information for administrators. They have many flags to control the information they output. If desired, they can show user connection information, SQL queries, and detailed performance statistics.

When the postmaster starts, its output should be sent to a file in the POSTGRESQL home directory. That file can then be used to monitor database activity. See the postmaster and postgres manual pages for a complete list of output options. To specify the flags to be passed to each postgres process, use the postmaster -*o* flag.

Another way to monitor the database is by using ps. The ps operating system command displays information about processes, including data about the postmaster and postgres processes. This tool is helpful for analyzing POSTGRESQL activity, particularly for diagnosing problems. The ps command can display information about the following aspects of a process:

- Current CPU usage

- Total CPU usage

- Start time

- Memory usage

- Disk operations (on some operating systems)

Each operating system uses different ps flags to output these values. A typical display is

```
                                      ┌ blocks read
                                      ┌ blocks written
USER       PID %CPU    TIME STARTED   VSZ INBLK OUBLK COMMAND
...
postgres 18923 45.4  0:27.79  1:15PM  2140   34    1 /usr/local/postgres/ ...
```

In this case, process 18923 is using 45.4% of the CPU, has used 27.79 seconds of CPU time, was started at 1:15 P.M., has read 34 blocks, and has written 1 block.

To identify who is using each postgres process, most operating systems allow ps to display the following connection information:

- User name

- User's network address

- Database

- SQL command keyword (SELECT, INSERT, UPDATE, DELETE, CREATE, idle, …)

The ps command displays this information next to the name of each postgres process. A typical display is

```
    PID  TT  STAT     TIME COMMAND
    ...                                                    user       host    db    cmd
    18923 ??  S       0:27.79 /usr/local/postgres/bin/postgres demouser localhost test SELECT
    ...
```

In this example, demouser, using process ID 18923, is connecting from the local machine to database *test* and executing a SELECT. Administrators can use ps to analyze who is connected to each database, the query command being run, and the system resources used.

20.8 Performance

Chapter 11 covered the performance of SQL queries. This chapter discusses more general performance considerations.

One of the most important administrative tasks is the scheduling of the vacuumdb -a command, which vacuums all databases. It should be run when the databases are least busy. Section 11.4 describes the purpose of vacuuming. Vacuum analyze should also be performed periodically; it is covered in Section 11.5. The vacuumdb command can perform analyzing as well. See the vacuumdb manual page for more information.

Both postmaster and postgres have several flags that can improve performance. In POSTGRESQL release 7.0 and earlier, the postgres *-F* flag prevents the database server from flushing all data to disk at the end of each transaction. This improves performance, but if the operating system abnormally shuts down, the database can be left in an inconsistent state. Later releases may not use this flag.

The postmaster *-B* flag controls the amount of shared buffer memory allocated. The postgres *-S* flag controls the amount of sort memory allocated. While these flags consume system resources, they also improve performance by reducing disk access.

Name	Contents
pg_aggregate	aggregates
pg_attribute	columns
pg_class	tables
pg_database	databases
pg_description	comments
pg_group	groups
pg_index	indexes
pg_log	transaction status
pg_operator	operators
pg_proc	functions
pg_rewrite	rules and views
pg_shadow	users
pg_trigger	triggers
pg_type	types

Table 20.1: Commonly used system tables

You can also improve database performance by moving databases to different disk drives. This strategy spreads disk access among multiple drives. The initlocation utility allows new database locations to be created on different drives; createdb can then use these locations for new databases.

POSTGRESQL stores tables and indexes in operating system files. Using operating system symbolic links, you can move databases, tables, and indexes to different disk drives, which often improves performance.

20.9 System Tables

A great deal of data is stored in POSTGRESQL system tables. The names of these tables begin with *pg_*. The tables contain information about data types, functions, operators, databases, users, and groups. Table 20.1 shows the most commonly used tables.

The *pg_log* table is a binary file rather than a real table. The *pg_shadow* table contains user passwords and is not visible to ordinary users. The *pg_user* table (not listed in Table 20.1) is a view of *pg_shadow* that does not display the password field. Several other system views are available as well. Most system tables are joined using OIDs (see Section 7.1). Psql's \dS command lists all system tables and views.

20.10   Internationalization

POSTGRESQL supports several features important for international use. Multibyte encoding allows non-ASCII character sets to be accurately stored in the database. It can be specified during POSTGRESQL initialization, at database creation, or inside psql. POSTGRESQL can also be installed to support international character sets, called locales.

POSTGRESQL can read and display dates in a variety of formats. The default date format can be specified as a postgres flag, using SET DATESTYLE from inside psql, or using the PGDATESTYLE environment variable.

20.11   Upgrading

The process of upgrading from previous POSTGRESQL releases is covered in the documentation distributed with each version. Sometimes the pg_upgrade utility can be used. In other cases, a pg_dumpall and reload are required.

20.12   Summary

This chapter merely summarizes the basic administrative tasks. Each utility has many other options not covered here.

Administration can prove quite challenging. It takes skill and experience. This chapter has supplied enough information that you should be able to start exploring topics of interest. The manual pages and *Administrator's Guide* mentioned in Appendix A.2 contain even more valuable information.

Appendix A

Additional Resources

A.1 Mailing List Support

There are a variety of mailing lists available for discussing POSTGRESQL topics, getting help, and reporting bugs. This information can be found at `http://www.postgresql.org/lists/mailing-list.html`.

A.2 Supplied Documentation

POSTGRESQL comes with a variety of documentation. There is a general user guide, and specific guides for administrators and programmers. There is also a tutorial. These can be all found at:

`http://www.postgresql.org/docs/index.html`.

A.3 Commercial Support

Currently, commercial support is provided by three companies:

- POSTGRESQL, Inc., `http://www.pgsql.com/`.

- Software Research Associates, `http://osb.sra.co.jp/`.

- Great Bridge LLC, `http://www.greatbridge.com/`.

A.4 Modifying the Source Code

POSTGRESQL allows users access to all of its source code. The Web page is at

`http://www.postgresql.org/docs/index.html`

It has a *Developers* section with many developer resources.

A.5   Frequently Asked Questions (FAQs)

Frequently Asked Questions (FAQ) for POSTGRESQL
Last updated: Wed Jul 26 13:31:44 EDT 2000
Current maintainer: Bruce Momjian (pgman@candle.pha.pa.us)
The most recent version of this document can be viewed at
`http://www.PostgreSQL.org/docs/faq-english.html`.
Platform-specific questions are answered at `http://www.PostgreSQL.org/docs/`.

General Questions

1.1) What is POSTGRESQL?
1.2) What's the copyright on POSTGRESQL?
1.3) What Unix platforms does POSTGRESQL run on?
1.4) What non-Unix ports are available?
1.5) Where can I get POSTGRESQL?
1.6) Where can I get support?
1.7) What is the latest release?
1.8) What documentation is available?
1.9) How do I find out about known bugs or missing features?
1.10) How can I learn SQL?
1.11) Is POSTGRESQL Y2K compliant?
1.12) How do I join the development team?
1.13) How do I submit a bug report?
1.14) How does POSTGRESQL compare to other DBMS's?

User Client Questions

2.1) Are there ODBC drivers for POSTGRESQL?
2.2) What tools are available for hooking POSTGRESQL to Web pages?
2.3) Does POSTGRESQL have a graphical user interface? A report generator? An embedded query language interface?
2.4) What languages are available to communicate with POSTGRESQL?

Administrative Questions

3.1) Why does *initdb* fail?
3.2) How do I install POSTGRESQL somewhere other than */usr/local/pgsql?*
3.3) When I start the *postmaster*, I get a *Bad System Call* or core dumped message. Why?
3.4) When I try to start the *postmaster*, I get *IpcMemoryCreate* errors. Why?
3.5) When I try to start the *postmaster*, I get *IpcSemaphoreCreate* errors. Why?

3.6) How do I prevent other hosts from accessing my POSTGRESQL database?

3.7) Why can't I connect to my database from another machine?

3.8) Why can't I access the database as the *root* user?

3.9) All my servers crash under concurrent table access. Why?

3.10) How do I tune the database engine for better performance?

3.11) What debugging features are available?

3.12) I get *"Sorry, too many clients"* when trying to connect. Why?

3.13) What are the *pg_sorttempNNN.NN* files in my database directory?

Operational Questions

4.1) Why is the system confused about commas, decimal points, and date formats?

4.2) What is the exact difference between binary cursors and normal cursors?

4.3) How do I SELECT only the first few rows of a query?

4.4) How do I get a list of tables or other things I can see in *psql?*

4.5) How do you remove a column from a table?

4.6) What is the maximum size for a row, table, database?

4.7) How much database disk space is required to store data from a typical text file?

4.8) How do I find out what indices or operations are defined in the database?

4.9) My queries are slow or don't make use of the indexes. Why?

4.10) How do I see how the query optimizer is evaluating my query?

4.11) What is an R-tree index?

4.12) What is Genetic Query Optimization?

4.13) How do I do regular expression searches and case-insensitive regular expression searches?

4.14) In a query, how do I detect if a field is NULL?

4.15) What is the difference between the various character types?

4.16.1) How do I create a serial/auto-incrementing field?

4.16.2) How do I get the value of a SERIAL insert?

4.16.3) Don't *currval()* and *nextval()* lead to a race condition with other users?

4.17) What is an OID? What is a TID?

4.18) What is the meaning of some of the terms used in POSTGRESQL?

4.19) Why do I get the error "*FATAL: palloc failure: memory exhausted?*"

4.20) How do I tell what POSTGRESQL version I am running?

4.21) My large-object operations get *invalid large obj descriptor.* Why?

4.22) How do I create a column that will default to the current time?

4.23) Why are my subqueries using IN so slow?

4.24) How do I do an *outer* join?

Extending POSTGRESQL

5.1) I wrote a user-defined function. When I run it in *psql,* why does it dump core?

5.2) What does the message *"NOTICE:PortalHeapMemoryFree: 0x402251d0 not in alloc set!"* mean?

5.3) How can I contribute some nifty new types and functions to POSTGRESQL?

5.4) How do I write a C function to return a tuple?

5.5) I have changed a source file. Why does the recompile not see the change?

General Questions

1.1) What is POSTGRESQL?

POSTGRESQL is an enhancement of the Postgres management system, a next-generation DBMS research prototype. While POSTGRESQL retains the powerful data model and rich data types of Postgres, it replaces the POSTQUEL query language with an extended subset of SQL. POSTGRESQL is free and the complete source is available.

POSTGRESQL development is performed by a team of Internet developers who all subscribe to the POSTGRESQL development mailing list. The current coordinator is Marc G. Fournier (scrappy@PostgreSQL.org). (See below on how to join). This team is now responsible for all development of POSTGRESQL.

The authors of POSTGRESQL 1.01 were Andrew Yu and Jolly Chen. Many others have contributed to the porting, testing, debugging, and enhancement of the code. The original Postgres code, from which POSTGRESQL is derived, was the effort of many graduate students, undergraduate students, and staff programmers working under the direction of Professor Michael Stonebraker at the University of California, Berkeley.

The original name of the software at Berkeley was Postgres. When SQL functionality was added in 1995, its name was changed to Postgres95. The name was changed at the end of 1996 to POSTGRESQL.

It is pronounced *Post-Gres-Q-L.*

1.2) What's the copyright on POSTGRESQL?

POSTGRESQL is subject to the following COPYRIGHT:

POSTGRESQL Data Base Management System

Portions copyright (c) 1996-2000, PostgreSQL, Inc Portions Copyright (c) 1994-6 Regents of the University of California

Permission to use, copy, modify, and distribute this software and its documentation for any purpose, without fee, and without a written agreement is hereby granted, provided that the above copyright notice and this paragraph and the following two paragraphs appear in all copies.

IN NO EVENT SHALL THE UNIVERSITY OF CALIFORNIA BE LIABLE TO ANY PARTY FOR DIRECT, INDIRECT, SPECIAL, INCIDENTAL, OR CONSEQUENTIAL DAMAGES, IN-CLUDING LOST PROFITS, ARISING OUT OF THE USE OF THIS SOFTWARE AND ITS DOCUMENTATION, EVEN IF THE UNIVERSITY OF CALIFORNIA HAS BEEN ADVISED OF THE POSSIBILITY OF SUCH DAMAGE.

THE UNIVERSITY OF CALIFORNIA SPECIFICALLY DISCLAIMS ANY WARRANTIES, IN-CLUDING, BUT NOT LIMITED TO, THE IMPLIED WARRANTIES OF MERCHANTABILITY AND FITNESS FOR A PARTICULAR PURPOSE. THE SOFTWARE PROVIDED HEREUNDER IS ON AN "AS IS" BASIS, AND THE UNIVERSITY OF CALIFORNIA HAS NO OBLIGATIONS TO PROVIDE MAINTENANCE, SUPPORT, UPDATES, ENHANCEMENTS, OR MODIFICA-TIONS.

1.3) What Unix platforms does POSTGRESQL run on?

The authors have compiled and tested POSTGRESQL on the following platforms (some of these compiles require gcc):

- aix - IBM on AIX 3.2.5 or 4.x

- alpha - DEC Alpha AXP on Digital Unix 2.0, 3.2, 4.0

- BSD44_derived - OSs derived from 4.4-lite BSD (NetBSD, FreeBSD)

- bsdi - BSD/OS 2.x, 3.x, 4.x

- dgux - DG/UX 5.4R4.11

- hpux - HP PA-RISC on HP-UX 9.*, 10.*

- i386_solaris - i386

- Irix5 - SGI MIPS

- MIPS on IRIX 5.3

- linux - Intel i86 Alpha SPARC PPC M68k

- sco - SCO 3.2v5

- Unixware

- sparc_solaris - SUN SPARC on Solaris 2.4, 2.5, 2.5.1

- sunos4 - SUN SPARC on SunOS 4.1.3

- svr4 - Intel x86 on Intel SVR4 and MIPS

- ultrix4 - DEC MIPS on Ultrix 4.4

1.4) What non-Unix ports are available?

It is possible to compile the *libpq* C library, *psql,* and other interfaces and binaries to run on MS Windows platforms. In this case, the client is running on MS Windows, and communicates via TCP/IP to a server running on one of our supported Unix platforms.

A file *win31.mak* is included in the distribution for making a Win32 *libpq* library and *psql.*

The database server is now working on Windows NT using the Cygnus Unix/NT porting library. See *pgsql/doc/FAQ_NT* in the distribution.

1.5) Where can I get POSTGRESQL?

The primary anonymous ftp site for POSTGRESQL is ftp://ftp.PostgreSQL.org/pub. For mirror sites, see our main Web site.

1.6) Where can I get support?

There is no support for POSTGRESQL from the University of California, Berkeley. It is maintained through volunteer effort.

The main mailing list is: pgsql-general@PostgreSQL.org. It is available for discussion of matters pertaining to POSTGRESQL. To subscribe, send mail with the following lines in the body (not the subject line):

```
subscribe
end
```

to pgsql-general-request@PostgreSQL.org.

There is also a digest list available. To subscribe to this list, send email to: pgsql-general-digest-request@PostgreSQL.org with a body of:

```
subscribe
end
```

Digests are sent out to members of this list whenever the main list has received around 30k of messages.

The bugs mailing list is available. To subscribe to this list, send email to pgsql-bugs-request@PostgreSQL.org with a body of:

```
subscribe
end
```

There is also a developers discussion mailing list available. To subscribe to this list, send email to pgsql-hackers-request@PostgreSQL.org with a body of:

```
subscribe
end
```

Additional mailing lists and information about POSTGRESQL can be found via the POSTGRESQL WWW home page at: `http://www.PostgreSQL.org`.

There is also an IRC channel on EFNet, channel *#PostgreSQL*. I use the Unix command `irc -c '#PostgreSQL' "$USER" irc.phoenix.net`. Commercial support for POSTGRESQL is available at `http://www.pgsql.com/`.

1.7) What is the latest release?

The latest release of POSTGRESQL is version 7.0.2. We plan to have major releases every four months.

1.8) What documentation is available?

Several manuals, manual pages, and some small test examples are included in the distribution. See the */doc* directory. You can also browse the manual online at `http://www.postgresql.org/docs/postgres`.

There is a POSTGRESQL book available at `http://www.postgresql.org/docs/awbook.html`.

psql has some nice backslash commands to show information about types, operators, functions, aggregates, etc.

Our Web site contains even more documentation.

1.9) How do I find out about known bugs or missing features?

POSTGRESQL supports an extended subset of SQL-92. See our TODO list for known bugs, missing features, and future plans.

1.10) How can I learn SQL?

The POSTGRESQL book at:

```
http://www.postgresql.org/docs/awbook.html
```

teaches SQL. There is a nice tutorial at

```
http://w3.one.net/~jhoffman/sqltut.htm
```
and at
```
http://ourworld.compuserve.com/homepages/graeme_birchall/HTM_COOK.HTM.
```

Another one is *Teach Yourself SQL in 21 Days, Second Edition* at:

```
http://members.tripod.com/er4ebus/sql/index.htm
```

Many of our users like *The Practical SQL Handbook*, Bowman, Judith S., et al., Addison–Wesley. Others like *The Complete Reference SQL*, Groff et al., McGraw–Hill.

1.11) Is POSTGRESQL Y2K compliant?

Yes, we easily handle dates past the year 2000AD, and before 2000BC.

1.12) How do I join the development team?

First, download the latest source and read the POSTGRESQL Developers documentation on our Web site, or in the distribution. Second, subscribe to the *pgsql-hackers* and *pgsql-patches* mailing lists. Third, submit high-quality patches to pgsql-patches.

There are about a dozen people who have commit privileges to the POSTGRESQL CVS archive. They each have submitted so many high-quality patches that it was impossible for the existing committers to keep up, and we had confidence that patches they committed were of high quality.

1.13) How do I submit a bug report?

Fill out the *bug-template* file and send it to: pgsql-bugs@PostgreSQL.org

Also check out our ftp site, `ftp://ftp.PostgreSQL.org/pub`, to see if there is a more recent POSTGRESQL version or patches.

1.14) How does POSTGRESQL compare to other DBMS's?

There are several ways of measuring software: features, performance, reliability, support, and price.

Features

POSTGRESQL has most features present in large commercial DBMS's, like transactions, subselects, triggers, views, foreign key referential integrity, and sophisticated locking. We have some features they don't have, like user-defined types, inheritance, rules, and multi-version concurrency control to reduce lock contention. We don't have outer joins, but are working on them.

Performance

POSTGRESQL runs in two modes. Normal *fsync* mode flushes every completed transaction to disk, guaranteeing that if the OS crashes or loses power in the next few seconds, all your data is safely stored on disk. In this mode, we are slower than most commercial databases, partly because few of them do such conservative flushing to disk in their default modes. In *no-fsync* mode, we are usually faster than commercial databases, though in this mode, an OS crash could cause data corruption.

We are working to provide an intermediate mode that suffers less performance overhead than full fsync mode, and will allow data integrity within 30 seconds of an OS crash.

In comparison to MySQL or leaner database systems, we are slower on inserts/updates because we have transaction overhead. Of course, MySQL doesn't have any of the features mentioned in the *Features* section above. We are built for flexibility and features, though we continue to improve performance through profiling and source code analysis. There is an interesting Web page comparing POSTGRESQL to MySQL at `http://openacs.org/why-not-mysql.html`.

We handle each user connection by creating a Unix process. Backend processes share data buffers and locking information. With multiple CPU's, multiple backends can easily run on different CPU's.

Reliability

We realize that a DBMS must be reliable, or it is worthless. We strive to release well-tested, stable code that has a minimum of bugs. Each release has at least one month of beta testing, and our release history shows that we can provide stable, solid releases that are ready for production use. We believe we compare favorably to other database software in this area.

Support

Our mailing list provides a large group of developers and users to help resolve any problems encountered. While we can not guarantee a fix, commercial DBMS's don't always supply a fix either. Direct access to developers, the user community, manuals, and the source code often make POSTGRESQL support superior to other DBMS's. There is commercial per-incident support available for those who need it. (See support FAQ item.)

Price

We are free for all use, both commercial and non-commercial. You can add our code to your product with no limitations, except those outlined in our BSD-style license stated above.

User Client Questions

2.1) Are there ODBC drivers for POSTGRESQL?

There are two ODBC drivers available, PsqlODBC and OpenLink ODBC.

PsqlODBC is included in the distribution. More information about it can be gotten from:

```
ftp://ftp.PostgreSQL.org/pub/odbc/
```

OpenLink ODBC can be gotten from `http://www.openlinksw.com`. It works with their standard ODBC client software so you'll have POSTGRESQL ODBC available on every client platform they support (Win, Mac, Unix, VMS).

They will probably be selling this product to people who need commercial-quality support, but a freeware version will always be available. Questions to postgres95@openlink.co.uk.

See also the ODBC chapter of the Programmer's Guide.

2.2) What tools are available for hooking POSTGRESQL to Web pages?

A nice introduction to Database-backed Web pages can be seen at `http://www.webtools.com`.
There is also one at `http://www.phone.net/home/mwm/hotlist/`.
For Web integration, PHP is an excellent interface. It is at `http://www.php.net`
For complex cases, many use the Perl interface and CGI.pm.
A WWW gateway based on WDB using Perl can be downloaded from
`http://www.eol.ists.ca/dunlop/wdb-p95`.

2.3) Does POSTGRESQL have a graphical user interface? A report generator? An embedded query language interface?

We have a nice graphical user interface called *pgaccess,* which is shipped as part of the distribution.
Pgaccess also has a report generator. The Web page is `http://www.flex.ro/pgaccess`.

We also include *ecpg,* which is an embedded SQL query language interface for C.

2.4) What languages are available to communicate with POSTGRESQL?

We have:

- C (libpq)

- C++ (libpq++)

- Embedded C (ecpg)

- Java (jdbc)

- Perl (perl5)

- ODBC (odbc)

- Python (PyGreSQL)

- TCL (libpgtcl)

- C Easy API (libpgeasy)

- Embedded HTML (PHP from `http://www.php.net`)

Administrative Questions

3.1) Why does *initdb* fail?

Try these:

- check that you don't have any of the previous version's binaries in your path

- check to see that you have the proper paths set

- check that the *postgres* user owns the proper files

3.2) How do I install POSTGRESQL somewhere other than */usr/local/pgsql?*

The simplest way is to specify the –prefix option when running *configure*. If you forgot to do that, you can edit *Makefile.global* and change POSTGRESDIR accordingly, or create a *Makefile.custom* and define POSTGRESDIR there.

3.3) When I start the *postmaster*, I get a *Bad System Call* or core dumped message. Why?

It could be a variety of problems, but first check to see that you have System V extensions installed in your kernel. POSTGRESQL requires kernel support for shared memory and semaphores.

3.4) When I try to start the *postmaster*, I get *IpcMemoryCreate* errors. Why?

You either do not have shared memory configured properly in your kernel or you need to enlarge the shared memory available in the kernel. The exact amount you need depends on your architecture and how many buffers and backend processes you configure for the *postmaster*. For most systems, with default numbers of buffers and processes, you need a minimum of ˜1MB.

3.5) When I try to start the *postmaster*, I get *IpcSemaphoreCreate* errors. Why?

If the error message is *IpcSemaphoreCreate: semget failed (No space left on device)* then your kernel is not configured with enough semaphores. Postgres needs one semaphore per potential backend process. A temporary solution is to start the *postmaster* with a smaller limit on the number of backend processes. Use *-N* with a parameter less than the default of 32. A more permanent solution is to increase your kernel's SEMMNS and SEMMNI parameters.

If the error message is something else, you might not have semaphore support configured in your kernel at all.

3.6) How do I prevent other hosts from accessing my POSTGRESQL database?

By default, POSTGRESQL only allows connections from the local machine using Unix domain sockets. Other machines will not be able to connect unless you add the *-i* flag to the *postmaster,* and enable host-based authentication by modifying the file *$PGDATA/pg_hba.conf* accordingly. This will allow TCP/IP connections.

3.7) Why can't I connect to my database from another machine?

The default configuration allows only Unix domain socket connections from the local machine. To enable TCP/IP connections, make sure the *postmaster* has been started with the *-i* option, and add an appropriate host entry to the file *pgsql/data/pg_hba.conf*.

3.8) Why can't I access the database as the *root* user?

You should not create database users with user id 0 (root). They will be unable to access the database. This is a security precaution because of the ability of users to dynamically link object modules into the database engine.

3.9) All my servers crash under concurrent table access. Why?

This problem can be caused by a kernel that is not configured to support semaphores.

3.10) How do I tune the database engine for better performance?

Certainly, indices can speed up queries. The EXPLAIN command allows you to see how POSTGRESQL is interpreting your query, and which indices are being used.

If you are doing a lot of INSERTs, consider doing them in a large batch using the COPY command. This is much faster than individual INSERTs. Second, statements not in a BEGIN WORK/COMMIT transaction block are considered to be in their own transaction. Consider performing several statements in a single transaction block. This reduces the transaction overhead. Also consider dropping and recreating indices when making large data changes.

There are several tuning options. You can disable *fsync()* by starting the *postmaster* with a *-o -F* option. This will prevent *fsync()'s* from flushing to disk after every transaction.

You can also use the *postmaster -B* option to increase the number of shared memory buffers used by the backend processes. If you make this parameter too high, the *postmaster* may not start because you've exceeded your kernel's limit on shared memory space. Each buffer is 8K and the default is 64 buffers.

You can also use the backend *-S* option to increase the maximum amount of memory used by the backend process for temporary sorts. The *-S* value is measured in kilobytes, and the default is 512 (ie, 512K).

You can also use the CLUSTER command to group data in tables to match an index. See the CLUSTER manual page for more details.

3.11) What debugging features are available?

POSTGRESQL has several features that report status information that can be valuable for debugging purposes.

First, by running *configure* with the –enable-cassert option, many *assert()'s* monitor the progress of the backend and halt the program when something unexpected occurs.

Both *postmaster* and *postgres* have several debug options available. First, whenever you start the *postmaster*, make sure you send the standard output and error to a log file, like:

```
cd /usr/local/pgsql
./bin/postmaster > server.log 2>&1 &
```

This will put a server.log file in the top-level POSTGRESQL directory. This file contains useful information about problems or errors encountered by the server. *Postmaster* has a -*d* option that allows even more detailed information to be reported. The -*d* option takes a number that specifies the debug level. Be warned that high debug level values generate large log files.

If the *postmaster* is not running, you can actually run the *postgres* backend from the command line, and type your SQL statement directly. This is recommended **only** for debugging purposes. Note that a newline terminates the query, not a semicolon. If you have compiled with debugging symbols, you can use a debugger to see what is happening. Because the backend was not started from the *postmaster*, it is not running in an identical environment and locking/backend interaction problems may not be duplicated.

If the *postmaster* is running, start *psql* in one window, then find the PID of the *postgres* process used by *psql*. Use a debugger to attach to the *postgres* PID. You can set breakpoints in the debugger and issue queries from *psql*. If you are debugging *postgres* start-up, you can set PGOPTIONS="-W n", then start *psql*. This will cause start-up to delay for *n* seconds so you can attach with the debugger and trace through the start-up sequence.

The *postgres* program has -*s, -A,* and -*t* options that can be very useful for debugging and performance measurements.

You can also compile with profiling to see what functions are taking execution time. The backend profile files will be deposited in the *pgsql/data/base/dbname* directory. The client profile file will be put in the client's current directory.

3.12) I get *"Sorry, too many clients"* when trying to connect. Why?

You need to increase the *postmaster's* limit on how many concurrent backend processes it can start.

In POSTGRESQL 6.5 and up, the default limit is 32 processes. You can increase it by restarting the *postmaster* with a suitable -*N* value. With the default configuration you can set -*N* as large as

1024. If you need more, increase MAXBACKENDS in *include/config.h* and rebuild. You can set the default value of *-N* at configuration time, if you like, using *configure's –with-maxbackends* switch.

Note that if you make *-N* larger than 32, you must also increase *-B* beyond its default of 64; *-B* must be at least twice *-N*, and probably should be more than that for best performance. For large numbers of backend processes, you are also likely to find that you need to increase various Unix kernel configuration parameters. Things to check include the maximum size of shared memory blocks, SHMMAX; the maximum number of semaphores, SEMMNS and SEMMNI; the maximum number of processes, NPROC; the maximum number of processes per user, MAXUPRC; and the maximum number of open files, NFILE and NINODE. The reason that POSTGRESQL has a limit on the number of allowed backend processes is so your system won't run out of resources.

In POSTGRESQL versions prior to 6.5, the maximum number of backends was 64, and changing it required a rebuild after altering the MaxBackendId constant in *include/storage/sinvaladt.h.*

3.13) What are the *pg_sorttempNNN.NN* files in my database directory?

They are temporary files generated by the query executor. For example, if a sort needs to be done to satisfy an ORDER BY, and the sort requires more space than the backend's *-S* parameter allows, then temporary files are created to hold the extra data.

The temporary files should be deleted automatically, but might not if a backend crashes during a sort. If you have no backends running at the time, it is safe to delete the pg_tempNNN.NN files.

Operational Questions

4.1) Why is the system confused about commas, decimal points, and date formats?

Check your locale configuration. POSTGRESQL uses the locale setting of the user that ran the *postmaster* process. There are postgres and *psql* SET commands to control the date format. Set those accordingly for your operating environment.

4.2) What is the exact difference between binary cursors and normal cursors?

See the DECLARE manual page for a description.

4.3) How do I SELECT only the first few rows of a query?

See the FETCH manual page, or use SELECT...LIMIT....

The entire query may have to be evaluated, even if you only want the first few rows. Consider a query that has an ORDER BY. If there is an index that matches the ORDER BY, POSTGRESQL may be able to evaluate only the first few records requested, or the entire query may have to be evaluated until the desired rows have been generated.

4.4) How do I get a list of tables or other information I see in *psql?*

You can read the source code for *psql* in file *pgsql/src/bin/psql/psql.c.* It contains SQL commands that generate the output for *psql's* backslash commands. You can also start *psql* with the *-E* option so it will print out the queries it uses to execute the commands you give.

4.5) How do you remove a column from a table?

We do not support ALTER TABLE DROP COLUMN, but do this:

```
SELECT ... -- select all columns but the one you want to remove
INTO TABLE new_table
FROM old_table;
DROP TABLE old_table;
ALTER TABLE new_table RENAME TO old_table;
```

4.6) What is the maximum size for a row, table, database?

These are the limits:

- Maximum size for a database? unlimited (60GB databases exist)

- Maximum size for a table? unlimited on all operating systems

- Maximum size for a row? 8k, configurable to 32k

- Maximum number of rows in a table? unlimited

- Maximum number of columns in a table? unlimited

- Maximum number of indexes on a table? unlimited

Of course, these are not actually unlimited, but limited to available disk space.

To change the maximum row size, edit *include/config.h* and change BLCKSZ. To use attributes larger than 8K, you can also use the large object interface.

The row length limit will be removed in 7.1.

4.7) How much database disk space is required to store data from a typical text file?

A POSTGRESQL database may need six-and-a-half times the disk space required to store the data in a flat file.

Consider a file of 300,000 lines with two integers on each line. The flat file is 2.4MB. The size of the POSTGRESQL database file containing this data can be estimated at 14MB:

```
  36 bytes: each row header (approximate)
+  8 bytes: two int fields @ 4 bytes each
+  4 bytes: pointer on page to tuple
----------------------------------------
 48 bytes per row
```

```
The data page size in PostgreSQL is 8192 bytes (8 KB), so:
```

```
8192 bytes per page
------------------- = 171 rows per database page (rounded up)
  48 bytes per row
```

```
300000 data rows
-------------------- = 1755 database pages
   171 rows per page
```

```
1755 database pages * 8192 bytes per page = 14,376,960 bytes (14MB)
```

Indexes do not require as much overhead, but do contain the data that is being indexed, so they can be large also.

4.8) How do I find out what indices or operations are defined in the database?

psql has a variety of backslash commands to show such information. Use \? to see them.

Also try the file *pgsql/src/tutorial/syscat.source*. It illustrates many of the SELECTs needed to get information from the database system tables.

4.9) My queries are slow or don't make use of the indexes. Why?

POSTGRESQL does not automatically maintain statistics. VACUUM must be run to update the statistics. After statistics are updated, the optimizer knows how many rows in the table, and can better decide if it should use indices. Note that the optimizer does not use indices in cases when the table is small because a sequential scan would be faster.

For column-specific optimization statistics, use VACUUM ANALYZE. VACUUM ANALYZE is important for complex multijoin queries, so the optimizer can estimate the number of rows returned from each table, and choose the proper join order. The backend does not keep track of column statistics on its own, so VACUUM ANALYZE must be run to collect them periodically.

Indexes are usually not used for ORDER BY operations: a sequential scan followed by an explicit sort is faster than an indexscan of all tuples of a large table, because it takes fewer disk accesses.

When using wild-card operators such as LIKE or ˜, indices can only be used if the beginning of the search is anchored to the start of the string. So, to use indices, LIKE searches should not begin with %, and ˜(regular expression searches) should start with ^.

4.10) How do I see how the query optimizer is evaluating my query?

See the EXPLAIN manual page.

4.11) What is an R-tree index?

An R-tree index is used for indexing spatial data. A hash index can't handle range searches. A B-tree index only handles range searches in a single dimension. R-tree's can handle multi-dimensional data. For example, if an R-tree index can be built on an attribute of type *point,* the system can more efficiently answer queries such as "select all points within a bounding rectangle."

The canonical paper that describes the original R-tree design is:

Guttman, A. "R-trees: A Dynamic Index Structure for Spatial Searching." Proc of the 1984 ACM SIGMOD Int'l Conf on Mgmt of Data, 45-57.

You can also find this paper in Stonebraker's "Readings in Database Systems"

Built-in R-trees can handle polygons and boxes. In theory, R-trees can be extended to handle higher number of dimensions. In practice, extending R-trees requires a bit of work and we don't currently have any documentation on how to do it.

4.12) What is Genetic Query Optimization?

The GEQO module speeds query optimization when joining many tables by means of a Genetic Algorithm (GA). It allows the handling of large join queries through nonexhaustive search.

4.13) How do I do regular expression searches and case-insensitive regular expression searches?

The ˜ operator does regular expression matching, and ˜* does case-insensitive regular expression matching. There is no case-insensitive variant of the LIKE operator, but you can get the effect of case-insensitive LIKE with this:

```
WHERE lower(textfield) LIKE lower(pattern)
```

4.14) In a query, how do I detect if a field is NULL?

You test the column with IS NULL and IS NOT NULL.

4.15) What is the difference between the various character types?

Type	Internal Name	Notes
"CHAR"	char	1 character
CHAR(#)	bpchar	blank padded to the specified fixed length
VARCHAR(#)	varchar	size specifies maximum length, no padding
TEXT	text	length limited only by maximum row length
BYTEA	bytea	variable-length array of bytes

You will see the internal name when examining system catalogs and in some error messages.

The last four types above are VARLENA types (i.e., the first four bytes are the length, followed by the data). CHAR(#) allocates the maximum number of bytes no matter how much data is stored in the field. TEXT, VARCHAR(#), and BYTEA all have variable length on the disk, and because of this, there is a small performance penalty for using them. Specifically, the penalty is for access to all columns after the first column of this type.

4.16.1) How do I create a serial/auto-incrementing field?

POSTGRESQL supports a SERIAL data type. It auto-creates a sequence and index on the column. For example, this:

```
CREATE TABLE person ( id SERIAL, name TEXT );
```

is automatically translated into this:

```
CREATE SEQUENCE person_id_seq;
CREATE TABLE person ( id INT4 NOT NULL DEFAULT nextval('person_id_seq'),
                      name TEXT );
CREATE UNIQUE INDEX person_id_key ON person ( id );
```

See the CREATE_SEQUENCE manual page for more information about sequences. You can also use each row's OID field as a unique value. However, if you need to dump and reload the database, you need to use *pg_dump's -o* option or COPY WITH OIDS option to preserve the OIDs.

4.16.2) How do I get the value of a SERIAL insert?

One approach is to to retrieve the next SERIAL value from the sequence object with the *nextval()* function *before* inserting and then insert it explicitly. Using the example table in 4.16.1, that might look like this:

```
$newSerialID = nextval('person_id_seq');
INSERT INTO person (id, name) VALUES ($newSerialID, 'Blaise Pascal');
```

You would then also have the new value stored in $newSerialID for use in other queries (e.g., as a foreign key to the person table). Note that the name of the automatically created SEQUENCE object will be named *<table>_<serialcolumn>_seq*, where *table* and *serialcolumn* are the names of your table and your SERIAL column, respectively.

Alternatively, you could retrieve the assigned SERIAL value with the *currval()* function *after* it was inserted by default, e.g.,

```
INSERT INTO person (name) VALUES ('Blaise Pascal');
$newID = currval('person_id_seq');
```

Finally, you could use the OID returned from the INSERT statement to look up the default value, though this is probably the least portable approach. In Perl, using DBI with Edmund Mergl's DBD::Pg module, the OID value is made available via *$sth->{pg_oid_status}* *after $sth->execute()*.

4.16.3) Don't *currval()* and *nextval()* lead to a race condition with other users?

No. This is handled by the backends.

4.17) What is an OID? What is a TID?

OIDs are POSTGRESQL'S answer to unique row ids. Every row that is created in POSTGRESQL gets a unique OID. All OIDs generated during *initdb* are less than 16384 (from *backend/access/transam.h*). All user-created OIDs are equal to or greater than this. By default, all these OIDs are unique not only within a table or database, but unique within the entire POSTGRESQL installation.

POSTGRESQL uses OIDs in its internal system tables to link rows between tables. These OIDs can be used to identify specific user rows and used in joins. It is recommended you use column type OID to store OID values. You can create an index on the OID field for faster access.

OIDs are assigned to all new rows from a central area that is used by all databases. If you want to change the OID to something else, or if you want to make a copy of the table, with the original OID's, there is no reason you can't do it:

```
CREATE TABLE new_table(old_oid oid, mycol int);
SELECT old_oid, mycol INTO new FROM old;
COPY new TO '/tmp/pgtable';
DELETE FROM new;
COPY new WITH OIDS FROM '/tmp/pgtable';
```

TIDs are used to identify specific physical rows with block and offset values. TIDs change after rows are modified or reloaded. They are used by index entries to point to physical rows.

4.18) What is the meaning of some of the terms used in POSTGRESQL?

Some of the source code and older documentation use terms that have more common usage. Here are some:

- table, relation, class
- row, record, tuple
- column, field, attribute
- retrieve, select
- replace, update
- append, insert
- OID, serial value
- portal, cursor
- range variable, table name, table alias

4.19) Why do I get the error *"FATAL: palloc failure: memory exhausted?"*

It is possible you have run out of virtual memory on your system, or your kernel has a low limit for certain resources. Try this before starting the *postmaster:*

```
ulimit -d 65536
limit datasize 64m
```

Depending on your shell, only one of these may succeed, but it will set your process data segment limit much higher and perhaps allow the query to complete. This command applies to the current process, and all subprocesses created after the command is run. If you are having a problem with the SQL client because the backend is returning too much data, try it before starting the client.

4.20) How do I tell what POSTGRESQL version I am running?

From *psql,* type `select version();`

4.21) My large-object operations get *invalid large obj descriptor.* Why?

You need to put BEGIN WORK and COMMIT around any use of a large object handle, that is, surrounding `lo_open ... lo_close`. Currently POSTGRESQL enforces the rule by closing large object handles at transaction commit. So the first attempt to do anything with the handle will draw *invalid large obj descriptor.* So code that used to work (at least most of the time) will now generate that error message if you fail to use a transaction.

If you are using a client interface like ODBC you may need to set auto-commit off.

4.22) How do I create a column that will default to the current time?

Use *now()*:

```
CREATE TABLE test (x int, modtime timestamp DEFAULT now() );
```

4.23) Why are my subqueries using IN so slow?

Currently, we join subqueries to outer queries by sequentially scanning the result of the subquery for each row of the outer query. A workaround is to replace IN with EXISTS:

```
SELECT * FROM tab WHERE col1 IN (SELECT col2 FROM TAB2)
```

to:

```
SELECT * FROM tab WHERE EXISTS (SELECT col2 FROM TAB2 WHERE col1 = col2)
```

We hope to fix this limitation in a future release.

4.24) How do I do an outer join?

POSTGRESQL does not support outer joins in the current release. They can be simulated using UNION and NOT IN. For example, when joining *tab1* and *tab2,* the following query does an *outer* join of the two tables:

```
SELECT tab1.col1, tab2.col2
FROM tab1, tab2
WHERE tab1.col1 = tab2.col1
UNION ALL
SELECT tab1.col1, NULL
FROM tab1
WHERE tab1.col1 NOT IN (SELECT tab2.col1 FROM tab2)
ORDER BY tab1.col1
```

Extending POSTGRESQL

5.1) I wrote a user-defined function. When I run it in *psql*, why does it dump core?

The problem could be a number of things. Try testing your user-defined function in a stand-alone test program first.

5.2) What does the message *"NOTICE:PortalHeapMemoryFree: 0x402251d0 not in alloc set!"* mean?

You are *pfree*'ing something that was not *palloc*'ed. Beware of mixing *malloc/free* and *palloc/pfree*.

5.3) How can I contribute some nifty new types and functions to POSTGRESQL?

Send your extensions to the *pgsql-hackers* mailing list, and they will eventually end up in the *contrib/* subdirectory.

5.4) How do I write a C function to return a tuple?

This requires wizardry so extreme that the authors have never tried it, though in principle it can be done.

5.5) I have changed a source file. Why does the recompile not see the change?

The *Makefiles* do not have the proper dependencies for include files. You have to do a *make clean* and then another *make*.

Appendix B

Installation

Getting POSTGRESQL

The POSTGRESQL software is distributed in several formats:

- Tar-gzipped file with a file extension of *.tar.gz*

- Prepackaged file with a file extension of *.rpm*

- Another prepackaged format

- CD-ROM

Because so many formats exist, this appendix will cover only the general steps needed to install POSTGRESQL. Each distribution comes with an INSTALL or README file with more specific instructions.

Creating the POSTGRESQL User

It is best to create a separate user to own the POSTGRESQL files and processes that will be installed. The user name is typically *postgres*.

Configuration

Many distributions use a `configure` command that allows users to choose various options before compiling and installing the software.

Compilation

POSTGRESQL is usually distributed in source code format. As a consequence, C source code must be compiled into a format that is understood by the CPU. This process is usually handled by a *compiler,* often called cc or gcc. Several distribution formats automatically perform these steps for the user.

Installation

The installation process involves copying all compiled programs into a directory that will serve as the home of all POSTGRESQL activity. It will also contain all POSTGRESQL programs, databases, and log files. The directory is typically called /usr/local/pgsql.

Initialization

Initialization creates a database called *template1* in the POSTGRESQL home directory. This database is used to create all other databases. Initdb performs this initialization step.

Starting the Server

Once *template1* is created, the database server can be started. This step typically involves running the program called postmaster.

Creating a Database

Once the database server is running, you can create databases by running createdb from the operating system prompt. Chapter 20 covers POSTGRESQL administration in detail.

postgres / postgres 03

Appendix C

PostgreSQL Nonstandard Features by Chapter

This appendix outlines the nonstandard features covered in this book.

Chapter 1 None.

Chapter 2 Psql is a unique feature of POSTGRESQL.

Chapter 3 None.

Chapter 4 Use of regular expressions, SET, SHOW, and RESET are features unique to POSTGRESQL.

Chapter 5 None.

Chapter 6 None.

Chapter 7 OIDs, sequences, and SERIAL are unique features of POSTGRESQL.

Chapter 8 FROM in UPDATE is a unique feature of POSTGRESQL. Some databases support the creation of tables by SELECT.

Chapter 9 Most databases support only a few of the many data types, functions, and operators included in POSTGRESQL. Arrays are a unique features of POSTGRESQL. Large objects are implemented differently by other database systems.

Chapter 10 None.

Chapter 11 CLUSTER, VACUUM, and EXPLAIN are features unique to POSTGRESQL.

Chapter 12 LIMIT is implemented by a few other database systems.

Chapter 13 Inheritance, RULES, LISTEN, and NOTIFY are features unique to POSTGRESQL.

Chapter 14 None.

Chapter 15 COPY is a unique feature of POSTGRESQL.

Chapter 16 Psql and pgaccess are unique features of POSTGRESQL.

Chapter 17 All of the programming interfaces except ECPG and Java are implemented differently by other database systems.

Chapter 18 Server-side functions and triggers are implemented differently by other database systems.

Chapter 19 Using C to enhance the database is a unique POSTGRESQL feature.

Chapter 20 The administrative utilities are unique to POSTGRESQL.

Appendix D

Reference Manual

The following is a copy of the reference manual pages *(man pages)* as they appeared in POSTGRESQL 7.0.2. The most current version is available at:

- `http://www.postgresql.org/docs/user/sql-commands.htm`

- `http://www.postgresql.org/docs/user/applications.htm`

These are part of the POSTGRESQL *User's Guide*.

D.1 ABORT

Name

ABORT — Aborts the current transaction
    ABORT [WORK | TRANSACTION]

Inputs

None.

Outputs

ROLLBACK Message returned if successful.

NOTICE: ROLLBACK: no transaction in progress If there is not any transaction currently in progress.

Description

ABORT rolls back the current transaction and causes all the updates made by the transaction to be discarded. This command is identical in behavior to the SQL92 command **ROLLBACK**, and is present only for historical reasons.

Notes

Use **COMMIT** to successfully terminate a transaction.

Usage

To abort all changes:

```
ABORT WORK;
```

Compatibility

SQL92

This command is a Postgres extension present for historical reasons. **ROLLBACK** is the SQL92 equivalent command.

D.2   ALTER GROUP

Name

ALTER GROUP — Add users to a group, remove users from a group
    ALTER GROUP *name* ADD USER *username* [, ...]
    ALTER GROUP *name* DROP USER *username* [, ...]

Inputs

name   The name of the group to modify.

username   Users which are to be added or removed from the group. The user names must exist.

Outputs

ALTER GROUP Message returned if the alteration was successful.

Description

ALTER GROUP is used to add or remove users from a group. Only database superusers can use this command. Adding a user to a group does not create the user. Similarly, removing a user from a group does not drop the user itself.

Use *CREATE GROUP* to create a new group and *DROP GROUP* to remove a group.

Usage

Add users to a group:

```
ALTER GROUP staff ADD USER karl, john
```

Remove a user from a group:

```
ALTER GROUP workers DROP USER beth
```

Compatibility

SQL92

There is no **ALTER GROUP** statement in SQL92. The concept of roles is similar.

D.3   ALTER TABLE

Name

ALTER TABLE — Modifies table properties
    ALTER TABLE *table* [*] ADD [COLUMN] *column type*
    ALTER TABLE *table* [*] ALTER [COLUMN] *column* { SET DEFAULT *value* | DROP DEFAULT }
    ALTER TABLE *table* [*] RENAME [COLUMN] *column* TO *newcolumn*
    ALTER TABLE *table* RENAME TO *newtable*
    ALTER TABLE *table* ADD *table constraint definition*

Inputs

table The name of an existing table to alter.

column Name of a new or existing column.

type Type of the new column.

newcolumn New name for an existing column.

newtable   New name for the table.

table constraint definition   New table constraint for the table

Outputs

ALTER Message returned from column or table renaming.

ERROR Message returned if table or column is not available.

Description

ALTER TABLE changes the definition of an existing table. The ADD COLUMN form adds a new column to the table using the same syntax as *CREATE TABLE*. The ALTER COLUMN form allows you to set or remove the default for the column. Note that defaults only apply to newly inserted rows. The RENAME clause causes the name of a table or column to change without changing any of the data contained in the affected table. Thus, the table or column will remain of the same type and size after this command is executed. The ADD *table constraint definition* clause adds a new constraint to the table using the same syntax as *CREATE TABLE*.

You must own the table in order to change its schema.

Notes

The keyword COLUMN is noise and can be omitted.

An asterisk (*) following a name of a table indicates that the statement should be run over that table and all tables below it in the inheritance hierarchy; by default, the attribute will not be added to or renamed in any of the subclasses. This should always be done when adding or modifying an attribute in a superclass. If it is not, queries on the inheritance hierarchy such as SELECT NewColumn FROM SuperClass * will not work because the subclasses will be missing an attribute found in the superclass.

In the current implementation, default and constraint clauses for the new column will be ignored. You can use the SET DEFAULT form of **ALTER TABLE** to set the default later. (You will also have to update the already existing rows to the new default value, using *UPDATE*.)

In the current implementation, only FOREIGN KEY constraints can be added to a table. To create or remove a unique constraint, create a unique index (see *CREATE INDEX*). To add check constraints you need to recreate and reload the table, using other parameters to the *CREATE TABLE* command.

You must own the class in order to change its schema. Renaming any part of the schema of a system catalog is not permitted. The *PostgreSQL User's Guide* has further information on inheritance.

Refer to **CREATE TABLE** for a further description of valid arguments.

Usage

To add a column of type VARCHAR to a table:

```
ALTER TABLE distributors ADD COLUMN address VARCHAR(30);
```

To rename an existing column:

```
ALTER TABLE distributors RENAME COLUMN address TO city;
```

To rename an existing table:

```
ALTER TABLE distributors RENAME TO suppliers;
```

To add a foreign key constraint to a table:

```
ALTER TABLE distributors ADD CONSTRAINT distfk FOREIGN KEY (address) REFER-
ENCES addresses(address) MATCH FULL;
```

Compatibility

SQL92

The ADD COLUMN form is compliant with the exception that it does not support defaults and constraints, as explained above. The ALTER COLUMN form is in full compliance.

SQL92 specifies some additional capabilities for **ALTER TABLE** statement which are not yet directly supported by Postgres:

ALTER TABLE *table* **DROP CONSTRAINT** *constraint* **{ RESTRICT | CASCADE }**
Removes a table constraint (such as a check constraint, unique constraint, or foreign key constraint). To remove a unique constraint, drop a unique index. To remove other kinds of constraints you need to recreate and reload the table, using other parameters to the *CREATE TABLE* command.

For example, to drop any constraints on a table *distributors:*

```
CREATE TABLE temp AS
SELECT * FROM distributors;
DROP TABLE distributors;
CREATE TABLE distributors AS
SELECT * FROM temp;
DROP TABLE temp;
```

ALTER TABLE *table* **DROP [COLUMN** *column* **{ RESTRICT | CASCADE }]** Removes a column from a table. Currently, to remove an existing column the table must be recreated and reloaded:

```
CREATE TABLE temp AS
SELECT did, city
FROM distributors;
DROP TABLE distributors;
CREATE TABLE distributors (
                        did DECIMAL(3) DEFAULT 1,
                        name VARCHAR(40) NOT NULL
);
INSERT INTO distributors
SELECT *
FROM temp;
DROP TABLE temp;
```

The clauses to rename columns and tables are Postgres extensions from SQL92.

D.4 ALTER USER

Name

ALTER USER — Modifies user account information
    ALTER USER *username*
    [WITH PASSWORD *'password'*]
    [CREATEDB | NOCREATEDB]
    [CREATEUSER | NOCREATEUSER]
    [VALID UNTIL *'abstime'*]

Inputs

username   The name of the user whose details are to be altered.

password   The new password to be used for this account.

CREATEDB, NOCREATEDB   These clauses define a user's ability to create databases.   If CREATEDB is specified, the user being defined will be allowed to create his own databases. Using NOCREATEDB will deny a user the ability to create databases.

CREATEUSER, NOCREATEUSER   These clauses determine whether a user will be permitted to create new users himself. This option will also make the user a superuser who can override all access restrictions.

abstime   The date (and, optionally, the time) at which this user's password is to expire.

Outputs

ALTER USER Message returned if the alteration was successful.

ERROR: ALTER USER: user "username" does not exist Error message returned if the specified user is not known to the database.

Description

ALTER USER is used to change the attributes of a user's Postgres account. Only a database superuser can change privileges and password expiration with this command. Ordinary users can only change their own password.

Use *CREATE USER* to create a new user and *DROP USER* to remove a user.

Usage

Change a user password:

```
ALTER USER davide WITH PASSWORD 'hu8jmn3';
```

Change a user's valid until date:

```
ALTER USER manuel VALID UNTIL 'Jan 31 2030';
```

Change a user's valid until date, specifying that his authorization should expire at midday on 4th May 1998 using the time zone which is one hour ahead of UTC:

```
ALTER USER chris VALID UNTIL 'May 4 12:00:00 1998 +1';
```

Give a user the ability to create other users and new databases:

```
ALTER USER miriam CREATEUSER CREATEDB;
```

Compatibility

SQL92

There is no **ALTER USER** statement in SQL92. The standard leaves the definition of users to the implementation.

D.5 BEGIN

Name

BEGIN — Begins a transaction in chained mode
    BEGIN [WORK | TRANSACTION]

Inputs

WORK, TRANSACTION Optional keywords. They have no effect.

Outputs

BEGIN This signifies that a new transaction has been started.

NOTICE: BEGIN: already a transaction in progress This indicates that a transaction was already in progress. The current transaction is not affected.

Description

By default, Postgres executes transactions in *unchained mode* (also known as *autocommit* in other database systems). In other words, each user statement is executed in its own transaction and a commit is implicitly performed at the end of the statement (if execution was successful, otherwise a rollback is done). **BEGIN** initiates a user transaction in chained mode, i.e., all user statements after **BEGIN** command will be executed in a single transaction until an explicit *COMMIT*, *ROLLBACK*, or execution abort. Statements in chained mode are executed much faster, because transaction start/commit requires significant CPU and disk activity. Execution of multiple statements inside a transaction is also required for consistency when changing several related tables.

The default transaction isolation level in Postgres is READ COMMITTED, where queries inside the transaction see only changes committed before query execution. So, you have to use **SET TRANSACTION ISOLATION LEVEL SERIALIZABLE** just after **BEGIN** if you need more rigorous transaction isolation. In SERIALIZABLE mode queries will see only changes committed before the entire transaction began (actually, before execution of the first DML statement in a serializable transaction).

If the transaction is committed, Postgres will ensure either that all updates are done or else that none of them are done. Transactions have the standard ACID (atomic, consistent, isolatable, and durable) property.

Notes

Refer to *LOCK* for further information about locking tables inside a transaction.

Use *COMMIT* or *ROLLBACK* to terminate a transaction.

Usage

To begin a user transaction:

```
BEGIN WORK;
```

Compatibility

SQL92

BEGIN is a Postgres language extension. There is no explicit **BEGIN** command in SQL92; transaction initiation is always implicit and it terminates either with a **COMMIT** or **ROLLBACK** statement. **Note:** Many relational database systems offer an autocommit feature as a convenience.

Incidentally, the BEGIN keyword is used for a different purpose in embedded SQL. You are advised to be careful about the transaction semantics when porting database applications.

SQL92 also requires SERIALIZABLE to be the default transaction isolation level.

D.6   CLOSE

Name

CLOSE — Close a cursor
    CLOSE *cursor*

Inputs

cursor The name of an open cursor to close.

Outputs

CLOSE Message returned if the cursor is successfully closed.

NOTICE PerformPortalClose: portal "*cursor*" not found This warning is given if *cursor* is not declared or has already been closed.

Description

CLOSE frees the resources associated with an open cursor. After the cursor is closed, no subsequent operations are allowed on it. A cursor should be closed when it is no longer needed.

An implicit close is executed for every open cursor when a transaction is terminated by **COMMIT** or **ROLLBACK**.

Notes

Postgres does not have an explicit **OPEN** cursor statement; a cursor is considered open when it is declared. Use the **DECLARE** statement to declare a cursor.

Usage

Close the cursor *liahona:*

```
CLOSE liahona;
```

Compatibility

SQL92

CLOSE is fully compatible with SQL92.

D.7   CLUSTER

Name

CLUSTER — Gives storage clustering advice to the server
     CLUSTER *indexname* ON *table*

Inputs

indexname The name of an index.

table The name of a table.

Outputs

CLUSTER   The clustering was done successfully.

ERROR: relation *<tablerelation_number>* inherits "*table*"

ERROR: Relation *table* does not exist!

Description

CLUSTER instructs Postgres to cluster the class specified by *table* approximately based on the index specified by *indexname*. The index must already have been defined on *classname*.

When a class is clustered, it is physically reordered based on the index information. The clustering is static. In other words, as the class is updated, the changes are not clustered. No attempt is made to keep new instances or updated tuples clustered. If one wishes, one can re-cluster manually by issuing the command again.

Notes

The table is actually copied to a temporary table in index order, then renamed back to the original name. For this reason, all grant permissions and other indexes are lost when clustering is performed.

In cases where you are accessing single rows randomly within a table, the actual order of the data in the heap table is unimportant. However, if you tend to access some data more than others, and there is an index that groups them together, you will benefit from using **CLUSTER**.

Another place where **CLUSTER** is helpful is in cases where you use an index to pull out several rows from a table. If you are requesting a range of indexed values from a table, or a single indexed value that has multiple rows that match, **CLUSTER** will help because once the index identifies the heap page for the first row that matches, all other rows that match are probably already on the same heap page, saving disk accesses and speeding up the query.

There are two ways to cluster data. The first is with the **CLUSTER** command, which reorders the original table with the ordering of the index you specify. This can be slow on large tables because the rows are fetched from the heap in index order, and if the heap table is unordered, the entries are on random pages, so there is one disk page retrieved for every row moved. Postgres has a cache, but the majority of a big table will not fit in the cache.

Another way to cluster data is to use:

```
SELECT columnlist INTO TABLE newtable
FROM table ORDER BY columnlist
```

which uses the Postgres sorting code in the ORDER BY clause to match the index, and which is much faster for unordered data. You then drop the old table, use **ALTER TABLE/RENAME** to rename *temp* to the old name, and recreate any indexes. The only problem is that OIDs will not be preserved. From then on, **CLUSTER** should be fast because most of the heap data has already been ordered, and the existing index is used.

Usage

Cluster the employees relation on the basis of its salary attribute:

```
CLUSTER emp_ind ON emp;
```

Compatibility

SQL92

There is no **CLUSTER** statement in SQL92.

D.8　COMMENT

Name

COMMENT — Add comment to an object

COMMENT ON [[DATABASE | INDEX | RULE | SEQUENCE | TABLE | TYPE | VIEW
] *object_name* |
　　COLUMN *table_name.column_name* |
　　AGGREGATE *agg_name agg_type* |
　　FUNCTION *func_name* (*arg1* , *arg2* , ...)|
　　OPERATOR *op* (*leftoperand_type rightoperand_type*) |
　　TRIGGER *trigger_name* ON *table_name*]
　　IS *'text'*

Inputs

object_name, table_name, column_name, agg_name, func_name, op, trigger_name　The name
　　of the object to be be commented.

text　The comment to add.

Outputs

COMMENT　Message returned if the table is successfully commented.

Description

COMMENT adds a comment to an object that can be easily retrieved with *psql*'s *\dd* command. To
remove a comment, use NULL. Comments are automatically dropped when the object is dropped.

Usage

Comment the table *mytable:*

```
COMMENT ON mytable IS 'This is my table.';
```

Some more examples:

```
COMMENT ON DATABASE my_database IS 'Development Database';
COMMENT ON INDEX my_index IS 'Enforces uniqueness on employee id';
COMMENT ON RULE my_rule IS 'Logs UPDATES of employee records';
COMMENT ON SEQUENCE my_sequence IS 'Used to generate primary keys';
COMMENT ON TABLE my_table IS 'Employee Information';
```

```
COMMENT ON TYPE my_type IS 'Complex Number support';
COMMENT ON VIEW my_view IS 'View of departmental costs';
COMMENT ON COLUMN my_table.my_field IS 'Employee ID number';
COMMENT ON AGGREGATE my_aggregate float8 IS 'Computes sample variance';
COMMENT ON FUNCTION my_function (datetime) IS 'Returns Roman Numeral';
COMMENT ON OPERATOR ^ (text, text) IS 'Performs intersection of two text';
COMMENT ON TRIGGER my_trigger ON my_table IS 'Used for R.I.';
```

Compatibility

SQL92

There is no **COMMENT** in SQL92.

D.9 COMMIT

Name

COMMIT — Commits the current transaction
   COMMIT [WORK | TRANSACTION]

Inputs

WORK, TRANSACTION Optional keywords. They have no effect.

Outputs

COMMIT Message returned if the transaction is successfully committed.

NOTICE: COMMIT: no transaction in progress If there is no transaction in progress.

Description

COMMIT commits the current transaction. All changes made by the transaction become visible to others and are guaranteed to be durable if a crash occurs.

Notes

The keywords WORK and TRANSACTION are noise and can be omitted.
   Use *ROLLBACK* to abort a transaction.

Usage

To make all changes permanent:

```
COMMIT WORK;
```

Compatibility

SQL92

SQL92 only specifies the two forms COMMIT and COMMIT WORK. Otherwise full compatibility.

D.10   COPY

Name

COPY — Copies data between files and tables

COPY [BINARY] *table* [WITH OIDS]
FROM { *'filename'* | stdin } [[USING] DELIMITERS *'delimiter'*] [WITH NULL AS *'null string'*]

COPY [BINARY] *table* [WITH OIDS]
TO { *'filename'* | stdout } [[USING] DELIMITERS *'delimiter'*] [WITH NULL AS *'null string'*]

Inputs

BINARY Changes the behavior of field formatting, forcing all data to be stored or read in binary format rather than as text.

table The name of an existing table.

WITH OIDS Copies the internal unique object id (OID) for each row.

filename The absolute Unix pathname of the input or output file.

stdin Specifies that input comes from a pipe or terminal.

stdout Specifies that output goes to a pipe or terminal.

delimiter A character that delimits the input or output fields.

null print A string to represent NULL values. The default is \N (backslash-N). You might prefer an empty string, for example.

> **Note:** On a copy in, any data item that matches this string will be stored as a NULL value, so you should make sure that you use the same string as you used on copy out.

Outputs

COPY The copy completed successfully.

ERROR: *reason* The copy failed for the reason stated in the error message.

Description

COPY moves data between Postgres tables and standard file-system files. **COPY** instructs the Postgres backend to directly read from or write to a file. The file must be directly visible to the backend and the name must be specified from the viewpoint of the backend. If stdin or stdout are specified, data flows through the client frontend to the backend.

Notes

The BINARY keyword will force all data to be stored/read as binary format rather than as text. It is somewhat faster than the normal copy command, but is not generally portable, and the files generated are somewhat larger, although this factor is highly dependent on the data itself.

By default, a text copy uses a tab (\t) character as a delimiter. The delimiter may also be changed to any other single character with the keyword phrase USING DELIMITERS. Characters in data fields which happen to match the delimiter character will be backslash quoted.

You must have *select access* on any table whose values are read by **COPY**, and either *insert* or *update access* to a table into which values are being inserted by **COPY**. The backend also needs appropriate Unix permissions for any file read or written by **COPY**.

The keyword phrase USING DELIMITERS specifies a single character to be used for all delimiters between columns. If multiple characters are specified in the delimiter string, only the first character is used. **Tip:** Do not confuse **COPY** with the psql instruction **copy**.

COPY neither invokes rules nor acts on column defaults. It does invoke triggers, however.

COPY stops operation at the first error. This should not lead to problems in the event of a **COPY FROM**, but the target relation will, of course, be partially modified in a **COPY TO**. **VACUUM** should be used to clean up after a failed copy.

Because the Postgres backend's current working directory is not usually the same as the user's working directory, the result of copying to a file "foo" (without additional path information) may yield unexpected results for the naive user. In this case, foo will wind up in $PGDATA/foo. In general, the full pathname as it would appear to the backend server machine should be used when specifying files to be copied.

Files used as arguments to **COPY** must reside on or be accessible to the database server machine by being either on local disks or on a networked file system.

When a TCP/IP connection from one machine to another is used, and a target file is specified, the target file will be written on the machine where the backend is running rather than the user's machine.

File Formats

Text Format

When **COPY TO** is used without the BINARY option, the file generated will have each row (instance) on a single line, with each column (attribute) separated by the delimiter character. Embedded delimiter characters will be preceded by a backslash character (\ ). The attribute values themselves are strings generated by the output function associated with each attribute type. The output function for a type should not try to generate the backslash character; this will be handled by **COPY** itself.

The actual format for each instance is <attr1> <*separator*> <attr2> <*separator*> ...<*separator*> <attr*n*> <newline>. The oid is placed on the beginning of the line if WITH OIDS is specified.

If **COPY** is sending its output to standard output instead of a file, it will send a backslash (\ ) and a period (.) followed immediately by a newline, on a separate line, when it is done. Similarly, if **COPY** is reading from standard input, it will expect a backslash (\ ) and a period (.) followed by a newline, as the first three characters on a line to denote end-of-file. However, **COPY** will terminate (followed by the backend itself) if a true EOF is encountered before this special end-of-file pattern is found.

The backslash character has other special meanings. A literal backslash character is represented as two consecutive backslashes (\\ ). A literal tab character is represented as a backslash and a tab. A literal newline character is represented as a backslash and a newline. When loading text data not generated by Postgres, you will need to convert backslash characters (\ ) to double-backslashes (\\ ) to ensure that they are loaded properly.

Binary Format

In the case of **COPY BINARY**, the first four bytes in the file will be the number of instances in the file. If this number is zero, the **COPY BINARY** command will read until end-of-file is encountered. Otherwise, it will stop reading when this number of instances has been read. Remaining data in the file will be ignored.

The format for each instance in the file is as follows. Note that this format must be followed *exactly*. Unsigned four-byte integer quantities are called uint32 in the table below.

Contents of a binary copy file

Type	Meaning
uint32	number of tuples
	For every tuple
uint32	total length of tuple data
uint32	oid (if specified)
uint32	number of null attributes
[uint32,...,uint32]	attribute numbers of attributes, counting from 0

Alignment of Binary Data

On Sun-3s, 2-byte attributes are aligned on two-byte boundaries, and all larger attributes are aligned on four-byte boundaries. Character attributes are aligned on single-byte boundaries. On most other machines, all attributes larger than 1 byte are aligned on four-byte boundaries. Note that variable length attributes are preceded by the attribute's length; arrays are simply contiguous streams of the array element type.

Usage

The following example copies a table to standard output, using a pipe (|) as the field delimiter:

```
COPY country TO stdout USING DELIMITERS '|';
```

To copy data from a Unix file into a table *country:*

```
COPY country FROM '/usr1/proj/bray/sql/country_data';
```

Here is a sample of data suitable for copying into a table from stdin (so it has the termination sequence on the last line):

```
AF AFGHANISTAN
AL ALBANIA
DZ ALGERIA ...
ZM ZAMBIA
ZW ZIMBABWE
\.
```

The following is the same data, output in binary format on a Linux/i586 machine. The data is shown after filtering through the Unix utility **od -c**. The table has three fields; the first is char(2) and the second is text. All the rows have a null value in the third field. Notice how the char(2) field is padded with nulls to four bytes and the text field is preceded by its length:

```
355   \0   \0   \0 027   \0   \0   \0 001   \0   \0   \0 002   \0   \0   \0
006   \0   \0   \0    A    F   \0   \0 017   \0   \0   \0    A    F    G    H
  A    N    I    S    T    A    N 023   \0   \0   \0 001   \0   \0   \0 002
 \0   \0   \0 006   \0   \0   \0    A    L   \0   \0   \v   \0   \0   \0    A
  L    B    A    N    I    A 023   \0   \0   \0 001   \0   \0   \0 002   \0
 \0   \0 006   \0   \0   \0    D    Z   \0   \0   \v   \0   \0   \0    A    L
  G    E    R    I    A
...
 \n   \0   \0   \0    Z    A    M    B    I    A 024   \0
 \0   \0 001   \0   \0   \0 002   \0   \0   \0 006   \0   \0   \0    Z    W
 \0   \0   \f   \0   \0   \0    Z    I    M    B    A    B    W    E
```

Compatibility

SQL92

There is no **COPY** statement in SQL92.

D.11   CREATE AGGREGATE

Name

CREATE AGGREGATE — Defines a new aggregate function
    CREATE AGGREGATE *name* (
    BASETYPE = *input_data_type*
    [, SFUNC1 = *sfunc1* , STYPE1 = *state1_type*]
    [, SFUNC2 = *sfunc2* , STYPE2 = *state2_type*]
    [, FINALFUNC = *ffunc*]
    [, INITCOND1 = *initial_condition1*]
    [, INITCOND2 = *initial_condition2*])

Inputs

name   The name of an aggregate function to create.

input_data_type   The input data type on which this aggregate function operates.

sfunc1   A state transition function to be called for every non-NULL input data value. This must be a function of two arguments, the first being of type *state1_type* and the second of type *input_data_type*. The function must return a value of type *state1_type*. This function takes the current state value 1 and the current input data item, and returns the next state value 1.

state1_type   The data type for the first state value of the aggregate.

sfunc2 A state transition function to be called for every non-NULL input data value. This must be a function of one argument of type *state2_type*, returning a value of the same type. This function takes the current state value 2 and returns the next state value 2.

state2_type The data type for the second state value of the aggregate.

ffunc The final function called to compute the aggregate's result after all input data has been traversed. If both state values are used, the final function must take two arguments of types *state1_type* and *state2_type*. If only one state value is used, the final function must take a single argument of that state value's type. The output data type of the aggregate is defined as the return type of this function.

initial_condition1 The initial value for state value 1.

initial_condition2 The initial value for state value 2.

Outputs

CREATE Message returned if the command completes successfully.

Description

CREATE AGGREGATE allows a user or programmer to extend Postgres functionality by defining new aggregate functions. Some aggregate functions for base types such as *min(int4)* and *avg(float8)* are already provided in the base distribution. If one defines new types or needs an aggregate function not already provided, then **CREATE AGGREGATE** can be used to provide the desired features.

An aggregate function is identified by its name and input data type. Two aggregates can have the same name if they operate on different input types. To avoid confusion, do not make an ordinary function of the same name and input data type as an aggregate.

An aggregate function is made from between one and three ordinary functions: two state transition functions, *sfunc1* and *sfunc2*, and a final calculation function, *ffunc*. These are used as follows:

> *sfunc1* (internal-state1, next-data-item) —> next-internal-state1
>
> *sfunc2* (internal-state2) —> next-internal-state2
>
> *ffunc* (internal-state1, internal-state2) —> aggregate-value

Postgres creates one or two temporary variables (of data types *stype1* and/or *stype2*) to hold the current internal states of the aggregate. At each input data item, the state transition function(s) are invoked to calculate new values for the internal state values. After all the data has been processed, the final function is invoked once to calculate the aggregate's output value.

ffunc must be specified if both transition functions are specified. If only one transition function is used, then *ffunc* is optional. The default behavior when *ffunc* is not provided is to return the ending value of the internal state value being used (and, therefore, the aggregate's output type is the same as that state value's type).

An aggregate function may also provide one or two initial conditions, that is, initial values for the internal state values being used. These are specified and stored in the database as fields of type text, but they must be valid external representations of constants of the state value data types. If *sfunc1* is specified without an *initcond1* value, then the system does not call *sfunc1* at the first input item; instead, the internal state value 1 is initialized with the first input value, and *sfunc1* is called beginning at the second input item. This is useful for aggregates like MIN and MAX. Note that an aggregate using this feature will return NULL when called with no input values. There is no comparable provision for state value 2; if *sfunc2* is specified then an *initcond2* is required.

Notes

Use **DROP AGGREGATE** to drop aggregate functions.

The parameters of **CREATE AGGREGATE** can be written in any order, not just the order illustrated above.

It is possible to specify aggregate functions that have varying combinations of state and final functions. For example, the count aggregate requires *sfunc2* (an incrementing function) but not *sfunc1* or *ffunc*, whereas the sum aggregate requires *sfunc1* (an addition function) but not *sfunc2* or *ffunc*, and the avg aggregate requires both state functions as well as a *ffunc* (a division function) to produce its answer. In any case, at least one state function must be defined, and any *sfunc2* must have a corresponding *initcond2*.

Usage

Refer to the chapter on aggregate functions in the *PostgreSQL Programmer's Guide* for complete examples of usage.

Compatibility

SQL92

CREATE AGGREGATE is a Postgres language extension. There is no **CREATE AGGREGATE** in SQL92.

D.12   CREATE CONSTRAINT TRIGGER

Name

CREATE CONSTRAINT TRIGGER — Create a trigger to support a constraint

CREATE CONSTRAINT TRIGGER *name*
AFTER *events* ON *relation constraint attributes*
FOR EACH ROW
EXECUTE PROCEDURE *func* '(' *args* ')'

Inputs

name The name of the constraint trigger.

events The event categories for which this trigger should be fired.

relation Table name of the triggering relation.

constraint Actual constraint specification.

attributes Constraint attributes.

func (args) Function to call as part of the trigger processing.

Outputs

CREATE CONSTRAINT Message returned if successful.

Description

CREATE CONSTRAINT TRIGGER is used from inside of **CREATE/ALTER TABLE** and by
pg_dump to create the special triggers for referential integrity.
   It is not intended for general use.

D.13   CREATE DATABASE

Name

CREATE DATABASE — Creates a new database
   CREATE DATABASE *name* [WITH LOCATION = '*dbpath* ']

Inputs

name The name of a database to create.

dbpath An alternate location where to store the new database in the filesystem. See below for
   caveats.

Outputs

CREATE DATABASE Message returned if the command completes successfully.

ERROR: user '*username*' is not allowed to create/drop databases You must have the special CREATEDB privilege to create databases. See *CREATE USER*.

ERROR: createdb: database "*name*" already exists This occurs if a database with the *name* specified already exists.

ERROR: Single quotes are not allowed in database names., ERROR: Single quotes are not allowed in database paths. The database *name* and *dbpath* cannot contain single quotes. This is required so that the shell commands that create the database directory can execute safely.

ERROR: The path 'xxx' is invalid. The expansion of the specified *dbpath* (see below) failed. Check the path you entered or make sure that the environment variable you are referencing does exist.

ERROR: createdb: May not be called in a transaction block. If you have an explicit transaction block in progress you cannot call **CREATE DATABASE**. You must finish the transaction first.

ERROR: Unable to create database directory '*path*'., ERROR: Could not initialize database directory. These are most likely related to insufficient permissions on the data directory, a full disk, or other file system problems. The user under which the database server is running must have access to the location.

Description

CREATE DATABASE creates a new Postgres database. The creator becomes the owner of the new database.

An alternate location can be specified in order to, for example, store the database on a different disk. The path must have been prepared with the initlocation command.

If the path contains a slash, the leading part is interpreted as an environment variable, which must be known to the server process. This way the database administrator can exercise control over at which locations databases can be created. (A customary choice is, e.g., 'PGDATA2'.) If the server is compiled with ALLOW_ABSOLUTE_DBPATHS (not so by default), absolute path names, as identified by a leading slash (e.g., '/usr/local/pgsql/data'), are allowed as well.

Notes

CREATE DATABASE is a Postgres language extension.
Use *DROP DATABASE* to remove a database.

The program createdb is a shell script wrapper around this command, provided for convenience.

There are security and data integrity issues involved with using alternate database locations specified with absolute path names, and by default only an environment variable known to the backend may be specified for an alternate location. See the Administrator's Guide for more information.

Usage

To create a new database:

```
olly=>  create database lusiadas;
```

To create a new database in an alternate area /private_db:

```
$ mkdir private_db
$ initlocation /private_db
```

Creating Postgres database system directory */home/olly/private_db/base:*

```
$ psql olly
Welcome to psql, the PostgreSQL interactive terminal.

Type: \copyright for distribution terms
      \h for help with SQL commands
      \? for help on internal slash commands
      \g or terminate with semicolon to execute query
      \q to quit
                                    test
olly=> CREATE DATABASE elsewhere WITH LOCATION = '/home/olly/private_db';
CREATE DATABASE                   db name
```

Compatibility

SQL92

There is no **CREATE DATABASE** statement in SQL92. Databases are equivalent to catalogs whose creation is implementation-defined.

D.14 CREATE FUNCTION

Name

CREATE FUNCTION — Defines a new function

CREATE FUNCTION *name* ([*ftype* [, ...]])
RETURNS *rtype*
AS *definition*
LANGUAGE *'langname'* [WITH (*attribute* [, ...])]

CREATE FUNCTION *name* ([*ftype* [, ...]])
RETURNS *rtype*
AS *obj_file* , *link_symbol*
LANGUAGE 'C' [WITH (*attribute* [, ...])]

Inputs

name The name of a function to create.

ftype The data type of function arguments. The input types may be base or complex types, or *opaque*. Opaque indicates that the function accepts arguments of an invalid type such as char *.

rtype The return data type. The output type may be specified as a base type, complex type, setof type, or opaque. The setof modifier indicates that the function will return a set of items, rather than a single item.

attribute An optional piece of information about the function, used for optimization. The only attribute currently supported is iscachable. Iscachable indicates that the function always returns the same result when given the same input values (i.e., it does not do database lookups or otherwise use information not directly present in its parameter list). The optimizer uses iscachable to know whether it is safe to pre-evaluate a call of the function.

definition A string defining the function; the meaning depends on the language. It may be an internal function name, the path to an object file, an SQL query, or text in a procedural language.

obj_file* , *link_symbol This form of the **AS** clause is used for dynamically linked, C language functions when the function name in the C language source code is not the same as the name of the SQL function. The string *obj_file* is the name of the file containing the dynamically loadable object, and *link_symbol*, is the object's link symbol which is the same as the name of the function in the C language source code.

langname May be 'C', 'sql', 'internal' or *'plname'*, where *'plname'* is the name of a created procedural language. See *CREATE LANGUAGE* for details.

Outputs

CREATE This is returned if the command completes successfully.

Description

CREATE FUNCTION allows a Postgres user to register a function with a database. Subsequently, this user is considered the owner of the function.

Notes

Refer to the chapter in the *PostgreSQL Programmer's Guide* on the topic of extending Postgres via functions for further information on writing external functions.

Use **DROP FUNCTION** to remove user-defined functions.

Postgres allows function "overloading"; that is, the same name can be used for several different functions so long as they have distinct argument types. This facility must be used with caution for internal and C-language functions, however.

The full SQL92 type syntax is allowed for input arguments and return value. However, some details of the type specification (e.g., the precision field for numeric types) are the responsibility of the underlying function implementation and are silently swallowed (e.g., not recognized or enforced) by the **CREATE FUNCTION** command.

Two internal functions cannot have the same C name without causing errors at link time. To get around that, give them different C names (for example, use the argument types as part of the C names), then specify those names in the AS clause of **CREATE FUNCTION**. If the AS clause is left empty, then **CREATE FUNCTION** assumes the C name of the function is the same as the SQL name.

When overloading SQL functions with C-language functions, give each C-language instance of the function a distinct name, and use the alternative form of the **AS** clause in the **CREATE FUNCTION** syntax to ensure that overloaded SQL functions names are resolved to the correct dynamically linked objects.

A C function cannot return a set of values.

Usage

To create a simple SQL function:

```
CREATE FUNCTION one()
RETURNS int4 AS 'SELECT 1 AS RESULT'
LANGUAGE 'sql';
SELECT one() AS answer;
answer

--------
 1
```

This example creates a C function by calling a routine from a user-created shared library. This particular routine calculates a check digit and returns TRUE if the check digit in the function parameters is correct. It is intended for use in a CHECK constraint.

```
CREATE FUNCTION ean_checkdigit(bpchar, bpchar)
RETURNS bool
AS '/usr1/proj/bray/sql/funcs.so'
LANGUAGE 'c';

CREATE TABLE product (
    id        char(8) PRIMARY KEY,
    eanprefix char(8) CHECK (eanprefix ~ '[0-9]{2}-[0-9]{5}')
                      REFERENCES brandname(ean_prefix),
    eancode   char(6) CHECK (eancode ~ '[0-9]{6}'),
    CONSTRAINT ean    CHECK (ean_checkdigit(eanprefix, eancode))
);
```

This example creates a function that does type conversion between the user-defined type complex, and the internal type point. The function is implemented by a dynamically loaded object that was compiled from C source. For Postgres to find a type conversion function automatically, the sql function has to have the same name as the return type, and overloading is unavoidable. The function name is overloaded by using the second form of the **AS** clause in the SQL definition:

```
CREATE FUNCTION point(complex) RETURNS point
AS '/home/bernie/pgsql/lib/complex.so', 'complex_to_point'
LANGUAGE 'c';
```

The C declaration of the function is:

```
Point * complex_to_point (Complex *z)
{
        Point *p;
        p = (Point *) palloc(sizeof(Point));
        p->x = z->x;
        p->y = z->y;

        return p;
}
```

Compatibility

SQL92

CREATE FUNCTION is a Postgres language extension.

SQL/PSM

Note: PSM stands for Persistent Stored Modules. It is a procedural language and it was originally hoped that PSM would be ratified as an official standard by late 1996. As of mid-1998, this has not yet happened, but it is hoped that PSM will eventually become a standard. SQL/PSM **CREATE FUNCTION** has the following syntax:

CREATE FUNCTION name
([[IN | OUT | INOUT] type [, ...]])
RETURNS rtype
LANGUAGE 'langname'
ESPECIFIC routine
SQL-statement

D.15   CREATE GROUP

Name

CREATE GROUP — Creates a new group
CREATE GROUP *name*
[WITH [SYSID *gid*]
[USER *username* [, ...]]]

Inputs

name The name of the group.

gid The SYSID clause can be used to choose the Postgres group id of the new group. It is not necessary to do so, however.

If this is not specified, the highest assigned group id plus one, starting at 1, will be used as default.

username A list of users to include in the group. The users must already exist.

Outputs

CREATE GROUP Message returned if the command completes successfully.

Description

CREATE GROUP will create a new group in the database installation. Refer to the administrator's guide for information about using groups for authentication. You must be a database superuser to use this command.

Use *ALTER GROUP* to change a group's membership, and *DROP GROUP* to remove a group.

Usage

Create an empty group:

```
CREATE GROUP staff
```

Create a group with members:

```
CREATE GROUP marketing WITH USER jonathan, david
```

Compatibility

SQL92

There is no **CREATE GROUP** statement in SQL92. Roles are similar in concept to groups.

D.16   CREATE INDEX

Name

CREATE INDEX — Constructs a secondary index
    CREATE [UNIQUE] INDEX *index_name* ON *table*
    [USING *acc_name*] (*column* [*ops_name*] [, ...])

    CREATE [UNIQUE] INDEX *index_name* ON *table*
    [USING *acc_name*] (*func_name* (*column* [, ...]) [*ops_name*])

Inputs

UNIQUE Causes the system to check for duplicate values in the table when the index is created (if data already exist) and each time data is added. Attempts to insert or update data which would result in duplicate entries will generate an error.

index_name The name of the index to be created.

table The name of the table to be indexed.

acc_name The name of the access method to be used for the index. The default access method is BTREE. Postgres provides three access methods for indexes:

default **BTREE** an implementation of Lehman-Yao high-concurrency btrees.

    RTREE implements standard rtrees using Guttman's quadratic split algorithm.

> **HASH** an implementation of Litwin's linear hashing.

column The name of a column of the table.

ops_name An associated operator class. See below for details.

func_name A function, which returns a value that can be indexed.

Outputs

CREATE The message returned if the index is successfully created.

ERROR: Cannot create index: 'index_name' already exists. This error occurs if it is impossible to create the index.

Description

CREATE INDEX constructs an index *index_name* on the specified *table*. **Tip:** Indexes are primarily used to enhance database performance. But inappropriate use will result in slower performance.

In the first syntax shown above, the key field(s) for the index are specified as column names. Multiple fields can be specified if the index access method supports multi-column indexes.

In the second syntax shown above, an index is defined on the result of a user-specified function *func_name* applied to one or more attributes of a single class. These *functional indices* can be used to obtain fast access to data based on operators that would normally require some transformation to apply them to the base data.

Postgres provides btree, rtree and hash access methods for indices. The btree access method is an implementation of Lehman-Yao high-concurrency btrees. The rtree access method implements standard rtrees using Guttman's quadratic split algorithm. The hash access method is an implementation of Litwin's linear hashing. We mention the algorithms used solely to indicate that all of these access methods are fully dynamic and do not have to be optimized periodically (as is the case with, for example, static hash access methods).

Use *DROP INDEX* to remove an index.

Notes

The Postgres query optimizer will consider using a btree index whenever an indexed attribute is involved in a comparison using one of: $<, <=, =, >=, >$

The Postgres query optimizer will consider using an rtree index whenever an indexed attribute is involved in a comparison using one of: $<<, \&<, \&>, >>, @, \tilde{} =, \&\&$

The Postgres query optimizer will consider using a hash index whenever an indexed attribute is involved in a comparison using the $=$ operator.

Currently, only the btree access method supports multi-column indexes. Up to 16 keys may be specified by default (this limit can be altered when building Postgres).

An *operator class* can be specified for each column of an index. The operator class identifies the operators to be used by the index for that column. For example, a btree index on four-byte integers would use the int4_ops class; this operator class includes comparison functions for four-byte integers. In practice the default operator class for the field's data type is usually sufficient. The main point of having operator classes is that for some data types, there could be more than one meaningful ordering. For example, we might want to sort a complex-number data type either by absolute value or by real part. We could do this by defining two operator classes for the data type and then selecting the proper class when making an index. There are also some operator classes with special purposes:

- The operator classes box_ops and bigbox_ops both support rtree indices on the box data type. The difference between them is that bigbox_ops scales box coordinates down, to avoid floating-point exceptions from doing multiplication, addition, and subtraction on very large floating-point coordinates. If the field on which your rectangles lie is about 20,000 units square or larger, you should use bigbox_ops.

- The int24_ops operator class is useful for constructing indices on int2 data, and doing comparisons against int4 data in query qualifications. Similarly, int42_ops support indices on int4 data that is to be compared against int2 data in queries.

The following query shows all defined operator classes:

```
SELECT am.amname AS acc_name,
       opc.opcname AS ops_name,
       opr.oprname AS ops_comp
FROM pg_am am, pg_amop amop, pg_opclass opc, pg_operator opr
WHERE amop.amopid = am.oid AND
      amop.amopclaid = opc.oid AND
      amop.amopopr = opr.oid
ORDER BY acc_name, ops_name, ops_comp
```

Usage

To create a btree index on the field title in the table films:

```
CREATE UNIQUE INDEX title_idx ON films (title);
```

Compatibility

SQL92

CREATE INDEX is a Postgres language extension.

There is no **CREATE INDEX** command in SQL92.

D.17 CREATE LANGUAGE

Name

CREATE LANGUAGE — Defines a new language for functions
    CREATE [TRUSTED] PROCEDURAL LANGUAGE *'langname'*
    HANDLER *call_handler*
    LANCOMPILER *'comment'*

Inputs

TRUSTED TRUSTED specifies that the call handler for the language is safe; that is, it offers an unprivileged user no functionality to bypass access restrictions. If this keyword is omitted when registering the language, only users with the Postgres superuser privilege can use this language to create new functions (like the C language).

langname The name of the new procedural language. The language name is case insensitive. A procedural language cannot override one of the built-in languages of Postgres.

HANDLER *call_handler* *call_handler* is the name of a previously registered function that will be called to execute the PL procedures.

comment The LANCOMPILER argument is the string that will be inserted in the LANCOMPILER attribute of the new pg_language entry. At present, Postgres does not use this attribute in any way.

Outputs

CREATE This message is returned if the language is successfully created.

ERROR: PL handler function *funcname* () doesn't exist This error is returned if the function *funcname* () is not found.

Description

Using **CREATE LANGUAGE**, a Postgres user can register a new language with Postgres. Subsequently, functions and trigger procedures can be defined in this new language. The user must have the Postgres superuser privilege to register a new language.

Writing PL handlers

The call handler for a procedural language must be written in a compiler language such as C and registered with Postgres as a function taking no arguments and returning the opaque type, a placeholder for unspecified or undefined types. This prevents the call handler from being called directly as a function from queries.

However, arguments must be supplied on the actual call when a PL function or trigger procedure in the language offered by the handler is to be executed.

- When called from the trigger manager, the only argument is the object ID from the procedure's pg_proc entry. All other information from the trigger manager is found in the global CurrentTriggerData pointer.

- When called from the function manager, the arguments are the object ID of the procedure's pg_proc entry, the number of arguments given to the PL function, the arguments in a FmgrValues structure, and a pointer to a boolean where the function tells the caller if the return value is the SQL NULL value.

It's up to the call handler to fetch the pg_proc entry and to analyze the argument and return types of the called procedure. The AS clause from the **CREATE FUNCTION** of the procedure will be found in the prosrc attribute of the pg_proc table entry. This may be the source text in the procedural language itself (like for PL/Tcl), a pathname to a file, or anything else that tells the call handler what to do in detail.

Notes

Use **CREATE FUNCTION** to create a function.

Use **DROP LANGUAGE** to drop procedural languages.

Refer to the table pg_language for further information:

```
            Table "pg_language"
     Attribute    |  Type   | Modifier
   ---------------+---------+----------
    lanname       | name    |
    lanispl       | boolean |
    lanpltrusted  | boolean |
    lanplcallfoid | oid     |
    lancompiler   | text    |

    lanname  | lanispl | lanpltrusted | lanplcallfoid | lancompiler
   ----------+---------+--------------+---------------+-------------
    internal | f       | f            |             0 | n/a
```

```
C          | f      | f                      | 0 | /bin/cc
sql        | f      | f                      | 0 | postgres
```

Since the call handler for a procedural language must be registered with Postgres in the C language, it inherits all the capabilities and restrictions of C functions.

At present, the definitions for a procedural language cannot be changed once they have been created.

Usage

This is a template for a PL handler written in C:

```c
#include "executor/spi.h"
#include "commands/trigger.h"
#include "utils/elog.h"
#include "fmgr.h"          /* for FmgrValues struct */
#include "access/heapam.h"
#include "utils/syscache.h"
#include "catalog/pg_proc.h"
#include "catalog/pg_type.h"
Datum
plsample_call_handler(
    Oid         prooid,
    int         pronargs,
    FmgrValues      *proargs,
    bool        *isNull)
{
    Datum           retval;
    TriggerData     *trigdata;
    if (CurrentTriggerData == NULL) {
        /*
         * Called as a function
         */
        retval = ...
    } else {
        /*
         * Called as a trigger procedure
         */
        trigdata = CurrentTriggerData;
        CurrentTriggerData = NULL;
        retval = ...
```

```
        }
        *isNull = false;
        return retval;
    }
```

Only a few thousand lines of code have to be added instead of the dots to complete the PL call handler. See **CREATE FUNCTION** for information on how to compile it into a loadable module.

The following commands then register the sample procedural language:

```
CREATE FUNCTION plsample_call_handler () RETURNS opaque
AS '/usr/local/pgsql/lib/plsample.so'
LANGUAGE 'C';

CREATE PROCEDURAL LANGUAGE 'plsample'
HANDLER plsample_call_handler
LANCOMPILER 'PL/Sample';
```

Compatibility

SQL92

CREATE LANGUAGE is a Postgres extension. There is no **CREATE LANGUAGE** statement in SQL92.

D.18   CREATE OPERATOR

Name

CREATE OPERATOR — Defines a new user operator
    CREATE OPERATOR *name* (
    PROCEDURE = *func_name*
    [, LEFTARG = *type1*]
    [, RIGHTARG = *type2*]
    [, COMMUTATOR = *com_op*]
    [, NEGATOR = *neg_op*]
    [, RESTRICT = *res_proc*]
    [, JOIN = *join_proc*]
    [, HASHES]
    [, SORT1 = *left_sort_op*]
    [, SORT2 = *right_sort_op*])

Inputs

name The operator to be defined. See below for allowable characters.

func_name The function used to implement this operator.

type1 The type of the left-hand argument of the operator, if any. This option would be omitted for a left-unary operator.

type2 The type of the right-hand argument of the operator, if any. This option would be omitted for a right-unary operator.

com_op The commutator of this operator.

neg_op The negator of this operator.

res_proc The restriction selectivity estimator function for this operator.

join_proc The join selectivity estimator function for this operator.

HASHES Indicates this operator can support a hash join.

left_sort_op If this operator can support a merge join, the operator that sorts the left-hand data type of this operator.

right_sort_op If this operator can support a merge join, the operator that sorts the right-hand data type of this operator.

Outputs

CREATE Message returned if the operator is successfully created.

Description

CREATE OPERATOR defines a new operator, *name*. The user who defines an operator becomes its owner.

The operator *name* is a sequence of up to NAMEDATALEN-1 (31 by default) characters from the following list:

```
+ - * / < > = ~ ! @ # % ^ & | ' ? $ :
```

There are a few restrictions on your choice of name:

- "$" and ":" cannot be defined as single-character operators, although they can be part of a multi-character operator name.

- "–" and "/*" cannot appear anywhere in an operator name, since they will be taken as the start of a comment.

- A multi-character operator name cannot end in "+" or "-", unless the name also contains at least one of these characters:

  ⁻ ! @ # % ^ & | ' ? $:

  For example, @- is an allowed operator name, but *- is not. This restriction allows Postgres to parse SQL-compliant queries without requiring spaces between tokens.

Note: When working with non-SQL-standard operator names, you will usually need to separate adjacent operators with spaces to avoid ambiguity. For example, if you have defined a left-unary operator named "@", you cannot write X*@Y; you must write X*@Y to ensure that Postgres reads it as two operator names not one.

The operator "!=" is mapped to "<>" on input, so these two names are always equivalent.

At least one of LEFTARG and RIGHTARG must be defined. For binary operators, both should be defined. For right unary operators, only LEFTARG should be defined, while for left unary operators only RIGHTARG should be defined.

The *func_name* procedure must have been previously defined using **CREATE FUNCTION** and must be defined to accept the correct number of arguments (either one or two) of the indicated types.

The commutator operator should be identified if one exists, so that Postgres can reverse the order of the operands if it wishes. For example, the operator area-less-than, $<<<$, would probably have a commutator operator, area-greater-than, $>>>$. Hence, the query optimizer could freely convert:

```
box '((0,0), (1,1))' >>> MYBOXES.description
```
to
```
MYBOXES.description <<< box '((0,0), (1,1))'.
```

This allows the execution code to always use the latter representation and simplifies the query optimizer somewhat.

Similarly, if there is a negator operator then it should be identified. Suppose that an operator, area-equal, $===$, exists, as well as an area not equal, $!==$. The negator link allows the query optimizer to simplify

```
NOT MYBOXES.description === box '((0,0), (1,1))'
```
to
```
MYBOXES.description !== box '((0,0), (1,1))'.
```

If a commutator operator name is supplied, Postgres searches for it in the catalog. If it is found and it does not yet have a commutator itself, then the commutator's entry is updated to have the newly created operator as its commutator. This applies to the negator, as well. This is to allow the definition of two operators that are the commutators or the negators of each other. The first operator should be defined without a commutator or negator (as appropriate). When the second operator is defined, name the first as the commutator or negator. The first will be updated as a side effect. (As of Postgres 6.5, it also works to just have both operators refer to each other.)

The HASHES, SORT1, and SORT2 options are present to support the query optimizer in performing joins. Postgres can always evaluate a join (i.e., processing a clause with two tuple variables separated by an operator that returns a boolean) by iterative substitution [WONG76]. In addition, Postgres can use a hash-join algorithm along the lines of [SHAP86]; however, it must know whether this strategy is applicable. The current hash-join algorithm is only correct for operators that represent equality tests; furthermore, equality of the data type must mean bitwise equality of the representation of the type. (For example, a data type that contains unused bits that don't matter for equality tests could not be hashjoined.) The HASHES flag indicates to the query optimizer that a hash join may safely be used with this operator.

Similarly, the two sort operators indicate to the query optimizer whether merge-sort is a usable join strategy and which operators should be used to sort the two operand classes. Sort operators should only be provided for an equality operator, and they should refer to less-than operators for the left and right side data types respectively.

If other join strategies are found to be practical, Postgres will change the optimizer and run-time system to use them and will require additional specification when an operator is defined. Fortunately, the research community invents new join strategies infrequently, and the added generality of user-defined join strategies was not felt to be worth the complexity involved.

The RESTRICT and JOIN options assist the query optimizer in estimating result sizes. If a clause of the form: `MYBOXES.description <<< box '((0,0), (1,1))'`

is present in the qualification, then Postgres may have to estimate the fraction of the instances in MYBOXES that satisfy the clause. The function *res_proc* must be a registered function (meaning it is already defined using **CREATE FUNCTION**) which accepts arguments of the correct data types and returns a floating point number. The query optimizer simply calls this function, passing the parameter ((0,0), (1,1)) and multiplies the result by the relation size to get the expected number of instances.

Similarly, when the operands of the operator both contain instance variables, the query optimizer must estimate the size of the resulting join. The function join_proc will return another floating point number which will be multiplied by the cardinalities of the two classes involved to compute the expected result size.

The difference between the function

`my_procedure_1 (MYBOXES.description, box '((0,0), (1,1))')`

and the operator

`MYBOXES.description === box '((0,0), (1,1))'`

is that Postgres attempts to optimize operators and can decide to use an index to restrict the search space when operators are involved. However, there is no attempt to optimize functions, and they are performed by brute force. Moreover, functions can have any number of arguments while operators are restricted to one or two.

Notes

Refer to the chapter on operators in the *PostgreSQL User's Guide* for further information. Refer to
DROP OPERATOR to delete user-defined operators from a database.

Usage

The following command defines a new operator, area-equality, for the BOX data type:

```
CREATE OPERATOR === (
                LEFTARG = box,
                RIGHTARG = box,
                PROCEDURE = area_equal_procedure,
                COMMUTATOR = ===,
                NEGATOR = !==,
                RESTRICT = area_restriction_procedure,
                JOIN = area_join_procedure,
                HASHES, SORT1 = <<< ,
                SORT2 = <<<
    );
```

Compatibility

SQL92

CREATE OPERATOR is a Postgres extension. There is no **CREATE OPERATOR** statement
in SQL92.

ex 149

D.19   CREATE RULE

Name

CREATE RULE — Defines a new rule
   CREATE RULE *name* AS ON *event*
   TO *object*
   [WHERE *condition*]
   DO [INSTEAD] [*action* | NOTHING]

Inputs

name The name of a rule to create.

event Event is one of select, update, delete or insert.

object Object is either *table* or *table.column*.

condition Any SQL WHERE clause, new or old, can appear instead of an instance variable whenever an instance variable is permissible in SQL.

action Any SQL statement, new or old, can appear instead of an instance variable whenever an instance variable is permissible in SQL.

Outputs

CREATE Message returned if the rule is successfully created.

Description

The Postgres *rule system* allows one to define an alternate action to be performed on inserts, updates, or deletions from database tables or classes. Currently, rules are used to implement table views.

The semantics of a rule is that at the time an individual instance is accessed, inserted, updated, or deleted, there is an old instance (for selects, updates and deletes) and a new instance (for inserts and updates). If the *event* specified in the ON clause and the *condition* specified in the WHERE clause are true for the old instance, the *action* part of the rule is executed. First, however, values from fields in the old instance and/or the new instance are substituted for old.*attribute-name* and new.*attribute-name*.

The *action* part of the rule executes with the same command and transaction identifier as the user command that caused activation.

Notes

A caution about SQL rules is in order. If the same class name or instance variable appears in the *event, condition* and *action* parts of a rule, they are all considered different tuple variables. More accurately, new and old are the only tuple variables that are shared between these clauses. For example, the following two rules have the same semantics:

```
ON UPDATE TO emp.salary
WHERE emp.name = "Joe" DO
UPDATE emp SET ...
WHERE ...

ON UPDATE TO emp-1.salary
WHERE emp-2.name = "Joe" DO
UPDATE emp-3 SET ...
WHERE ...
```

Each rule can have the optional tag INSTEAD. Without this tag, *action* will be performed in addition
to the user command when the *event* in the *condition* part of the rule occurs. Alternately, the *action*
part will be done instead of the user command. In this latter case, the *action* can be the keyword
NOTHING.

It is very important to note to avoid circular rules. For example, though each of the following
two rule definitions are accepted by Postgres, the select command will cause Postgres to report
an error because the query cycled too many times:

Example of a circular rewrite rule combination.

```
CREATE RULE bad_rule_combination_1 AS
ON SELECT TO emp DO INSTEAD
SELECT TO toyemp;

CREATE RULE bad_rule_combination_2 AS
ON SELECT TO toyemp DO INSTEAD
SELECT TO emp;
```

This attempt to select from EMP will cause Postgres to issue an error because the queries cycled
too many times:

```
SELECT * FROM emp;
```

You must have rule definition access to a class in order to define a rule on it. Use **GRANT** and
REVOKE to change permissions.

The object in a SQL rule cannot be an array reference and cannot have parameters.

Aside from the "oid" field, system attributes cannot be referenced anywhere in a rule. Among
other things, this means that functions of instances (e.g., foo(emp) where emp is a class) cannot
be called anywhere in a rule.

The rule system stores the rule text and query plans as text attributes. This implies that
creation of rules may fail if the rule plus its various internal representations exceed some value
that is on the order of one page (8KB).

Usage

Make Sam get the same salary adjustment as Joe:

```
CREATE RULE example_1 AS
ON UPDATE emp.salary
WHERE old.name = "Joe" DO
UPDATE emp SET salary = new.salary
WHERE emp.name = "Sam";
```

At the time Joe receives a salary adjustment, the event will become true and Joe's old instance and proposed new instance are available to the execution routines. Hence, his new salary is substituted into the action part of the rule which is subsequently executed. This propagates Joe's salary on to Sam.

Make Bill get Joe's salary when it is accessed:

```
CREATE RULE example_2 AS
ON SELECT TO EMP.salary
WHERE old.name = "Bill" DO INSTEAD
SELECT emp.salary
FROM emp
WHERE emp.name = "Joe";
```

Deny Joe access to the salary of employees in the shoe department (current_user returns the name of the current user):

```
CREATE RULE example_3 AS
ON SELECT TO emp.salary
WHERE old.dept = "shoe" AND current_user = "Joe" DO INSTEAD
NOTHING;
```

Create a view of the employees working in the toy department:

```
CREATE toyemp(name = char16, salary = int4);
CREATE RULE example_4 AS
ON SELECT TO toyemp DO INSTEAD
SELECT emp.name, emp.salary
FROM emp
WHERE emp.dept = "toy";
```

All new employees must make 5,000 or less:

```
CREATE RULE example_5 AS
ON INERT TO emp
WHERE new.salary > 5000 DO
UPDATE emp SET salary = 5000
WHERE emp.oid = new.oid;
```

Compatibility

SQL92

CREATE RULE statement is a Postgres language extension. There is no **CREATE RULE** statement in SQL92.

D.20   CREATE SEQUENCE

Name

CREATE SEQUENCE — Creates a new sequence number generator
      CREATE SEQUENCE *seqname*
      [INCREMENT *increment*]
      [MINVALUE *minvalue*]
      [MAXVALUE *maxvalue*]
      [START *start*]
      [CACHE *cache*]
      [CYCLE]

Inputs

seqname The name of a sequence to be created.

increment The INCREMENT *increment* clause is optional. A positive value will make an ascending sequence, a negative one a descending sequence. The default value is one (1).

minvalue The optional clause MINVALUE *minvalue* determines the minimum value a sequence can generate. The defaults are 1 and -2147483647 for ascending and descending sequences, respectively.

maxvalue Use the optional clause MAXVALUE *maxvalue* to determine the maximum value for the sequence. The defaults are 2147483647 and -1 for ascending and descending sequences, respectively.

start The optional START *start* clause enables the sequence to begin anywhere. The default starting value is *minvalue* for ascending sequences and *maxvalue* for descending ones.

cache The CACHE *cache* option enables sequence numbers to be preallocated and stored in memory for faster access. The minimum value is 1 (only one value can be generated at a time, i.e., no cache) and this is also the default.

CYCLE The optional CYCLE keyword may be used to enable the sequence to continue when the *maxvalue* or *minvalue* has been reached by an ascending or descending sequence respectively. If the limit is reached, the next number generated will be whatever the *minvalue* or *maxvalue* is, as appropriate.

Outputs

CREATE Message returned if the command is successful.

ERROR: Relation *'seqname'* already exists If the sequence specified already exists.

ERROR: DefineSequence: MINVALUE (*start*) can't be >= MAXVALUE (*max*) If the specified starting value is out of range.

ERROR: DefineSequence: START value (*start*) can't be < MINVALUE (*min*) If the specified starting value is out of range.

ERROR: DefineSequence: MINVALUE (*min*) can't be >= MAXVALUE (*max*) If the minimum and maximum values are inconsistent.

Description

CREATE SEQUENCE will enter a new sequence number generator into the current data base. This involves creating and initializing a new single-row table with the name *seqname*. The generator will be "owned" by the user issuing the command.

After a sequence is created, you may use the function nextval(*seqname*) to get a new number from the sequence. The function currval('*seqname*') may be used to determine the number returned by the last call to nextval(*seqname*) for the specified sequence in the current session. The function setval('*seqname*', *newvalue*) may be used to set the current value of the specified sequence. The next call to nextval(*seqname*) will return the given value plus the sequence increment.

Use a query like `SELECT * FROM seqname;` to get the parameters of a sequence. As an alternative to fetching the parameters from the original definition as above, you can use `SELECT last_value FROM seqname;` to obtain the last value allocated by any backend.

Low-level locking is used to enable multiple simultaneous calls to a generator.

Notes

Use **DROP SEQUENCE** to remove a sequence.

Each backend uses its own cache to store allocated numbers. Numbers that are cached but not used in the current session will be lost, resulting in "holes" in the sequence.

Usage

Create an ascending sequence called serial, starting at 101:

```
CREATE SEQUENCE serial START 101;
```

Select the next number from this sequence:

```
SELECT NEXTVAL ('serial');
nextval
```

```
-------
  114
```

Use this sequence in an INSERT:

```
INSERT INTO distributors
VALUES (NEXTVAL('serial'),'nothing');
```

Set the sequence value after a COPY FROM:

```
CREATE FUNCTION distributors_id_max()
RETURNS INT4 AS '
    SELECT max(id)
    FROM distributors'
LANGUAGE 'sql';
BEGIN;
    COPY distributors FROM 'input_file';
    SELECT setval('serial', distributors_id_max());
END;
```

Compatibility

SQL92

CREATE SEQUENCE is a Postgres language extension. There is no **CREATE SEQUENCE** statement in SQL92.

D.21   CREATE TABLE

Name

CREATE TABLE — Creates a new table
    CREATE [TEMPORARY | TEMP] TABLE *table* (
    column type [NULL | NOT NULL] [UNIQUE] [DEFAULT *value*] [*column_constraint_clause*
    | PRIMARY KEY } [...]] [, ...]
    [, PRIMARY KEY (*column* [, ...])] [, CHECK (*condition*)] [, *table_constraint_clause*]
) [INHERITS (*inherited_table* [, ...])]

Inputs

TEMPORARY The table is created only for this session, and is automatically dropped on session
    exit. Existing permanent tables with the same name are not visible while the temporary
    table exists.

table The name of a new class or table to be created.

column The name of a column.

type The type of the column. This may include array specifiers. Refer to the *PostgreSQL User's Guide* for further information about data types and arrays.

DEFAULT *value* A default value for a column. See the DEFAULT clause for more information.

column_constraint_clause The optional column constraint clauses specify a list of integrity constraints or tests which new or updated entries must satisfy for an insert or update operation to succeed. Each constraint must evaluate to a boolean expression. Although SQL92 requires the *column_constraint_clause* to refer to that column only, Postgres allows multiple columns to be referenced within a single column constraint. See the column constraint clause for more information.

table_constraint_clause The optional table CONSTRAINT clause specifies a list of integrity constraints which new or updated entries must satisfy for an insert or update operation to succeed. Each constraint must evaluate to a boolean expression. Multiple columns may be referenced within a single constraint. Only one PRIMARY KEY clause may be specified for a table; PRIMARY KEY *column* (a table constraint) and PRIMARY KEY (a column constraint) are mutually exclusive. See the table constraint clause for more information.

INHERITS *inherited_table* The optional INHERITS clause specifies a collection of table names from which this table automatically inherits all fields. If any inherited field name appears more than once, Postgres reports an error. Postgres automatically allows the created table to inherit functions on tables above it in the inheritance hierarchy.

Outputs

CREATE Message returned if table is successfully created.

ERROR Message returned if table creation failed. This is usually accompanied by some descriptive text, such as: ERROR: Relation *'table'* already exists, which occurs at runtime if the table specified already exists in the database.

ERROR: DEFAULT: type mismatched If data type of default value doesn't match the column definition's data type.

Description

CREATE TABLE will enter a new class or table into the current data base. The table will be "owned" by the user issuing the command.

Each *type* may be a simple type, a complex type (set) or an array type. Each attribute may be specified to be non-null and each may have a default value, specified by the *DEFAULT Clause*.

Note: Consistent array dimensions within an attribute are not enforced. This will likely change in a future release.

The optional INHERITS clause specifies a collection of class names from which this class automatically inherits all fields. If any inherited field name appears more than once, Postgres reports an error. Postgres automatically allows the created class to inherit functions on classes above it in the inheritance hierarchy. Inheritance of functions is done according to the conventions of the Common Lisp Object System (CLOS).

Each new table or class *table* is automatically created as a type. Therefore, one or more instances from the class are automatically a type and can be used in *ALTER TABLE* or other **CREATE TABLE** statements.

The new table is created as a heap with no initial data. A table can have no more than 1600 columns (realistically, this is limited by the fact that tuple sizes must be less than 8192 bytes), but this limit may be configured lower at some sites. A table cannot have the same name as a system catalog table.

DEFAULT Clause

DEFAULT *value*

Inputs

value The possible values for the default value expression are:

- a literal value
- a user function
- a niladic function

Outputs

None.

Description

The DEFAULT clause assigns a default data value to a column (via a column definition in the CREATE TABLE statement). The data type of a default value must match the column definition's data type.

An INSERT operation that includes a column without a specified default value will assign the NULL value to the column if no explicit data value is provided for it. Default *literal* means that the default is the specified constant value. Default *niladic-function* or *user-function* means that the default is the value of the specified function at the time of the INSERT.

There are two types of niladic functions:

niladic USER

    CURRENT_USER / USER See CURRENT_USER function

    SESSION_USER See CURRENT_USER function

    SYSTEM_USER Not implemented

niladic datetime

    CURRENT_DATE See CURRENT_DATE function

    CURRENT_TIME See CURRENT_TIME function

    CURRENT_TIMESTAMP See CURRENT_TIMESTAMP function

Usage

To assign a constant value as the default for the columns *did* and *number,* and a string literal to the column *did:*

```
CREATE TABLE video_sales (
                    did VARCHAR(40) DEFAULT 'luso films',
                    number INTEGER DEFAULT 0,
                    total CASH DEFAULT '$0.0'
);
```

To assign an existing sequence as the default for the column *did,* and a literal to the column *name:*

```
CREATE TABLE distributors (
                    did DECIMAL(3) DEFAULT NEXTVAL('serial'),
                    name VARCHAR(40) DEFAULT 'luso films'
);
```

Column CONSTRAINT Clause

[CONSTRAINT *name*] {
   [NULL | NOT NULL] | UNIQUE | PRIMARY KEY | CHECK *constraint* |
   REFERENCES *reftable* (*refcolumn*) [MATCH *matchtype*] [ON DELETE *action*] [ON UPDATE
action] [[NOT] DEFERRABLE] [INITIALLY *checktime*] } [, ...]

Inputs

name An arbitrary name given to the integrity constraint. If *name* is not specified, it is generated from the table and column names, which should ensure uniqueness for *name*.

NULL The column is allowed to contain NULL values. This is the default.

NOT NULL The column is not allowed to contain NULL values. This is equivalent to the column constraint CHECK (*column* NOT NULL).

UNIQUE The column must have unique values. In Postgres this is enforced by an implicit creation of a unique index on the table.

PRIMARY KEY This column is a primary key, which implies that uniqueness is enforced by the system and that other tables may rely on this column as a unique identifier for rows. See PRIMARY KEY for more information.

constraint The definition of the constraint.

Description

The optional constraint clauses specify constraints or tests which new or updated entries must satisfy for an insert or update operation to succeed. Each constraint must evaluate to a boolean expression. Multiple attributes may be referenced within a single constraint. The use of PRIMARY KEY as a table constraint is mutually incompatible with PRIMARY KEY as a column constraint.

A constraint is a named rule: an SQL object which helps define valid sets of values by putting limits on the results of INSERT, UPDATE or DELETE operations performed on a Base Table.

There are two ways to define integrity constraints: table constraints, covered later, and column constraints, covered here.

A column constraint is an integrity constraint defined as part of a column definition, and logically becomes a table constraint as soon as it is created. The column constraints available are:

```
PRIMARY KEY
REFERENCES
UNIQUE
CHECK
NOT NULL
```

NOT NULL Constraint

[CONSTRAINT *name*] NOT NULL

The NOT NULL constraint specifies a rule that a column may contain only non-null values. This is a column constraint only, and not allowed as a table constraint.

Outputs

status ERROR: ExecAppend: Fail to add null value in not null attribute *"column* ". This error occurs at runtime if one tries to insert a null value into a column which has a NOT NULL constraint.

Description

Usage

Define two NOT NULL column constraints on the table distributors, one of which being a named constraint:

```
CREATE TABLE distributors (
                        did DECIMAL(3) CONSTRAINT no_null NOT NULL,
                        name VARCHAR(40) NOT NULL
    );
```

UNIQUE Constraint

[CONSTRAINT *name*] UNIQUE

Inputs

CONSTRAINT *name* An arbitrary label given to a constraint.

Outputs

status

> **ERROR: Cannot insert a duplicate key into a unique index.** This error occurs at runtime if one tries to insert a duplicate value into a column.

Description

The UNIQUE constraint specifies a rule that a group of one or more distinct columns of a table may contain only unique values.

The column definitions of the specified columns do not have to include a NOT NULL constraint to be included in a UNIQUE constraint. Having more than one null value in a column without a NOT NULL constraint, does not violate a UNIQUE constraint. (This deviates from the SQL92 definition, but is a more sensible convention. See the section on compatibility for more details.)

Each UNIQUE column constraint must name a column that is different from the set of columns named by any other UNIQUE or PRIMARY KEY constraint defined for the table.

Note: Postgres automatically creates a unique index for each UNIQUE constraint, to assure data integrity. See CREATE INDEX for more information.

Usage

Defines a UNIQUE column constraint for the table distributors. UNIQUE column constraints can only be defined on one column of the table:

```
CREATE TABLE distributors ( did DECIMAL(3),
                            name VARCHAR(40) UNIQUE
);
```

which is equivalent to the following specified as a table constraint:

```
CREATE TABLE distributors ( did DECIMAL(3),
                            name VARCHAR(40),
                            UNIQUE(name)
);
```

The CHECK Constraint

[CONSTRAINT *name*] CHECK (*condition* [, ...])

Inputs

name   An arbitrary name given to a constraint.

condition   Any valid conditional expression evaluating to a boolean result.

Outputs

status

> **ERROR: ExecAppend: rejected due to CHECK constraint "*table_column*".** This error occurs at runtime if one tries to insert an illegal value into a column subject to a CHECK constraint.

Description

The CHECK constraint specifies a restriction on allowed values within a column. The CHECK constraint is also allowed as a table constraint.

The SQL92 CHECK column constraints can only be defined on, and refer to, one column of the table. Postgres does not have this restriction.

PRIMARY KEY Constraint

[CONSTRAINT *name*] PRIMARY KEY

Inputs

CONSTRAINT *name* An arbitrary name for the constraint.

Outputs

ERROR: Cannot insert a duplicate key into a unique index. This occurs at runtime if one tries to insert a duplicate value into a column subject to a PRIMARY KEY constraint.

Description

The PRIMARY KEY column constraint specifies that a column of a table may contain only unique (non-duplicate), non-NULL values. The definition of the specified column does not have to include an explicit NOT NULL constraint to be included in a PRIMARY KEY constraint.

Only one PRIMARY KEY can be specified for a table.

Notes

Postgres automatically creates a unique index to assure data integrity (see CREATE INDEX statement).

The PRIMARY KEY constraint should name a set of columns that is different from other sets of columns named by any UNIQUE constraint defined for the same table, since it will result in duplication of equivalent indexes and unproductive additional runtime overhead. However, Postgres does not specifically disallow this.

REFERENCES Constraint

[CONSTRAINT *name*] REFERENCES *reftable* [(*refcolumn*)] [MATCH *matchtype*] [ON DELETE *action*] [ON UPDATE *action*] [[NOT] DEFERRABLE] [INITIALLY *checktime*]

The REFERENCES constraint specifies a rule that a column value is checked against the values of another column. REFERENCES can also be specified as part of a FOREIGN KEY table constraint.

Inputs

CONSTRAINT *name* An arbitrary name for the constraint.

reftable The table that contains the data to check against.

refcolumn   The column in *reftable* to check the data against. If this is not specified, the PRIMARY KEY of the *reftable* is used.

MATCH *matchtype*   There are three match types: MATCH FULL, MATCH PARTIAL, and a default match type if none is specified. MATCH FULL will not allow one column of a multi-column foreign key to be NULL unless all foreign key columns are NULL. The default MATCH type allows some foreign key columns to be NULL while other parts of the foreign key are not NULL. MATCH PARTIAL is currently not supported.

ON DELETE *action*   The action to do when a referenced row in the referenced table is being deleted. There are the following actions.

  NO ACTION   Produce error if foreign key violated. This is the default.

  RESTRICT   Same as NO ACTION.

  CASCADE   Delete any rows referencing the deleted row.

  SET NULL   Set the referencing column values to NULL.

  SET DEFAULT   Set the referencing column values to their default value.

ON UPDATE *action*   The action to do when a referenced column in the referenced table is being updated to a new value. If the row is updated, but the referenced column is not changed, no action is done. There are the following actions.

  NO ACTION   Produce error if foreign key violated. This is the default.

  RESTRICT   Same as NO ACTION.

  CASCADE   Update the value of the referencing column to the new value of the referenced column.

  SET NULL   Set the referencing column values to NULL.

  SET DEFAULT   Set the referencing column values to their default value.

[NOT DEFERRABLE]   This controls whether the constraint can be deferred to the end of the transaction. If DEFERRABLE, SET CONSTRAINTS ALL DEFERRED will cause the foreign key to be checked only at the end of the transaction. NOT DEFERRABLE is the default.

INITIALLY *checktime*   *checktime* has two possible values which specify the default time to check the constraint.

  DEFERRED   Check constraint only at the end of the transaction.

  IMMEDIATE   Check constraint after each statement. This is the default.

Outputs

status

ERROR: *name* **referential integrity violation - key referenced from** *table* **not found in**
reftable This error occurs at runtime if one tries to insert a value into a column which does
not have a matching column in the referenced table.

Description

The REFERENCES column constraint specifies that a column of a table must only contain values
which match against values in a referenced column of a referenced table.

A value added to this column is matched against the values of the referenced table and referenced
column using the given match type. In addition, when the referenced column data is changed,
actions are run upon this column's matching data.

Notes

Currently Postgres only supports MATCH FULL and a default match type. In addition, the
referenced columns are supposed to be the columns of a UNIQUE constraint in the referenced
table, however Postgres does not enforce this.

Table CONSTRAINT Clause

[CONSTRAINT name] { PRIMARY KEY | UNIQUE } (*column* [, ...]) [CONSTRAINT name
] CHECK (*constraint*) [CONSTRAINT name] FOREIGN KEY (*column* [, ...]) REFERENCES
reftable
   (*refcolumn* [, ...]) [MATCH *matchtype*] [ON DELETE *action*] [ON UPDATE *action*] [[NOT
] DEFERRABLE] [INITIALLY *checktime*]

Inputs

CONSTRAINT *name* An arbitrary name given to an integrity constraint.

column [, ...] The column name(s) for which to define a unique index and, for PRIMARY KEY, a
NOT NULL constraint.

CHECK (*constraint* **)** A boolean expression to be evaluated as the constraint.

Outputs

The possible outputs for the table constraint clause are the same as for the corresponding portions
of the column constraint clause.

Description

A table constraint is an integrity constraint defined on one or more columns of a base table. The four variations of "Table Constraint" are:

```
UNIQUE
CHECK
PRIMARY KEY
FOREIGN KEY
```

UNIQUE Constraint

[CONSTRAINT *name*] UNIQUE (*column* [, ...])

Inputs

CONSTRAINT *name* An arbitrary name given to a constraint.

column A name of a column in a table.

Outputs

status

> **ERROR: Cannot insert a duplicate key into a unique index** This error occurs at run-time if one tries to insert a duplicate value into a column.

Description

The UNIQUE constraint specifies a rule that a group of one or more distinct columns of a table may contain only unique values. The behavior of the UNIQUE table constraint is the same as that for column constraints, with the additional capability to span multiple columns.

See the section on the UNIQUE column constraint for more details.

Usage

Define a UNIQUE table constraint for the table distributors:

```
CREATE TABLE distributors (
                    did DECIMAL(3),
                    name VARCHAR(40),
                    UNIQUE(name)
    );
```

PRIMARY KEY Constraint

[CONSTRAINT *name*] PRIMARY KEY (*column* [, ...])

Inputs

CONSTRAINT *name* An arbitrary name for the constraint.

column [, ...] The names of one or more columns in the table.

Outputs

status

> **ERROR: Cannot insert a duplicate key into a unique index.** This occurs at run-time if one tries to insert a duplicate value into a column subject to a PRIMARY KEY constraint.

Description

The PRIMARY KEY constraint specifies a rule that a group of one or more distinct columns of a table may contain only unique (nonduplicate), non-null values. The column definitions of the specified columns do not have to include a NOT NULL constraint to be included in a PRIMARY KEY constraint.

The PRIMARY KEY table constraint is similar to that for column constraints, with the additional capability of encompassing multiple columns.

Refer to the section on the PRIMARY KEY column constraint for more information.

REFERENCES Constraint

[CONSTRAINT *name*] FOREIGN KEY (*column* [, ...]) REFERENCES *reftable* [(*refcolumn* [, ...])] [MATCH *matchtype*] [ON DELETE *action*] [ON UPDATE *action*] [[NOT] DEFERRABLE] [INITIALLY *checktime*]

The REFERENCES constraint specifies a rule that a column value is checked against the values of another column. REFERENCES can also be specified as part of a FOREIGN KEY table constraint.

Inputs

CONSTRAINT *name* An arbitrary name for the constraint.

column [, ...] The names of one or more columns in the table.

reftable The table that contains the data to check against.

referenced column [, ...] One or more column in the *reftable* to check the data against. If this is not specified, the PRIMARY KEY of the *reftable* is used.

MATCH *matchtype* There are three match types: MATCH FULL, MATCH PARTIAL, and a default match type if none is specified. MATCH FULL will not allow one column of a multi-column foreign key to be NULL unless all foreign key columns are NULL. The default MATCH type allows a some foreign key columns to be NULL while other parts of the foreign key are not NULL. MATCH PARTIAL is currently not supported.

ON DELETE *action* The action to do when a referenced row in the referenced table is being deleted. There are the following actions.

> **NO ACTION** Produce error if foreign key violated. This is the default.

> **RESTRICT** Same as NO ACTION.

> **CASCADE** Delete any rows referencing the deleted row.

> **SET NULL** Set the referencing column values to NULL.

> **SET DEFAULT** Set the referencing column values to their default value.

ON UPDATE *action* The action to do when a referenced column in the referenced table is being updated to a new value. If the row is updated, but the referenced column is not changed, no action is done. There are the following actions.

> **NO ACTION** Produce error if foreign key violated. This is the default.

> **RESTRICT** Disallow update of row being referenced.

> **CASCADE** Update the value of the referencing column to the new value of the referenced column.

> **SET NULL** Set the referencing column values to NULL.

> **SET DEFAULT** Set the referencing column values to their default value.

[NOT DEFERRABLE] This controls whether the constraint can be deferred to the end of the transaction. If DEFERRABLE, SET CONSTRAINTS ALL DEFERRED will cause the foreign key to be checked only at the end of the transaction. NOT DEFERRABLE is the default.

INITIALLY *checktime* *checktime* has two possible values which specify the default time to check the constraint.

> **IMMEDIATE** Check constraint after each statement. This is the default.

> **DEFERRED** Check constraint only at the end of the transaction.

Outputs

status

> **ERROR:** *name* **referential integrity violation — key referenced from** *table* **not found in** *reftable* This error occurs at runtime if one tries to insert a value into a column which does not have a matching column in the referenced table.

Description

The FOREIGN KEY constraint specifies a rule that a group of one or more distinct columns of a table is related to a group of distinct columns in the referenced table.

The FOREIGN KEY table constraint is similar to that for column constraints, with the additional capability of encompassing multiple columns.

Refer to the section on the FOREIGN KEY column constraint for more information.

Usage

Create table films and table distributors:

```
CREATE TABLE films (
    code      CHARACTER(5) CONSTRAINT firstkey PRIMARY KEY,
    title     CHARACTER VARYING(40) NOT NULL,
    did       DECIMAL(3) NOT NULL,
    date_prod DATE,
    kind      CHAR(10),
    len       INTERVAL HOUR TO MINUTE
);

CREATE TABLE distributors (
    did       DECIMAL(3) PRIMARY KEY DEFAULT NEXTVAL('serial'),
    name      VARCHAR(40) NOT NULL CHECK (name <> '')
);
```

Create a table with a 2-dimensional array:

```
CREATE TABLE array (
        vector INT[][]
);
```

Define a UNIQUE table constraint for the table films. UNIQUE table constraints can be defined on one or more columns of the table:

```
CREATE TABLE films (
    code        CHAR(5),
    title       VARCHAR(40),
    did         DECIMAL(3),
    date_prod DATE,
    kind        CHAR(10),
    len         INTERVAL HOUR TO MINUTE,
    CONSTRAINT production UNIQUE(date_prod)
);
```

Define a CHECK column constraint:

```
CREATE TABLE distributors (
    did         DECIMAL(3) CHECK (did > 100),
    name        VARCHAR(40)
);
```

Define a CHECK table constraint:

```
CREATE TABLE distributors (
    did         DECIMAL(3),
    name        VARCHAR(40)
    CONSTRAINT con1 CHECK (did > 100 AND name > '')
);
```

Define a PRIMARY KEY table constraint for the table films. PRIMARY KEY table constraints can be defined on one or more columns of the table:

```
CREATE TABLE films (
    code        CHAR(5),
    title       VARCHAR(40),
    did         DECIMAL(3),
    date_prod DATE,
    kind        CHAR(10),
    len         INTERVAL HOUR TO MINUTE,
    CONSTRAINT code_title PRIMARY KEY(code,title)
);
```

Defines a PRIMARY KEY column constraint for table distributors. PRIMARY KEY column constraints can only be defined on one column of the table (the following two examples are equivalent):

```
CREATE TABLE distributors (
    did      DECIMAL(3),
    name     CHAR VARYING(40),
    PRIMARY KEY(did)
);

CREATE TABLE distributors (
    did      DECIMAL(3) PRIMARY KEY,
    name     VARCHAR(40)
);
```

Notes

CREATE TABLE/INHERITS is a Postgres language extension.

Compatibility

SQL92

In addition to the locally visible temporary table, SQL92 also defines a CREATE GLOBAL TEM-
PORARY TABLE statement, and optionally an ON COMMIT clause:

CREATE GLOBAL TEMPORARY TABLE *table* (*column type* [DEFAULT *value*] [CON-
STRAINT *column_constraint*] [, ...]) [CONSTRAINT *table_constraint*] [ON COMMIT {
DELETE | PRESERVE } ROWS]

For temporary tables, the CREATE GLOBAL TEMPORARY TABLE statement names a new
table visible to other clients and defines the table's columns and constraints.

The optional ON COMMIT clause of CREATE TEMPORARY TABLE specifies whether or
not the temporary table should be emptied of rows whenever COMMIT is executed. If the ON
COMMIT clause is omitted, the default option, ON COMMIT DELETE ROWS, is assumed.

To create a temporary table:

```
CREATE TEMPORARY TABLE actors (
    id       DECIMAL(3),
    name     VARCHAR(40),
    CONSTRAINT actor_id CHECK (id < 150)
) ON COMMIT DELETE ROWS;
```

UNIQUE clause

SQL92 specifies some additional capabilities for UNIQUE:
Table Constraint definition:

```
[ CONSTRAINT name ] UNIQUE ( column [, ...] ) [ {  INITIALLY DEFERRED | INI-
TIALLY IMMEDIATE }  ] [ [ NOT ] DEFERRABLE ]
```

Column Constraint definition:

```
[ CONSTRAINT name ] UNIQUE [ { INITIALLY DEFERRED | INITIALLY IMMEDI-
ATE} ] [ [ NOT ] DEFERRABLE ]
```

NULL clause

The NULL "constraint" (actually a non-constraint) is a Postgres extension to SQL92 is included for symmetry with the NOT NULL clause. Since it is the default for any column, its presence is simply noise. [CONSTRAINT *name*] NULL

NOT NULL clause

SQL92 specifies some additional capabilities for NOT NULL:

```
[ CONSTRAINT name ] NOT NULL [ { INITIALLY DEFERRED | INITIALLY IMMEDI-
ATE} ] [ [ NOT ] DEFERRABLE ]
```

CONSTRAINT clause

SQL92 specifies some additional capabilities for constraints, and also defines assertions and domain constraints. **Note:** Postgres does not yet support either domains or assertions.

An assertion is a special type of integrity constraint and shares the same namespace as other constraints. However, an assertion is not necessarily dependent on one particular base table as constraints are, so SQL-92 provides the CREATE ASSERTION statement as an alternate method for defining a constraint:

```
CREATE ASSERTION name CHECK ( condition )
```

Domain constraints are defined by CREATE DOMAIN or ALTER DOMAIN statements:

Domain constraint:

```
[ CONSTRAINT name ] CHECK constraint
[ { INITIALLY DEFERRED | INITIALLY IMMEDIATE} ] [ [ NOT ] DEFERRABLE ]
```

Table constraint definition:

```
[ CONSTRAINT name ] { PRIMARY KEY ( column , ... ) | FOREIGN KEY con-
straint | UNIQUE constraint | CHECK constraint } [ { INITIALLY DEFERRED | INI-
TIALLY IMMEDIATE} ] [ [ NOT ] DEFERRABLE ]
```

Column constraint definition:

```
[ CONSTRAINT name ] { NOT NULL | PRIMARY KEY | FOREIGN KEY con-
straint | UNIQUE | CHECK constraint } [ { INITIALLY DEFERRED | INITIALLY IMME-
DIATE} ] [ [ NOT ] DEFERRABLE ]
```

A CONSTRAINT definition may contain one deferment attribute clause and/or one initial constraint mode clause, in any order.

NOT DEFERRABLE The constraint must be checked at the end of each statement. SET CONSTRAINTS ALL DEFERRED will have no effect on this type of constraint.

DEFERRABLE This controls whether the constraint can be deferred to the end of the transaction. If SET CONSTRAINTS ALL DEFERRED is used or the constraint is set to INITIALLY DEFERRED, this will cause the foreign key to be checked only at the end of the transaction.

SET CONSTRAINT changes the foreign key constraint mode only for the current transaction.

INITIALLY IMMEDIATE Check constraint only at the end of the transaction. This is the default

INITIALLY DEFERRED Check constraint after each statement.

CHECK clause

SQL92 specifies some additional capabilities for CHECK in either table or column constraints. table constraint definition:

```
[ CONSTRAINT name ] CHECK ( VALUE condition ) [ { INITIALLY DEFERRED | INI-
TIALLY IMMEDIATE} ] [ [ NOT ] DEFERRABLE ]
```

column constraint definition:

```
[ CONSTRAINT name ] CHECK ( VALUE condition ) [ { INITIALLY DEFERRED | INI-
TIALLY IMMEDIATE} ] [ [ NOT ] DEFERRABLE ]
```

PRIMARY KEY clause

SQL92 specifies some additional capabilities for PRIMARY KEY:
Table Constraint definition:

```
[ CONSTRAINT name ] PRIMARY KEY ( column [, ...] ) [ { INITIALLY DE-
FERRED | INITIALLY IMMEDIATE} ] [ [ NOT ] DEFERRABLE ]
```

Column Constraint definition:

```
[ CONSTRAINT name ] PRIMARY KEY [ { INITIALLY DEFERRED | INITIALLY IMMEDI-
ATE} ] [ [ NOT ] DEFERRABLE ]
```

D.22   CREATE TABLE AS

Name

CREATE TABLE AS — Creates a new table
CREATE TABLE *table* [(*column* [, ...])] AS *select_clause*

Inputs

table The name of a new table to be created.

column The name of a column. Multiple column names can be specified using a comma-delimited list of column names.

select_clause A valid query statement. Refer to SELECT for a description of the allowed syntax.

Outputs

Refer to **CREATE TABLE** and **SELECT** for a summary of possible output messages.

Description

CREATE TABLE AS enables a table to be created from the contents of an existing table. It is functionality equivalent to *SELECT INTO*, but with perhaps a more direct syntax.

D.23   CREATE TRIGGER

Name

CREATE TRIGGER — Creates a new trigger
     CREATE TRIGGER *name* { BEFORE | AFTER } { *event* [OR ...] }
     ON *table*
     FOR EACH { ROW | STATEMENT }
     EXECUTE PROCEDURE *func* (*arguments*)

Inputs

name The name of an existing trigger.

table The name of a table.

event One of INSERT, DELETE or UPDATE.

funcname A user-supplied function.

Outputs

CREATE This message is returned if the trigger is successfully created.

Description

CREATE TRIGGER will enter a new trigger into the current data base. The trigger will be associated with the relation *relname* and will execute the specified function *funcname*.

The trigger can be specified to fire either before BEFORE the operation is attempted on a tuple (before constraints are checked and the **INSERT, UPDATE** or **DELETE** is attempted) or AFTER the operation has been attempted (e.g., after constraints are checked and the **INSERT, UPDATE** or **DELETE** has completed). If the trigger fires before the event, the trigger may skip the operation for the current tuple, or change the tuple being inserted (for **INSERT** and **UPDATE** operations only). If the trigger fires after the event, all changes, including the last insertion, update, or deletion, are "visible" to the trigger.

Refer to the chapters on SPI and Triggers in the *PostgreSQL Programmer's Guide* for more information.

Notes

CREATE TRIGGER is a Postgres language extension.

Only the relation owner may create a trigger on this relation.

As of the current release (v7.0), STATEMENT triggers are not implemented.

Refer to **DROP TRIGGER** for information on how to remove triggers.

Usage

Check if the specified distributor code exists in the distributors table before appending or updating a row in the table films:

```
CREATE TRIGGER if_dist_exists
BEFORE INSERT OR UPDATE ON films
FOR EACH ROW
EXECUTE PROCEDURE check_primary_key ('did', 'distributors', 'did');
```

Before cancelling a distributor or updating its code, remove every reference to the table films:

```
CREATE TRIGGER if_film_exists
BEFORE DELETE OR UPDATE ON distributors
FOR EACH ROW
EXECUTE PROCEDURE check_foreign_key (1, 'CASCADE', 'did', 'films', 'did');
```

Compatibility

SQL92

There is no **CREATE TRIGGER** in SQL92.

The second example above may also be done by using a FOREIGN KEY constraint as in:

```
CREATE TABLE distributors (
                        did DECIMAL(3),
                        name VARCHAR(40),
                        CONSTRAINT if_film_exists FOREIGN KEY(did)
                        REFERENCES films ON UPDATE CASCADE ON DELETE CASCADE
);
```

D.24   CREATE TYPE

Name

CREATE TYPE — Defines a new base data type
    CREATE TYPE *typename* (
    INPUT = *input_function* ,
    OUTPUT = *output_function,*
    INTERNALLENGTH = { *internallength* | VARIABLE }
    [, EXTERNALLENGTH = { *externallength* | VARIABLE }]
    [, DEFAULT = "*default* "]
    [, ELEMENT = *element*]
    [, DELIMITER = *delimiter*]
    [, SEND = *send_function*]
    [, RECEIVE = *receive_function*]
    [, PASSEDBYVALUE])

Inputs

typename   The name of a type to be created.

internallength   A literal value, which specifies the internal length of the new type.

externallength   A literal value, which specifies the external length of the new type.

input_function   The name of a function, created by **CREATE FUNCTION**, which converts data from its external form to the type's internal form.

output_function   The name of a function, created by **CREATE FUNCTION,** which converts data from its internal form to a form suitable for display.

element   The type being created is an array; this specifies the type of the array elements.

delimiter   The delimiter character for the array.

default   The default text to be displayed to indicate "data not present."

send_function The name of a function, created by **CREATE FUNCTION**, which converts data of this type into a form suitable for transmission to another machine.

receive_function The name of a function, created by **CREATE FUNCTION**, which converts data of this type from a form suitable for transmission from another machine to internal form.

Outputs

CREATE Message returned if the type is successfully created.

Description

CREATE TYPE allows the user to register a new user data type with Postgres for use in the current data base. The user who defines a type becomes its owner. *typename* is the name of the new type and must be unique within the types defined for this database.

CREATE TYPE requires the registration of two functions (using create function) before defining the type. The representation of a new base type is determined by *input_function*, which converts the type's external representation to an internal representation usable by the operators and functions defined for the type. Naturally, *output_function* performs the reverse transformation. Both the input and output functions must be declared to take one or two arguments of type "opaque".

New base data types can be fixed length, in which case *internallength* is a positive integer, or variable length, in which case Postgres assumes that the new type has the same format as the Postgres-supplied data type, "text". To indicate that a type is variable length, set *internallength* to VARIABLE. The external representation is similarly specified using the *externallength* keyword.

To indicate that a type is an array and to indicate that a type has array elements, indicate the type of the array element using the element keyword. For example, to define an array of 4-byte integers ("int4"), specify ELEMENT = int4

To indicate the delimiter to be used on arrays of this type, *delimiter* can be set to a specific character. The default delimiter is the comma (",").

A default value is optionally available in case a user wants some specific bit pattern to mean "data not present." Specify the default with the DEFAULT keyword.

The optional arguments *send_function* and *receive_function* are used when the application program requesting Postgres services resides on a different machine. In this case, the machine on which Postgres runs may use a format for the data type different from that used on the remote machine. In this case it is appropriate to convert data items to a standard form when sending from the server to the client and converting from the standard format to the machine specific format when the server receives the data from the client. If these functions are not specified, then it is assumed that the internal format of the type is acceptable on all relevant machine architectures. For example, single characters do not have to be converted if passed from a Sun-4 to a DECstation, but many other types do.

The optional flag, PASSEDBYVALUE, indicates that operators and functions which use this data type should be passed an argument by value rather than by reference. Note that you may not pass by value types whose internal representation is more than four bytes.

For new base types, a user can define operators, functions and aggregates using the appropriate facilities described in this section.

Array Types

Two generalized built-in functions, array_in and array_out, exist for quick creation of variable length array types. These functions operate on arrays of any existing Postgres type.

Large Object Types

A "regular" Postgres type can only be 8192 bytes in length. If you need a larger type you must create a Large Object type. The interface for these types is discussed at length in the *PostgreSQL Programmer's Guide*. The length of all large object types is always VARIABLE.

Examples

This command creates the box data type and then uses the type in a class definition:

```
CREATE TYPE box (INTERNALLENGTH = 8,
                 INPUT = my_procedure_1,
                 OUTPUT = my_procedure_2);
CREATE TABLE myboxes (id INT4, description box);
```

This command creates a variable length array type with integer elements:

```
CREATE TYPE int4array (INPUT = array_in,
                       OUTPUT = array_out,
                       INTERNALLENGTH = VARIABLE,
                       ELEMENT = int4);
CREATE TABLE myarrays (id int4, numbers int4array);
```

This command creates a large object type and uses it in a class definition:

```
CREATE TYPE bigobj (INPUT = lo_filein,
                    OUTPUT = lo_fileout,
                    INTERNALLENGTH = VARIABLE);
CREATE TABLE big_objs (id int4, obj bigobj);
```

Notes

Type names cannot begin with the underscore character ("_") and can only be 31 characters long. This is because Postgres silently creates an array type for each base type with a name consisting of the base type's name prepended with an underscore.

Refer to **DROP TYPE** to remove an existing type.

See also **CREATE FUNCTION**, **CREATE OPERATOR** and the chapter on Large Objects in the *PostgreSQL Programmer's Guide*.

Compatibility

SQL3

CREATE TYPE is an SQL3 statement.

D.25   CREATE USER

Name

CREATE USER — Creates a new database user

      CREATE USER *username*
      [WITH [SYSID *uid*]
      [PASSWORD *'password'*]]
      [CREATEDB | NOCREATEDB]
      [CREATEUSER | NOCREATEUSER]
      [IN GROUP *groupname* [, ...]]
      [VALID UNTIL *'abstime'*]

Inputs

username The name of the user.

uid The SYSID clause can be used to choose the Postgres user id of the user that is being created. It is not at all necessary that those match the UNIX user ids, but some people choose to keep the numbers the same.

If this is not specified, the highest assigned user id plus one will be used as default.

password Sets the user's password. If you do not plan to use password authentication you can omit this option, otherwise the user won't be able to connect to a password-authenticated server. See pg_hba.conf(5) or the administrator's guide for details on how to set up authentication mechanisms.

CREATEDB, NOCREATEDB These clauses define a user's ability to create databases. If CREATEDB is specified, the user being defined will be allowed to create his own databases. Using NOCREATEDB will deny a user the ability to create databases. If this clause is omitted, NOCREATEDB is used by default.

CREATEUSER, NOCREATEUSER These clauses determine whether a user will be permitted to create new users himself. This option will also make the user a superuser who can override all access restrictions. Omitting this clause will set the user's value of this attribute to be NOCREATEUSER.

groupname A name of a group into which to insert the user as a new member.

abstime The VALID UNTIL clause sets an absolute time after which the user's password is no longer valid. If this clause is omitted the login will be valid for all time.

Outputs

CREATE USER Message returned if the command completes successfully.

Description

CREATE USER will add a new user to an instance of Postgres. Refer to the administrator's guide for information about managing users and authentication. You must be a database superuser to use this command.

Use *ALTER USER* to change a user's password and privileges, and *DROP USER* to remove a user. Use **ALTER GROUP** to add or remove the user from other groups. Postgres comes with a script *createuser* which has the same functionality as this command (in fact, it calls this command) but can be run from the command shell.

Usage

Create a user with no password:

```
CREATE USER jonathan
```

Create a user with a password:

```
CREATE USER davide WITH PASSWORD 'jw8s0F4'
```

Create a user with a password, whose account is valid until the end of 2001. Note that after one second has ticked in 2002, the account is not valid:

```
CREATE USER miriam WITH PASSWORD 'jw8s0F4' VALID UNTIL 'Jan 1 2002'
```

Create an account where the user can create databases:

```
CREATE USER manuel WITH PASSWORD 'jw8s0F4'
CREATEDB
```

Compatibility

SQL92

There is no **CREATE USER** statement in SQL92.

D.26 CREATE VIEW

Name

CREATE VIEW — Constructs a virtual table
    CREATE VIEW *view* AS SELECT *query*

Inputs

view The name of a view to be created.

query An SQL query which will provide the columns and rows of the view.

    Refer to the SELECT statement for more information about valid arguments.

Outputs

CREATE The message returned if the view is successfully created.

ERROR: Relation '*view*' already exists This error occurs if the view specified already exists in the database.

NOTICE create: attribute named "*column*" has an unknown type The view will be created having a column with an unknown type if you do not specify it. For example, the following command gives a warning:

```
CREATE VIEW vista AS SELECT 'Hello World'
```

whereas this command does not:

```
CREATE VIEW vista AS SELECT text 'Hello World'
```

Description

CREATE VIEW will define a view of a table or class. This view is not physically materialized. Specifically, a query rewrite retrieve rule is automatically generated to support retrieve operations on views.

Notes

Currently, views are read only.
Use the **DROP VIEW** statement to drop views.

Usage

Create a view consisting of all Comedy films:

```
                    Comedies
CREATE VIEW kinds AS
SELECT *
FROM films
WHERE kind = 'Comedy';
SELECT *
                comedies
FROM kinds;
 code  |              title           | did | date_prod  |  kind  | len
-------+------------------------------+-----+------------+--------+-------
 UA502 | Bananas                      | 105 | 1971-07-13 | Comedy | 01:22
 C_701 | There's a Girl in my Soup    | 107 | 1970-06-11 | Comedy | 01:36
(2 rows)
```

Compatibility

SQL92

SQL92 specifies some additional capabilities for the **CREATE VIEW** statement:
    CREATE VIEW *view* [*column* [, ...]] AS
    SELECT *expression* [AS *colname*] [, ...]
    FROM *table*
    [WHERE *condition*]
    [WITH [CASCADE | LOCAL] CHECK OPTION]
    The optional clauses for the full SQL92 command are:

CHECK OPTION This option is to do with updatable views. All INSERTs and UPDATEs on the view will be checked to ensure data satisfy the view-defining condition. If they do not, the update will be rejected.

LOCAL Check for integrity on this view.

CASCADE Check for integrity on this view and on any dependent view. CASCADE is assumed if neither CASCADE nor LOCAL is specified.

D.27   createdb

Name

createdb — Create a new Postgres database
createdb [*options*] *dbname* [*description*]

Inputs

-h, –host *host* Specifies the hostname of the machine on which the postmaster is running.

-p, –port *port* Specifies the Internet TCP/IP port or local Unix domain socket file extension on which the postmaster is listening for connections.

-U, –username *username* Username to connect as.

-W, –password Force password prompt.

-e, –echo Echo the queries that createdb generates and sends to the backend.

-q, –quiet Do not display a response.

-D, –location *datadir* Specifies the alternate database location for this database installation. This is the location of the installation system tables, not the location of this specific database, which may be different.

-E, –encoding *encoding* Specifies the character encoding scheme to be used with this database.

dbname Specifies the name of the database to be created. The name must be unique among all Postgres databases in this installation. The default is to create a database with the same name as the current system user.

description This optionally specifies a comment to be associated with the newly created database.

The options -h, -p, -U, -W, and -e are passed on literally to *psql*.

Outputs

CREATE DATABASE The database was successfully created.

createdb: Database creation failed. (Says it all.)

createdb: Comment creation failed. (Database was created.) The comment/description for
the database could not be created. the database itself will have been created already. You can
use the SQL command **COMMENT ON DATABASE** to create the comment later on.

If there is an error condition, the backend error message will be displayed. See *CREATE
DATABASE* and *psql* for possibilities.

Description

createdb creates a new Postgres database. The user who executes this command becomes the
database owner.

createdb is a shell script wrapper around the SQL command *CREATE DATABASE* via the
Postgres interactive terminal *psql*. Thus, there is nothing special about creating databases via this
or other methods. This means that the *psql* must be found by the script and that a database server
is running at the targeted host. Also, any default settings and environment variables available to
psql and the libpq front-end library do apply.

Usage

To create the database demo using the default database server:

```
$ createdb demo
```

CREATE DATABASE The response is the same as you would have gotten from running the
CREATE DATABASE SQL command.

To create the database demo using the postmaster on host eden, port 5000, using the LATIN1
encoding scheme with a look at the underlying query:

```
$ createdb -p 5000 -h eden -E LATIN1 -e demo
```

or

```
CREATE DATABASE "demo" WITH ENCODING = 'LATIN1' CREATE DATABASE
```

D.28 createlang

Name

createlang — Add a new programming language to a Postgres database
    createlang [*connection options*] [*langname* [*dbname*]]
    createlang [*connection options*] –list | -l [*dbname*]

Inputs

createlang accepts the following command line arguments:

langname Specifies the name of the backend programming language to be defined. createlang
    will prompt for *langname* if it is not specified on the command line.

-d, –dbname *dbname* Specifies which database the language should be added.

-l, –list Shows a list of already installed languages in the target database (which must be specified).

createlang also accepts the following command line arguments for connection parameters:

-h, –host *host* Specifies the hostname of the machine on which the postmaster is running.

-p, –port *port* Specifies the Internet TCP/IP port or local Unix domain socket file extension on
    which the postmaster is listening for connections.

-U, –username *username* Username to connect as.

-W, –password Force password prompt.

Outputs

Most error messages are self-explanatory. If not, run createlang with the –echo option and see
under the respective SQL command for details. Check also under *psql* for more possibilities.

Description

createlang is a utility for adding a new programming language to a Postgres database. createlang
currently accepts two languages, plsql and pltcl.

    Although backend programming languages can be added directly using several SQL commands,
it is recommended to use createlang because it performs a number of checks and is much easier
to use. See *CREATE LANGUAGE* for more.

Notes

Use *droplang* to remove a language.

Usage

To install pltcl:

```
$ createlang pltcl
```

D.29   createuser

Name

createuser — Create a new Postgres user
    createuser [*options*] [*username*]

Inputs

-h, –host *host* Specifies the hostname of the machine on which the postmaster is running.

-p, –port *port* Specifies the Internet TCP/IP port or local Unix domain socket file extension on which the postmaster is listening for connections.

-e, –echo Echo the queries that createdb generates and sends to the backend.

-q, –quiet Do not display a response.

-d, –createdb Allows the new user to create databases.

-D, –no-createdb Forbids the new user to create databases.

-a, –adduser Allows the new user to create other users.

-A, –no-adduser Forbids the new user to create other users.

-P, –pwprompt If given, createuser will issue a prompt for the password of the new user. This is not necessary if you do not plan on using password authentication.

-i, –sysid *uid* Allows you to pick a non-default user id for the new user. This is not necessary, but some people like it.

username Specifies the name of the Postgres user to be created. This name must be unique among all Postgres users.

You will be prompted for a name and other missing information if it is not specified on the command line. The options -h, -p, and -e, are passed on literally to *psql*. The *psql* options -U and -W are available as well, but their use can be confusing in this context.

Outputs

CREATE USER All is well.

createuser: creation of user "*username*" failed Something went wrong. The user was not created.

If there is an error condition, the backend error message will be displayed. See *CREATE USER* and *psql* for possibilities.

Description

createuser creates a new Postgres user. Only users with *usesuper* set in the pg_shadow class can create new Postgres users.

createuser is a shell script wrapper around the SQL command *CREATE USER* via the Postgres interactive terminal *psql*. Thus, there is nothing special about creating users via this or other methods. This means that the *psql* must be found by the script and that a database server is running at the targeted host. Also, any default settings and environment variables available to *psql* and the libpq front-end library do apply.

Usage

To create a user joe on the default database server:

```
$ createuser joe
Is the new user allowed to create databases? (y/n) n
Shall the new user be allowed to create more new users? (y/n) n
CREATE USER
```

To create the same user joe using the postmaster on host eden, port 5000, avoiding the prompts and taking a look at the underlying query:

```
$ createuser -p 5000 -h eden -D -A -e joe
CREATE USER "joe" NOCREATEDB NOCREATEUSER CREATE USER
```

D.30 DECLARE

Name

DECLARE — Defines a cursor for table access
    DECLARE *cursorname* [BINARY] [INSENSITIVE] [SCROLL]
    CURSOR FOR *query*
    [FOR { READ ONLY | UPDATE [OF *column* [, ...]]]]

Inputs

cursorname The name of the cursor to be used in subsequent FETCH operations.

BINARY Causes the cursor to fetch data in binary rather than in text format.

INSENSITIVE SQL92 keyword indicating that data retrieved from the cursor should be unaffected by updates from other processes or cursors. Since cursor operations occur within transactions in Postgres this is always the case. This keyword has no effect.

SCROLL SQL92 keyword indicating that data may be retrieved in multiple rows per FETCH operation. Since this is allowed at all times by Postgres this keyword has no effect.

query An SQL query which will provide the rows to be governed by the cursor. Refer to the SELECT statement for further information about valid arguments.

READ ONLY SQL92 keyword indicating that the cursor will be used in a read only mode. Since this is the only cursor access mode available in Postgres this keyword has no effect.

UPDATE SQL92 keyword indicating that the cursor will be used to update tables. Since cursor updates are not currently supported in Postgres this keyword provokes an informational error message.

column Column(s) to be updated. Since cursor updates are not currently supported in Postgres the UPDATE clause provokes an informational error message.

Outputs

SELECT The message returned if the SELECT is run successfully.

NOTICE BlankPortalAssignName: portal "*cursorname* " already exists This error occurs if *cursorname* is already declared.

ERROR: Named portals may only be used in begin/end transaction blocks This error occurs if the cursor is not declared within a transaction block.

Description

DECLARE allows a user to create cursors, which can be used to retrieve a small number of rows at a time out of a larger query. Cursors can return data either in text or in binary format using *FETCH*.

Normal cursors return data in text format, either ASCII or another encoding scheme depending on how the Postgres backend was built. Since data is stored natively in binary format, the system must do a conversion to produce the text format. In addition, text formats are often larger in size than the corresponding binary format. Once the information comes back in text form, the client application may need to convert it to a binary format to manipulate it. BINARY cursors give you back the data in the native binary representation.

As an example, if a query returns a value of one from an integer column, you would get a string of '1' with a default cursor whereas with a binary cursor you would get a 4-byte value equal to control-A (^A).

BINARY cursors should be used carefully. User applications such as *psql* are not aware of binary cursors and expect data to come back in a text format.

String representation is architecture-neutral whereas binary representation can differ between different machine architectures and *Postgres does not resolve byte ordering or representation issues for binary cursors*. Therefore, if your client machine and server machine use different representations (e.g., "big-endian" versus "little-endian"), you will probably not want your data returned in binary format. However, binary cursors may be a little more efficient since there is less conversion overhead in the server to client data transfer. **Tip:** If you intend to display the data in ASCII, getting it back in ASCII will save you some effort on the client side.

Notes

Cursors are only available in transactions. Use to *BEGIN*, *COMMIT* and *ROLLBACK* to define a transaction block.

In SQL92 cursors are only available in embedded SQL (ESQL) applications. The Postgres backend does not implement an explicit **OPEN cursor** statement; a cursor is considered to be open when it is declared. However, ecpg, the embedded SQL preprocessor for Postgres, supports the SQL92 cursor conventions, including those involving DECLARE and OPEN statements.

Usage

To declare a cursor:

```
DECLARE liahona CURSOR FOR
SELECT * FROM films;
```

Compatibility

SQL92

SQL92 allows cursors only in embedded SQL and in modules. Postgres permits cursors to be used interactively. SQL92 allows embedded or modular cursors to update database information. All Postgres cursors are read only. The BINARY keyword is a Postgres extension.

D.31   DELETE

Name

DELETE — Removes rows from a table
    DELETE FROM *table* [WHERE *condition*]

Inputs

table The name of an existing table.

condition This is an SQL selection query which returns the rows which are to be deleted.

Refer to the SELECT statement for further description of the WHERE clause.

Outputs

DELETE *count* Message returned if items are successfully deleted. The *count* is the number of rows deleted.

If *count* is 0, no rows were deleted.

Description

DELETE removes rows which satisfy the WHERE clause from the specified table.

If the *condition* (WHERE clause) is absent, the effect is to delete all rows in the table. The result is a valid, but empty table. **Tip:** *TRUNCATE* is a Postgres extension which provides a faster mechanism to remove all rows from a table.

You must have write access to the table in order to modify it, as well as read access to any table whose values are read in the *condition*.

Usage

Remove all films but musicals:

```
DELETE FROM films
WHERE kind <>  'Musical';
SELECT * FROM films;
  code  |          title          | did | date_prod  |  kind   | len
--------+-------------------------+-----+------------+---------+-------
 UA501  | West Side Story         | 105 | 1961-01-03 | Musical | 02:32
 TC901  | The King and I          | 109 | 1956-08-11 | Musical | 02:13
 WD101  | Bed Knobs and Broomsticks | 111 |            | Musical | 01:57
(3 rows)
```

Clear the table films:

```
DELETE FROM films;
SELECT * FROM films;
 code | title | did | date_prod | kind | len
------+-------+-----+-----------+------+-----
(0 rows)
```

Compatibility

SQL92

SQL92 allows a positioned DELETE statement:

```
DELETE FROM table WHERE CURRENT OF cursor
```

where *cursor* identifies an open cursor. Interactive cursors in Postgres are read-only.

D.32   DROP AGGREGATE

Name

DROP AGGREGATE — Removes the definition of an aggregate function
    DROP AGGREGATE *name type*

Inputs

name   The name of an existing aggregate function.

type   The type of an existing aggregate function. (Refer to the *PostgreSQL User's Guide* for further information about data types).

Outputs

DROP Message returned if the command is successful.

NOTICE RemoveAggregate: aggregate 'agg ' for 'type ' does not exist This message occurs if the aggregate function specified does not exist in the database.

Description

DROP AGGREGATE will remove all references to an existing aggregate definition. To execute this command the current user must be the owner of the aggregate.

Notes

Use *CREATE AGGREGATE* to create aggregate functions.

Usage

To remove the myavg aggregate for type int4:

```
DROP AGGREGATE myavg int4;
```

Compatibility

SQL92

There is no **DROP AGGREGATE** statement in SQL92; the statement is a Postgres language extension.

D.33   DROP DATABASE

Name

DROP DATABASE — Removes an existing database
    DROP DATABASE *name*

Inputs

name   The name of an existing database to remove.

Outputs

DROP DATABASE   This message is returned if the command is successful.

ERROR: user '*username*' is not allowed to create/drop databases   You must have the special CREATEDB privilege to drop databases. See *CREATE USER*.

ERROR: dropdb: cannot be executed on the template database   The template1 database cannot be removed. It's not in your interest.

ERROR: dropdb: cannot be executed on an open database   You cannot be connected to the database your are about to remove. Instead, you could connect to template1 or any other database and run this command again.

ERROR: dropdb: database '*name*' does not exist   This message occurs if the specified database does not exist.

ERROR: dropdb: database *'name '* is not owned by you You must be the owner of the database. Being the owner usually means that you created it as well.

ERROR: dropdb: May not be called in a transaction block. You must finish the transaction in progress before you can call this command.

NOTICE: The database directory 'xxx' could not be removed. The database was dropped (unless other error messages came up), but the directory where the data is stored could not be removed. You must delete it manually.

Description

DROP DATABASE removes the catalog entries for an existing database and deletes the directory containing the data. It can only be executed by the database owner (usually the user that created it).

Notes

This command cannot be executed while connected to the target database. Thus, it might be more convenient to use the shell script dropdb, which is a wrapper around this command, instead.

Refer to *CREATE DATABASE* for information on how to create a database.

Compatibility

SQL92

DROP DATABASE statement is a Postgres language extension; there is no such command in SQL92.

D.34   DROP FUNCTION

Name

DROP FUNCTION — Removes a user-defined C function
DROP FUNCTION *name* ([*type* [, ...]])

Inputs

name The name of an existing function.

type The type of function parameters.

Outputs

DROP Message returned if the command completes successfully.

NOTICE RemoveFunction: Function "*name* " ("*types* ") does not exist This message is given
   if the function specified does not exist in the current database.

Description

DROP FUNCTION will remove references to an existing C function. To execute this command
the user must be the owner of the function. The input argument types to the function must be
specified, as only the function with the given name and argument types will be removed.

Notes

Refer to *CREATE FUNCTION* for information on creating aggregate functions.
   No checks are made to ensure that types, operators or access methods that rely on the function
have been removed first.

Usage

This command removes the square root function:

```
DROP FUNCTION sqrt(int4);
```

Compatibility

SQL92

DROP FUNCTION is a Postgres language extension.

SQL/PSM

SQL/PSM is a proposed standard to enable function extensibility. The SQL/PSM DROP FUNC-
TION statement has the following syntax:
   DROP [SPECIFIC] FUNCTION *name* { RESTRICT | CASCADE }

D.35   DROP GROUP

Name

DROP GROUP — Removes a group
   DROP GROUP *name*

Inputs

name The name of an existing group.

Outputs

DROP GROUP The message returned if the group is successfully deleted.

Description

DROP GROUP removes the specified group from the database. The users in the group are not deleted.

Use *CREATE GROUP* to add new groups, and *ALTER GROUP* to change a group's membership.

Usage

To drop a group:

```
DROP GROUP staff;
```

Compatibility

SQL92

There is no **DROP GROUP** in SQL92.

D.36 DROP INDEX

Name

DROP INDEX — Removes an index from a database
DROP INDEX *index_name*

Inputs

index_name The name of the index to remove.

Outputs

DROP The message returned if the index is successfully dropped.

ERROR: index "*index_name*" nonexistent This message occurs if *index_name* is not an index in the database.

Description

DROP INDEX drops an existing index from the database system. To execute this command you must be the owner of the index.

Notes

DROP INDEX is a Postgres language extension.
Refer to *CREATE INDEX* for information on how to create indexes.

Usage

This command will remove the title_idx index:

```
DROP INDEX title_idx;
```

Compatibility

SQL92

SQL92 defines commands by which to access a generic relational database. Indexes are an implementation-dependent feature and hence there are no index-specific commands or definitions in the SQL92 language.

D.37   DROP LANGUAGE

Name

DROP LANGUAGE — Removes a user-defined procedural language
    DROP PROCEDURAL LANGUAGE *'name'*

Inputs

name   The name of an existing procedural language.

Outputs

DROP   This message is returned if the language is successfully dropped.

ERROR: Language "*name*" doesn't exist   This message occurs if a language called *name* is not found in the database.

Description

DROP PROCEDURAL LANGUAGE will remove the definition of the previously registered procedural language called *name*.

Notes

The **DROP PROCEDURAL LANGUAGE** statement is a Postgres language extension.

Refer to *CREATE LANGUAGE* for information on how to create procedural languages.

No checks are made if functions or trigger procedures registered in this language still exist. To re-enable them without having to drop and recreate all the functions, the pg_proc's prolang attribute of the functions must be adjusted to the new object ID of the recreated pg_language entry for the PL.

Usage

This command removes the PL/Sample language:

```
DROP PROCEDURAL LANGUAGE 'plsample';
```

Compatibility

SQL92

There is no **DROP PROCEDURAL LANGUAGE** in SQL92.

D.38   DROP OPERATOR

Name

DROP OPERATOR — Removes an operator from the database

DROP OPERATOR *id* (*type* | NONE [,...])

Inputs

id   The identifier of an existing operator.

type   The type of function parameters.

Outputs

DROP The message returned if the command is successful.

ERROR: RemoveOperator: binary operator 'oper' taking 'type' and 'type2' does not exist
This message occurs if the specified binary operator does not exist.

ERROR: RemoveOperator: left unary operator 'oper ' taking 'type' does not exist This message occurs if the left unary operator specified does not exist.

ERROR: RemoveOperator: right unary operator 'oper' taking 'type' does not exist This message occurs if the right unary operator specified does not exist.

Description

DROP OPERATOR drops an existing operator from the database. To execute this command you must be the owner of the operator.

The left or right type of a left or right unary operator, respectively, may be specified as NONE.

Notes

The **DROP OPERATOR** statement is a Postgres language extension.

Refer to *CREATE OPERATOR* for information on how to create operators.

It is the user's responsibility to remove any access methods and operator classes that rely on the deleted operator.

Usage

Remove power operator aˆn for int4:

```
DROP OPERATOR ^ (int4, int4);
```

Remove left unary negation operator (b !) for booleans:

```
DROP OPERATOR ! (none, bool);
```

Remove right unary factorial operator (! i) for int4:

```
DROP OPERATOR ! (int4, none);
```

Compatibility

SQL92

There is no **DROP OPERATOR** in SQL92.

D.39   DROP RULE

Name

DROP RULE — Removes an existing rule from the database
DROP RULE *name*

Inputs

name   The name of an existing rule to drop.

Outputs

DROP   Message returned if successful.

ERROR: RewriteGetRuleEventRel: rule "*name*" not found   This message occurs if the specified rule does not exist.

Description

DROP RULE drops a rule from the specified Postgres rule system. Postgres will immediately cease enforcing it and will purge its definition from the system catalogs.

Notes

The **DROP RULE** statement is a Postgres language extension.
Refer to **CREATE RULE** for information on how to create rules.
Once a rule is dropped, access to historical information the rule has written may disappear.

Usage

To drop the rewrite rule *newrule*:

```
DROP RULE newrule;
```

Compatibility

SQL92

There is no **DROP RULE** in SQL92.

D.40   DROP SEQUENCE

Name

DROP SEQUENCE — Removes an existing sequence
  DROP SEQUENCE *name* [, ...]

Inputs

name   The name of a sequence.

Outputs

DROP   The message returned if the sequence is successfully dropped.

NOTICE: Relation "*name*" does not exist. This message occurs if the specified sequence does not exist.

Description

DROP SEQUENCE removes sequence number generators from the data base. With the current implementation of sequences as special tables it works just like the **DROP TABLE** statement.

Notes

The **DROP SEQUENCE** statement is a Postgres language extension.
  Refer to the **CREATE SEQUENCE** statement for information on how to create a sequence.

Usage

To remove sequence serial from database:

```
DROP SEQUENCE serial;
```

Compatibility

SQL92

There is no **DROP SEQUENCE** in SQL92.

D.41 DROP TABLE

Name

DROP TABLE — Removes existing tables from a database
    DROP TABLE *name* [, ...]

Inputs

name   The name of an existing table or view to drop.

Outputs

DROP   The message returned if the command completes successfully.

ERROR Relation "*name*" Does Not Exist!   If the specified table or view does not exist in the database.

Description

DROP TABLE removes tables and views from the database. Only its owner may destroy a table or view. A table may be emptied of rows, but not destroyed, by using **DELETE**.

   If a table being destroyed has secondary indexes on it, they will be removed first. The removal of just a secondary index will not affect the contents of the underlying table.

Notes

Refer to **CREATE TABLE** and **ALTER TABLE** for information on how to create or modify tables.

Usage

To destroy two tables, films and distributors:

```
DROP TABLE films, distributors;
```

Compatibility

SQL92

SQL92 specifies some additional capabilities for DROP TABLE:

```
DROP TABLE table { RESTRICT | CASCADE }
```

RESTRICT Ensures that only a table with no dependent views or integrity constraints can be destroyed.

CASCADE Any referencing views or integrity constraints will also be dropped.

Tip: At present, to remove a referenced view you must drop it explicitly.

D.42   DROP TRIGGER

Name

DROP TRIGGER — Removes the definition of a trigger
   DROP TRIGGER *name* ON *table*

Inputs

name The name of an existing trigger.

table The name of a table.

Outputs

DROP The message returned if the trigger is successfully dropped.

ERROR: DropTrigger: there is no trigger *name* on relation "*table*" This message occurs if the trigger specified does not exist.

Description

DROP TRIGGER will remove all references to an existing trigger definition. To execute this command the current user must be the owner of the trigger.

Notes

DROP TRIGGER is a Postgres language extension.
   Refer to **CREATE TRIGGER** for information on how to create triggers.

Usage

Destroy the if_dist_exists trigger on table films:

```
DROP TRIGGER if_dist_exists ON films;
```

Compatibility

SQL92

There is no **DROP TRIGGER** statement in SQL92.

D.43 DROP TYPE

Name

DROP TYPE — Removes a user-defined type from the system catalogs
  DROP TYPE *typename*

Inputs

typename The name of an existing type.

Outputs

DROP The message returned if the command is successful.

ERROR: RemoveType: type *'typename'* does not exist This message occurs if the specified
  type is not found.

Description

DROP TYPE will remove a user type from the system catalogs.
  Only the owner of a type can remove it.

Notes

DROP TYPE statement is a Postgres language extension.
  Refer to **CREATE TYPE** for information on how to create types.
  It is the user's responsibility to remove any operators, functions, aggregates, access methods,
subtypes, and classes that use a deleted type.
  If a built-in type is removed, the behavior of the backend is unpredictable.

Usage

To remove the box type:

```
DROP TYPE box;
```

Compatibility

SQL3

DROP TYPE is a SQL3 statement.

D.44   DROP USER

Name

DROP USER — Removes a user
      DROP USER *name*

Inputs

name   The name of an existing user.

Outputs

DROP USER The message returned if the user is successfully deleted.

ERROR: DROP USER: user "*name*" does not exist This message occurs if the username is
      not found.

DROP USER: user "*name* " owns database "*name*", cannot be removed You must drop the
      database first or change its ownership.

Description

DROP USER removes the specified user from the database. It does not remove tables, views, or
other objects owned by the user. If the user owns any database you get an error.
      Use *CREATE USER* to add new users, and *ALTER USER* to change a user's properties.
Postgres comes with a script *dropuser* which has the same functionality as this command (in fact,
it calls this command) but can be run from the command shell.

Usage

To drop a user account:

```
DROP USER jonathan;
```

Compatibility

SQL92

There is no **DROP USER** in SQL92.

D.45   DROP VIEW

Name

DROP VIEW — Removes an existing view from a database
   DROP VIEW *name*

Inputs

name   The name of an existing view.

Outputs

DROP   The message returned if the command is successful.

ERROR: RewriteGetRuleEventRel: rule "_RET*name*" not found   This message occurs if the specified view does not exist in the database.

Description

DROP VIEW drops an existing view from the database. To execute this command you must be the owner of the view.

Notes

The Postgres **DROP TABLE** statement also drops views.
   Refer to **CREATE VIEW** for information on how to create views.

Usage

This command will remove the view called kinds:

```
DROP VIEW kinds;
```

Compatibility

SQL92

SQL92 specifies some additional capabilities for **DROP VIEW** :

```
DROP VIEW view {  RESTRICT | CASCADE }
```

Inputs

RESTRICT Ensures that only a view with no dependent views or integrity constraints can be destroyed.

CASCADE Any referencing views and integrity constraints will be dropped as well.

Notes

At present, to remove a referenced view from a Postgres database, you must drop it explicitly.

D.46   dropdb

Name

dropdb — Remove an existing Postgres database
    dropdb [*options*] *dbname*

Inputs

-h, –host *host* Specifies the hostname of the machine on which the postmaster is running.

-p, –port *port* Specifies the Internet TCP/IP port or local Unix domain socket file extension on which the postmaster is listening for connections.

-U, –username *username* Username to connect as.

-W, –password Force password prompt.

-e, –echo Echo the queries that dropdb generates and sends to the backend.

-q, –quiet Do not display a response.

-i, –interactive Issues a verification prompt before doing anything destructive.

dbname Specifies the name of the database to be removed. The database must be one of the existing Postgres databases in this installation.

The options -h, -p, -U, -W, and -e are passed on literally to *psql*.

Outputs

DROP DATABASE The database was successfully removed.

dropdb: Database removal failed. Something didn't work out.

If there is an error condition, the backend error message will be displayed. See *DROP DATABASE* and *psql* for possibilities.

Description

dropdb destroys an existing Postgres database. The user who executes this command must be a database superuser or the owner of the database.

dropdb is a shell script wrapper around the SQL command *DROP DATABASE* via the Postgres interactive terminal *psql*. Thus, there is nothing special about dropping databases via this or other methods. This means that the *psql* must be found by the script and that a database server is running at the targeted host. Also, any default settings and environment variables available to *psql* and the libpq front-end library do apply.

Usage

To destroy the database demo on the default database server:

```
$ dropdb demo
DROP DATABASE
```

To destroy the database demo using the postmaster on host eden, port 5000, with verification and a peek at the underlying query:

```
$ dropdb -p 5000 -h eden -i -e demo
Database "demo" will be permanently deleted. Are you sure? (y/n) y
DROP DATABASE "demo" DROP DATABASE
```

D.47   droplang

Name

droplang — Remove a programming language from a Postgres database
    droplang [*connection options*] [*langname* [*dbname*]]
    droplang [*connection options*] –list | -l

Inputs

droplang accepts the following command line arguments:

langname Specifies the name of the backend programming language to be removed. droplang
will prompt for *langname* if it is not specified on the command line.

[-d, –dbname *dbname*] Specifies from which database the language should be removed.

-l, –list Shows a list of already installed languages in the target database (which must be specified).

droplang also accepts the following command line arguments for connection parameters:

-h, –host *host* Specifies the hostname of the machine on which the postmaster is running.

-p, –port *port* Specifies the Internet TCP/IP port or local Unix domain socket file extension on
which the postmaster is listening for connections.

-U, –username *username* Username to connect as.

-W, –password Force password prompt.

Outputs

Most error messages are self-explanatory. If not, run droplang with the –echo option and see under
the respective SQL command for details. Check also under *psql* for more possibilities.

Description

droplang is a utility for removing an existing programming language from a Postgres database.
droplang currently accepts two languages, plsql and pltcl.

Although backend programming languages can be removed directly using several SQL commands, it is recommended to use droplang because it performs a number of checks and is much
easier to use. See *DROP LANGUAGE* for more.

Notes

Use createlang to add a language.

Usage

To remove pltcl:

```
$ droplang pltcl
```

D.48   dropuser

Name

dropuser — Drops (removes) a Postgres user
     dropuser [*options*] [*username*]

Inputs

-h, –host *host* Specifies the hostname of the machine on which the postmaster is running.

-p, –port *port* Specifies the Internet TCP/IP port or local Unix domain socket file extension on which the postmaster is listening for connections.

-e, –echo Echo the queries that createdb generates and sends to the backend.

-q, –quiet Do not display a response.

-i, –interactive Prompt for confirmation before actually removing the user.

username Specifies the name of the Postgres user to be removed. This name must exist in the Postgres installation. You will be prompted for a name if none is specified on the command line.

The options -h, -p, and -e, are passed on literally to *psql*. The *psql* options -U and -W are available as well, but they can be confusing in this context.

Outputs

DROP USER All is well.

dropuser: deletion of user "*username*" failed Something went wrong. The user was not removed.

If there is an error condition, the backend error message will be displayed. See *DROP USER* and *psql* for possibilities.

Description

dropuser removes an existing Postgres user *and* the databases which that user owned. Only users with usesuper set in the pg_shadow class can destroy Postgres users.

     dropuser is a shell script wrapper around the SQL command *DROP USER* via the Postgres interactive terminal *psql*. Thus, there is nothing special about removing users via this or other methods. This means that the *psql* must be found by the script and that a database server is running at the targeted host. Also, any default settings and environment variables available to *psql* and the libpq front-end library do apply.

Usage

To remove user joe from the default database server:

```
$ dropuser joe
DROP USER
```

To remove user joe using the postmaster on host eden, port 5000, with verification and a peek at the underlying query:

```
$ dropuser -p 5000 -h eden -i -e joe
User "joe" and any owned databases will be permanently deleted. Are you sure?
(y/n) y
DROP USER "joe" DROP USER
```

D.49   ecpg

Name

ecpg — Embedded SQL C preprocessor

   ecpg [-v] [-t] [-I include-path] [-o outfile] file1 [file2] [...]

Inputs

ecpg accepts the following command line arguments:

-v Print version information.

-t Turn off auto-transaction mode.

-I *path* Specify an additional include path. Defaults are /usr/local/include, the Postgres include path which is defined at compile time (default: /usr/local/pgsql/lib), and /usr/include.

-o Specifies that ecpg should write all its output to outfile. If no such option is given the output is written to *name*.c, assuming the input file was named *name*.pgc. If the input file does have the expected .pgc suffix, then the output file will have .pgc appended to the input file name.

file The files to be processed.

Outputs

ecpg will create a file or write to stdout.

return value ecpg returns 0 to the shell on successful completion, -1 for errors.

Description

ecpg is an embedded SQL preprocessor for the C language and the Postgres. It enables development of C programs with embedded SQL code.

Linus Tolke was the original author of ecpg (up to version 0.2). Michael Meskes is the current author and maintainer of ecpg. Thomas Good is the author of the last revision of the ecpg man page, on which this document is based.

Usage

Preprocessing for Compilation

An embedded SQL source file must be preprocessed before compilation:

```
ecpg [ -d ] [ -o file ] file .pgc
```

where the optional -d flag turns on debugging. The .pgc extension is an arbitrary means of denoting ecpg source.

You may want to redirect the preprocessor output to a log file.

Compiling and Linking

Assuming the Postgres binaries are in /usr/local/pgsql, you will need to compile and link your preprocessed source file:

```
gcc -g -I /usr/local/pgsql/include [ -o file ] file.c -L /usr/local/pgsql/lib -lecpg -lpq
```

Grammar

Libraries

The preprocessor will prepend two directives to the source:

```
#include <ecpgtype.h>
#include <ecpglib.h>
```

Variable Declaration

Variables declared within ecpg source code must be prepended with:

```
EXEC SQL BEGIN DECLARE SECTION;
```

Similarly, variable declaration sections must terminate with:

```
EXEC SQL END DECLARE SECTION;
```

Note: Prior to version 2.1.0, each variable had to be declared on a separate line. As of version 2.1.0 multiple variables may be declared on a single line:

```
char foo(16), bar(16);
```

Error Handling

The SQL communication area is defined with:

```
EXEC SQL INCLUDE sqlca;
```

Note: The sqlca is in lowercase. While SQL convention may be followed, i.e., using uppercase to separate embedded SQL from C statements, sqlca (which includes the sqlca.h header file) MUST be lowercase. This is because the EXEC SQL prefix indicates that this INCLUDE will be parsed by ecpg. ecpg observes case sensitivity (SQLCA.h will not be found). **EXEC SQL INCLUDE** can be used to include other header files as long as case sensitivity is observed.

The sqlprint command is used with the EXEC SQL WHENEVER statement to turn on error handling throughout the program:

```
EXEC SQL WHENEVER sqlerror sqlprint;
```

and

```
EXEC SQL WHENEVER not found sqlprint;
```

Note: This is *not* an exhaustive example of usage for the **EXEC SQL WHENEVER** statement. Further examples of usage may be found in SQL manuals (e.g., *The LAN TIMES Guide to SQL* by Groff and Weinberg).

Connecting to the Database Server

One connects to a database using the following:

```
EXEC SQL CONNECT dbname;
```

where the database name is not quoted. Prior to version 2.1.0, the database name was required to be inside single quotes.

Specifying a server and port name in the connect statement is also possible. The syntax is:

```
dbname [@server ][:port ]
```

or

```
<tcp|unix> :postgresql://server [:port ][/dbname ][?options ]
```

Queries

In general, SQL queries acceptable to other applications such as *psql* can be embedded into your C code. Here are some examples of how to do that.

Create Table:

```
EXEC SQL CREATE TABLE foo (number int4, ascii char(16));
EXEC SQL CREATE UNIQUE index num1 on foo(number);
EXEC SQL COMMIT;
```

Insert:

```
EXEC SQL INSERT INTO foo (number, ascii) VALUES (9999, 'doodad');
EXEC SQL COMMIT;
```

Delete:

```
EXEC SQL DELETE FROM foo WHERE number = 9999;
EXEC SQL COMMIT;
```

Singleton Select:

```
EXEC SQL SELECT foo INTO :FooBar FROM table1 WHERE ascii = 'doodad';
```

Select using Cursors:

```
EXEC SQL DECLARE foo_bar CURSOR FOR
SELECT number, ascii
FROM foo ORDER BY ascii;
EXEC SQL FETCH foo_bar INTO :FooBar, DooDad;
...
EXEC SQL CLOSE foo_bar;
EXEC SQL COMMIT;
```

Updates:

```
EXEC SQL UPDATE foo SET ascii = 'foobar' WHERE number = 9999;
EXEC SQL COMMIT;
```

Notes

There is no **EXEC SQL PREPARE** statement.

The complete structure definition MUST be listed inside the declare section.

See the TODO file in the source for some more missing features.

D.50   END

Name

END — Commits the current transaction
    END [WORK | TRANSACTION]

Inputs

WORK, TRANSACTION Optional keywords. They have no effect.

Outputs

COMMIT Message returned if the transaction is successfully committed.

NOTICE: COMMIT: no transaction in progress If there is no transaction in progress.

Description

END is a Postgres extension, and is a synonym for the SQL92-compatible *COMMIT*.

Notes

The keywords WORK and TRANSACTION are noise and can be omitted.
    Use *ROLLBACK* to abort a transaction.

Usage

To make all changes permanent:

```
END WORK;
```

Compatibility

SQL92

END is a PostgreSQL extension which provides functionality equivalent to *COMMIT*.

D.51   EXPLAIN

Name

EXPLAIN — Shows statement execution plan
    EXPLAIN [VERBOSE] *query*

Inputs

VERBOSE Flag to show detailed query plan.

query Any *query*.

Outputs

NOTICE: QUERY PLAN: *plan* Explicit query plan from the Postgres backend.

EXPLAIN Flag sent after query plan is shown.

Description

This command displays the execution plan that the Postgres planner generates for the supplied query. The execution plan shows how the table(s) referenced by the query will be scanned—by plain sequential scan, index scan, etc.—and if multiple tables are referenced, what join algorithms will be used to bring together the required tuples from each input table.

The most critical part of the display is the estimated query execution cost, which is the planner's guess at how long it will take to run the query (measured in units of disk page fetches). Actually two numbers are shown: the start-up time before the first tuple can be returned, and the total time to return all the tuples. For most queries the total time is what matters, but in contexts such as an EXISTS sub-query the planner will choose the smallest start-up time instead of the smallest total time (since the executor will stop after getting one tuple, anyway). Also, if you limit the number of tuples to return with a LIMIT clause, the planner makes an appropriate interpolation between the endpoint costs to estimate which plan is really the cheapest.

The VERBOSE option emits the full internal representation of the plan tree, rather than just a summary (and sends it to the postmaster log file, too). Usually this option is only useful for debugging Postgres.

Notes

There is only sparse documentation on the optimizer's use of cost information in Postgres. General information on cost estimation for query optimization can be found in database textbooks. Refer to the *Programmer's Guide* in the chapters on indexes and the genetic query optimizer for more information.

Usage

To show a query plan for a simple query on a table with a single int4 column and 128 rows:

```
EXPLAIN SELECT * FROM foo;
NOTICE: QUERY PLAN:
```

```
Seq Scan on foo (cost=0.00..2.28 rows=128 width=4)
EXPLAIN
```

For the same table with an index to support an *equijoin* condition on the query, **EXPLAIN** will show a different plan:

```
EXPLAIN SELECT * FROM foo WHERE i = 4;
NOTICE: QUERY PLAN:
Index Scan using fi on foo (cost=0.00..0.42 rows=1 width=4)
EXPLAIN
```

And finally, for the same table with an index to support an *equijoin* condition on the query, **EXPLAIN** will show the following for a query using an aggregate function:

```
EXPLAIN SELECT sum(i) FROM foo WHERE i = 4;
NOTICE: QUERY PLAN:
Aggregate (cost=0.42..0.42 rows=1 width=4) -
> Index Scan using fi on foo (cost=0.00..0.42 rows=1 width=4)
```

Note that the specific numbers shown, and even the selected query strategy, may vary between Postgres releases due to planner improvements.

Compatibility

SQL92

There is no **EXPLAIN** statement defined in SQL92.

D.52 FETCH

Name

FETCH — Gets rows using a cursor

 FETCH [*direction*] [*count*] { IN | FROM } *cursor*

 FETCH [FORWARD | BACKWARD | RELATIVE] [{ [# | ALL | NEXT | PRIOR] }] { IN | FROM } *cursor*

Inputs

direction   *selector* defines the fetch direction. It can be one of the following:

> **FORWARD** fetch next row(s). This is the default if *selector* is omitted.
>
> **BACKWARD** fetch previous row(s).

RELATIVE Noise word for SQL92 compatibility.

count *count* determines how many rows to fetch. It can be one of the following:

   # A signed integer that specifies how many rows to fetch. Note that a negative integer is equivalent to changing the sense of FORWARD and BACKWARD.

   ALL Retrieve all remaining rows.

   NEXT Equivalent to specifying a count of **1**.

   PRIOR Equivalent to specifying a count of **-1**.

cursor An open cursor's name.

Outputs

FETCH returns the results of the query defined by the specified cursor. The following messages will be returned if the query fails:

NOTICE: PerformPortalFetch: portal "*cursor* " not found If *cursor* is not previously declared. The cursor must be declared within a transaction block.

NOTICE: FETCH/ABSOLUTE not supported, using RELATIVE Postgres does not support absolute positioning of cursors.

ERROR: FETCH/RELATIVE at current position is not supported SQL92 allows one to repetitively retrieve the cursor at its "current position" using the syntax FETCH RELATIVE 0 FROM *cursor*.

   Postgres does not currently support this notion; in fact the value zero is reserved to indicate that all rows should be retrieved and is equivalent to specifying the ALL keyword. If the RELATIVE keyword has been used, Postgres assumes that the user intended SQL92 behavior and returns this error message.

Description

FETCH allows a user to retrieve rows using a cursor. The number of rows retrieved is specified by **#**. If the number of rows remaining in the cursor is less than **#**, then only those available are fetched. Substituting the keyword ALL in place of a number will cause all remaining rows in the cursor to be retrieved. Instances may be fetched in both FORWARD and BACKWARD directions. The default direction is FORWARD. **Tip:** Negative numbers are allowed to be specified for the row count. A negative number is equivalent to reversing the sense of the FORWARD and BACKWARD keywords. For example, **FORWARD -1** is the same as **BACKWARD 1**.

Notes

Note that the FORWARD and BACKWARD keywords are Postgres extensions. The SQL92 syntax is also supported, specified in the second form of the command. See below for details on compatibility issues.

Updating data in a cursor is not supported by Postgres, because mapping cursor updates back to base tables is not generally possible, as is also the case with VIEW updates. Consequently, users must issue explicit UPDATE commands to replace data.

Cursors may only be used inside of transactions because the data that they store spans multiple user queries.

Use *MOVE* to change cursor position. *DECLARE* will define a cursor. Refer to *BEGIN*, *COMMIT*, and *ROLLBACK* for further information about transactions.

Usage

The following examples traverse a table using a cursor:

```
-- Set up and use a cursor:
BEGIN WORK;
DECLARE liahona CURSOR FOR
SELECT * FROM films;
-- Fetch first 5 rows in the cursor liahona:
FETCH FORWARD 5 IN liahona;
 code  |          title          | did | date_prod  |   kind   | len
-------+-------------------------+-----+------------+----------+-------
 BL101 | The Third Man           | 101 | 1949-12-23 | Drama    | 01:44
 BL102 | The African Queen       | 101 | 1951-08-11 | Romantic | 01:43
 JL201 | Une Femme est une Femme | 102 | 1961-03-12 | Romantic | 01:25
 P_301 | Vertigo                 | 103 | 1958-11-14 | Action   | 02:08
 P_302 | Becket                  | 103 | 1964-02-03 | Drama    | 02:28
-- Fetch previous row:
FETCH BACKWARD 1 IN liahona;
 code  | title   | did | date_prod  | kind   | len
-------+---------+-----+------------+--------+-------
 P_301 | Vertigo | 103 | 1958-11-14 | Action | 02:08
-- close the cursor and commit work:
CLOSE liahona;
COMMIT WORK;
```

Compatibility

SQL92

Note: The non-embedded use of cursors is a Postgres extension. The syntax and usage of cursors is being compared against the embedded form of cursors defined in SQL92.

SQL92 allows absolute positioning of the cursor for FETCH, and allows placing the results into explicit variables:

FETCH ABSOLUTE #

FROM *cursor*

INTO :*variable* [, ...]

ABSOLUTE The cursor should be positioned to the specified absolute row number. All row numbers in Postgres are relative numbers so this capability is not supported.

:***variable*** Target host variable(s).

D.53 GRANT

revoke 424

Name

GRANT — Grants access privilege to a user, a group or all users

GRANT *privilege* [, ...] ON *object* [, ...] TO { PUBLIC | GROUP *group* | *username* }

Inputs

privilege The possible privileges are:

SELECT Access all of the columns of a specific table/view.

INSERT Insert data into all columns of a specific table.

UPDATE Update all columns of a specific table.

DELETE Delete rows from a specific table.

RULE Define rules on the table/view (See CREATE RULE statement).

ALL Grant all privileges.

object The name of an object to which to grant access. The possible objects are:

- table
- view
- sequence

PUBLIC A short form representing all users.

GROUP *group*   A *group* to whom to grant privileges.

username   The name of a user to whom to grant privileges. PUBLIC is a short form representing all users.

Outputs

CHANGE   Message returned if successful.

ERROR: ChangeAcl: class "*object*" not found   Message returned if the specified object is not available or if it is impossible to give privileges to the specified group or users.

Description

GRANT allows the creator of an object to give specific permissions to all users (PUBLIC) or to a certain user or group. Users other than the creator don't have any access permission unless the creator GRANTs permissions, after the object is created.

Once a user has a privilege on an object, he is enabled to exercise that privilege. There is no need to GRANT privileges to the creator of an object, the creator automatically holds ALL privileges, and can also drop the object.

Notes

Currently, to grant privileges in Postgres to only a few columns, you must create a view having desired columns and then grant privileges to that view.

Use **psql \z** for further information about permissions on existing objects:

```
    Database   = lusitania
    +-----------------+-------------------------------------------+
    | Relation        |          Grant/Revoke Permissions         |
    +-----------------+-------------------------------------------+
    | mytable         | {"=rw","miriam=arwR","group todos=rw"}    |
    +-----------------+-------------------------------------------+
Legend:
        uname=arwR -- privileges granted to a user
 group gname=arwR -- privileges granted to a GROUP
          =arwR -- privileges granted to PUBLIC
            r -- SELECT
            w -- UPDATE/DELETE
            a -- INSERT
            R -- RULE
         arwR -- ALL
```

Refer to REVOKE statements to revoke access privileges.

Usage

Grant insert privilege to all users on table films:

```
GRANT INSERT ON films TO PUBLIC;
```

Grant all privileges to user manuel on view kinds:

```
GRANT ALL ON kinds TO manuel;
```

Compatibility

SQL92

The SQL92 syntax for GRANT allows setting privileges for individual columns within a table, and allows setting a privilege to grant the same privileges to others:

```
GRANT privilege [, ...]
ON object [ ( column [, ...] ) ] [, ...]
TO { PUBLIC | username [, ...] }
[ WITH GRANT OPTION ]
```

Fields are compatible with those in the Postgres implementation, with the following additions:

privilege SQL92 permits additional privileges to be specified:

SELECT

REFERENCES Allowed to reference some or all of the columns of a specific table/view in integrity constraints.

USAGE Allowed to use a domain, character set, collation or translation. If an object specifies anything other than a table/view, *privilege* must specify only USAGE.

object

[**TABLE** *table*] SQL92 allows the additional non-functional keyword TABLE.

CHARACTER SET Allowed to use the specified character set.

COLLATION Allowed to use the specified collation sequence.

TRANSLATION Allowed to use the specified character set translation.

DOMAIN Allowed to use the specified domain.

WITH GRANT OPTION Allowed to grant the same privilege to others.

D.54   initdb

Name

initdb — Create a new Postgres database installation

    initdb
    [–pgdata | -D *dbdir*]
    [–sysid | -i *sysid*]
    [–pwprompt | -W]
    [–encoding | -E *encoding*]
    [–pglib | -L *libdir*]
    [–noclean | -n]
    [–debug | -d]
    [–template | -t]

Inputs

–pgdata=*dbdir* , -D *dbdir* , PGDATA This option specifies where in the file system the database
should be stored. This is the only information required by initdb, but you can avoid it by setting the PGDATA environment variable, which can be convenient since the database server
(postmaster) can find the database directory later by the same variable.

–sysid=*sysid* , -i *sysid* Selects the system id of the database superuser. This defaults to the
effective user id of the user running initdb. It is really not important what the superuser's
sysid is, but one might choose to start the numbering at some number like 0 or 1.

–pwprompt, -W Makes initdb prompt for a password of the database superuser. If you don't plan
on using password authentication, this is not important. Otherwise you won't be able to use
password authentication until you have a password set up.

–encoding=*encoding* , -E *encoding* Selects the multibyte encoding of the template database.
This will also be the default encoding of any database you create later, unless you override
it there. To use the multibyte encoding feature, you must specify so at build time, at which
time you also select the default for this option.

Other, less commonly used, parameters are also available:

–pglib=*libdir* , -l *libdir* initdb needs a few input files to initialize the database. This option
tells where to find them. You normally don't have to worry about this since initdb knows
about the most common installation layouts and will find the files itself. You will be told
if you need to specify their location explicitly. If that happens, one of the files is called
global1.bki.source and is traditionally installed along with the others in the library directory
(e.g., /usr/local/pgsql/lib).

–template, -t Replace the template1 database in an existing database system, and don't touch anything else. This is useful when you need to upgrade your template1 database using initdb from a newer release of Postgres, or when your template1 database has become corrupted by some system problem. Normally the contents of template1 remain constant throughout the life of the database system. You can't destroy anything by running initdb with the –template option.

–noclean, -n By default, when initdb determines that an error prevented it from completely creating the database system, it removes any files it may have created before determining that it can't finish the job. This option inhibits any tidying-up and is thus useful for debugging.

–debug, -d Print debugging output from the bootstrap backend and a few other messages of lesser interest for the general public. The bootstrap backend is the program initdb uses to create the catalog tables. This option generates a tremendous amount of output.

Outputs

initdb will create files in the specified data area which are the system tables and framework for a complete installation.

Description

initdb creates a new Postgres database system. A database system is a collection of databases that are all administered by the same Unix user and managed by a single postmaster.

Creating a database system consists of creating the directories in which the database data will live, generating the shared catalog tables (tables that don't belong to any particular database), and creating the template1 database. When you create a new database, everything in the template1 database is copied. It contains catalog tables filled in for things like the built-in types.

You must not execute initdb as root. This is because you cannot run the database server as root either, but the server needs to have access to the files initdb creates. Furthermore, during the initialization phase, when there are no users and no access controls installed, Postgres will only connect with the name of the current Unix user, so you must log in under the account that will own the server process.

Although initdb will attempt to create the respective data directory, chances are that it won't have the permission to do so. Thus it is a good idea to create the data directory before running initdb *and* to hand over the ownership of it to the database superuser.

D.55   initlocation

Name

initlocation — Create a secondary Postgres database storage area
   initlocation *directory*

Inputs

directory   Where in your Unix filesystem do you want alternate databases to go?

Outputs

initlocation will create directories in the specified place.

Description

initlocation creates a new Postgres secondary database storage area. See the discussion under *CREATE DATABASE* about how to manage and use secondary storage areas. If the argument does not contain a slash and is not valid as a path, it is assumed to be an environment variable, which is referenced. See the examples at the end.

In order to use this command you must be logged in (using 'su', for example) as the database superuser.

Usage

To create a database in an alternate location, using an environment variable:

```
$ export PGDATA2=/opt/postgres/data
```

Start and stop postmaster so it sees the $PGDATA2 environment variable. The system must be configured so the postmaster sees $PGDATA2 every time it starts.

```
$ initlocation PGDATA2
$ createdb -D 'PGDATA2' 'testdb'
```

Alternatively, if you allow absolute paths you could write:

```
$ initlocation /opt/postgres/data
$ createdb -D '/opt/postgres/data/testdb' testdb
```

D.56   INSERT

Name

INSERT — Inserts new rows into a table
    INSERT INTO *table* [(*column* [, ...])]
    { VALUES (*expression* [, ...]) | SELECT *query* }

Inputs

table The name of an existing table.

column The name of a column in *table*.

expression A valid expression or value to assign to *column*.

query A valid query. Refer to the SELECT statement for a further description of valid arguments.

Outputs

INSERT *oid* 1 Message returned if only one row was inserted. *oid* is the numeric OID of the inserted row.

INSERT 0 # Message returned if more than one rows were inserted. # is the number of rows inserted.

Description

INSERT allows one to insert new rows into a class or table. One can insert a single row at a time or several rows as a result of a query. The columns in the target list may be listed in any order.

Each column not present in the target list will be inserted using a default value, either a declared DEFAULT value or NULL. Postgres will reject the new column if a NULL is inserted into a column declared NOT NULL.

If the expression for each column is not of the correct data type, automatic type coercion will be attempted.

You must have insert privilege to a table in order to append to it, as well as select privilege on any table specified in a WHERE clause.

Usage

Insert a single row into table films:

```
INSERT INTO films
VALUES ('UA502','Bananas',105,'1971-07-13','Comedy',INTERVAL '82 minute');
```

In this second example the column date_prod is omitted and therefore it will have the default value of NULL:

```
INSERT INTO films (code, title, did, date_prod, kind)
VALUES ('T_601', 'Yojimbo', 106, DATE '1961-06-16', 'Drama');
```

Insert a single row into table distributors; note that only column name is specified, so the omitted column *did* will be assigned its default value:

```
INSERT INTO distributors (name)
VALUES ('British Lion');
```

Insert several rows into table films from table tmp:

```
INSERT INTO films
SELECT * FROM tmp;
```

Insert into arrays (refer to the *PostgreSQL User's Guide* for further information about arrays):

```
-- Create an empty 3x3 gameboard for noughts-and-crosses
-- (all of these queries create the same board attribute)
INSERT INTO tictactoe (game, board[1:3][1:3])
VALUES (1,'{{"","",""},{},{"",""}}');
INSERT INTO tictactoe (game, board[3][3])
VALUES (2,'{}');
INSERT INTO tictactoe (game, board)
VALUES (3,'{{,,},{,,},{,,}}');
```

Compatibility

SQL92

INSERT is fully compatible with SQL92. Possible limitations in features of the *query* clause are documented for *SELECT*.

D.57   ipcclean

Name

ipcclean — Clean up shared memory and semaphores from aborted backends
    ipcclean

Inputs

None.

Outputs

None.

Description

ipcclean cleans up shared memory and semaphore space from aborted backends by deleting all instances owned by user postgres. Only the DBA should execute this program as it can cause bizarre behavior (i.e., crashes) if run during multi-user execution. This program should be executed if messages such as *semget: No space left on device* are encountered when starting up the postmaster or the backend server.

If this command is executed while postmaster is running, the shared memory and semaphores allocated by the postmaster will be deleted. This will result in a general failure of the backend servers started by that postmaster.

This script is a hack, but in the many years since it was written, no one has come up with an equally effective and portable solution. Suggestions are welcome.

The script makes assumption about the format of output of the *ipcs* utility which may not be true across different operating systems. Therefore, it may not work on your particular OS.

D.58 LISTEN   NOTIFY 380

Name

LISTEN — Listen for a response on a notify condition
    LISTEN *name*

Inputs

name Name of notify condition.

Outputs

LISTEN Message returned upon successful completion of registration.

NOTICE Async_Listen: We are already listening on *name* If this backend is already registered for that notify condition.

Description

LISTEN registers the current Postgres backend as a listener on the notify condition *name*.

Whenever the command **NOTIFY *name*** is invoked, either by this backend or another one connected to the same database, all the backends currently listening on that notify condition are notified, and each will in turn notify its connected frontend application. See the discussion of **NOTIFY** for more information.

A backend can be unregistered for a given notify condition with the **UNLISTEN** command. Also, a backend's listen registrations are automatically cleared when the backend process exits.

The method a frontend application must use to detect notify events depends on which Postgres application programming interface it uses. With the basic libpq library, the application issues **LISTEN** as an ordinary SQL command, and then must periodically call the routine PQnotifies to find out whether any notify events have been received. Other interfaces such as libpgtcl provide higher-level methods for handling notify events; indeed, with libpgtcl the application programmer should not even issue **LISTEN** or **UNLISTEN** directly. See the documentation for the library you are using for more details.

NOTIFY contains a more extensive discussion of the use of **LISTEN** and **NOTIFY**.

Notes

name can be any string valid as a name; it need not correspond to the name of any actual table. If *notifyname* is enclosed in double-quotes, it need not even be a syntactically valid name, but can be any string up to 31 characters long.

In some previous releases of Postgres, *name* had to be enclosed in double-quotes when it did not correspond to any existing table name, even if syntactically valid as a name. That is no longer required.

Usage

Configure and execute a listen/notify sequence from *psql*:

```
LISTEN virtual;
NOTIFY virtual;
Asynchronous NOTIFY 'virtual' from backend with pid '8448' received.
```

Compatibility

SQL92

There is no **LISTEN** in SQL92.

D.59 LOAD

Name

LOAD — Dynamically loads an object file
    LOAD *'filename'*

Inputs

filename Object file for dynamic loading.

Outputs

LOAD Message returned on successful completion.

ERROR: LOAD: could not open file *'filename'* Message returned if the specified file is not found. The file must be visible *to the Postgres backend*, with the appropriate full path name specified, to avoid this message.

Description

Loads an object (or ".o") file into the Postgres backend address space. Once a file is loaded, all functions in that file can be accessed. This function is used in support of user-defined types and functions.

If a file is not loaded using **LOAD**, the file will be loaded automatically the first time the function is called by Postgres. **LOAD** can also be used to reload an object file if it has been edited and recompiled. Only objects created from C language files are supported at this time.

Notes

Functions in loaded object files should not call functions in other object files loaded through the **LOAD** command. For example, all functions in file A should call each other, functions in the standard or math libraries, or in Postgres itself. They should not call functions defined in a different loaded file B. This is because if B is reloaded, the Postgres loader is not able to relocate the calls from the functions in A into the new address space of B. If B is not reloaded, however, there will not be a problem.

Object files must be compiled to contain position independent code. For example, on DECstations you must use /bin/cc with the -G 0 option when compiling object files to be loaded.

Note that if you are porting Postgres to a new platform, **LOAD** will have to work in order to support ADTs.

Usage

Load the file /usr/postgres/demo/circle.o:

```
LOAD '/usr/postgres/demo/circle.o'
```

Compatibility

SQL92

There is no **LOAD** in SQL92.

D.60 LOCK

Name

LOCK — Explicitly lock a table inside a transaction
    LOCK [TABLE] *name*
    LOCK [TABLE] *name* IN [ROW | ACCESS] { SHARE | EXCLUSIVE } MODE
    LOCK [TABLE] *name* IN SHARE ROW EXCLUSIVE MODE

Inputs

name   The name of an existing table to lock.

ACCESS SHARE MODE Note: This lock mode is acquired automatically over tables being queried.

This is the least restrictive lock mode. It conflicts only with ACCESS EXCLUSIVE mode. It is used to protect a table from being modified by concurrent **ALTER TABLE**, **DROP TABLE** and **VACUUM** commands.

ROW SHARE MODE Note: Automatically acquired by **SELECT...FOR UPDATE**. While it is a shared lock, may be upgraded later to a ROW EXCLUSIVE lock.

Conflicts with EXCLUSIVE and ACCESS EXCLUSIVE lock modes.

ROW EXCLUSIVE MODE Note: Automatically acquired by **UPDATE**, **DELETE**, and **INSERT** statements.

Conflicts with SHARE, SHARE ROW EXCLUSIVE, EXCLUSIVE and ACCESS EXCLUSIVE modes.

SHARE MODE Note: Automatically acquired by **CREATE INDEX**. Share-locks the entire table.

Conflicts with ROW EXCLUSIVE, SHARE ROW EXCLUSIVE, EXCLUSIVE and ACCESS EXCLUSIVE modes. This mode protects a table against concurrent updates.

SHARE ROW EXCLUSIVE MODE Note: This is like EXCLUSIVE MODE, but allows SHARE ROW locks by others.

Conflicts with ROW EXCLUSIVE, SHARE, SHARE ROW EXCLUSIVE, EXCLUSIVE and ACCESS EXCLUSIVE modes.

EXCLUSIVE MODE Note: This mode is yet more restrictive than SHARE ROW EXCLUSIVE. It blocks all concurrent ROW SHARE/SELECT..FOR UPDATE queries.

Conflicts with ROW SHARE, ROW EXCLUSIVE, SHARE, SHARE ROW EXCLUSIVE, EXCLUSIVE and ACCESS EXCLUSIVE modes.

ACCESS EXCLUSIVE MODE Note: Automatically acquired by **ALTER TABLE, DROP TABLE, VACUUM** statements. This is the most restrictive lock mode which conflicts with all other lock modes and protects a locked table from any concurrent operations.

> **Note:** This lock mode is also acquired by an unqualified **LOCK TABLE** (i.e., the command without an explicit lock mode option).

Outputs

LOCK TABLE The lock was successfully applied.

ERROR *name* : Table does not exist. Message returned if *name* does not exist.

Description

LOCK TABLE controls concurrent access to a table for the duration of a transaction. Postgres always uses the least restrictive lock mode whenever possible. **LOCK TABLE** provides for cases when you might need more restrictive locking.

RDBMS locking uses the following terminology:

EXCLUSIVE Exclusive lock that prevents other locks from being granted.

SHARE Allows others to share lock. Prevents EXCLUSIVE locks.

ACCESS Locks table schema.

ROW Locks individual rows.

Note: If EXCLUSIVE or SHARE are not specified, EXCLUSIVE is assumed. Locks exist for the duration of the transaction.

For example, an application runs a transaction at READ COMMITTED isolation level and needs to ensure the existence of data in a table for the duration of the transaction. To achieve this you could use SHARE lock mode over the table before querying. This will protect data from concurrent changes and provide any further read operations over the table with data in their actual current state, because SHARE lock mode conflicts with any ROW EXCLUSIVE one acquired by writers, and your **LOCK TABLE *name* IN SHARE MODE** statement will wait until any concurrent write operations commit or rollback. **Note:** To read data in their real current state when running a transaction at the SERIALIZABLE isolation level you have to execute a LOCK TABLE statement before executing any DML statement, when the transaction defines what concurrent changes will be visible to itself.

In addition to the requirements above, if a transaction is going to change data in a table, then SHARE ROW EXCLUSIVE lock mode should be acquired to prevent deadlock conditions when two concurrent transactions attempt to lock the table in SHARE mode and then try to change data in this table, both (implicitly) acquiring ROW EXCLUSIVE lock mode that conflicts with a concurrent SHARE lock.

To continue with the deadlock (when two transaction wait for one another) issue raised above, you should follow two general rules to prevent deadlock conditions:

- Transactions have to acquire locks on the same objects in the same order.

  For example, if one application updates row R1 and than updates row R2 (in the same transaction) then the second application shouldn't update row R2 if it's going to update row R1 later (in a single transaction). Instead, it should update rows R1 and R2 in the same order as the first application.

- Transactions should acquire two conflicting lock modes only if one of them is self-conflicting (i.e., may be held by one transaction at time only). If multiple lock modes are involved, then transactions should always acquire the most restrictive mode first.

  An example for this rule was given previously when discussing the use of SHARE ROW EXCLUSIVE mode rather than SHARE mode.

Note: Postgres does detect deadlocks and will rollback at least one waiting transaction to resolve the deadlock.

Notes

LOCK is a Postgres language extension.

Except for ACCESS SHARE/EXCLUSIVE lock modes, all other Postgres lock modes and the **LOCK TABLE** syntax are compatible with those present in Oracle.

LOCK works only inside transactions.

Usage

Illustrate a SHARE lock on a primary key table when going to perform inserts into a foreign key table:

```
BEGIN WORK;
LOCK TABLE films IN SHARE MODE;
SELECT id
FROM films
WHERE name = 'Star Wars: Episode I - The Phantom Menace';
-- Do ROLLBACK if record was not returned
INSERT INTO films_user_comments
VALUES (_id_, 'GREAT! I was waiting for it for so long!');
COMMIT WORK;
```

Take a SHARE ROW EXCLUSIVE lock on a primary key table when going to perform a delete operation:

```
BEGIN WORK; LOCK TABLE films IN SHARE ROW EXCLUSIVE MODE;
DELETE FROM films_user_comments
WHERE id IN (SELECT id
             FROM films
             WHERE rating < 5);
DELETE FROM films
WHERE rating < 5;
COMMIT WORK;
```

Compatibility

SQL92

There is no **LOCK TABLE** in SQL92, which instead uses **SET TRANSACTION** to specify concurrency levels on transactions. We support that too; see *SET* for details.

D.61 MOVE

Name

MOVE — Moves cursor position
    MOVE [*direction*] [*count*] { IN | FROM } *cursor*

Description

MOVE allows a user to move cursor position a specified number of rows. **MOVE** works like the **FETCH** command, but only positions the cursor and does not return rows.
    Refer to *FETCH* for details on syntax and usage.

Notes

MOVE is a Postgres language extension.
    Refer to *FETCH* for a description of valid arguments. Refer to *DECLARE* to define a cursor. Refer to *BEGIN*, *COMMIT*, and *ROLLBACK* for further information about transactions.

Usage

Set up and use a cursor:

```
BEGIN WORK;
DECLARE liahona CURSOR FOR
SELECT * FROM films;
-- Skip first 5 rows:
MOVE FORWARD 5 IN liahona;
MOVE
-- Fetch 6th row in the cursor liahona:
FETCH 1 IN liahona;
FETCH
 code  |  title  | did | date_prod |  kind  | len
-------+---------+-----+-----------+--------+-------
 P_303 | 48 Hrs  | 103 | 1982-10-22| Action | 01:37
(1 row)
-- close the cursor liahona and commit work:
CLOSE liahona;
COMMIT WORK;
```

Compatibility

SQL92

There is no SQL92 **MOVE** statement. Instead, SQL92 allows one to **FETCH** rows from an absolute cursor position, implicitly moving the cursor to the correct position.

D.62 NOTIFY   LISTEN   373

Name

NOTIFY — Signals all frontends and backends listening on a notify condition
  NOTIFY *name*

Inputs

notifyname Notify condition to be signaled.

Outputs

NOTIFY Acknowledgement that notify command has executed.

Notify events Events are delivered to listening frontends; whether and how each frontend application reacts depends on its programming.

Description

The **NOTIFY** command sends a notify event to each frontend application that has previously executed **LISTEN** *notifyname* for the specified notify condition in the current database.

The information passed to the frontend for a notify event includes the notify condition name and the notifying backend process's PID. It is up to the database designer to define the condition names that will be used in a given database and what each one means.

Commonly, the notify condition name is the same as the name of some table in the database, and the notify event essentially means "I changed this table, take a look at it to see what's new". But no such association is enforced by the **NOTIFY** and **LISTEN** commands. For example, a database designer could use several different condition names to signal different sorts of changes to a single table.

NOTIFY provides a simple form of signal or IPC (interprocess communication) mechanism for a collection of processes accessing the same Postgres database. Higher-level mechanisms can be built by using tables in the database to pass additional data (beyond a mere condition name) from notifier to listener(s).

When **NOTIFY** is used to signal the occurrence of changes to a particular table, a useful programming technique is to put the **NOTIFY** in a rule that is triggered by table updates. In this way, notification happens automatically when the table is changed, and the application programmer can't accidentally forget to do it.

NOTIFY interacts with SQL transactions in some important ways. Firstly, if a **NOTIFY** is executed inside a transaction, the notify events are not delivered until and unless the transaction is committed. This is appropriate, since if the transaction is aborted we would like all the commands within it to have had no effect, including **NOTIFY**. But it can be disconcerting if one is expecting the notify events to be delivered immediately. Secondly, if a listening backend receives a notify signal while it is within a transaction, the notify event will not be delivered to its connected frontend until just after the transaction is completed (either committed or aborted). Again, the reasoning is that if a notify were delivered within a transaction that was later aborted, one would want the notification to be undone somehow—but the backend cannot "take back" a notify once it has sent it to the frontend. So notify events are only delivered between transactions. The upshot of this is that applications using **NOTIFY** for real-time signaling should try to keep their transactions short.

NOTIFY behaves like Unix signals in one important respect: if the same condition name is signaled multiple times in quick succession, recipients may get only one notify event for several executions of **NOTIFY**. So it is a bad idea to depend on the number of notifies received. Instead, use **NOTIFY** to wake up applications that need to pay attention to something, and use a database object (such as a sequence) to keep track of what happened or how many times it happened.

It is common for a frontend that sends **NOTIFY** to be listening on the same notify name itself. In that case it will get back a notify event, just like all the other listening frontends. Depending on the application logic, this could result in useless work —for example, re-reading a database table to find the same updates that that frontend just wrote out. In Postgres 6.4 and later, it is possible to avoid such extra work by noticing whether the notifying backend process's PID (supplied in the notify event message) is the same as one's own backend's PID (available from libpq). When they are the same, the notify event is one's own work bouncing back, and can be ignored. (Despite what was said in the preceding paragraph, this is a safe technique. Postgres keeps self-notifies separate from notifies arriving from other backends, so you cannot miss an outside notify by ignoring your own notifies.)

Notes

name can be any string valid as a name; it need not correspond to the name of any actual table. If *name* is enclosed in double-quotes, it need not even be a syntactically valid name, but can be any string up to 31 characters long.

In some previous releases of Postgres, *name* had to be enclosed in double-quotes when it did not correspond to any existing table name, even if syntactically valid as a name. That is no longer required.

In Postgres releases prior to 6.4, the backend PID delivered in a notify message was always the PID of the frontend's own backend. So it was not possible to distinguish one's own notifies from other clients' notifies in those earlier releases.

Usage

Configure and execute a listen/notify sequence from *psql*:

```
LISTEN virtual;
NOTIFY virtual;
Asynchronous NOTIFY 'virtual' from backend with pid '8448' received.
```

Compatibility

SQL92

There is no **NOTIFY** statement in SQL92.

D.63   pg_ctl

Name

pg_ctl — Starts, stops, and restarts postmaster
    pg_ctl [-w] [-D *datadir*][-p *path*] [-o "*options* "] start
    pg_ctl [-w] [-D *datadir*] [-m [s[mart]|f[ast]|i[mmediate]]] stop
    pg_ctl [-w] [-D *datadir*] [-m [s[mart]|f[ast]|i[mmediate]]] [-o "*options* "] restart
    pg_ctl [-D *datadir*] status

Inputs

-w Wait for the database server to come up, by watching for creation of the pid file (PG-DATA/postmaster.pid). Times out after 60 seconds.

-D *datadir* Specifies the database location for this database installation.

-p *path* Specifies the path to the postmaster image.

-o *"options* " Specifies options to be passed directly to postmaster.

The parameters are usually surrounded by single or double quotes to ensure that they are passed through as a group.

-m *mode* Specifies the shutdown mode.

smart, s smart mode waits for all the clients to logout. This is the default.

fast, f Fast mode sends SIGTERM to the backends; that means active transactions get rolled back.

immediate, i Immediate mode sends SIGUSR1 to the backends and lets them abort. In this case, database recovery will be necessary on the next start-up.

start Start up postmaster.

stop Shut down postmaster.

restart Restart the postmaster, performing a stop/start sequence.

status Show the current state of postmaster.

Outputs

pg_ctl: postmaster is *state* **(pid: #)** Postmaster status.

If there is an error condition, the backend error message will be displayed.

Description

pg_ctl is a utility for starting, stopping or restarting postmaster.

Usage

Starting postmaster

To start up postmaster:

```
$ pg_ctl start
```

If -w is supplied, pg_ctl waits for the database server to come up, by watching for creation of the pid file (PGDATA/postmaster.pid), for up to 60 seconds.

Parameters to invoke postmaster are taken from the following sources:

- Path to postmaster: found in the command search path.

- Database directory: *PGDATA* environment variable.

- Other parameters: *PGDATA/postmaster.opts.default.*

postmaster.opts.default contains parameters for postmaster.

Note that *postmaster.opts.default* is installed by initdb from *lib/postmaster.opts.default.sample* under the Postgres installation directory (*lib/postmaster.opts.default.sample* is copied from *src/bin/pg_-ctl/postmaster.opts.default.sample* while installing Postgres).

To override the default parameters you can use -D, -p and -o options.

An example of starting the postmaster, blocking until postmaster comes up is:

```
$ pg_ctl -w start
```

To specify the postmaster binary path, try:

```
$ pg_ctl -p /usr/local/pgsql/bin/postmaster start
```

For a postmaster using port 5433, and running without fsync, use:

```
$ pg_ctl -o "-o -F -p 5433" start
```

Stopping postmaster

$ pg_ctl stop stops postmaster. Using the -m switch allows one to control *how* the backend shuts down. -w waits for postmaster to shut down. -m specifies the shut down mode.

Restarting postmaster

This is almost equivalent to stopping the postmaster then starting it again except that the parameters used before stopping it would be used too. This is done by saving them in $PG-DATA/postmaster.opts file. -w, -D, -m, -fast, -immediate and -o can also be used in the restarting mode and they have the same meanings as described above.

To restart postmaster in the simplest form:

```
$ pg_ctl restart
```

To restart postmaster, waiting for it to shut down and to come up:

```
$ pg_ctl -w restart
```

To restart using port 5433 and disabling fsync after restarting:

```
$ pg_ctl -o "-o -F -p 5433" restart
```

postmaster status

To get status information from postmaster:

```
$ pg_ctl status
```

Here is a sample output from pg_ctl:

```
pg_ctl: postmaster is running (pid: 13718)
options are:
/usr/local/src/pgsql/current/bin/postmaster
-p 5433
-D /usr/local/src/pgsql/current/data
-B 64
-b /usr/local/src/pgsql/current/bin/postgres
-N 32
-o '-F'
```

D.64   pg_dump

Name

pg_dump — Extract a Postgres database into a script file
    pg_dump [*dbname*]

    pg_dump [-h *host*] [-p *port*] [-t *table*] [-a] [-c] [-d] [-D] [-i] [-n] [-N] [-o] [-s] [-u] [-v] [-x] [*dbname*]

Inputs

pg_dump accepts the following command line arguments:

dbname Specifies the name of the database to be extracted. *dbname* defaults to the value of the USER environment variable.

-a Dump out only the data, no schema (definitions).

-c Clean (drop) schema prior to create.

-d Dump data as proper insert strings.

-D Dump data as inserts with attribute names

-i Ignore version mismatch between pg_dump and the database server. Since pg_dump knows a great deal about system catalogs, any given version of pg_dump is only intended to work with the corresponding release of the database server. Use this option if you need to override the version check (and if pg_dump then fails, don't say you weren't warned).

-n Suppress double quotes around identifiers unless absolutely necessary. This may cause trouble loading this dumped data if there are reserved words used for identifiers. This was the default behavior for pg_dump prior to v6.4.

-N Include double quotes around identifiers. This is the default.

-o Dump object identifiers (OIDs) for every table.

-s Dump out only the schema (definitions), no data.

-t *table* Dump data for *table* only.

-u Use password authentication. Prompts for username and password.

-v Specifies verbose mode.

-x Prevent dumping of ACLs (grant/revoke commands) and table ownership information.

pg_dump also accepts the following command line arguments for connection parameters:

-h *host* Specifies the hostname of the machine on which the postmaster is running. Defaults to using a local Unix domain socket rather than an IP connection.

-p *port* Specifies the Internet TCP/IP port or local Unix domain socket file extension on which the postmaster is listening for connections. The port number defaults to 5432, or the value of the PGPORT environment variable (if set).

-u Use password authentication. Prompts for *username* and *password*.

Outputs

pg_dump will create a file or write to stdout.

Connection to database 'template1' failed. connectDB() failed: Is the postmaster running and accepting connections at 'UNIX Socket' on port '*port*'? pg_dump could not attach to the postmaster process on the specified host and port. If you see this message, ensure that the postmaster is running on the proper host and that you have specified the proper port. If your site uses an authentication system, ensure that you have obtained the required authentication credentials.

Connection to database '*dbname*' failed. FATAL 1: SetUserId: user '*username*' is not in 'pg_shadow' You do not have a valid entry in the relation pg_shadow and and will not be allowed to access Postgres. Contact your Postgres administrator.

dumpSequence(*table*): SELECT failed You do not have permission to read the database. Contact your Postgres site administrator.

Note: pg_dump internally executes **SELECT** statements. If you have problems running pg_-dump, make sure you are able to select information from the database using, for example, *psql*.

Description

pg_dump is a utility for dumping out a Postgres database into a script file containing query commands. The script files are in text format and can be used to reconstruct the database, even on other machines and other architectures. pg_dump will produce the queries necessary to regenerate all user-defined types, functions, tables, indices, aggregates, and operators. In addition, all the data is copied out in text format so that it can be readily copied in again, as well as imported into tools for editing.

   pg_dump is useful for dumping out the contents of a database to move from one Postgres installation to another. After running pg_dump, one should examine the output script file for any warnings, especially in light of the limitations listed below.

Notes

pg_dump has a few limitations. The limitations mostly stem from difficulty in extracting certain meta-information from the system catalogs.

- pg_dump does not understand partial indices. The reason is the same as above; partial index predicates are stored as plans.

- pg_dump does not handle large objects. Large objects are ignored and must be dealt with manually.

- When doing a data only dump, pg_dump emits queries to disable triggers on user tables before inserting the data and queries to re-enable them after the data has been inserted. If the restore is stopped in the middle, the system catalogs may be left in the wrong state.

Usage

To dump a database of the same name as the user:

```
$ pg_dump > db.out
```

To reload this database:

```
$ psql -e database < db.out
```

D.65   pg_dumpall

Name

pg_dumpall — Extract all Postgres databases into a script file
    pg_dumpall [-h *host*] [-p *port*] [-a] [-d] [-D] [-O] [-s] [-u] [-v] [-x]

Inputs

pg_dumpall accepts the following command line arguments:

-a Dump out only the data, no schema (definitions).

-d Dump data as proper insert strings.

-D Dump data as inserts with attribute names

-n Suppress double quotes around identifiers unless absolutely necessary. This may cause trouble loading this dumped data if there are reserved words used for identifiers.

-o Dump object identifiers (OIDs) for every table.

-s Dump out only the schema (definitions), no data.

-u Use password authentication. Prompts for username and password.

-v Specifies verbose mode.

-x Prevent dumping ACLs (grant/revoke commands) and table ownership information.

pg_dumpall also accepts the following command line arguments for connection parameters:

-h *host* Specifies the hostname of the machine on which the postmaster is running. Defaults to using a local Unix domain socket rather than an IP connection.

-p *port* Specifies the Internet TCP/IP port or local Unix domain socket file extension on which the postmaster is listening for connections. The port number defaults to 5432, or the value of the PGPORT environment variable (if set).

-u Use password authentication. Prompts for *username* and *password*.

Outputs

pg_dumpall will create a file or write to stdout.

Connection to database 'template1' failed. connectDB() failed: Is the postmaster running and accepting connections at 'UNIX Socket' on port *'port* **'?** pg_dumpall could not attach to the postmaster process on the specified host and port. If you see this message, ensure that the postmaster is running on the proper host and that you have specified the proper port. If your site uses an authentication system, ensure that you have obtained the required authentication credentials.

Connection to database *'dbname'* **failed. FATAL 1: SetUserId: user 'username' is not in 'pg_shadow'** You do not have a valid entry in the relation pg_shadow and and will not be allowed to access Postgres. Contact your Postgres administrator.

dumpSequence(*table* **): SELECT failed** You do not have permission to read the database. Contact your Postgres site administrator.

Note: pg_dumpall internally executes **SELECT** statements. If you have problems running pg_-dumpall, make sure you are able to select information from the database using, for example, *psql*.

Description

pg_dumpall is a utility for dumping out all Postgres databases into one file. It also dumps the pg_shadow table, which is global to all databases. pg_dumpall includes in this file the proper commands to automatically create each dumped database before loading.

pg_dumpall takes all pg_dump options, but -f, -t and *dbname* should be omitted.

Refer to pg_dump for more information on this capability.

Usage

To dump all databases:

```
$ pg_dumpall > db.out
```

Tip: You can use most pg_dump options for pg_dumpall.

    To reload this database:

```
$ psql -e template1 < db.out
```

Tip: You can use most *psql* options when reloading.

D.66   pg_passwd

Name

pg_passwd — Manipulate the flat password file
   pg_passwd *filename*

Description

pg_passwd is a tool to manipulate the flat password file functionality of Postgres. This style of password authentication is not *required* in an installation, but is one of several supported security mechanisms.

    Specify the password file in the same style of Ident authentication in $PGDATA/pg_hba.conf:

```
host unv 133.65.96.250 255.255.255.255 password passwd
```

where the above line allows access from 133.65.96.250 using the passwords listed in $PG-DATA/passwd. The format of the password file follows those of /etc/passwd and /etc/shadow. The first field is the user name, and the second field is the encrypted password. The rest is completely ignored. Thus the following three sample lines specify the same user and password pair:

```
pg_guest:/nB7.w5Auq.BY:10031::::::
pg_guest:/nB7.w5Auq.BY:93001:930::/home/guest:/bin/tcsh
pg_guest:/nB7.w5Auq.BY:93001
```

Supply the password file to the pg_passwd command. In the case described above, after changing the working directory to PGDATA, the following command execution specifies the new password for pg_guest:

```
$ pg_passwd passwd
        Username: pg_guest
        Password:
        Re-enter password:
```

where the *Password:* and *Re-enter password:* prompts require the same password input which are not displayed on the terminal. The original password file is renamed to *passwd.bk*.

psql uses the -u option to invoke this style of authentication.

The following lines show the sample usage of the option:

```
$ psql -h hyalos -u unv
Username: pg_guest
Password:
Welcome to the POSTGRESQL interactive sql monitor:
  Please read the file COPYRIGHT for copyright terms of POSTGRESQL
  type \? for help on slash commands
  type \q to quit
  type \g or terminate with semicolon to execute query
 You are currently connected to the database: unv
unv=>
```

Perl5 authentication uses the new style of the Pg.pm like this:

```
$conn = Pg::connectdb("host=hyalos dbname=unv user=pg_guest password=xxxxxxx");
```

For more details, refer to src/interfaces/perl5/Pg.pm.

Pg{tcl,tk}sh authentication uses the pg_connect command with the -conninfo option thusly:

```
% set conn [pg_connect -conninfo \\
              "host=hyalos dbname=unv \\
              user=pg_guest password=xxxxxxx "]
```

You can list all of the keys for the option by executing the following command:

```
% puts [ pg_conndefaults]
```

D.67   pg_upgrade

Name

pg_upgrade — Allows upgrade from a previous release without reloading data

pg_upgrade [-f *filename*] *old_data_dir*

Description

pg_upgrade is a utility for upgrading from a previous Postgres release without reloading all the data. Not all Postgres release transitions can be handled this way. Check the release notes for details on your installation.

Upgrading Postgres with pg_upgrade

1. Back up your existing data directory, preferably by making a complete dump with pg_dumpall.

2. Then do:

```
$ pg_dumpall -s > db.out
```

3. to dump out your old database's table definitions without any data.

4. Stop the old postmaster and all backends.

5. Rename (using mv) your old pgsql data/ directory to data.old/.

6. Do:

```
$ make install
```

7. to install the new binaries.

8. Run initdb to create a new template1 database containing the system tables for the new release.

9. Start the new postmaster. (Note: it is critical that no users connect to the database until the upgrade is complete. You may wish to start the postmaster without -i and/or alter pg_hba.conf temporarily.)

10. Change your working directory to the pgsql main directory, and type:

```
$ pg_upgrade -f db.out data.old
```

11. The program will do some checking to make sure everything is properly configured, and will run your db.out script to recreate all the databases and tables you had, but with no data. It will then physically move the data files containing non-system tables and indexes from data.old/ into the proper data/ subdirectories, replacing the empty data files created during the db.out script.

12. Restore your old *pg_hba.conf* if needed to allow user logins.

13. Stop and restart the postmaster.

14. *Carefully* examine the contents of the upgraded database. If you detect problems, you'll need to recover by restoring from your full pg_dump backup. You can delete the data.old/ directory when you are satisfied.

15. The upgraded database will be in an un-vacuumed state. You will probably want to run a **VACUUM ANALYZE** before beginning production work.

D.68   pgaccess

Name

pgaccess — Postgres graphical interactive client
  pgaccess [*dbname*]

Inputs

dbname   The name of an existing database to access.

Outputs

Description

pgaccess provides a graphical interface for Postgres where you can manage your tables, edit them, define queries, sequences and functions.

Another way of accessing Postgres through tcl is to use pgtclsh or pgtksh.

pgaccess can:

- Open any database on a specified host at the specified port, username and password.

- Execute *VACUUM*.

- Save preferences in ˜/.pgaccessrc file.

For tables, pgaccess can:

- Open multiple tables for viewing, max n records (configurable).

- Resize columns by dragging the vertical grid lines.

- Wrap text in cells.

- Dynamically adjust row height when editing.

- Save table layout for every table.

- Import/export to external files (SDF,CSV).

- Use filter capabilities; enter filter like price > 3.14.

- Specify sort order; enter manually the sort field(s).

- Edit in place; double click the text you want to change.

- Delete records; point to the record, press Del key.

- Add new records; save new row with right-button-click.

- Create tables with an assistant.

- Rename and delete (drop) tables.

- Retrieve information on tables, including owner, field information, indices.

For queries, pgaccess can:

- Define, edit and store *user defined queries*.

- Save view layouts.

- Store queries as views.

- Execute with optional user input parameters; e.g., select * from invoices where year=[parameter "Year of selection"].

- View any select query result.

- Run action queries (insert, update, delete).

- Construct queries using a visual query builder with drag & drop support, table aliasing.

For sequences, pgaccess can:

- Define new instances.

- Inspect existing instances.

- Delete.

For views, pgaccess can:

- Define them by saving queries as views.

- View them, with filtering and sorting capabilities.

- Design new views.

- Delete (drop) existing views.

For functions, pgaccess can:

- Define.

- Inspect.

- Delete.

For reports, pgaccess can:

- Generate simple reports from a table (beta stage).

- Change font, size and style of fields and labels.

- Load and save reports from the database.

- Preview tables, sample postscript print.

For forms, pgaccess can:

- Open user defined forms.

- Use a form design module.

- Access record sets using a query widget.

For scripts, pgaccess can:

- Define.

- Modify.

- Call user defined scripts.

D.69 pgtclsh

Name

pgtclsh — Postgres TCL shell client
   pgtclsh [*dbname*]

Inputs

dbname   The name of an existing database to access.

Outputs

Description

pgtclsh provides a TCL shell interface for Postgres.
   Another way of accessing Postgres through tcl is to use pgtksh or pgaccess.

D.70   pgtksh

Name

pgtksh — Postgres graphical TCL/TK shell
   pgtksh [*dbname*]

Inputs

dbname   The name of an existing database to access.

Outputs

Description

pgtksh provides a graphical TCL/TK shell interface for Postgres.
   Another way of accessing Postgres through TCL is to use pgtclsh or pgaccess.

D.71   postgres

Name

postgres — Run a Postgres single-user backend
   postgres [*dbname*]
   postgres [-B *nBuffers*] [-C] [-D *DataDir*] [-E] [-F] [-O] [-P] [-Q] [-S *SortSize*] [-d [
DebugLevel]] [-e] [-o] [*OutputFile*] [-s] [-v *protocol*] [*dbname*]

Inputs

postgres accepts the following command line arguments:

dbname   The optional argument *dbname* specifies the name of the database to be accessed. *dbname*
   defaults to the value of the USER environment variable.

-B *nBuffers*   If the backend is running under the postmaster, *nBuffers* is the number of shared-
   memory buffers that the postmaster has allocated for the backend server processes that it
   starts. If the backend is running stand-alone, this specifies the number of buffers to allocate.
   This value defaults to 64 buffers, where each buffer is 8k bytes (or whatever BLCKSZ is set
   to in config.h).

-C   Do not show the server version number.

-D *DataDir* Specifies the directory to use as the root of the tree of database directories. If -D is not given, the default data directory name is the value of the environment variable PGDATA. If PGDATA is not set, then the directory used is $POSTGRESHOME/data. If neither environment variable is set and this command-line option is not specified, the default directory that was set at compile-time is used.

-E Echo all queries.

-F Disable an automatic fsync() call after each transaction. This option improves performance, but an operating system crash while a transaction is in progress may cause the loss of the most recently entered data. Without the fsync() call the data is buffered by the operating system, and written to disk sometime later.

-O Override restrictions, so system table structures can be modified. These tables are typically those with a leading *pg_* in the table name.

-P Ignore system indexes to scan/update system tuples. The **REINDEX** for system tables/indexes requires this option. System tables are typically those with a leading *pg_* in the table name.

-Q Specifies "quiet" mode.

-S *SortSize* Specifies the amount of memory to be used by internal sorts and hashes before resorting to temporary disk files. The value is specified in kilobytes, and defaults to 512 kilobytes. Note that for a complex query, several sorts and/or hashes might be running in parallel, and each one will be allowed to use as much as *SortSize* kilobytes before it starts to put data into temporary files.

-d [*DebugLevel*] The optional argument *DebugLevel* determines the amount of debugging output the backend servers will produce. If *DebugLevel* is one, the postmaster will trace all connection traffic, and nothing else. For levels two and higher, debugging is turned on in the backend process and the postmaster displays more information, including the backend environment and process traffic. Note that if no file is specified for backend servers to send their debugging output then this output will appear on the controlling tty of their parent postmaster.

-e This option controls how dates are interpreted upon input to and output from the database. If the -e option is supplied, then dates passed to and from the frontend processes will be assumed to be in "European" format (DD-MM-YYYY), otherwise dates are assumed to be in "American" format (MM-DD-YYYY). Dates are accepted by the backend in a wide variety of formats, and for input dates this switch mostly affects the interpretation for ambiguous cases. See the *PostgreSQL User's Guide* for more information.

-o *OutputFile* Sends all debugging and error output to *OutputFile*. If the backend is running under the postmaster, error messages are still sent to the frontend process as well as to

OutputFile, but debugging output is sent to the controlling tty of the postmaster (since only one file descriptor can be sent to an actual file).

-s Print time information and other statistics at the end of each query. This is useful for bench-marking or for use in tuning the number of buffers.

-v *protocol* Specifies the number of the frontend/backend protocol to be used for this particular session.

There are several other options that may be specified, used mainly for debugging purposes. These are listed here only for the use by Postgres system developers. *Use of any of these options is highly discouraged.* Furthermore, any of these options may disappear or change at any time.

These special-case options are:

-A [n | r | b | Q | X] This option generates a tremendous amount of output.

-L Turns off the locking system.

-N Disables use of newline as a query delimiter.

-f [s | i | m | n | h] Forbids the use of particular scan and join methods: *s* and *i* disable se-quential and index scans respectively, while *n, m,* and *h* disable nested-loop, merge and hash joins respectively. **Note:** Neither sequential scans nor nested-loop joins can be disabled completely; the *-fs* and *-fn* options simply discourage the optimizer from using those plan types if it has any other alternative.

-i Prevents query execution, but shows the plan tree.

-p *dbname* Indicates to the backend server that it has been started by a postmaster and makes different assumptions about buffer pool management, file descriptors, etc. Switches following *-p* are restricted to those considered "secure".

-t pa[rser | pl[anner] | e[xecutor]] Print timing statistics for each query relating to each of the major system modules. This option cannot be used with -s.

Outputs

Of the nigh-infinite number of error messages you may see when you execute the backend server directly, the most common will probably be:

semget: No space left on device If you see this message, you should run the ipcclean command. After doing this, try starting postmaster again. If this still doesn't work, you probably need to configure your kernel for shared memory and semaphores as described in the installation notes. If you have a kernel with particularly small shared memory and/or semaphore limits, you may have to reconfigure your kernel to increase its shared memory or semaphore parameters. **Tip:** You may be able to postpone reconfiguring your kernel by decreasing -B to reduce Postgres' shared memory consumption.

Description

The Postgres backend server can be executed directly from the user shell. This should be done only while debugging by the DBA, and should not be done while other Postgres backends are being managed by a postmaster on this set of databases.

Some of the switches explained here can be passed to the backend through the "database options" field of a connection request, and thus can be set for a particular backend without going to the trouble of restarting the postmaster. This is particularly handy for debugging-related switches.

The optional argument *dbname* specifies the name of the database to be accessed. *dbname* defaults to the value of the USER environment variable.

Notes

Useful utilities for dealing with shared memory problems include ipcs(1), ipcrm(1), and ipcclean(1). See also postmaster.

D.72   postmaster

Name

postmaster — Run the Postgres multi-user backend
postmaster [-B *nBuffers*] [-D *DataDir*] [-N *maxBackends*] [-S] [-d *DebugLevel*] [-i] [-l] [-o *BackendOptions*] [-p *port*] [-n | -s]

Inputs

postmaster accepts the following command line arguments:

-B *nBuffers* Sets the number of shared-memory disk buffers for the postmaster to allocate for use by the backend server processes that it starts. This value defaults to 64 buffers, where each buffer is 8k bytes (or whatever BLCKSZ is set to in src/include/config.h).

-D *DataDir* Specifies the directory to use as the root of the tree of database directories. If -D is not given, the default data directory name is the value of the environment variable PGDATA. If PGDATA is not set, then the directory used is $POSTGRESHOME/data. If neither environment variable is set and this command-line option is not specified, the default directory that was set at compile-time is used.

-N *maxBackends* Sets the maximum number of backend server processes that this postmaster is allowed to start. By default, this value is 32, but it can be set as high as 1024 if your system will support that many processes. (Note that -B is required to be at least twice -N, so you'll need to increase -B if you increase -N.) Both the default and upper limit values for -N can be altered when building Postgres (see src/include/config.h).

-S Specifies that the postmaster process should start up in silent mode. That is, it will disassociate from the user's (controlling) tty, start its own process group, and redirect its standard output and standard error to */dev/null.*

Note that using this switch makes it very difficult to troubleshoot problems, since all tracing and logging output that would normally be generated by this postmaster and its child backends will be discarded.

-d *DebugLevel* Determines the amount of debugging output the backend servers will produce. If *DebugLevel* is one, the postmaster will trace all connection traffic. Levels two and higher turn on increasing amounts of debug output from the backend processes, and the postmaster displays more information including the backend environment and process traffic. Note that unless the postmaster's standard output and standard error are redirected into a log file, all this output will appear on the controlling tty of the postmaster.

-i Allows clients to connect via TCP/IP (Internet domain) connections. Without this option, only local Unix domain socket connections are accepted.

-l Enables secure connections using SSL. The -i option is also required. You must have compiled with SSL enabled to use this option.

-o *BackendOptions* The postgres option(s) specified in *BackendOptions* are passed to all backend server processes started by this postmaster. If the option string contains any spaces, the entire string must be quoted.

-p *port* Specifies the TCP/IP port or local Unix domain socket file extension on which the postmaster is to listen for connections from frontend applications. Defaults to the value of the PGPORT environment variable, or if PGPORT is not set, then defaults to the value established when Postgres was compiled (normally 5432). If you specify a port other than the default port, then all frontend applications (including psql) must specify the same port using either command-line options or PGPORT.

Two additional command line options are available for debugging problems that cause a backend to die abnormally. These options control the behavior of the postmaster in this situation, and *neither option is intended for use in ordinary operation.*

The ordinary strategy for this situation is to notify all other backends that they must terminate and then reinitialize the shared memory and semaphores. This is because an errant backend could have corrupted some shared state before terminating.

These special-case options are:

-n postmaster will not reinitialize shared data structures. A knowledgeable system programmer can then use a debugger to examine shared memory and semaphore state.

-s postmaster will stop all other backend processes by sending the signal SIGSTOP, but will not cause them to terminate. This permits system programmers to collect core dumps from all backend processes by hand.

Outputs

semget: No space left on device If you see this message, you should run the ipcclean command. After doing so, try starting postmaster again. If this still doesn't work, you probably need to configure your kernel for shared memory and semaphores as described in the installation notes. If you run multiple instances of postmaster on a single host, or have a kernel with particularly small shared memory and/or semaphore limits, you may have to reconfigure your kernel to increase its shared memory or semaphore parameters. **Tip:** You may be able to postpone reconfiguring your kernel by decreasing -B to reduce Postgres' shared memory consumption, and/or by reducing -N to reduce Postgres' semaphore consumption.

StreamServerPort: cannot bind to port If you see this message, you should make certain that there is no other postmaster process already running on the same port number. The easiest way to determine this is by using the command $ `ps -ax | grep postmaster` on BSD-based systems, or $ `ps -e | grep postmast` for System V-like or POSIX-compliant systems such as HP-UX.

If you are sure that no other postmaster processes are running and you still get this error, try specifying a different port using the -p option. You may also get this error if you terminate the postmaster and immediately restart it using the same port; in this case, you must simply wait a few seconds until the operating system closes the port before trying again. Finally, you may get this error if you specify a port number that your operating system considers to be reserved. For example, many versions of Unix consider port numbers under 1024 to be *trusted* and only permit the Unix superuser to access them.

IpcMemoryAttach: shmat() failed: Permission denied A likely explanation is that another user attempted to start a postmaster process on the same port which acquired shared resources and then died. Since Postgres shared memory keys are based on the port number assigned to the postmaster, such conflicts are likely if there is more than one installation on a single host. If there are no other postmaster processes currently running (see above), run ipcclean and try again. If other postmaster images are running, you will have to find the owners of those processes to coordinate the assignment of port numbers and/or removal of unused shared memory segments.

Description

postmaster manages the communication between frontend and backend processes, as well as allocating the shared buffer pool and SysV semaphores (on machines without a test-and-set instruction). postmaster does not itself interact with the user and should be started as a background process.

Only one postmaster should be running at a time in a given Postgres installation. Here, an installation means a database directory and postmaster port number. You can run more than one postmaster on a machine only if each one has a separate directory and port number.

Notes

If at all possible, *do not* use SIGKILL when killing the postmaster. SIGHUP, SIGINT, or SIGTERM (the default signal for kill(1))" should be used instead. Using `$ kill -KILL` or its alternative form `$ kill -9` will prevent postmaster from freeing the system resources (e.g., shared memory and semaphores) that it holds before dying. Use SIGTERM instead to avoid having to clean up manually (as described earlier).

Useful utilities for dealing with shared memory problems include ipcs(1), ipcrm(1), and ipc-clean(1).

Usage

To start postmaster using default values, type:

```
$ nohup postmaster > logfile 2>&1
```

This command will start up postmaster on the default port (5432). This is the simplest and most common way to start the postmaster.

To start postmaster with a specific port:

```
$ nohup postmaster -p 1234 &
```

This command will start up postmaster communicating through the port 1234. In order to connect to this postmaster using psql, you would need to run it as:

```
$ psql -p 1234
```

or set the environment variable PGPORT:

```
$ export PGPORT 1234
$ psql
```

D.73   psql

Name

psql — Postgres interactive terminal
    psql [*options*] [*dbname* [*user*]]

Summary

psql is a terminal-based front-end to Postgres. It enables you to type in queries interactively, issue them to Postgres, and see the query results. Alternatively, input can be from a file. In addition, it provides a number of meta-commands and various shell-like features to facilitate writing scripts and automating a wide variety of tasks.

Description

Connecting To A Database

psql is a regular Postgres client application. In order to connect to a database you need to know the name of your target database, the hostname and port number of the server and what user name you want to connect as. psql can be told about those parameters via command line options, namely -d, -h, -p, and -U respectively. If an argument is found that does not belong to any option it will be interpreted as the database name (or the user name, if the database name is also given). Not all these options are required, defaults do apply. If you omit the host name psql will connect via a Unix domain socket to a server on the local host. The default port number is compile-time determined. Since the database server uses the same default, you will not have to specify the port in most cases. The default user name is your Unix username, as is the default database name. Note that you can't just connect to any database under any username. Your database administrator should have informed you about your access rights. To save you some typing you can also set the environment variables PGDATABASE, PGHOST, PGPORT and PGUSER to appropriate values.

If the connection could not be made for any reason (e.g., insufficient privileges, postmaster is not running on the server, etc.), psql will return an error and terminate.

Entering Queries

In normal operation, psql provides a prompt with the name of the database to which psql is currently connected, followed by the string "=>". For example,

```
$ psql testdb
Welcome to psql, the PostgreSQL interactive terminal.
Type:  \copyright for distribution terms
       \h for help with SQL commands
       \? for help on internal slash commands
       \g or terminate with semicolon to execute query
       \q to quit
testdb=>
```

At the prompt, the user may type in SQL queries. Ordinarily, input lines are sent to the backend when a query-terminating semicolon is reached. An end of line does not terminate a query! Thus queries can be spread over several lines for clarity. If the query was sent and without error, the query results are displayed on the screen.

Whenever a query is executed, psql also polls for asynchronous notification events generated by *LISTEN* and *NOTIFY*.

psql Meta-Commands

Anything you enter in psql that begins with an unquoted backslash is a psql meta-command that is processed by psql itself. These commands are what makes psql interesting for administration or scripting. Meta-commands are more commonly called slash or backslash commands.

The format of a psql command is the backslash, followed immediately by a command verb, then any arguments. The arguments are separated from the command verb and each other by any number of whitespace characters.

To include whitespace into an argument you must quote it with a single quote. To include a single quote into such an argument, precede it by a backslash. Anything contained in single quotes is furthermore subject to C-like substitutions for \n (new line), \t (tab), \\digits, \\0digits, and \\0x*digits* (the character with the given decimal, octal, or hexadecimal code).

If an unquoted argument begins with a colon (:), it is taken as a variable and the value of the variable is taken as the argument instead.

Arguments that are quoted in backticks (`) are taken as a command line that is passed to the shell. The output of the command (with a trailing newline removed) is taken as the argument value. The above escape sequences also apply in backticks.

Some commands take the name of an SQL identifier (such as a table name) as argument. These arguments follow the syntax rules of SQL regarding double quotes: an identifier without double quotes is coerced to lower-case. For all other commands double quotes are not special and will become part of the argument.

Parsing for arguments stops when another unquoted backslash occurs. This is taken as the beginning of a new meta-command. The special sequence \\ (two backslashes) marks the end of arguments and continues parsing SQL queries, if any. That way SQL and psql commands can be freely mixed on a line. But in any case, the arguments of a meta-command cannot continue beyond the end of the line.

The following meta-commands are defined:

\a If the current table output format is unaligned, switch to aligned. If it is not unaligned, set it to unaligned. This command is kept for backwards compatibility. See **\pset** for a general solution.

\C [*title*] Set the title of any tables being printed as the result of a query or unset any such title. This command is equivalent to \pset title *title*. (The name of this command derives from *caption,* as it was previously only used to set the caption in an HTML table.)

\connect (or \c) [*dbname* [*username*]] Establishes a connection to a new database and/or under a user name. The previous connection is closed. If *dbname* is - the current database name is assumed.

If *username* is omitted the current user name is assumed.

As a special rule, **\connect** without any arguments will connect to the default database as the default user (as you would have gotten by starting psql without any arguments).

If the connection attempt failed (wrong username, access denied, etc.), the previous connection will be kept if and only if psql is in interactive mode. When executing a non-interactive script, processing will immediately stop with an error. This distinction was chosen as a user convenience against typos on the one hand, and a safety mechanism that scripts are not accidentally acting on the wrong database on the other hand.

\copy *table* [with oids { from | to } *filename* | stdin | stdout [using delimiters *'characters'*] [with null as *'string'*]] Performs a frontend (client) copy. This is an operation that runs an SQL *COPY* command, but instead of the backend's reading or writing the specified file, and consequently requiring backend access and special user privilege, as well as being bound to the file system accessible by the backend, psql reads or writes the file and routes the data between the backend and the local file system.

The syntax of the command is similar to that of the SQL **COPY** command (see its description for the details). Note that, because of this, special parsing rules apply to the **\copy** command. In particular, the variable substitution rules and backslash escapes do not apply.

Tip: This operation is not as efficient as the SQL **COPY** command because all data must pass through the client/server IP or socket connection. For large amounts of data the other technique may be preferable.

Note: Note the difference in interpretation of stdin and stdout between frontend and backend copies: in a frontend copy these always refer to psql's input and output stream. On a backend copy stdin comes from wherever the **COPY** itself came from (for example, a script run with the -f option), and stdout refers to the query output stream (see **\o** meta-command below).

\copyright Shows the copyright and distribution terms of Postgres.

\d *relation* Shows all columns of *relation* (which could be a table, view, index, or sequence), their types, and any special attributes such as NOT NULL or defaults, if any. If the relation is, in fact, a table, any defined indices are also listed. If the relation is a view, the view definition is also shown.

The command form **\d+** is identical, but any comments associated with the table columns are shown as well.

Note: If **\d** is called without any arguments, it is equivalent to **\dtvs** which will show a list of all tables, views, and sequences. This is purely a convenience measure.

\da [*pattern*] Lists all available aggregate functions, together with the data type they operate on. If *pattern* (a regular expression) is specified, only matching aggregates are shown.

\dd [*object*] Shows the descriptions of *object* (which can be a regular expression), or of all objects if no argument is given. (*Object* covers aggregates, functions, operators, types, relations (tables, views, indices, sequences, large objects), rules, and triggers.) For example:

```
=>  \dd version
Object descriptions
    Name  |   What   | Description
 ---------+----------+--------------------------
  version | function | PostgreSQL version string
(1 row)
```

Descriptions for objects can be generated with the **COMMENT ON** SQL command.

Note: Postgres stores the object descriptions in the pg_description system table.

\df [*pattern*] Lists available functions, together with their argument and return types. If *pattern* (a regular expression) is specified, only matching functions are shown. If the form \df+ is used, additional information about each function, including language and description, is shown.

\distvS [*pattern*] This is not the actual command name: The letters *i, s, t, v, S* stand for index, sequence, table, view, and system table, respectively. You can specify any or all of them in any order to obtain a listing of them, together with who the owner is.

If *pattern* is specified, it is a regular expression that restricts the listing to those objects whose name matches. If one appends a + to the command name, each object is listed with its associated description, if any.

\dl This is an alias for **\lo_list**, which shows a list of large objects.

\do [*name*] Lists available operators with their operand and return types. If *name* is specified, only operators with that name will be shown.

\dp [*pattern*] This is an alias for **\z** which was included for its greater mnemonic value (*display permissions*).

\dT [*pattern*] Lists all data types or only those that match *pattern*. The command form \dT+ shows extra information.

\edit (or \e) [*filename*] If *filename* is specified, the file is edited; after the editor exits, its content is copied back to the query buffer. If no argument is given, the current query buffer is copied to a temporary file which is then edited in the same fashion.

The new query buffer is then re-parsed according to the normal rules of psql, where the whole buffer is treated as a single line. (Thus you cannot make scripts this way. Use \i for that.) This means also that if the query ends with (or rather contains) a semicolon, it is immediately executed. In other cases it will merely wait in the query buffer.

Tip: psql searches the environment variables PSQL_EDITOR, EDITOR, and VISUAL (in that order) for an editor to use. If all of them are unset, */bin/vi* is run.

\echo *text* [...] Prints the arguments to the standard output, separated by one space and followed by a newline. This can be useful to intersperse information in the output of scripts. For example:

```
=>  \echo 'date'
Tue Oct 26 21:40:57 CEST 1999
```

If the first argument is an unquoted -n the the trailing newline is not written.

Tip: If you use the \o command to redirect your query output you may wish to use **\qecho** instead of this command.

\encoding [*encoding*] Sets the client encoding, if you are using multibyte encodings. Without an argument, this command shows the current encoding.

\f [*string*] Sets the field separator for unaligned query output. The default is pipe (|). See also \pset for a generic way of setting output options.

\g [{*filename* | |*command*}] Sends the current query input buffer to the backend and optionally saves the output in *filename* or pipes the output into a separate Unix shell to execute *command*. A bare \g is virtually equivalent to a semicolon. A \g with argument is a *one-shot* alternative to the \o command.

\help (or \h) [*command*] Give syntax help on the specified SQL command. If *command* is not specified, then psql will list all the commands for which syntax help is available. If *command* is an asterisk (*), then syntax help on all SQL commands is shown.

Note: To simplify typing, commands that consists of several words do not have to be quoted. Thus it is fine to type **\help alter table**.

\H Turns on HTML query output format. If the HTML format is already on, it is switched back to the default aligned text format. This command is for compatibility and convenience, but see \pset about setting other output options.

\i *filename* Reads input from the file *filename* and executes it as though it had been typed on the keyboard.

Note: If you want to see the lines on the screen as they are read you must set the variable ECHO to all.

\l (or \list) List all the databases in the server as well as their owners. Append a + to the command name to see any descriptions for the databases as well. If your Postgres installation was compiled with multibyte encoding support, the encoding scheme of each database is shown as well.

\lo_export *loid filename* Reads the large object with OID *loid* from the database and writes it to *filename*. Note that this is subtly different from the server function lo_export, which acts with the permissions of the user that the database server runs as and on the server's file system.

> **Tip:** Use **\lo_list** to find out the large object's OID.

> **Note:** See the description of the LO_TRANSACTION variable for important information concerning all large object operations.

\lo_import *filename* [*comment*] Stores the file into a Postgres *large object*. Optionally, it associates the given comment with the object. Example:

```
foo=>  \lo_import '/home/peter/pictures/photo.xcf' 'a picture of me'
lo_import 152801
```

The response indicates that the large object received object id 152801 which one ought to remember if one wants to access the object ever again. For that reason it is recommended to always associate a human-readable comment with every object. Those can then be seen with the **\lo_list** command.

Note that this command is subtly different from the server-side lo_import because it acts as the local user on the local file system, rather than the server's user and file system.

> **Note:** See the description of the LO_TRANSACTION variable for important information concerning all large object operations.

\lo_list Shows a list of all Postgres *large objects* currently stored in the database along with their owners.

\lo_unlink *loid* Deletes the large object with OID *loid* from the database.

> **Tip:** Use **\lo_list** to find out the large object's OID.

> **Note:** See the description of the LO_TRANSACTION variable for important information concerning all large object operations.

\o [{*filename* | |*command*}] Saves future query results to the file *filename* or pipes future results into a separate Unix shell to execute *command*. If no arguments are specified, the query output will be reset to stdout.

> *Query results* includes all tables, command responses, and notices obtained from the database server, as well as output of various backslash commands that query the database (such as **\d**), but not error messages.

> **Tip:** To intersperse text output in between query results, use **\qecho**.

\p Print the current query buffer to the standard output.

\pset *parameter* [*value*] This command sets options affecting the output of query result tables. *parameter* describes which option is to be set. The semantics of *value* depend thereon.

Adjustable printing options are:

format Sets the output format to one of unaligned, aligned, html, or latex. Unique abbreviations are allowed. (That would mean one letter is enough.)

Unaligned writes all fields of a tuple on a line, separated by the currently active field separator. This is intended to create output that might be intended to be read in by other programs (tab-separated, comma-separated).

Aligned mode is the standard, human-readable, nicely formatted text output that is default. The HTML and LaTeX modes put out tables that are intended to be included in documents using the respective mark-up language. They are not complete documents! (This might not be so dramatic in HTML, but in LaTeX you must have a complete document wrapper.)

border The second argument must be a number. In general, the higher the number the more borders and lines the tables will have, but this depends on the particular format. In HTML mode, this will translate directly into the border=... attribute, in the others only values 0 (no border), 1 (internal dividing lines), and 2 (table frame) make sense.

expanded (or x) Toggles between regular and expanded format. When expanded format is enabled, all output has two columns with the field name on the left and the data on the right. This mode is useful if the data wouldn't fit on the screen in the normal *horizontal* mode.

Expanded mode is supported by all four output modes.

null The second argument is a string that should be printed whenever a field is null. The default is not to print anything, which can easily be mistaken for, say, an empty string. Thus, one might choose to write \pset null '(null)'.

fieldsep Specifies the field separator to be used in unaligned output mode. That way one can create, for example, tab- or comma-separated output, which other programs might prefer. To set a tab as field separator, type \pset fieldsep '\t'. The default field separator is pipe (|).

recordsep Specifies the record (line) separator to use in unaligned output mode. The default is a newline character.

tuples_only (or t) Toggles between tuples only and full display. Full display may show extra information such as column headers, titles, and various footers. In tuples only mode, only actual table data is shown.

title [*text*] Sets the table title for any subsequently printed tables. This can be used to give your output descriptive tags. If no argument is given, the title is unset.

Note: This formerly only affected HTML mode. You can now set titles in any output format.

tableattr (or T) [*text*] Allows you to specify any attributes to be placed inside the HTML table tag. This could for example be cellpadding or bgcolor. Note that you probably don't want to specify border here, as that is already taken care of by \pset border.

pager Toggles the list of a pager to do table output. If the environment variable PAGER is set, the output is piped to the specified program. Otherwise more is used.

In any case, psql only uses the pager if it seems appropriate. That means among other things that the output is to a terminal and that the table would normally not fit on the screen. Because of the modular nature of the printing routines it is not always possible to predict the number of lines that will actually be printed. For that reason psql might not appear very discriminating about when to use the pager and when not to.

Illustrations on how these different formats look can be seen in the *Examples* section. **Tip:** There are various shortcut commands for **pset**. See **a**, **C**, **H**, **t**, **T**, and **x**.

Note: It is an error to call **pset** without arguments. In the future this call might show the current status of all printing options.

\q Quit the psql program.

\qecho *text* [...] This command is identical to **echo** except that all output will be written to the query output channel, as set by **o**.

\r Resets (clears) the query buffer.

\s [*filename*] Print or save the command line history to *filename*. If *filename* is omitted, the history is written to the standard output. This option is only available if psql is configured to use the GNU history library.

Note: As of psql version 7.0 it is no longer necessary to save the command history, since that will be done automatically on program termination. The history is also loaded automatically every time psql starts up.

\set [*name* [*value* [...]]] Sets the internal variable *name* to *value* or, if more than one value is given, to the concatenation of all of them. If no second argument is given, the variable is just set with no value. To unset a variable, use the **unset** command.

Valid variable names can contain characters, digits, and underscores. See the section about psql variables for details.

Although you are welcome to set any variable to anything you want, psql treats several variables as special. They are documented in the section about variables.

Note: This command is totally separate from the SQL command *SET*.

\t Toggles the display of output column name headings and row count footer. This command is equivalent to \pset tuples_only and is provided for convenience.

\T *table_options* Allows you to specify options to be placed within the table tag in HTML tabular output mode. This command is equivalent to \pset tableattr *table_options*.

\w {*filename* | |*command*} Outputs the current query buffer to the file *filename* or pipes it to the Unix command *command*.

\x Toggles extended row format mode. As such it is equivalent to \pset expanded.

\z [*pattern*] Produces a list of all tables in the database with their appropriate access permissions listed. If an argument is given it is taken as a regular expression which limits the listing to those tables which match it.

```
test=> \z
Access permissions for database "test"
 Relation | Access permissions
----------+------------------------------------
 my_table | { "=r","joe=arwR", "group staff=ar"}
(1 row )
```

Read this as follows:

- "=r": PUBLIC has read (**SELECT**) permission on the table.

- "joe=arwR": User joe has read, write (**UPDATE, DELETE**), *append* (**INSERT**) permissions, and permission to create rules on the table.

- "group staff=ar": Group staff has **SELECT** and **INSERT** permission.

  The commands *GRANT* and *REVOKE* are used to set access permissions.

\! [*command*] Escapes to a separate Unix shell or executes the Unix command *command*. The arguments are not further interpreted, the shell will see them as is.

\? Get help information about the backslash (\ ) commands.

Command-line Options

If so configured, psql understands both standard Unix short options, and GNU-style long options. The latter are not available on all systems.

-a, –echo-all Print all the lines to the screen as they are read. This is more useful for script processing rather than interactive mode. This is equivalent to setting the variable ECHO to all.

-A, –no-align Switches to unaligned output mode. (The default output mode is otherwise aligned.)

-c, –command *query* Specifies that psql is to execute one query string, *query*, and then exit. This is useful in shell scripts.

query must be either a query string that is completely parseable by the backend (i.e., it contains no psql specific features), or it is a single backslash command. Thus you cannot mix SQL and psql meta-commands. To achieve that, you could pipe the string into psql, like this:

```
echo "\x \ \ select * from foo;" | psql.
```

-d, –dbname *dbname* Specifies the name of the database to connect to. This is equivalent to specifying *dbname* as the first non-option argument on the command line.

-e, –echo-queries Show all queries that are sent to the backend. This is equivalent to setting the variable ECHO to queries.

-E, –echo-hidden Echoes the actual queries generated by \d and other backslash commands. You can use this if you wish to include similar functionality into your own programs. This is equivalent to setting the variable ECHO_HIDDEN from within psql.

-f, –file *filename* Use the file *filename* as the source of queries instead of reading queries inter-actively. After the file is processed, psql terminates. This is in many ways equivalent to the internal command **\i**.

Using this option is subtly different from writing psql < *filename*. In general, both will do what you expect, but using -f enables some nice features such as error messages with line numbers. There is also a slight chance that using this option will reduce the start-up overhead. On the other hand, the variant using the shell's input redirection is (in theory) guaranteed to yield exactly the same output that you would have gotten had you entered everything by hand.

-F, –field-separator *separator* Use *separator* as the field separator. This is equivalent to **\pset fieldsep** or **\f**.

-h, –host *hostname* Specifies the host name of the machine on which the postmaster is running. Without this option, communication is performed using local Unix domain sockets.

-H, –html Turns on HTML tabular output. This is equivalent to **\pset format html** or the **\H** command.

-l, –list Lists all available databases, then exits. Other non-connection options are ignored. This is similar to the internal command **\list**.

-o, –output *filename* Put all query output into file *filename*. This is equivalent to the command **\o**.

-p, –port *port* Specifies the TCP/IP port or, by omission, the local Unix domain socket file extension on which the postmaster is listening for connections. Defaults to the value of the PGPORT environment variable or, if not set, to the port specified at compile time, usually 5432.

-P, –pset *assignment* Allows you to specify printing options in the style of **\pset** on the command line. Note that here you have to separate name and value with an equal sign instead of a space. Thus to set the output format to LATEX, you could write -P format=latex.

-q Specifies that psql should do its work quietly. By default, it prints welcome messages and various informational output. If this option is used, none of this happens. This is useful with the -c option. Within psql you can also set the QUIET variable to achieve the same effect.

-R, –record-separator *separator* Use *separator* as the record separator. This is equivalent to the **\pset recordsep** command.

-s, –single-step Run in single-step mode. That means the user is prompted before each query is sent to the backend, with the option to cancel execution as well. Use this to debug scripts.

-S, –single-line Runs in single-line mode where a newline terminates a query, as a semicolon does.

> **Note:** This mode is provided for those who insist on it, but you are not necessarily encouraged to use it. In particular, if you mix SQL and meta-commands on a line the order of execution might not always be clear to the inexperienced user.

-t, –tuples-only Turn off printing of column names and result row count footers, etc. It is completely equivalent to the **\t** meta-command.

-T, –table-attr *table_options* Allows you to specify options to be placed within the HTML table tag. See **\pset** for details.

-u Makes psql prompt for the user name and password before connecting to the database.

> This option is deprecated, as it is conceptually flawed. (Prompting for a non-default user name and prompting for a password because the backend requires it are really two different things.) You are encouraged to look at the -U and -W options instead.

-U, –username *username* Connects to the database as the user *username* instead of the default. (You must have permission to do so, of course.)

-v, –variable, –set *assignment* Performs a variable assignment, like the **\set** internal command. Note that you must separate name and value, if any, by an equal sign on the command line. To unset a variable, leave off the equal sign. These assignments are done during a very early state of start-up, so variables reserved for internal purposes might get overwritten later.

-V, –version Shows the psql version.

-W, –password Requests that psql should prompt for a password before connecting to a database. This will remain set for the entire session, even if you change the database connection with the meta-command **connect**.

As of version 7.0, psql automatically issues a password prompt whenever the backend requests password authentication. Because this is currently based on a hack, the automatic recognition might mysteriously fail, hence this option to force a prompt. If no password prompt is issued and the backend requires password authentication the connection attempt will fail.

-x, –expanded Turns on extended row format mode. This is equivalent to the command **x**.

-X, –no-psqlrc Do not read the start-up file /.psqlrc.

-?, –help Shows help about psql command line arguments.

Advanced features

Variables

psql provides variable substitution features similar to common Unix command shells. This feature is new and not very sophisticated, yet, but there are plans to expand it in the future. Variables are simply name/value pairs, where the value can be any string of any length. To set variables, use the psql meta-command **set**:

```
testdb=>  \set foo bar
```

sets the variable *foo* to the value *bar*. To retrieve the content of the variable, precede the name with a colon and use it as the argument of any slash command:

```
testdb=>  \echo :foo
bar
```

Note: The arguments of **set** are subject to the same substitution rules as with other commands. Thus you can construct interesting references such as \set :foo 'something' and get *soft links* or *variable variables,* of Perl or PHP fame, respectively. Unfortunately (or fortunately?), there is no way to do anything useful with these constructs. On the other hand, \set bar :foo is a perfectly valid way to copy a variable.

If you call **set** without a second argument, the variable is simply set, but has no value. To unset (or delete) a variable, use the command **unset**.

psql's internal variable names can consist of letters, numbers, and underscores in any order and any number of them. A number of regular variables are treated specially by psql. They indicate certain option settings that can be changed at runtime by altering the value of the variable or represent some state of the application. Although you can use these variables for any other purpose, this is not recommended, as the program behavior might grow really strange really quickly. By convention, all specially treated variables consist of all upper-case letters (and possibly numbers and underscores). To ensure maximum compatibility in the future, avoid such variables. A list of all specially treated variables follows.

DBNAME The name of the database you are currently connected to. This is set every time you connect to a database (including program start-up), but can be unset.

ECHO If set to *all,* all lines entered or from a script are written to the standard output before they are parsed or executed. To specify this on program start-up, use the switch -a. If set to *queries,* psql merely prints all queries as they are sent to the backend. The option for this is -e.

ECHO_HIDDEN When this variable is set and a backslash command queries the database, the query is first shown. This way you can study the Postgres internals and provide similar functionality in your own programs. If you set the variable to the value *noexec,* the queries are just shown but are not actually sent to the backend and executed.

ENCODING The current client multibyte encoding. If you are not set up to use multibyte characters, this variable will always contain SQL_ASCII.

HISTCONTROL If this variable is set to ignorespace, lines which begin with a space are not entered into the history list. If set to a value of ignoredups, lines matching the previous history line are not entered. A value of ignoreboth combines the two options. If unset, or if set to any other value than those above, all lines read in interactive mode are saved on the history list.

Note: This feature was shamelessly plagiarized from bash.

HISTSIZE The number of commands to store in the command history. The default value is 500.

Note: This feature was shamelessly plagiarized from bash.

HOST The database server host you are currently connected to. This is set every time you connect to a database (including program start-up), but can be unset.

IGNOREEOF If unset, sending an EOF character (usually Control-D) to an interactive session of psql will terminate the application. If set to a numeric value, that many EOF characters are ignored before the application terminates. If the variable is set but has no numeric value, the default is 10.

Note: This feature was shamelessly plagiarized from bash.

LASTOID The value of the last affected oid, as returned from an **INSERT** or **lo_insert** command. This variable is only guaranteed to be valid until after the result of the next SQL command has been displayed.

LO_TRANSACTION If you use the Postgres large object interface to specially store data that does not fit into one tuple, all the operations must be contained in a transaction block. (See the documentation of the large object interface for more information.) Since psql has no way to tell if you already have a transaction in progress when you call one of its internal commands (**\lo_export**, **\lo_import**, **\lo_unlink**) it must take some arbitrary action. This action could either be to roll back any transaction that might already be in progress, or to commit any such transaction, or to do nothing at all. In the last case you must provide your own **BEGIN TRANSACTION / COMMIT** block or the results will be unpredictable (usually resulting in the desired action's not being performed in any case).

To choose what you want to do you set this variable to one of *rollback, commit,* or *nothing*. The default is to roll back the transaction. If you just want to load one or a few objects this is fine. However, if you intend to transfer many large objects, it might be advisable to provide one explicit transaction block around all commands.

ON_ERROR_STOP By default, if non-interactive scripts encounter an error, such as a malformed SQL query or internal meta-command, processing continues. This has been the traditional behavior of psql but it is sometimes not desirable. If this variable is set, script processing will immediately terminate. If the script was called from another script it will terminate in the same fashion. If the outermost script was not called from an interactive psql session but rather using the -f option, psql will return error code 3, to distinguish this case from fatal error conditions (error code 1).

PORT The database server port to which you are currently connected. This is set every time you connect to a database (including program start-up), but can be unset.

PROMPT1, PROMPT2, PROMPT3 These specify what the prompt psql issues is supposed to look like. See *Prompting* below.

QUIET This variable is equivalent to the command line option -q. It is probably not too useful in interactive mode.

SINGLELINE This variable is set by the command line option -S. You can unset or reset it at run time.

SINGLESTEP This variable is equivalent to the command line option -s.

USER The database user you are currently connected as. This is set every time you connect to a database (including program start-up), but can be unset.

SQL Interpolation

An additional useful feature of psql variables is that you can substitute (*interpolate*) them into regular SQL statements. The syntax for this is again to prepend the variable name with a colon (:).

```
testdb=>  \set foo 'my_table'
testdb=>  SELECT * FROM :foo;
```

would then query the table my_table. The value of the variable is copied literally, so it can even contain unbalanced quotes or backslash commands. You must make sure that it makes sense where you put it. Variable interpolation will not be performed into quoted SQL entities.

A popular application of this facility is to refer to the last inserted OID in subsequent statements to build a foreign key scenario. Another possible use of this mechanism is to copy the contents of a file into a field. First load the file into a variable and then proceed as above.

```
testdb=>  \set content '\'' 'cat my_file.txt' '\''
testdb=>  INSERT INTO my_table VALUES (:content);
```

One possible problem with this approach is that my_file.txt might contain single quotes. These need to be escaped so that they don't cause a syntax error when the third line is processed. This could be done with the program sed:

```
testdb=>  \set content 'sed -e "s/'/\\\\\\'/g" < my_file.txt'
```

Observe the correct number of backslashes (6)! You can resolve it this way: After psql has parsed this line, it passes sed -e "s/'/\ \ \'/g" < my_file.txt to the shell. The shell will do it's own thing inside the double quotes and execute sed with the arguments -e and s/'/\\/'/g. When sed parses this it will replace the two backslashes with a single one and then do the substitution. Perhaps at one point you thought it was great that all Unix commands use the same escape character. And this is ignoring the fact that you might have to escape all backslashes as well because SQL text constants are also subject to certain interpretations. In that case you might be better off preparing the file externally.

Since colons may legally appear in queries, the following rule applies: If the variable is not set, the character sequence *colon* + *name* is not changed. In any case you can escape a colon with a backslash to protect it from interpretation. (The colon syntax for variables is standard SQL for embedded query languages, such as ecpg. The colon syntax for array slices and type casts are Postgres extensions, hence the conflict.)

Prompting

The prompts psql issues can be customized to your preference. The three variables PROMPT1, PROMPT2, and PROMPT3 contain strings and special escape sequences that describe the appearance of the prompt. Prompt 1 is the normal prompt that is issued when psql requests a new query. Prompt 2 is issued when more input is expected during query input because the query was not terminated with a semicolon or a quote was not closed. Prompt 3 is issued when you run an SQL **COPY** command and you are expected to type in the tuples on the terminal.

The value of the respective prompt variable is printed literally, except where a percent sign (%) is encountered. Depending on the next character, certain other text is substituted instead. Defined substitutions are:

%M The full hostname (with domain name) of the database server (or *localhost* if hostname information is not available).

%m The hostname of the database server, truncated after the first dot.

%> The port number at which the database server is listening.

%n The username you are connected as (not your local system user name).

%/ The name of the current database.

% Like %/, but the output is tilde (˜) if the database is your default database.

%# If the current user is a database superuser, then a #, otherwise a >.

%R In prompt 1 normally =, but ^ if in single-line mode, and ! if the session is disconnected from the database (which can happen if **connect** fails). In prompt 2 the sequence is replaced by -*, a single quote, or a double quote, depending on whether psql expects more input because the query wasn't terminated yet, because you are inside a /* ... */ comment, or because you are inside a quote. In prompt 3 the sequence doesn't resolve to anything.

%*digits* If *digits* starts with 0x the rest of the characters are interpreted as a hexadecimal digit and the character with the corresponding code is substituted. If the first digit is 0 the characters are interpreted as on octal number and the corresponding character is substituted. Otherwise a decimal number is assumed.

%:*name*: The value of the psql, variable *name*. See the section *Variables* for details.

%'*command*' The output of *command*, similar to ordinary *back-tick* substitution.

To insert a percent sign into your prompt, write %%. The default prompts are equivalent to '%/%R%# ' for prompts 1 and 2, and '> > ' for prompt 3. **Note:** This feature was shamelessly plagiarized from tcsh.

Miscellaneous

psql returns 0 to the shell if it finished normally, 1 if a fatal error of its own (out of memory, file not found) occurs, 2 if the connection to the backend went bad and the session is not interactive, and 3 if an error occurred in a script and the variable ON_ERROR_STOP was set.

Before starting up, psql attempts to read and execute commands from the file $HOME/.psqlrc. It could be used to set up the client or the server to taste (using the **set** and **SET** commands).

GNU readline

psql supports the readline and history libraries for convenient line editing and retrieval. The command history is stored in a file named .psql_history in your home directory and is reloaded when psql starts up. Tab-completion is also supported, although the completion logic makes no claim to be an SQL parser. When available, psql is automatically built to use these features. If for some reason you do not like the tab completion, you can turn if off by putting this in a file named .inputrc in your home directory:

```
$if psql
set disable-completion on
$endif
```

(This is not a psql but a readline feature. Read its documentation for further details.)

If you have the readline library installed but psql does not seem to use it, you must make sure that Postgres's top-level configure script finds it. configure needs to find both the library libreadline.a (or a shared library equivalent) *and* the header files readline.h and history.h (or readline/readline.h and readline/history.h) in appropriate directories. If you have the library and header files installed in an obscure place you must tell configure about them, for example:

```
$ ./configure --with-includes=/opt/gnu/include --with-libs=/opt/gnu/lib ...
```

Then you have to recompile psql (not necessarily the entire code tree).

The GNU readline library can be obtained from the GNU project's FTP server at ftp://ftp.gnu.org.

Examples

Note: This section only shows a few examples specific to psql. If you want to learn SQL or get familiar with Postgres, you might wish to read the Tutorial that is included in the distribution.

The first example shows how to spread a query over several lines of input. Notice the changing prompt:

```
testdb=>  CREATE TABLE my_table (
testdb(>                          first integer not null default 0,
testdb(>                          second text
testdb->  );
CREATE
```

Now look at the table definition again:

```
testdb=>  \d my_table
Table "my_table"
 Attribute |  Type  | Modifier
```

```
-----------+---------+--------------------
 first     | integer | not null default 0
 second    | text    |
```

At this point you decide to change the prompt to something more interesting:

```
testdb=>  \set PROMPT1 '%n@%m % %R%# '
peter@localhost testdb=>
```

Let's assume you have filled the table with data and want to take a look at it:

```
peter@localhost testdb=>  SELECT * FROM my_table;
 first | second
-------+--------
 1     | one
 2     | two
 3     | three
 4     | four
(4 rows)
```

You can make this table look differently by using the **\pset** command:

```
peter@localhost testdb=>  \pset border 2
Border style is 2.
peter@localhost testdb=>  SELECT * FROM my_table;
+-------+--------+
| first | second |
+-------+--------+
| 1     | one    |
| 2     | two    |
| 3     | three  |
| 4     | four   |
+-------+--------+
(4 rows)
peter@localhost testdb=>  \pset border 0
Border style is 0.
peter@localhost testdb=>  SELECT * FROM my_table;
first second
----- ------
 1     one
 2     two
 3     three
```

```
     4       four
(4 rows)
peter@localhost testdb=>  \pset border 1
Border style is 1.
peter@localhost testdb=>  \pset format unaligned
Output format is unaligned.
peter@localhost testdb=>  \pset fieldsep ","
Field separator is ",".
peter@localhost testdb=>  \pset tuples_only
Showing only tuples.
peter@localhost testdb=>  SELECT second, first FROM my_table;
one,1
two,2
three,3
four,4
```

Alternatively, use the short commands:

```
peter@localhost testdb=>  \a \t \x
Output format is aligned. Tuples only is off. Expanded display is on.
peter@localhost testdb=>  SELECT * FROM my_table;
-[ RECORD 1 ]- first | 1 second | one
-[ RECORD 2 ]- first | 2 second | two
-[ RECORD 3 ]- first | 3 second | three
-[ RECORD 4 ]- first | 4 second | four
```

Appendix

Bugs and Issues

- In some earlier life psql allowed the first argument to start directly after the (single-letter) command. For compatibility this is still supported to some extent but I am not going to explain the details here as this use is discouraged. But if you get strange messages, keep this in mind. For example:

    ```
    testdb=>  \foo
    ```

    Field separator is "oo", which is perhaps not what one would expect.

- psql only works smoothly with servers of the same version. That does not mean other combinations will fail outright, but subtle and not-so-subtle problems might come up.

- Pressing Control-C during a *copy in* (data sent to the server) doesn't show the most ideal of behaviors. If you get a message such as *PQexec:* you gotta get out of a COPY state yourself —simply reset the connection by entering \c - -.

D.74   REINDEX

Name

REINDEX — Recover corrupted system indexes under stand-alone Postgres
REINDEX { TABLE | DATABASE | INDEX } *name* [FORCE]

Inputs

TABLE Recreate all indexes of a specified table.

DATABASE Recreate all system indexes of a specified database.

INDEX Recreate a specified index.

name The name of the specific table/database/index to be be reindexed.

FORCE Recreate indexes forcedly. Without this keyword REINDEX does nothing unless target indexes are invalidated.

Outputs

REINDEX Message returned if the table is successfully reindexed.

Description

REINDEX is used to recover corrupted system indexes. In order to run REINDEX command, postmaster must be shut down and stand-alone Postgres should be started instead with options -O and -P (an option to ignore system indexes). Note that we couldn't rely on system indexes for the recovery of system indexes.

Usage

Recreate the table mytable:

```
REINDEX TABLE mytable;
```

Some more examples:

```
REINDEX DATABASE my_database FORCE;
REINDEX INDEX my_index;
```

Compatibility

SQL92

There is no **REINDEX** in SQL92.

D.75   RESET

Name

RESET — Restores run-time parameters for session to default values
    RESET *variable*

Inputs

variable Refer to *SET* for more information on available variables.

Outputs

RESET VARIABLE Message returned if *variable* is successfully reset to its default value.

Description

RESET restores variables to their default values. Refer to *SET* for details on allowed values and defaults. **RESET** is an alternate form for SET *variable* = DEFAULT.

Notes

See also *SET* and *SHOW* to manipulate variable values.

Usage

Set DateStyle to its default value:

```
RESET DateStyle;
```

Set Geqo to its default value:

```
RESET GEQO;
```

Compatibility

SQL92

There is no **RESET** in SQL92.

D.76   REVOKE   *grant   365*

Name

REVOKE — Revokes access privilege from a user, a group or all users.
   REVOKE *privilege* [, ...]
   ON *object* [, ...]
   FROM { PUBLIC | GROUP *groupname* | *username* }

Inputs

privilege   The possible privileges are:

> **SELECT** Privilege to access all of the columns of a specific table/view.
>
> **INSERT** Privilege to insert data into all columns of a specific table.
>
> **UPDATE** Privilege to update all columns of a specific table.
>
> **DELETE** Privilege to delete rows from a specific table.
>
> **RULE** Privilege to define rules on table/view. (See *CREATE RULE*).
>
> **ALL** Rescind all privileges.

object   The name of an object from which to revoke access. The possible objects are:

- table
- view
- sequence

group   The name of a group from whom to revoke privileges.

username   The name of a user from whom revoke privileges. Use the PUBLIC keyword to specify all users.

PUBLIC   Rescind the specified privilege(s) for all users.

Outputs

CHANGE   Message returned if successfully.

ERROR   Message returned if object is not available or impossible to revoke privileges from a group or users.

Description

REVOKE allows creator of an object to revoke permissions granted before, from all users (via PUBLIC) or a certain user or group.

Notes

Refer to \z command for further information about permissions on existing objects:

```
Database    = lusitania
+-----------------+-------------------------------------------+
| Relation        |          Grant/Revoke Permissions         |
+-----------------+-------------------------------------------+
| mytable         | {"=rw","miriam=arwR","group todos=rw"}    |
+-----------------+-------------------------------------------+
Legend:
    uname=arwR -- privileges granted to a user
    group gname=arwR -- privileges granted to a GROUP
    =arwR -- privileges granted to PUBLIC

    r -- SELECT
    w -- UPDATE/DELETE
    a -- INSERT
    R -- RULE
    arwR -- ALL
```

Tip: Currently, to create a GROUP you have to insert data manually into table pg_group as:

```
INSERT INTO pg_group VALUES ('todos');
CREATE USER miriam IN GROUP todos;
```

Usage

Revoke insert privilege from all users on table films:

```
REVOKE INSERT ON films FROM PUBLIC;
```

Revoke all privileges from user manuel on view kinds:

```
REVOKE ALL ON kinds FROM manuel;
```

Compatibility

SQL92

The SQL92 syntax for **REVOKE** has additional capabilities for rescinding privileges, including those on individual columns in tables:

REVOKE { SELECT | DELETE | USAGE | ALL PRIVILEGES } [...] ON *object*

> FROM { PUBLIC | *username* [, ... } { RESTRICT | CASCADE } REVOKE { INSERT | UPDATE | REFERENCES } [, ...] [(*column* [, ...])] ON *object*

> FROM { PUBLIC | *username* [, ...] } { RESTRICT | CASCADE }] Refer to *GRANT* for details on individual fields.

REVOKE GRANT OPTION FOR *privilege* [, ... ON *object*

> FROM { PUBLIC | *username* [, ...] } { RESTRICT | CASCADE }] Rescinds authority for a user to grant the specified privilege to others. Refer to *GRANT* for details on individual fields.

The possible objects are:

If user1 gives a privilege WITH GRANT OPTION to user2, and user2 gives it to user3 then user1 can revoke this privilege in cascade using the CASCADE keyword.

If user1 gives a privilege WITH GRANT OPTION to user2, and user2 gives it to user3, then if user1 tries to revoke this privilege it fails if he specifies the RESTRICT keyword.

D.77   ROLLBACK

Name

ROLLBACK — Aborts the current transaction
> ROLLBACK [WORK | TRANSACTION]

Inputs

None.

Outputs

ABORT Message returned if successful.

NOTICE: ROLLBACK: no transaction in progress If there is not any transaction currently in progress.

Description

ROLLBACK rolls back the current transaction and causes all the updates made by the transaction to be discarded.

Notes

Use *COMMIT* to successfully terminate a transaction. *ABORT* is a synonym for **ROLLBACK**.

Usage

To abort all changes:

```
ROLLBACK WORK;
```

Compatibility

SQL92

SQL92 only specifies the two forms ROLLBACK and ROLLBACK WORK. Otherwise full compatibility.

D.78 SELECT

Name

SELECT — Retrieve rows from a table or view.
    SELECT [ALL | DISTINCT [ON (*expression* [, ...])]]
    expression [AS *name*] [, ...]
    [INTO [TEMPORARY | TEMP] [TABLE] *new_table*]
    [FROM *table* [*alias*] [, ...]]
    [WHERE *condition*]
    [GROUP BY *column* [, ...]]
    [HAVING *condition* [, ...]]
    [{ UNION [ALL] | INTERSECT | EXCEPT } *select*]
    [ORDER BY *column* [ASC | DESC | USING *operator*] [, ...]]
    [FOR UPDATE [OF *class_name* [, ...]]]
    [LIMIT { *count* | ALL } [{ OFFSET | , } *start*]]

Inputs

expression The name of a table's column or an expression.

name Specifies another name for a column or an expression using the AS clause. This name is primarily used to label the column for display. It can also be used to refer to the column's value in ORDER BY and GROUP BY clauses. But the *name* cannot be used in the WHERE or HAVING clauses; write out the expression instead.

TEMPORARY, TEMP If TEMPORARY or TEMP is specified, the table is created unique to this session, and is automatically dropped on session exit.

new_table If the INTO TABLE clause is specified, the result of the query will be stored in a new table with the indicated name. The target table (*new_table*) will be created automatically and must not exist before this command. Refer to **SELECT INTO** for more information. **Note:** The **CREATE TABLE AS** statement will also create a new table from a select query.

table The name of an existing table referenced by the FROM clause.

alias An alternate name for the preceding *table*. It is used for brevity or to eliminate ambiguity for joins within a single table.

condition A boolean expression giving a result of true or false. See the WHERE clause.

column The name of a table's column.

select A select statement with all features except the ORDER BY and LIMIT clauses.

Outputs

Rows The complete set of rows resulting from the query specification.

count The count of rows returned by the query.

Description

SELECT will return rows from one or more tables. Candidates for selection are rows which satisfy the WHERE condition; if WHERE is omitted, all rows are candidates. (See *WHERE Clause*.)

   DISTINCT will eliminate duplicate rows from the result. **ALL** (the default) will return all candidate rows, including duplicates.

   DISTINCT ON eliminates rows that match on all the specified expressions, keeping only the first row of each set of duplicates. The DISTINCT ON expressions are interpreted using the same rules as for ORDER BY items; see below. Note that "the first row" of each set is unpredictable unless **ORDER BY** is used to ensure that the desired row appears first. For example,

```
SELECT DISTINCT ON (location) location, time, report
FROM weatherReports
ORDER BY location, time DESC;
```

retrieves the most recent weather report for each location. But if we had not used ORDER BY to force descending order of time values for each location, we'd have gotten a report of unpredictable age for each location.

The GROUP BY clause allows a user to divide a table into groups of rows that match on one or more values. (See *GROUP BY Clause*.)

The HAVING clause allows selection of only those groups of rows meeting the specified condition. (See *HAVING Clause*.)

The ORDER BY clause causes the returned rows to be sorted in a specified order. If ORDER BY is not given, the rows are returned in whatever order the system finds cheapest to produce. (See *ORDER BY Clause*.)

The UNION operator allows the result to be the collection of rows returned by the queries involved. (See *UNION Clause*.)

The INTERSECT operator gives you the rows that are common to both queries. (See *INTER-SECT Clause*.)

The EXCEPT operator gives you the rows returned by the first query but not the second query. (See *EXCEPT Clause*.)

The FOR UPDATE clause allows the SELECT statement to perform exclusive locking of selected rows.

The LIMIT clause allows a subset of the rows produced by the query to be returned to the user. (See *LIMIT Clause*.)

You must have SELECT privilege to a table to read its values (See the **GRANT /REVOKE** statements).

WHERE Clause

The optional WHERE condition has the general form:

```
WHERE boolean_expr
```

boolean_expr can consist of any expression which evaluates to a boolean value. In many cases, this expression will be:

```
expr cond_op expr
```

or

```
log_op expr
```

where *cond_op* can be one of: =, <, <=, >, >= or <>, a conditional operator like ALL, ANY, IN, LIKE, or a locally defined operator, and *log_op* can be one of: AND, OR, NOT. SELECT will ignore all rows for which the WHERE condition does not return TRUE.

GROUP BY Clause

GROUP BY specifies a grouped table derived by the application of this clause:

```
GROUP BY column [, ...]
```

GROUP BY will condense into a single row all selected rows that share the same values for the grouped columns. Aggregate functions, if any, are computed across all rows making up each group, producing a separate value for each group (whereas without GROUP BY, an aggregate produces a single value computed across all the selected rows). When GROUP BY is present, it is not valid for the SELECT output expression(s) to refer to ungrouped columns except within aggregate functions, since there would be more than one possible value to return for an ungrouped column.

An item in GROUP BY can also be the name or ordinal number of an output column (SELECT expression), or it can be an arbitrary expression formed from input-column values. In case of ambiguity, a GROUP BY name will be interpreted as an input-column name rather than an output column name.

HAVING Clause

The optional HAVING condition has the general form:

```
HAVING cond_expr
```

where *cond_expr* is the same as specified for the WHERE clause.

HAVING specifies a grouped table derived by the elimination of group rows that do not satisfy the *cond_expr*. HAVING is different from WHERE: WHERE filters individual rows before application of GROUP BY, while HAVING filters group rows created by GROUP BY.

Each column referenced in *cond_expr* shall unambiguously reference a grouping column, unless the reference appears within an aggregate function.

ORDER BY Clause

ORDER BY *column* [ASC | DESC] [, ...]

column can be either a result column name or an ordinal number.

The ordinal numbers refers to the ordinal (left-to-right) position of the result column. This feature makes it possible to define an ordering on the basis of a column that does not have a proper name. This is never absolutely necessary because it is always possible to assign a name to a result column using the AS clause, e.g.:

```
SELECT title, date_prod + 1 AS newlen
FROM films
ORDER BY newlen;
```

It is also possible to ORDER BY arbitrary expressions (an extension to SQL92), including fields that do not appear in the SELECT result list. Thus the following statement is legal:

```
SELECT name
FROM distributors
ORDER BY code;
```

Note that if an ORDER BY item is a simple name that matches both a result column name and an input column name, ORDER BY will interpret it as the result column name. This is the opposite of the choice that GROUP BY will make in the same situation. This inconsistency is mandated by the SQL92 standard.

Optionally one may add the keyword DESC (descending) or ASC (ascending) after each column name in the ORDER BY clause. If not specified, ASC is assumed by default. Alternatively, a specific ordering operator name may be specified. ASC is equivalent to USING '< ' and DESC is equivalent to USING '> '.

UNION Clause

table_query UNION [ALL] *table_query*

[ORDER BY *column* [ASC | DESC] [, ...]] where *table_query* specifies any select expression without an ORDER BY or LIMIT clause.

The UNION operator allows the result to be the collection of rows returned by the queries involved. The two SELECTs that represent the direct operands of the UNION must produce the same number of columns, and corresponding columns must be of compatible data types.

By default, the result of UNION does not contain any duplicate rows unless the ALL clause is specified.

Multiple UNION operators in the same SELECT statement are evaluated left to right. Note that the ALL keyword is not global in nature, being applied only for the current pair of table results.

INTERSECT Clause

table_query INTERSECT *table_query*

[ORDER BY *column* [ASC | DESC] [, ...]] where *table_query* specifies any select expression without an ORDER BY or LIMIT clause.

The INTERSECT operator gives you the rows that are common to both queries. The two SELECTs that represent the direct operands of the INTERSECT must produce the same number of columns, and corresponding columns must be of compatible data types.

Multiple INTERSECT operators in the same SELECT statement are evaluated left to right, unless parentheses dictate otherwise.

EXCEPT Clause

table_query EXCEPT *table_query*

[ORDER BY *column* [ASC | DESC] [, ...]] where *table_query* specifies any select expression without an ORDER BY or LIMIT clause.

The EXCEPT operator gives you the rows returned by the first query but not the second query. The two SELECTs that represent the direct operands of the EXCEPT must produce the same number of columns, and corresponding columns must be of compatible data types.

Multiple EXCEPT operators in the same SELECT statement are evaluated left to right, unless parentheses dictate otherwise.

LIMIT Clause

LIMIT { *count* | ALL } [{ OFFSET | , } *start*] OFFSET *start*

where *count* specifies the maximum number of rows to return, and *start* specifies the number of rows to skip before starting to return rows.

LIMIT allows you to retrieve just a portion of the rows that are generated by the rest of the query. If a limit count is given, no more than that many rows will be returned. If an offset is given, that many rows will be skipped before starting to return rows.

When using LIMIT, it is a good idea to use an ORDER BY clause that constrains the result rows into a unique order. Otherwise you will get an unpredictable subset of the query's rows —you may be asking for the tenth through twentieth rows, but tenth through twentieth in what ordering? You don't know what ordering, unless you specified ORDER BY.

As of Postgres 7.0, the query optimizer takes LIMIT into account when generating a query plan, so you are very likely to get different plans (yielding different row orders) depending on what you give for LIMIT and OFFSET. Thus, using different LIMIT/OFFSET values to select different subsets of a query result *will give inconsistent results* unless you enforce a predictable result ordering with ORDER BY. This is not a bug; it is an inherent consequence of the fact that SQL does not promise to deliver the results of a query in any particular order unless ORDER BY is used to constrain the order.

Usage

To join the table films with the table distributors:

```
SELECT f.title, f.did, d.name, f.date_prod, f.kind
FROM distributors d, films f
WHERE f.did = d.did
```

title	did	name	date_prod	kind
The Third Man	101	British Lion	1949-12-23	Drama
The African Queen	101	British Lion	1951-08-11	Romantic

```
Une Femme est une Femme   | 102 | Jean Luc Godard   | 1961-03-12 | Romantic
Vertigo                   | 103 | Paramount         | 1958-11-14 | Action
Becket                    | 103 | Paramount         | 1964-02-03 | Drama
48 Hrs                    | 103 | Paramount         | 1982-10-22 | Action
War and Peace             | 104 | Mosfilm           | 1967-02-12 | Drama
West Side Story           | 105 | United Artists    | 1961-01-03 | Musical
Bananas                   | 105 | United Artists    | 1971-07-13 | Comedy
Yojimbo                   | 106 | Toho              | 1961-06-16 | Drama
There's a Girl in my Soup | 107 | Columbia          | 1970-06-11 | Comedy
Taxi Driver               | 107 | Columbia          | 1975-05-15 | Action
Absence of Malice         | 107 | Columbia          | 1981-11-15 | Action
Storia di una donna       | 108 | Westward          | 1970-08-15 | Romantic
The King and I            | 109 | 20th Century Fox  | 1956-08-11 | Musical
Das Boot                  | 110 | Bavaria Atelier   | 1981-11-11 | Drama
Bed Knobs and Broomsticks | 111 | Walt Disney       |            | Musical
(17 rows)
```

To sum the column len of all films and group the results by kind:

```
SELECT kind, SUM(len) AS total
FROM films
GROUP BY kind;
 kind     | total
----------+-------
 Action   | 07:34
 Comedy   | 02:58
 Drama    | 14:28
 Musical  | 06:42
 Romantic | 04:38
(5 rows)
```

To sum the column len of all films, group the results by kind and show those group totals that are less than 5 hours:

```
SELECT kind, SUM(len) AS total
FROM films
GROUP BY kind
HAVING SUM(len) < INTERVAL '5 hour';
 kind     | total
----------+-------
 Comedy   | 02:58
 Romantic | 04:38
```

(2 rows)

The following two examples are identical ways of sorting the individual results according to the contents of the second column (name):

```
SELECT *
FROM distributors
ORDER BY name;

SELECT *
FROM distributors
ORDER BY 2;
```

```
 did |       name
-----+------------------
 109 | 20th Century Fox
 110 | Bavaria Atelier
 101 | British Lion
 107 | Columbia
 102 | Jean Luc Godard
 113 | Luso films
 104 | Mosfilm
 103 | Paramount
 106 | Toho
 105 | United Artists
 111 | Walt Disney
 112 | Warner Bros.
 108 | Westward
(13 rows)
```

This example shows how to obtain the union of the tables distributors and actors, restricting the results to those that begin with letter W in each table. Only distinct rows are wanted, so the ALL keyword is omitted:

```
distributors:              actors:
 did |     name             id |     name
-----+--------------       ----+----------------
 108 | Westward              1 | Woody Allen
 111 | Walt Disney           2 | Warren Beatty
 112 | Warner Bros.          3 | Walter Matthau
 ...                        ...
```

```
SELECT distributors.name
FROM    distributors
WHERE   distributors.name LIKE 'W%'
UNION
SELECT actors.name
FROM    actors
WHERE   actors.name LIKE 'W%'
        name
----------------
Walt Disney
Walter Matthau
Warner Bros.
Warren Beatty
Westward
Woody Allen
```

Compatibility

Extensions

Postgres allows one to omit the **FROM** clause from a query. This feature was retained from the original PostQuel query language:

```
SELECT distributors.*
WHERE name = 'Westwood';
 did | name
-----+----------
 108 | Westward
```

SQL92

SELECT Clause

In the SQL92 standard, the optional keyword "AS" is just noise and can be omitted without affecting the meaning. The Postgres parser requires this keyword when renaming columns because the type extensibility features lead to parsing ambiguities in this context.

The DISTINCT ON phrase is not part of SQL92. Nor are LIMIT and OFFSET.

In SQL92, an ORDER BY clause may only use result column names or numbers, while a GROUP BY clause may only use input column names. Postgres extends each of these clauses to allow the other choice as well (but it uses the standard's interpretation if there is ambiguity). Postgres also allows both clauses to specify arbitrary expressions. Note that names appearing in an expression will always be taken as input-column names, not as result-column names.

UNION Clause

The SQL92 syntax for UNION allows an additional CORRESPONDING BY clause:

```
table_query UNION [ALL] [CORRESPONDING [BY (column [,...])]] table_query
```

The CORRESPONDING BY clause is not supported by Postgres.

D.79   SELECT INTO

Name

SELECT INTO — Create a new table from an existing table or view
    SELECT [ALL | DISTINCT [ON (*expression* [, ...])]]
    expression [AS *name*] [, ...]
    [INTO [TEMPORARY | TEMP] [TABLE] *new_table*]
    [FROM *table* [*alias*] [, ...]]
    [WHERE *condition*]
    [GROUP BY *column* [, ...]]
    [HAVING *condition* [, ...]]
    [{ UNION [ALL] | INTERSECT | EXCEPT } *select*]
    [ORDER BY *column* [ASC | DESC | USING *operator*] [, ...]]
    [FOR UPDATE [OF *class_name* [, ...]]]
    [LIMIT { *count* | ALL } [{ OFFSET | , } *start*]]

Inputs

All input fields are described in detail for *SELECT*.

Outputs

All output fields are described in detail for *SELECT*.

Description

SELECT INTO creates a new table from the results of a query. Typically, this query draws data from an existing table, but any SQL query is allowed. **Note:** *CREATE TABLE AS* is functionally equivalent to the **SELECT INTO** command.

D.80 SET

Name

SET — Set run-time parameters for session
    SET *variable* { TO | = } { *value* | *'value'* | DEFAULT }
    SET CONSTRAINTS { ALL | *constraintlist* } *mode*
    SET TIME ZONE { *'timezone'* | LOCAL | DEFAULT }
    SET TRANSACTION ISOLATION LEVEL { READ COMMITTED | SERIALIZABLE }

Inputs

variable Settable global parameter.

value New value of parameter. DEFAULT can be used to specify resetting the parameter to its default value. Lists of strings are allowed, but more complex constructs may need to be single or double quoted.

The possible variables and allowed values are:

CLIENT_ENCODING | NAMES Sets the multibyte client encoding. Parameters are:

> ***value*** Sets the multibyte client encoding to *value*. The specified encoding must be supported by the backend.
>
> This option is only available if MULTIBYTE support was enabled during the configure step of building Postgres.

DATESTYLE Set the date/time representation style. Affects the output format, and in some cases it can affect the interpretation of input.

> **ISO** use ISO 8601-style dates and times
>
> **SQL** use Oracle/Ingres-style dates and times
>
> **Postgres** use traditional Postgres format
>
> **European** use dd/mm/yyyy for numeric date representations.
>
> **NonEuropean** use mm/dd/yyyy for numeric date representations.
>
> **German** use dd.mm.yyyy for numeric date representations.
>
> **US** same as NonEuropean
>
> **DEFAULT** restores the default values (ISO)
>
> Date format initialization may be done by:

- Setting the PGDATESTYLE environment variable. If PGDATESTYLE is set in the frontend environment of a client based on libpq, libpq will automatically set DATESTYLE to the value of PGDATESTYLE during connection start-up.

- Running postmaster using the option *-o -e* to set dates to the European convention.

SEED Sets the internal seed for the random number generator.

> *value* The value for the seed to be used by the random catalog function. Significant values are floating point numbers between 0 and 1, which are then multiplied by RAND_MAX. This product will silently overflow if a number outside the range is used.
>
> The seed can also be set by invoking the *setseed* SQL function:
>
> ```
> SELECT setseed(value);
> ```

This option is only available if MULTIBYTE support was enabled during the configure step of building Postgres.

SERVER_ENCODING Sets the multibyte server encoding to:

> *value* The identifying value for the server encoding.

This option is only available if MULTIBYTE support was enabled during the configure step of building Postgres.

CONSTRAINTS SET CONSTRAINTS affects the behavior of constraint evaluation in the current transaction. SET CONSTRAINTS, specified in SQL3, has these allowed parameters:

> *constraintlist* Comma separated list of deferrable constraint names.
>
> *mode* The constraint mode. Allowed values are DEFERRED and IMMEDIATE.

In IMMEDIATE mode, foreign key constraints are checked at the end of each query.

In DEFERRED mode, foreign key constraints marked as DEFERRABLE are checked only at transaction commit or until its mode is explicitly set to IMMEDIATE. This is actually only done for foreign key constraints, so it does not apply to UNIQUE or other constraints.

TIME ZONE, TIMEZONE The possible values for time zone depends on your operating system. For example, on Linux */usr/lib/zoneinfo* contains the database of time zones.

Here are some valid values for time zone:

PST8PDT set the time zone for California

> **Portugal** set time zone for Portugal.
>
> **'Europe/Rome'** set time zone for Italy.

DEFAULT set time zone to your local time zone (value of the TZ environment variable).

If an invalid time zone is specified, the time zone becomes GMT (on most systems anyway).

The second syntax shown above, allows one to set the time zone with a syntax similar to SQL92 **SET TIME ZONE**. The LOCAL keyword is just an alternate form of DEFAULT for SQL92 compatibility.

If the PGTZ environment variable is set in the frontend environment of a client based on libpq, libpq will automatically set TIMEZONE to the value of PGTZ during connection start-up.

TRANSACTION ISOLATION LEVEL Sets the isolation level for the current transaction.

> **READ COMMITTED** The current transaction queries read only rows committed before a query began. READ COMMITTED is the default.
>
> **Note:** SQL92 standard requires SERIALIZABLE to be the default isolation level.
>
> **SERIALIZABLE** The current transaction queries read only rows committed before first DML statement (**SELECT/INSERT/DELETE/UPDATE/FETCH/COPY_TO**) was executed in this transaction.

There are also several internal or optimization parameters which can be specified by the **SET** command:

PG_OPTIONS Sets various backend parameters.

RANDOM_PAGE_COST Sets the optimizer's estimate of the cost of a nonsequentially fetched disk page. This is measured as a multiple of the cost of a sequential page fetch.

> *float8* Set the cost of a random page access to the specified floating-point value.

CPU_TUPLE_COST Sets the optimizer's estimate of the cost of processing each tuple during a query. This is measured as a fraction of the cost of a sequential page fetch.

> *float8* Set the cost of per-tuple CPU processing to the specified floating-point value.

CPU_INDEX_TUPLE_COST Sets the optimizer's estimate of the cost of processing each index tuple during an index scan. This is measured as a fraction of the cost of a sequential page fetch.

> *float8* Set the cost of per-index-tuple CPU processing to the specified floating-point value.

CPU_OPERATOR_COST Sets the optimizer's estimate of the cost of processing each operator in a WHERE clause. This is measured as a fraction of the cost of a sequential page fetch.

> *float8* Set the cost of per-operator CPU processing to the specified floating-point value.

EFFECTIVE_CACHE_SIZE Sets the optimizer's assumption about the effective size of the disk cache (that is, the portion of the kernel's disk cache that will be used for Postgres data files). This is measured in disk pages, which are normally 8Kb apiece.

> ***float8*** Set the assumed cache size to the specified floating-point value.

ENABLE_SEQSCAN Enables or disables the planner's use of sequential scan plan types. (It's not possible to suppress sequential scans entirely, but turning this variable OFF discourages the planner from using one if there is any other method available.)

> **ON** enables use of sequential scans (default setting).
>
> **OFF** disables use of sequential scans.

ENABLE_INDEXSCAN Enables or disables the planner's use of index scan plan types.

> **ON** enables use of index scans (default setting).
>
> **OFF** disables use of index scans.

ENABLE_TIDSCAN Enables or disables the planner's use of TID scan plan types.

> **ON** enables use of TID scans (default setting).
>
> **OFF** disables use of TID scans.

ENABLE_SORT Enables or disables the planner's use of explicit sort steps. (It's not possible to suppress explicit sorts entirely, but turning this variable OFF discourages the planner from using one if there is any other method available.)

> **ON** enables use of sorts (default setting).
>
> **OFF** disables use of sorts.

ENABLE_NESTLOOP Enables or disables the planner's use of nested-loop join plans. (It's not possible to suppress nested-loop joins entirely, but turning this variable OFF discourages the planner from using one if there is any other method available.)

> **ON** enables use of nested-loop joins (default setting).
>
> **OFF** disables use of nested-loop joins.

ENABLE_MERGEJOIN Enables or disables the planner's use of mergejoin plans.

> **ON** enables use of merge joins (default setting).
>
> **OFF** disables use of merge joins.

ENABLE_HASHJOIN Enables or disables the planner's use of hashjoin plans.

ON enables use of hash joins (default setting).

OFF disables use of hash joins.

GEQO Sets the threshold for using the genetic optimizer algorithm.

ON enables the genetic optimizer algorithm for statements with 11 or more tables. (This is also the DEFAULT setting.)

ON=# Takes an integer argument to enable the genetic optimizer algorithm for statements with # or more tables in the query.

OFF disables the genetic optimizer algorithm.

See the chapter on GEQO in the Programmer's Guide for more information about query optimization.

If the PGGEQO environment variable is set in the frontend environment of a client based on libpq, libpq will automatically set GEQO to the value of PGGEQO during connection start-up.

KSQO *Key Set Query Optimizer* causes the query planner to convert queries whose WHERE clause contains many OR'ed AND clauses (such as "WHERE (a=1 AND b=2) OR (a=2 AND b=3) ...") into a UNION query. This method can be faster than the default implementation, but it doesn't necessarily give exactly the same results, since UNION implicitly adds a SELECT DISTINCT clause to eliminate identical output rows. KSQO is commonly used when working with products like Microsoft Access, which tend to generate queries of this form.

ON enables this optimization.

OFF disables this optimization (default setting).

DEFAULT Equivalent to specifying **SET KSQO=OFF**.

The KSQO algorithm used to be absolutely essential for queries with many OR'ed AND clauses, but in Postgres 7.0 and later the standard planner handles these queries fairly successfully.

MAX_EXPR_DEPTH Sets the maximum expression nesting depth that the parser will accept. The default value is high enough for any normal query, but you can raise it if you need to. (But if you raise it too high, you run the risk of backend crashes due to stack overflow.)

integer Maximum depth.

Outputs

SET VARIABLE Message returned if successful.

NOTICE: Bad value for *variable* (*value*) If the command fails to set the specified variable.

Description

SET will modify configuration parameters for variable during a session.

Current values can be obtained using **SHOW**, and values can be restored to the defaults using **RESET**. Parameters and values are case-insensitive. Note that the value field is always specified as a string, so is enclosed in single quotes.

SET TIME ZONE changes the session's default time zone offset. An SQL session always begins with an initial default time zone offset. The **SET TIME ZONE** statement is used to change the default time zone offset for the current SQL session.

Notes

The **SET** *variable* statement is a Postgres language extension.

Refer to **SHOW** and **RESET** to display or reset the current values.

Usage

Set the style of date to ISO (no quotes on the argument is required):

```
SET DATESTYLE TO ISO;
```

Enable GEQO for queries with 4 or more tables (note the use of single quotes to handle the equal sign inside the value argument):

```
SET GEQO = 'ON=4';
```

Set GEQO to default:

```
SET GEQO = DEFAULT;
```

Set the time zone for Berkeley, California, using double quotes to preserve the uppercase attributes of the time zone specifier:

```
SET TIME ZONE "PST8PDT"; SELECT CURRENT_TIMESTAMP AS today;
today
------------------------
1998-03-31 07:41:21-08
```

Set the time zone for Italy (note the required single or double quotes to handle the special characters):

```
SET TIME ZONE 'Europe/Rome';
SELECT CURRENT_TIMESTAMP AS today;
today
------------------------
1998-03-31 17:41:31+02
```

Compatibility

SQL92

There is no general **SET *variable*** in SQL92 (with the exception of **SET TRANSACTION ISOLATION LEVEL**). The SQL92 syntax for **SET TIME ZONE** is slightly different, allowing only a single integer value for time zone specification:

```
SET TIME ZONE {  interval_value_expression | LOCAL }
```

D.81   SHOW

Name

SHOW — Shows run-time parameters for session
   SHOW *keyword*

Inputs

keyword Refer to *SET* for more information on available variables.

Outputs

NOTICE: *variable* is *value* Message returned if successful.

NOTICE: Unrecognized variable *value* Message returned if variable does not exist.

NOTICE: Time zone is unknown If the TZ or PGTZ environment variable is not set.

Description

SHOW will display the current setting of a run-time parameter during a session.

   These variables can be set using the **SET** statement, and can be restored to the default values using the **RESET** statement. Parameters and values are case-insensitive.

Notes

See also *SET* and *RESET* to manipulate variable values.

Usage

Show the current DateStyle setting:

```
SHOW DateStyle;
NOTICE: DateStyle is ISO with US (NonEuropean) conventions
```

Show the current genetic optimizer (geqo) setting:

```
SHOW GEQO;
NOTICE: GEQO is ON beginning with 11 relations
```

Compatibility

SQL92

There is no **SHOW** defined in SQL92.

D.82   TRUNCATE

Name

TRUNCATE — Empty a table
    TRUNCATE [TABLE] *name*

Inputs

name   The name of the table to be truncated.

Outputs

TRUNCATE   Message returned if the table is successfully truncated.

Description

TRUNCATE quickly removes all rows from a table. It has the same effect as an unqualified **DELETE** but since it does not actually scan the table it is faster. This is most effective on large tables.

Usage

Truncate the table *bigtable*:

```
TRUNCATE TABLE bigtable;
```

Compatibility

SQL92

There is no **TRUNCATE** in SQL92.

D.83 UNLISTEN

Name

UNLISTEN — Stop listening for notification
 UNLISTEN { *notifyname* | * }

Inputs

notifyname Name of previously registered notify condition.

* All current listen registrations for this backend are cleared.

Outputs

UNLISTEN Acknowledgment that statement has executed.

Description

UNLISTEN is used to remove an existing **NOTIFY** registration. UNLISTEN cancels any existing registration of the current Postgres session as a listener on the notify condition *notifyname*. The special condition wildcard "*" cancels all listener registrations for the current session.

NOTIFY contains a more extensive discussion of the use of **LISTEN** and **NOTIFY**.

Notes

classname need not be a valid class name but can be any string valid as a name up to 32 characters long.

The backend does not complain if you UNLISTEN something you were not listening for. Each backend will automatically execute **UNLISTEN** * when exiting.

A restriction in some previous releases of Postgres that a *classname* which does not correspond to an actual table must be enclosed in double-quotes is no longer present.

Usage

To subscribe to an existing registration:

```
LISTEN virtual;
LISTEN
NOTIFY virtual;
NOTIFY
Asynchronous NOTIFY 'virtual' from backend with pid '8448' received
```

Once UNLISTEN has been executed, further NOTIFY commands will be ignored:

```
UNLISTEN virtual;
UNLISTEN
NOTIFY virtual;
NOTIFY
-- notice no NOTIFY event is received
```

Compatibility

SQL92

There is no **UNLISTEN** in SQL92.

D.84   UPDATE

Name

UPDATE — Replaces values of columns in a table
    UPDATE *table*
    SET *col = expression* [, ...]
    [FROM *fromlist*]
    [WHERE *condition*]

Inputs

table The name of an existing table.

column The name of a column in *table*.

expression A valid expression or value to assign to column.

fromlist A Postgres non-standard extension to allow columns from other tables to appear in the WHERE condition.

condition Refer to the SELECT statement for a further description of the WHERE clause.

Outputs

UPDATE # Message returned if successful. The # means the number of rows updated. If # is
0 no rows are updated.

Description

UPDATE changes the values of the columns specified for all rows which satisfy condition. Only
the columns to be modified need appear as columns in the statement.

Array references use the same syntax found in *SELECT*. That is, either single array elements,
a range of array elements or the entire array may be replaced with a single query.

You must have write access to the table in order to modify it, as well as read access to any table
whose values are mentioned in the WHERE condition.

Usage

Change word "Drama" with "Dramatic" on column kind:

```
UPDATE films
SET kind = 'Dramatic'
WHERE kind = 'Drama';
SELECT *
FROM films
WHERE kind = 'Dramatic' OR kind = 'Drama';
 code  |    title      | did | date_prod  |   kind   | len
-------+---------------+-----+------------+----------+-------
 BL101 | The Third Man | 101 | 1949-12-23 | Dramatic | 01:44
 P_302 | Becket        | 103 | 1964-02-03 | Dramatic | 02:28
 M_401 | War and Peace | 104 | 1967-02-12 | Dramatic | 05:57
 T_601 | Yojimbo       | 106 | 1961-06-16 | Dramatic | 01:50
 DA101 | Das Boot      | 110 | 1981-11-11 | Dramatic | 02:29
```

Compatibility

SQL92

SQL92 defines a different syntax for the positioned UPDATE statement:

```
UPDATE table
SET column = expression [, ...]
WHERE CURRENT OF cursor
```

where *cursor* identifies an open cursor.

D.85   VACUUM

Name

VACUUM — Clean and analyze a Postgres database
    VACUUM [VERBOSE] [ANALYZE] [*table*]
    VACUUM [VERBOSE] ANALYZE [*table* [(*column* [, ...])]]

Inputs

VERBOSE Prints a detailed vacuum activity report for each table.

ANALYZE Updates column statistics used by the optimizer to determine the most efficient way
    to execute a query.

table The name of a specific table to vacuum. Defaults to all tables.

column The name of a specific column to analyze. Defaults to all columns.

Outputs

VACUUM The command has been accepted and the database is being cleaned.

NOTICE: –Relation *table* – The report header for *table*.

**NOTICE: Pages 98: Changed 25, Reapped 74, Empty 0, New 0; Tup 1000: Vac 3000, Crash
0, UnUsed 0, MinLen 188, MaxLen 188; Re-using: Free/Avail. Space 586952/586952;
EndEmpty/Avail. Pages 0/74. Elapsed 0/0 sec.** The analysis for *table* itself.

NOTICE: Index *index* : Pages 28; Tuples 1000: Deleted 3000. Elapsed 0/0 sec. The analysis for an index on the target table.

Description

VACUUM serves two purposes in Postgres as both a means to reclaim storage and also a means
to collect information for the optimizer.

    VACUUM opens every class in the database, cleans out records from rolled back transactions,
and updates statistics in the system catalogs. The statistics maintained include the number of
tuples and number of pages stored in all classes.

    VACUUM ANALYZE collects statistics representing the dispersion of the data in each column.
This information is valuable when several query execution paths are possible.

    Running **VACUUM** periodically will increase the speed of the database in processing user
queries.

Notes

The open database is the target for **VACUUM**.

We recommend that active production databases be **VACUUM**-ed nightly, in order to remove expired rows. After copying a large class into Postgres or after deleting a large number of records, it may be a good idea to issue a **VACUUM ANALYZE** query. This will update the system catalogs with the results of all recent changes, and allow the Postgres query optimizer to make better choices in planning user queries.

Usage

The following is an example from running **VACUUM** on a table in the regression database:

```
regression=> vacuum verbose analyze onek;
NOTICE:  --Relation onek--
NOTICE:  Pages 98: Changed 25, Reapped 74, Empty 0, New 0;
         Tup 1000: Vac 3000, Crash 0, UnUsed 0, MinLen 188, MaxLen 188;
         Re-using: Free/Avail. Space 586952/586952; EndEmpty/Avail. Pages 0/74.
         Elapsed 0/0 sec.
NOTICE:  Index onek_-
stringu1: Pages 28; Tuples 1000: Deleted 3000. Elapsed 0/0 sec.
NOTICE:  Index onek_-
hundred: Pages 12; Tuples 1000: Deleted 3000. Elapsed 0/0 sec.
NOTICE:  Index onek_-
unique2: Pages 19; Tuples 1000: Deleted 3000. Elapsed 0/0 sec.
NOTICE:  Index onek_-
unique1: Pages 17; Tuples 1000: Deleted 3000. Elapsed 0/0 sec.
NOTICE:  Rel onek: Pages: 98 --> 25; Tuple(s) moved: 1000. Elapsed 0/1 sec.
NOTICE:  Index onek_-
stringu1: Pages 28; Tuples 1000: Deleted 1000. Elapsed 0/0 sec.
NOTICE:  Index onek_-
hundred: Pages 12; Tuples 1000: Deleted 1000. Elapsed 0/0 sec.
NOTICE:  Index onek_-
unique2: Pages 19; Tuples 1000: Deleted 1000. Elapsed 0/0 sec.
NOTICE:  Index onek_-
unique1: Pages 17; Tuples 1000: Deleted 1000. Elapsed 0/0 sec.
VACUUM
```

Compatibility

SQL92

There is no **VACUUM** statement in SQL92.

D.86   vacuumdb

Name

vacuumdb — Clean and analyze a Postgres database

vacuumdb [*options*] [–analyze | -z] [–alldb | -a] [–verbose | -v] [–table *'table* [(*column*
[,...])]'] [[-d] *dbname*]

Inputs

vacuumdb accepts the following command line arguments:

-d *dbname* , –dbname *dbname* Specifies the name of the database to be cleaned or analyzed.

-z, –analyze Calculate statistics on the database for use by the optimizer.

-a, –alldb Vacuum all databases.

-v, –verbose Print detailed information during processing.

-t *table* [(*column* [,...)], –table *table* [(*column* [,...])]] Clean or analyze *table* only. Column
names may be specified only in conjunction with the –analyze option.

> **Tip:** If you specify columns to vacuum, you probably have to escape the parentheses from
> the shell.

vacuumdb also accepts the following command line arguments for connection parameters:

-h *host* , –host *host* Specifies the hostname of the machine on which the postmaster is running.

-p *port* , –port *port* Specifies the Internet TCP/IP port or local Unix domain socket file extension
on which the postmaster is listening for connections.

-U *username* , –username *username* Username to connect as.

-W, –password Force password prompt.

-e, –echo Echo the commands that vacuumdb generates and sends to the backend.

-q, –quiet Do not display a response.

Outputs

VACUUM Everything went well.

vacuumdb: Vacuum failed. Something went wrong. vacuumdb is only a wrapper script. See *VACUUM* and *psql* for a detailed discussion of error messages and potential problems.

Description

vacuumdb is a utility for cleaning a Postgres database. vacuumdb will also generate internal statistics used by the Postgres query optimizer.

vacuumdb is a shell script wrapper around the backend command *VACUUM* via the Postgres interactive terminal *psql*. There is no effective difference between vacuuming databases via this or other methods. *psql* must be found by the script and a database server must be running at the targeted host. Also, any default settings and environment variables available to *psql* and the libpq front-end library do apply.

Usage

To clean the database test:

```
$ vacuumdb test
```

To analyze a database named *bigdb* for the optimizer:

```
$ vacuumdb --analyze bigdb
```

To analyze a single column bar in table foo in a database named *xyzzy* for the optimizer:

```
$ vacuumdb --analyze --verbose --table 'foo(bar)' xyzzy
```

Bibliography

[Bowman]   Bowman, Judith S., et al., *The Practical SQL Handbook, Third Edition,* Addison–Wesley, ISBN# 0201447878, Oct, 1996.

[Celko]   Celko, Joe, *Joe Celko's SQL For Smarties,* Morgan, Kaufmann, ISBN# 1558605762, October, 1999.

[Date, Standard]   Date, C. J., Darwen, Hugh, *A Guide to the SQL Standard,* Addison–Wesley, ISBN# 0201964260, Nov, 1996.

[Date, Introduction]   Date. C. J., *An Introduction to Database Systems,* Addison–Wesley, ISBN# 0201385902, Aug, 1999.

[Groff]   Groff, James R., Weinberg, Paul N., *SQL: The Complete Reference,* McGraw–Hill, ISBN# 0072118458, Feb, 1999.

[Hilton]   Hilton, Craig, Willis, Jeff, *Building Database Applications on the Web Using PHP3*, Addison–Wesley, ISBN# 0201657716, December, 1999.

[Administrator's Guide] POSTGRESQL Administrators Guide,
                         http://www.postgresql.org/docs/admin.

[Appendices]   POSTGRESQL Appendices,
                         http://www.postgresql.org/docs/postgres/part-appendix.htm.

[Programmer's Guide]   POSTGRESQL Programmer's Guide,
                         http://www.postgresql.org/docs/programmer.

[Tutorial]   POSTGRESQL Tutorial, http://www.postgresql.org/docs/tutorial.

[User's Guide]   POSTGRESQL User's Guide, http://www.postgresql.org/docs/user.

Index